Complete HORSE

Complete HORSE

Amanda Lang and Maria Costantino

Published by SILVERDALE BOOKS
An imprint of Bookmart Ltd
Registered number 2372865
Trading as Bookmart Ltd
Blaby Road
Wigston
Leicester LE18 4SE

D&S Books Ltd
Kerswell,
Parkham Ash, Bideford
Devon, England
EX39 5PR

e-mail us at:- enquiries@d-sbooks.co.uk

This edition printed 2006

ISBN 1-84509-294-5

DS0076. Complete Horse

Creative Director: Sarah King
Editor: Anna Southgate
Project editor: Judith Millidge
Designer: Debbie Fisher & Co.
Photographer: Paul Forrester

Fonts: Futura and Times New Roman

Material from this book previously appeared in The Horse Care Handbook and The Handbook of Horse Breeds.

Printed in Thailand

1 3 5 7 9 10 8 6 4 2

CONTENTS

INTRODUCTION

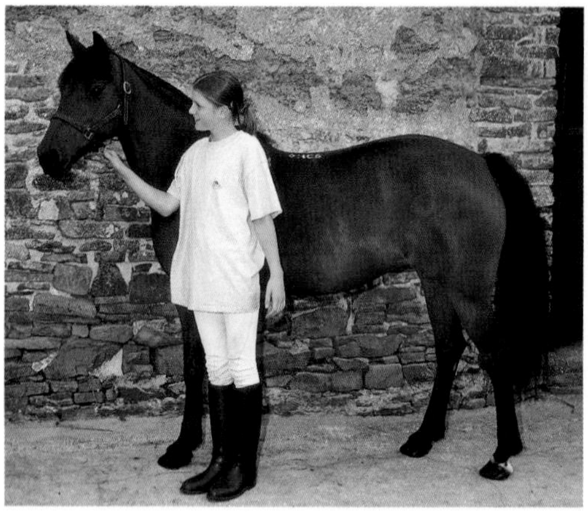

Having a pony of your own can be one of the best things about growing up. As a child I spent most of my time begging and pleading with my parents to buy me one. Of course, I was only six or seven years old at the time and had no idea how much of a responsibility caring for an animal actually was. Neither did I think about the costs – all I wanted was to gallop carefree along the beach on my own pony. So I continued to plead with my parents for years – at least twenty times a day and at every birthday and Christmas. Finally, one winter, when I was in my early teens, I got a pony on winter loan from the local riding school. He was short, fat and hairy, and I was sure we would take on the world together!

I spent most of my waking hours with my pony, and would have slept in the stable if I had been allowed to. While my teenage friends were experimenting with make-up and window-shopping for clothes, I would be out in my wellies and stinking of horses. Sadly, spring came round all too quickly and I was heartbroken when my pony had to be returned to the stables to work for the summer.

From that time on I worked at the stables at weekends and during school holidays in exchange for rides. When I left school I went on to study at an equestrian centre, where I became a working pupil. After two years I gained my qualifications as a riding instructor. Since then I have taught many children to ride and have owned and ridden many different horses and ponies. I believe a true love of horses stays with you for life, and the sight of them grazing quietly on a summer's day always fills me with immense pleasure.

I now live on a farm and have four daughters and, needless to say, a selection of ponies that I could only have dreamt of as a child. With this book, I would like to show you how to care for your pony properly so that you have a long and happy time together. If you are still waiting for that day to come, then at least when it does you will be well prepared.

CHAPTER 1

HORSE AND PONY BASICS

There are many breeds of horses and ponies, ranging from very small ponies just a few inches high, to large cart and heavy horses weighing over a ton. Horses are also categorised into types, as well as breeds, such as hunter or hack, for example.

HORSE BREEDS

There are many breeds of horses and ponies, ranging from very small ponies just a few feet high, to large cart and heavy horses weighing over a ton. Horses are also categorised into types, as well as breeds, such as hunter or hack, for example.

The characteristics of modern horse breeds have largely developed according to where in the world they originated. Some breeds show the influence of their Oriental forebears, for example, while others can trace their origins to European stock.

THOROUGHBRED.

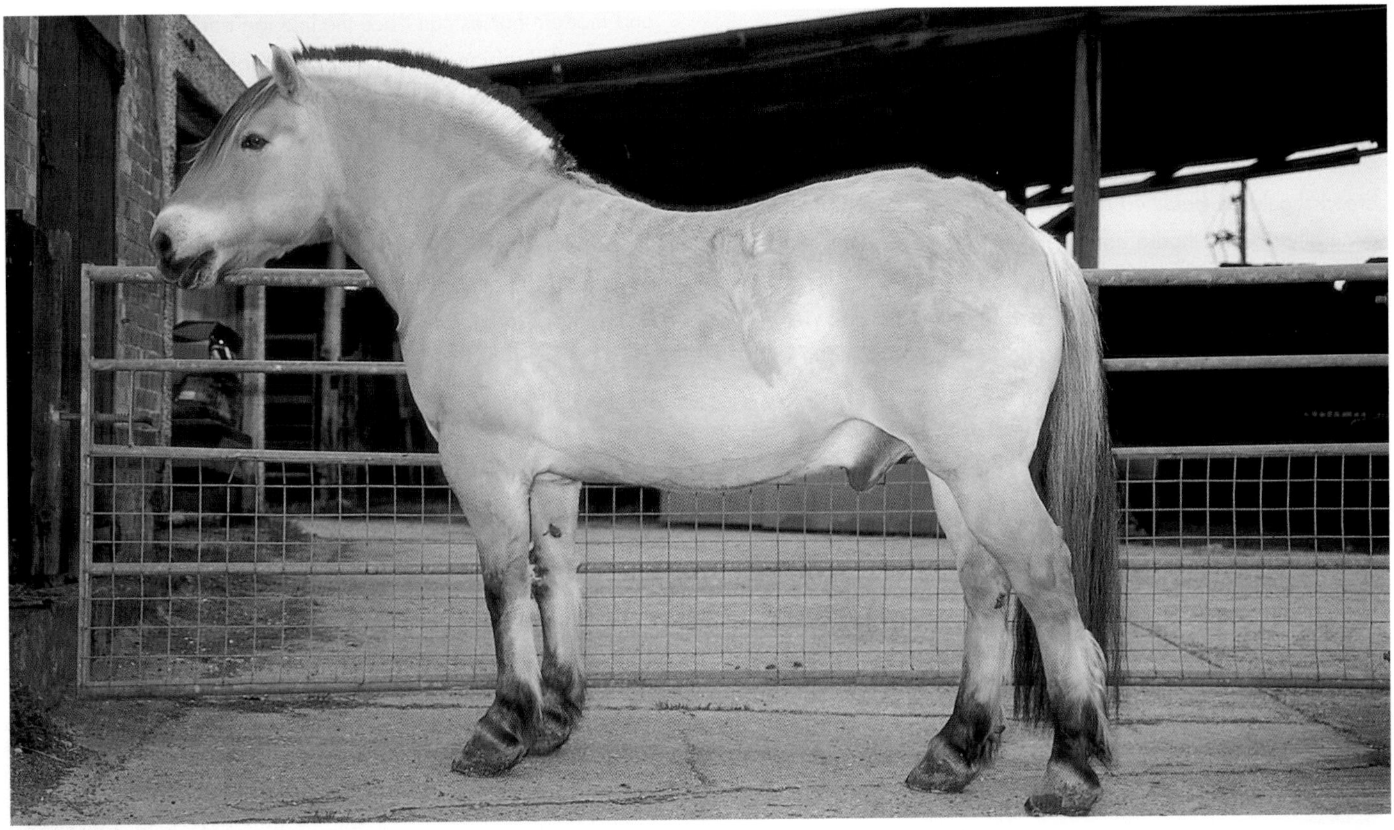

NORWEGIAN FJORD.

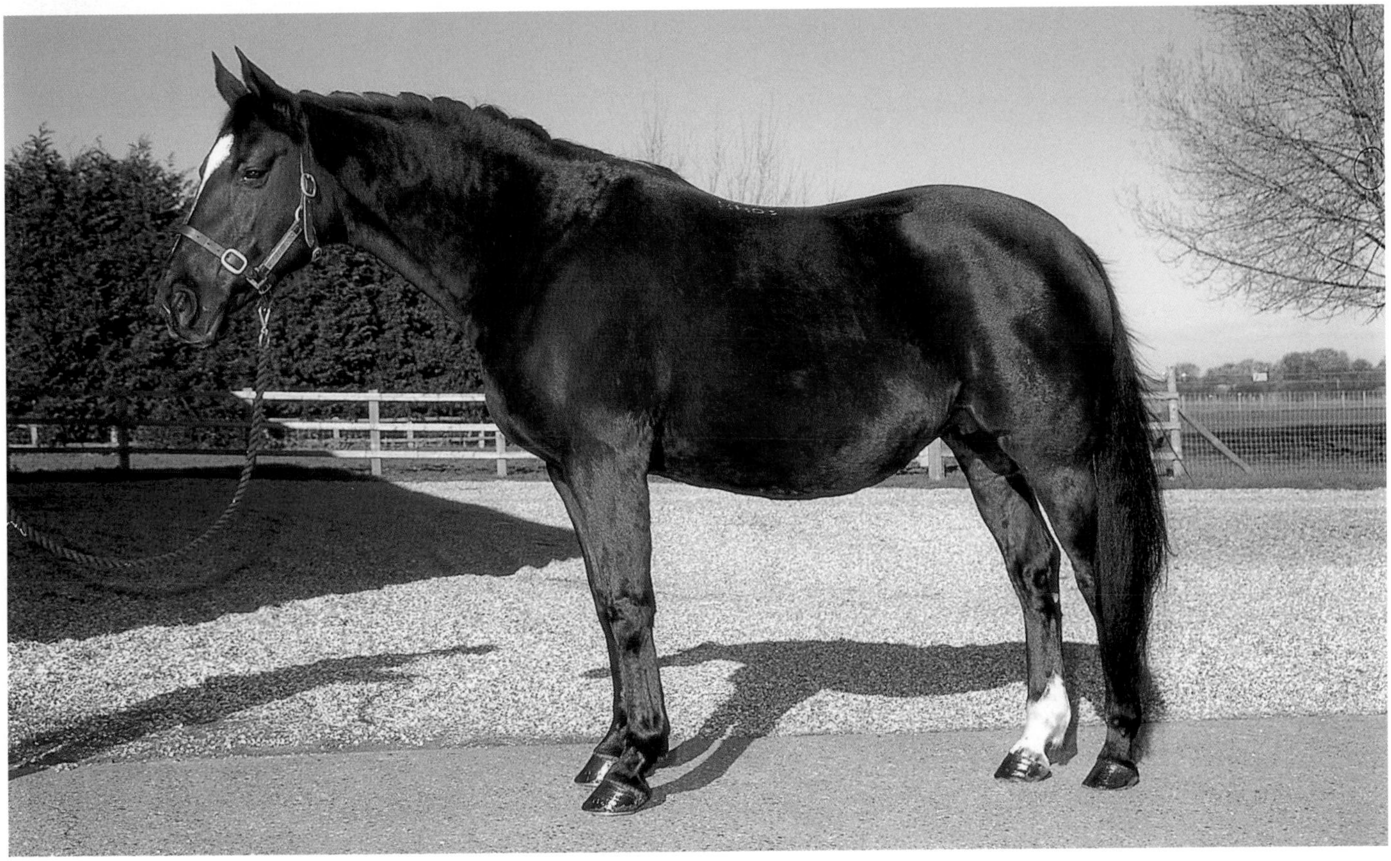

BRITISH WARMBLOOD.

There are three main types of horse – heavy (also known as coldbloods), Light (also known as warmbloods) and ponies. Cross breeding between the types makes some differences less distinct, but in general all horses fall within one of these types. In some cases there is a conflict of opinion as to whether a certain breed should be classified as a pony or horse, but a pony is generally stockier than a horse, and less than 15 hands high.

Breed classification is quite strict, and in order to classify as belonging to a particular breed, a horse needs to conform with certain key standards. Breed conformation largely depends on the purpose of the horse. The most important aspect being the physical proportions. These must be well-balanced in order for the horse to perform at its optimum level. Certain breeds also restrict colour variation.

The Thoroughbred horse is one of the most popular and easily recognisable breeds, thanks largely to its role as a racehorse, and modern horses can trace the lineage back to three sires – The Darley Arabian, The Godolphin Arabian and The Byerley Turk. Thoroughbred colours are generally brown or chestnut with height ranging between 14-17 hands.

The Shetland pony is one of the most well-known and loved of the pony breeds. IT is hardy, sturdy and generally even-tempered, and often found as a mount for young children. The Norwegian Fjord is another stocky pony, suitable for draft work.

The Russian Don is best known as being a cavalry warhorse, and its stamina and endurance make it eminently suitable as a long distance riding horse today. Its height is usually between 15-16.5 hands, with bay and chestnut being standard colours.

Used primarily in showjumping and other performance sports, the Dutch warmblood is generally 15-16 hands high, with any solid colour being allowed.

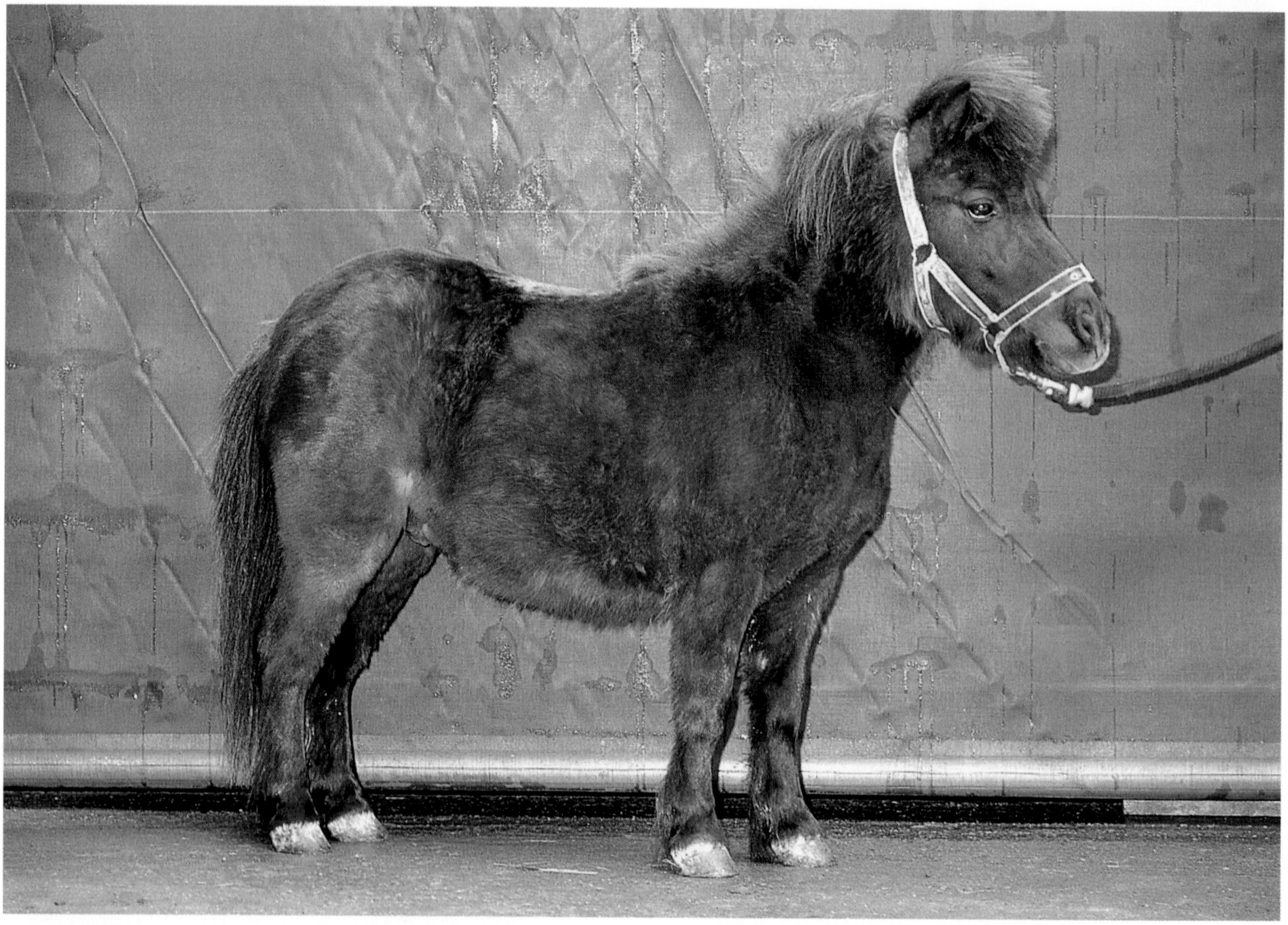

SHETLAND PONY.

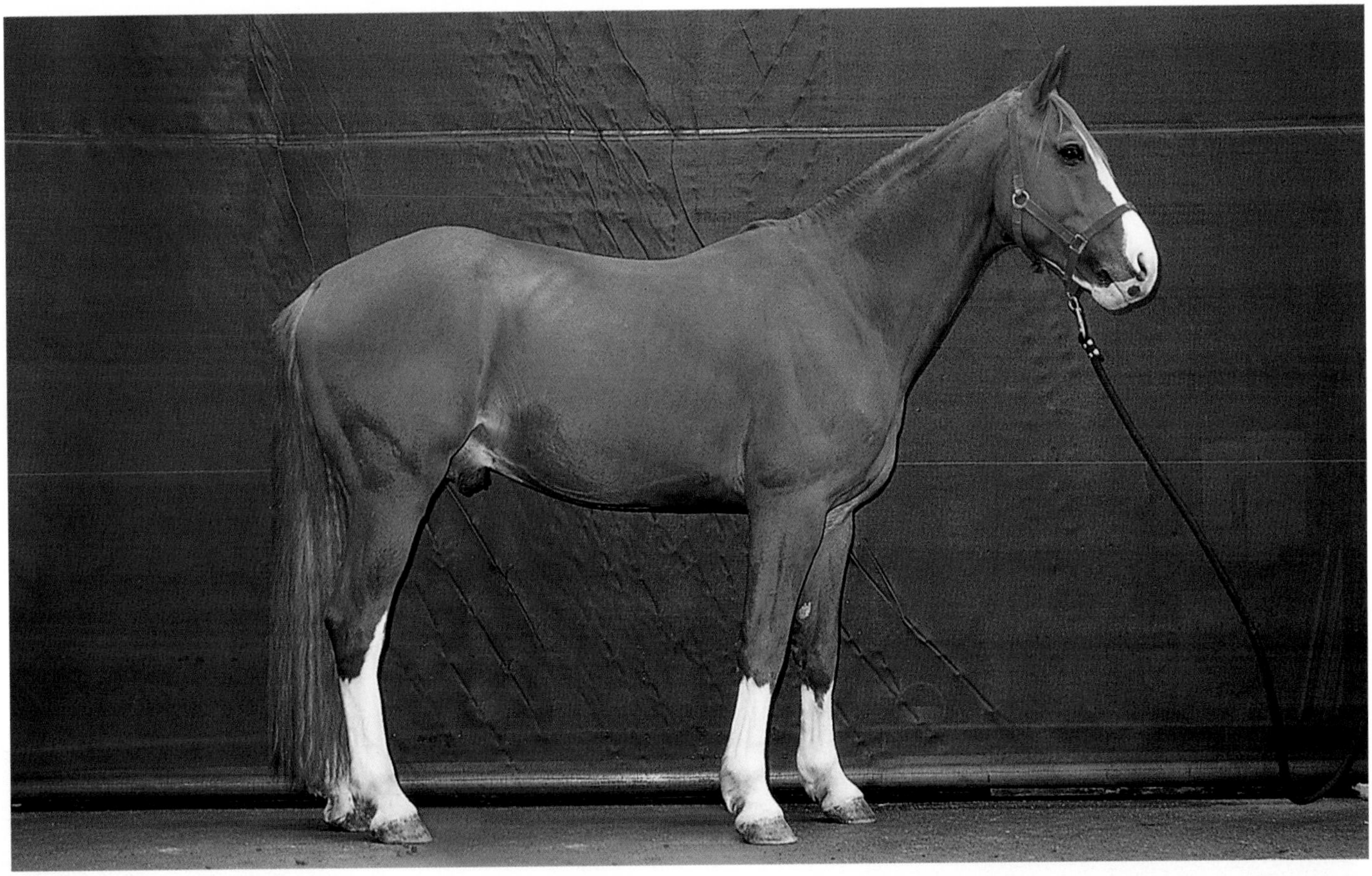

DON.

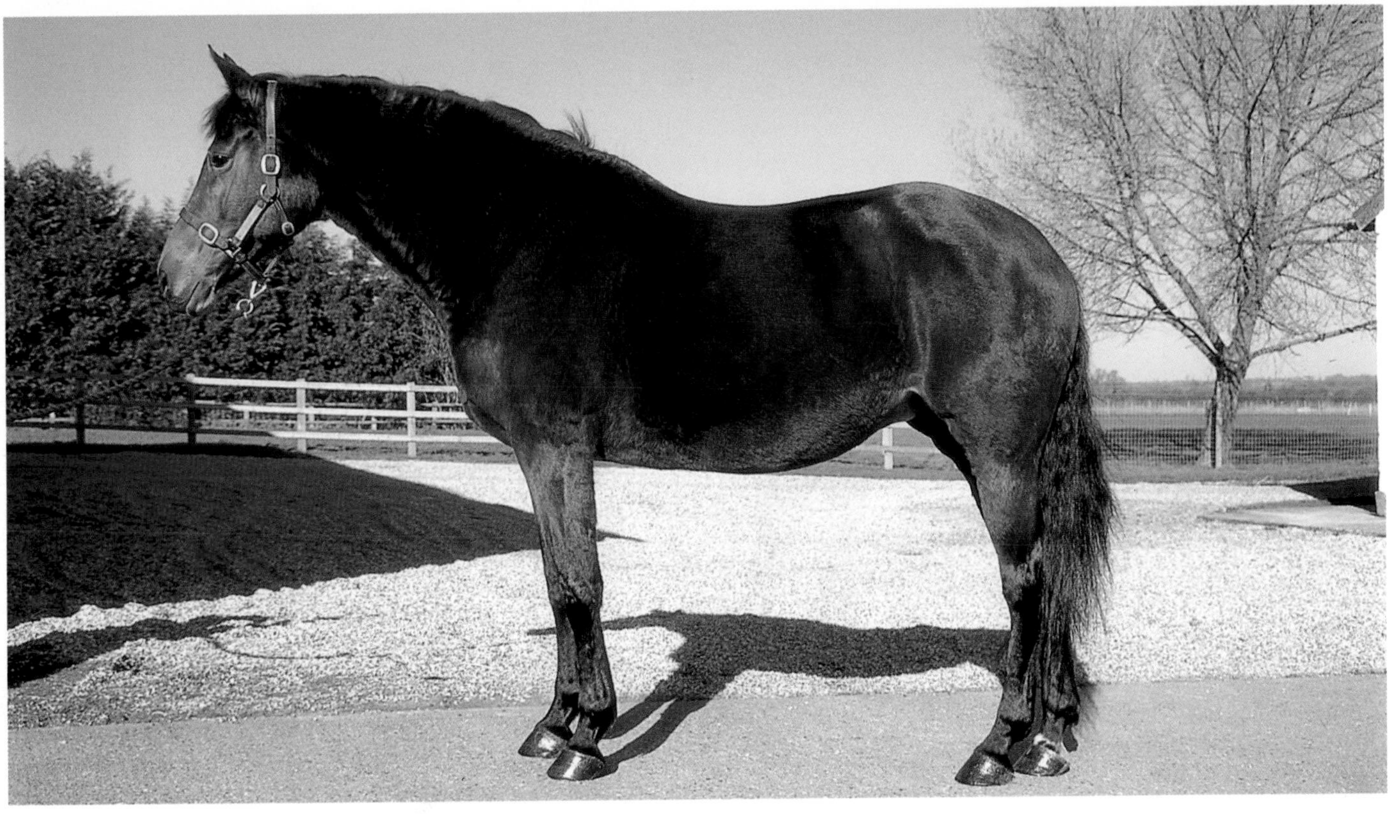

DUTCH WARMBLOOD.

COLOURS

Horses and ponies vary in colour from one season to another. Some breeds also change colour as they get older.

BLACK

Black horses and ponies are usually jet black all over, sometimes with a few white markings.

BROWN

Brown horses and ponies can be dark brown, (almost black) or brown. They have dark brown manes, tails and legs.

BAY

Bay colouring varies from light, reddish brown to dark brown. Bay horses and ponies have black manes and tails and are black below the knee or hock. Sometimes they also have some white markings.

SKEWBALD AT SHOW.

CHESTNUT

This is a ginger, reddish/orange colour and could be darker, more chestnut colour. The mane is a similar colour to the body. The lighter chestnuts sometimes have a cream-coloured mane and tail. This is known as a 'flaxen' mane and tail.

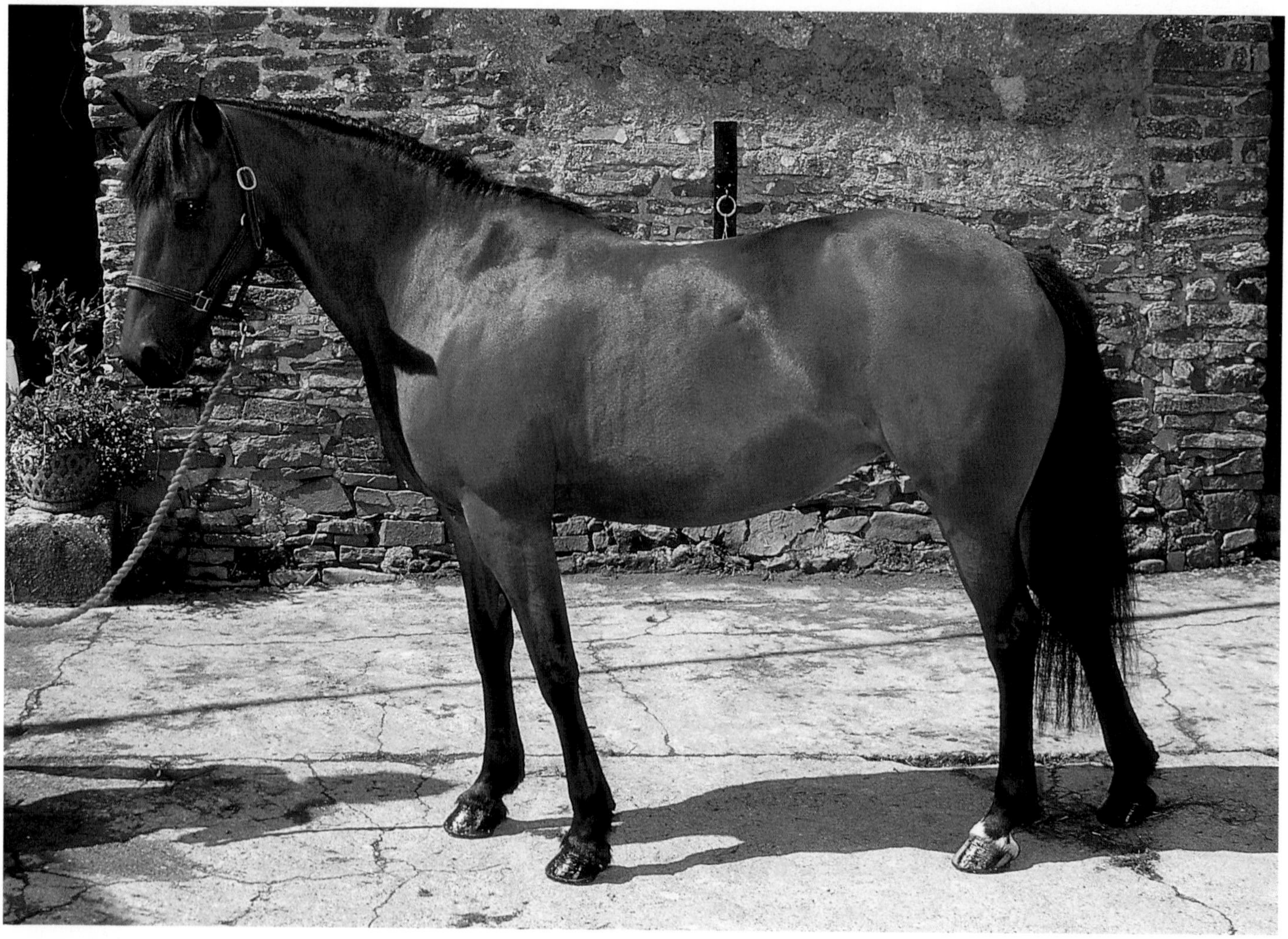

AN EXAMPLE OF BAY COLOURING.

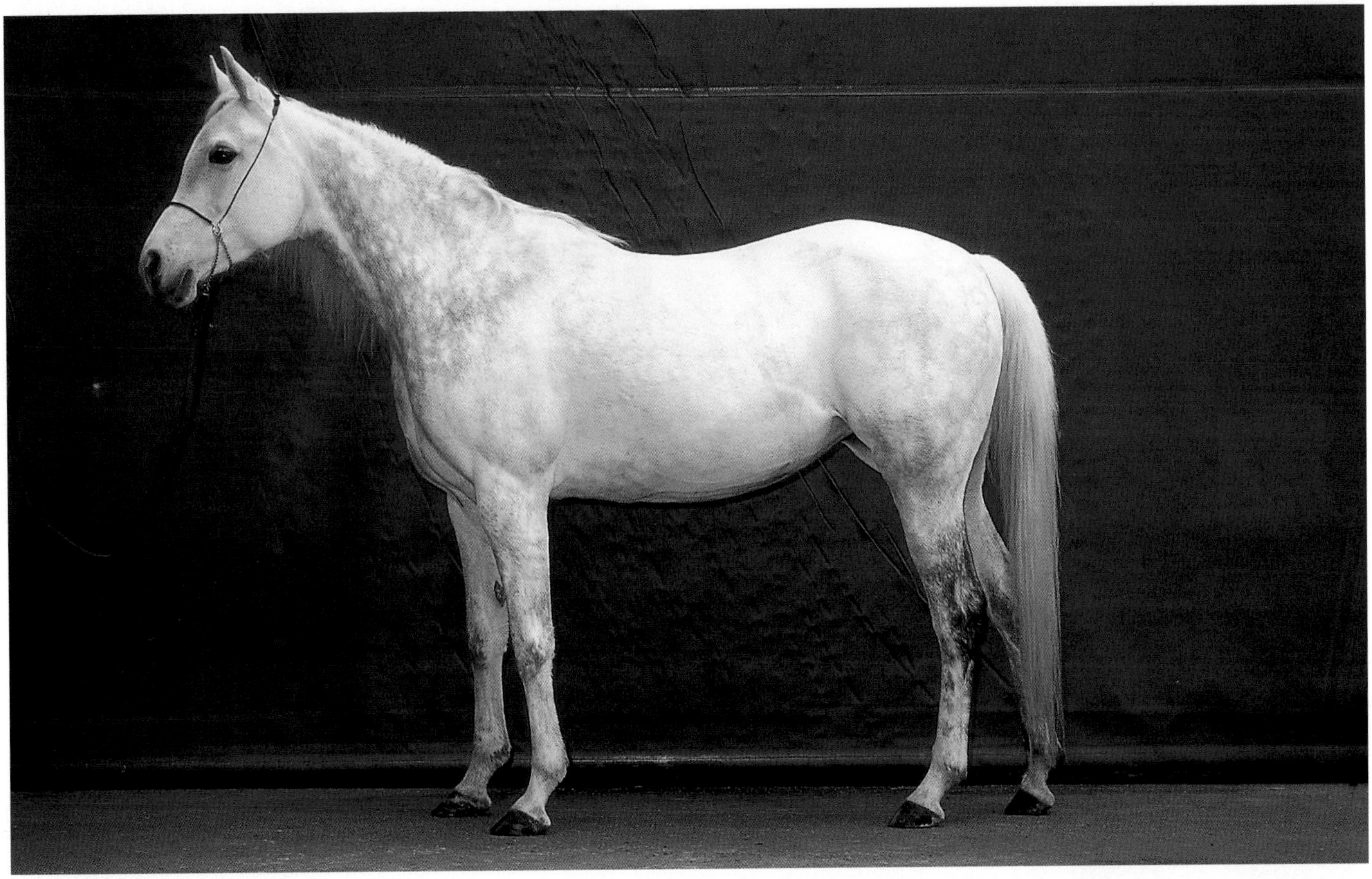

A FINE GREY.

GREY

Greys have black skin with white and black hairs. They vary from very light to dark iron-grey in colour and may have dappled areas. A flea-bitten grey is when the black hairs appear in tufts through the coat.

PALOMINO

Palomino horses and ponies are golden-yellow with a flaxen mane and tail.

PIEBALD

Piebald horses and ponies are black with large, irregular white patches.

SKEWBALD

Skewbald horses and ponies are any other colour with large patches of white.

DUN

Dun horses and ponies are a mousy colour, often with a black stripe along the spine and a black mane and tail.

ROAN

This is when the coat is mixed with white hairs. For example, a bay pony may have a lot of white hairs in its coat, giving it a red tinge. It could also have white markings. Chestnut or strawberry roan is when the coat is predominantly chestnut with white hairs mixed in it resulting in a strawberry colour. A blue roan is a predominantly black or very dark brown coat with white hairs mixed in, giving it a blue tinge. Blue roans usually have black legs below the knee and hock.

THE DISTINCTIVE PALOMINO COLOURING.

MARKINGS

Some horses and ponies have markings of white hair. Such markings are evident from birth rather than those that might grow following damage to the skin.

STAR

A patch of white hair found on a pony's forehead and which varies in shape and size.

STRIPE

A slim strip of white down a pony's face.

BLAZE

A white forehead and a white strip down the face, which is wider than the nasal bone.

SNIP

This is a small patch of white hair found between the nostrils.

STAR.

HAIR WHORLS

These are usually found on either side of the neck, on the crest or on the forehead. They are small patches where hair grows in a different direction to that of the rest of the coat.

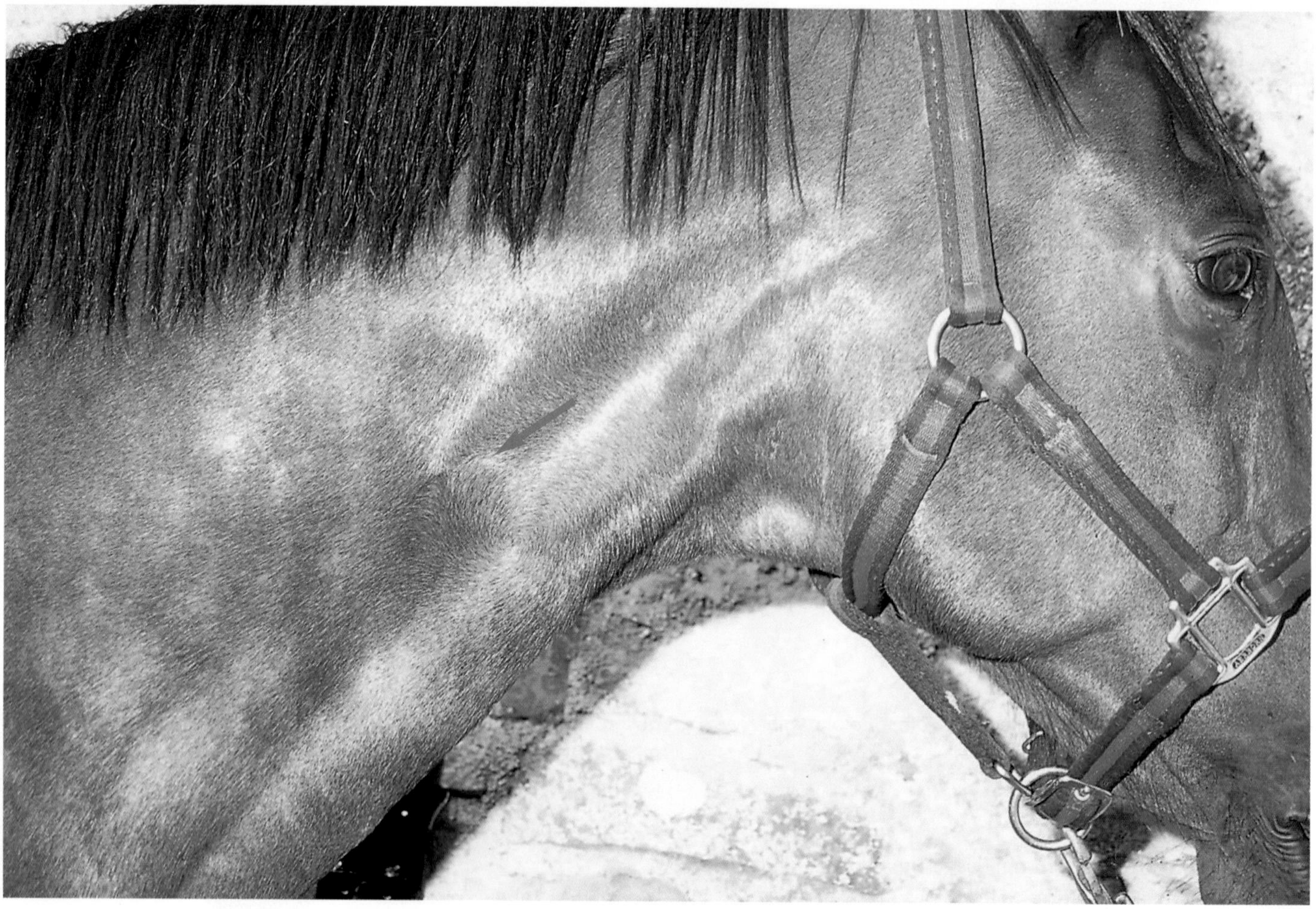

HAIR WHORL.

STRIPE AND SNIP AND ALSO WHITE MARKINGS ON THE LEGS.

WALL EYE

This is when a horse's or pony's eye looks very different, usually pale and blue. It is caused by a lack of pigment in the iris and often only affects one eye.

WHITE MARKINGS ON THE LEGS

This is described according to how far the white reaches up the leg. For example, white pastern, white coronet or white fetlock. White that extends above the fetlock and up the cannon bone is sometimes called a 'sock', and white that reaches just below the knee is sometimes called a 'stocking'.

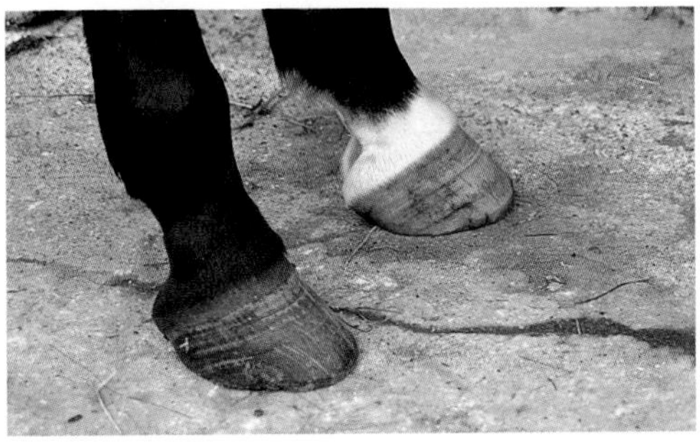

WHITE MARKINGS.

MEASURING

Horses and ponies are measured in hands. One hand is 4 inches, so a horse that is 131/2 hands would be described as 13.2 h. Another 2 inches and it would be described as 14.0 h. Ponies over 14.2 h high are often referred to as horses, although it is not just a matter of height – type needs to be taken into account as well. Shetland ponies are almost always measured in inches and so are described as 38 in., for example. Horses and ponies should be measured on level ground using a marked stick. Height is measured from the ground up to the highest point of the withers.

ALWAYS MEASURE A HORSE'S HEIGHT ON LEVEL GROUND.

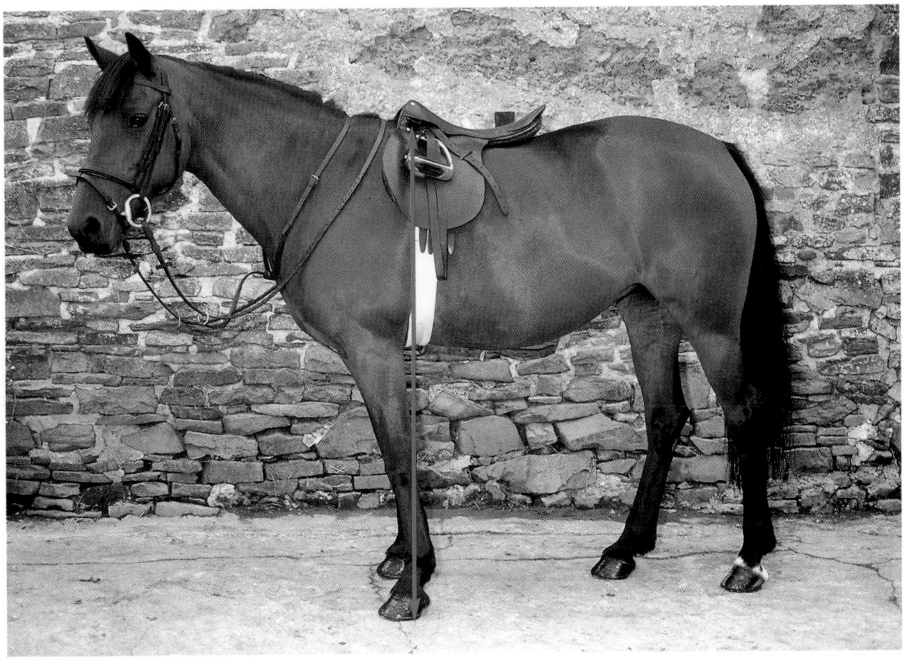

CHAPTER 2

CARE AND MANAGEMENT

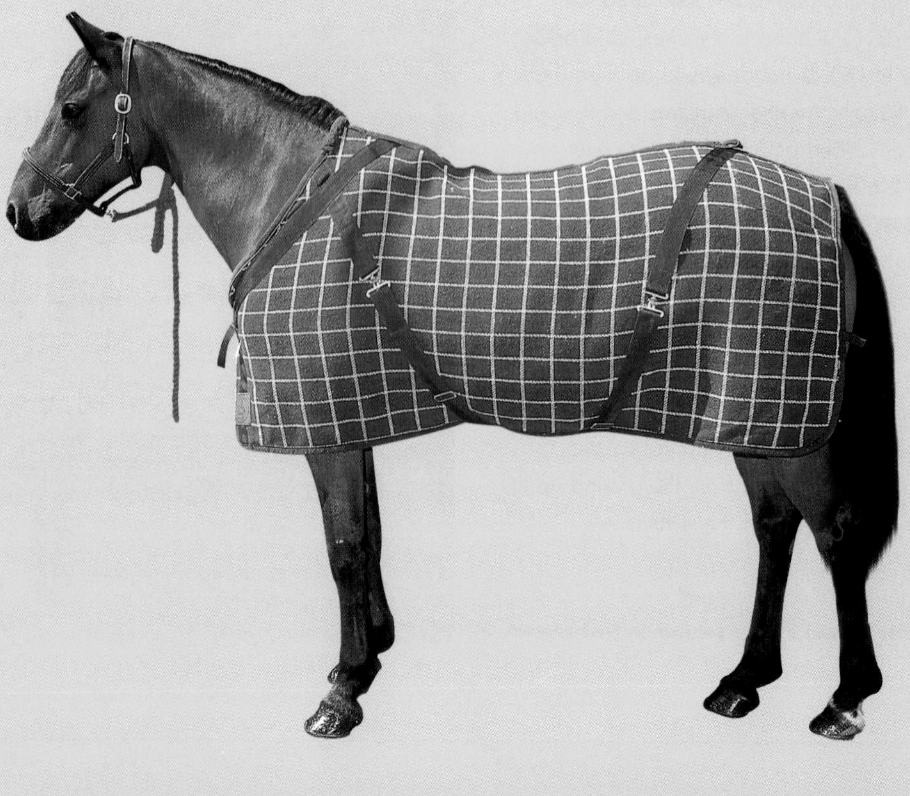

KEEPING A PONY AT LIVERY

In an ideal world all pony-mad children would have a stable and paddock at the bottom of their garden. If you don't have the facilities to keep a pony at home, however, you could consider the possibility of keeping one at a livery yard. Make sure you choose your livery yard or riding school carefully, as standards may vary. Take a knowledgeable friend along with you to visit prospective yards – they may spot things that you miss. A yard should be clean, well-maintained, and the ponies should be in good condition. Some riding schools run a working livery, with little or no money involved, where they use your pony to give lessons while you are not using him. This system can work well as long as you don't mind sharing your pony.

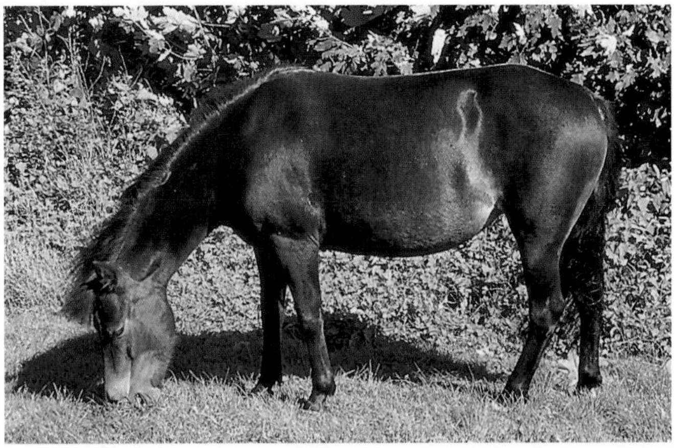

HARDY PONIES CAN LIVE OUTSIDE ALL YEAR.

Grass livery is probably the cheapest way to keep a pony if you have a hardy one that can live out all year round. You will still need to visit your pony twice a day, but if you are busy with school or work this method may suit you well. Native British ponies, such as Dartmoor and Exmoor ponies, are especially suited to a grass livery and are used to outdoor conditions.

HORSES ARE HERD ANIMALS AND NEED COMPANY.

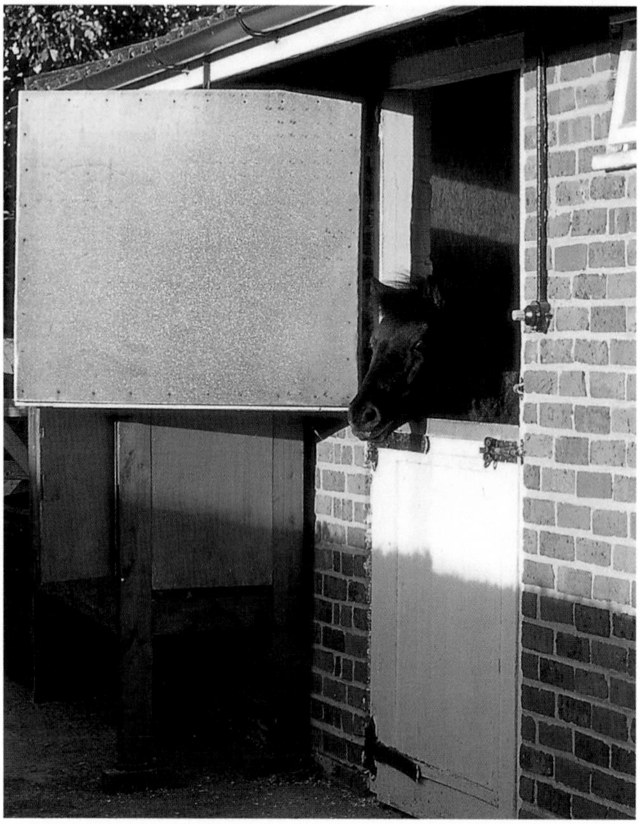

Full livery is when the pony is cared for completely, including feeding, mucking out, exercising and his general well being. This is a good option if you are very busy, but it can be expensive. You would also lose the fun and satisfaction of caring for your own pony. Do-it-yourself livery is another option where you care for the pony yourself, simply renting a field and /or a stable. This is a good option if you live nearby so that you can visit your pony twice a day. One advantage of this system is that your pony will probably have others for company. In some cases the livery yard owner may take on some of the responsibilities, such as feeding and turning out the pony in the morning to save you one visit a day.

Before taking your pony to his new home make sure you have a proper written agreement stating the terms and conditions you have agreed to. It is a good idea to make sure that you are insured just in case your pony kicks another pony or escapes onto the road and causes an accident. Keeping your pony at a livery yard can be fun, and you may be lucky enough to find new friends to ride with, as well a knowledgeable person to consult if you have any problems.

THERE ARE MANY ADVANTAGES TO STABLES.

KEEPING A PONY STABLED

Ponies can become stressed when confined in a stable, especially without company, and yet there are some advantages that cannot be overlooked. The first is that you always know where your pony is. With a stabled pony, it is obviously easier to monitor how warm he is, how much feed and hay he has eaten and how much water he has drunk. When you are mucking out you will easily notice any changes in the amount of dropping or urine, which could be an indication that the pony is not feeling well. It is also easier to get a pony fit when you can accurately monitor his feed and exercise. It is much easier to administer veterinary treatment in a safe, confined space. You can keep a stabled pony a lot cleaner, saving time when you want to ride him and helping to keep his skin healthy. You can clip him, which will keep him even drier and more comfortable when doing a lot of work. However, bear in mind that this means you will need rugs, which can be expensive, and looking after a clipped pony is more time-consuming, as rugs need to be changed, cleaned and repaired. Stabling a pony part-time is very useful in the management of certain conditions and particularly to restrict the grazing of an overweight pony.

STABLES OFFER PROTECTION AND SECURITY.

The disadvantages are that a pony can develop compulsive habits such as crib-biting, wind sucking and weaving, which may be copied by others in the yard. It is generally more expensive to keep a pony stabled, as you will have to provide a lot more feed, hay, rugs and bedding than for a grass-kept pony. It is also more time consuming. You must be sure to provide a stabled pony with plenty of interesting exercise, a thick comfortable bed, fresh clean water, a balanced diet, regular grooming and, as often as possible, the opportunity to be turned out with others to graze, roll and be free for a while.

SUITABLE STABLES

Your stable could be a modern purpose-built building or a converted barn. Both types have many potential dangers, and there are several aspects to consider in order ensure that your pony is safe. Firstly, it should be built on well-drained soil and facing away from the prevailing wind. It should be large, well ventilated, safe inside and strong enough to withstand a few kicks or the weight of the pony bumping against it.

The best form of stabling is a loose box. The box should be a minimum of 250–360 cm sq (10–12 ft sq) for a pony and 360 cm sq (12 ft–14 sq) for a horse. The animal should be able to move around freely and to lie down without getting 'cast' (stuck on his back). Other measures you can take to prevent him getting cast are to bank up the bedding around the walls on three sides of the box. The banks must be quite large in order to work. You can fix a 5 x 2 cm (2 x 1 in.) baton around the wall about 90 cm (three ft) from the floor all the way around the stable, which will help a horse to turn himself over.

Windows should be well maintained with any glass covered with a wire mesh to prevent the pony breaking the glass and cutting himself. A clear, non-breakable material would be preferable. Doors must be a minimum of 120 cm (4 ft) wide and should open outwards. Make sure that all the locks and

THESE BOXES LOOK SPACIOUS AND LIGHT WITH PLENTY OF VENTILATION.

bolts are in good working order. A kick bolt on the outside of the door at ground level is a good idea, where it will be out of reach for a pony. Some doors have a metal strip intended to stop the pony chewing the door. They need to be checked for any sharp edges that may cause harm. Full-height doors should be divided in two so that the top door can be hooked back for ventilation, allowing the horse to look out while the lower part remains secure. Some stables have a grille across the top half which is useful if a pony is likely to bite or weave. It will also prevent foals from trying to jump out. Fresh air is important for keeping your pony healthy. In most circumstances, it is best to leave the top door open.

Floors are usually concrete, which is cheap and easy to install, and should have a rough or grooved surface, to prevent it becoming slippery and dangerous. Rubber mats are quite expensive, but are ideal for putting over concrete as an extra precaution. They may save on bedding bills and, in the long run, on vet bills as well. A floor should slope slightly towards a drain either outside the stable or in the corner, and any drainage channels should be shallow and open.

MESH ON A WINDOW HELPS PREVENT INJURY IF THE GLASS BREAKS.

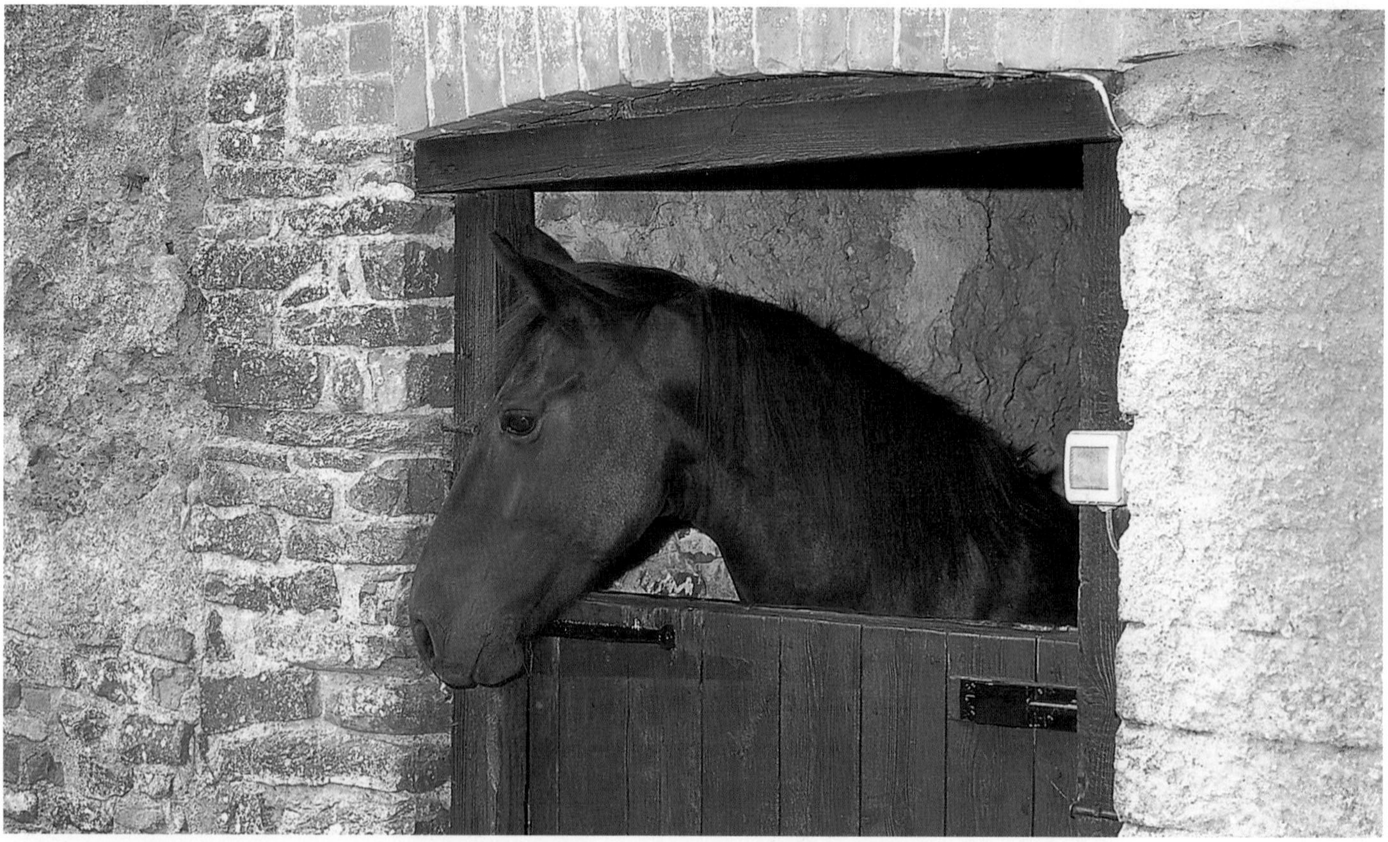

A DIVIDED DOOR ALLOWS A HORSE TO LOOK OUT.

HANG HAYNETS AT THE CORRECT HEIGHT.

Fit a couple of small metal rings to the wall, one to tie the pony up while you groom him, and one for the hay net. The first should be at about the height of the pony's head and should have a small loop of breakable string attached to it. Always tie the pony to the string in case he pulls back suddenly. He will break the string instead of hurting himself or you. The ring for the hay net should be higher up.

Water can be easily supplied by an automatic drinking bowl which must be cleaned and checked daily. Buckets must have handles removed (to prevent the pony getting his leg stuck) and all water containers must be safe. Use rubber type containers rather than ceramic sinks or old tin containers for feed. Hay nets can be a hazard and it is worth remembering when hanging them up that they hang much lower when empty, making it easy for ponies to get their legs trapped. It is best to tie them high enough up the wall, so that they hang a good 1 m (3 ft) from the floor when empty.

AN AUTOMATIC WATER CONTAINER.

If feeding a horse any concentrates, use a rubber bowl or trough at floor level. This is more natural for the animal and the rubber bowl is safe and easy to clean. However, a manger should be at chest height and in the corner or on a wall. A fixed manger can be hard to clean and the pony could get stuck beneath it when rolling. Removable mangers, which you hook over a door, are more convenient and easier to keep clean.

Electricity makes everything a little more comfortable and is useful for clipping and lighting on winter evenings, but make sure all fittings are out of a pony's reach, preferably outside the stable with waterproof switches. Always get an electrician to check wiring and switches when using a new or different stable. Fire extinguishers should be in obvious positions and everyone in the yard should be familiar with the fire drill and the whereabouts of the nearest phone. Extinguishers must be serviced regularly.

Stalls have the advantage of offering more accommodation in less space. However, the pony is usually tied up facing a wall and can become bored easily. He will have less fresh air and may be bullied by the pony next door. Some stalls can be divided by a solid partition from the floor at least 180 cm (6 ft) high. These must be fitted correctly. Dividing walls and partitions can be dangerous if made of a flimsy material such as plywood. Some thin woods will splinter if the pony kicks at them or rolls against them. Always use a strong solid material and make sure it reaches right to the floor – legs can become trapped in any gaps. If wooden bars are used, animals may kick at each other or become entangled when rolling. Stalls partitioned with a swing beam should be hung on ropes with a quick release knot, not wire. The beam should be slightly higher at the front end and should be the length of the stall.

THIS HAYNET IS TOO LOW.

THESE PONIES CAN EASILY SEE THEIR STABLE MATES.

STABLE EQUIPMENT

Stable equipment should be kept in good condition, particularly as some items are expensive. Quality is important, so always buy the best you can afford. Take care of it and it should give you years of use. The range of equipment – rugs, feeding items, protective clothing, bits, saddles and so on – is vast, but there are a few basic items you will need to start with. All the fashionable accessories can come later!

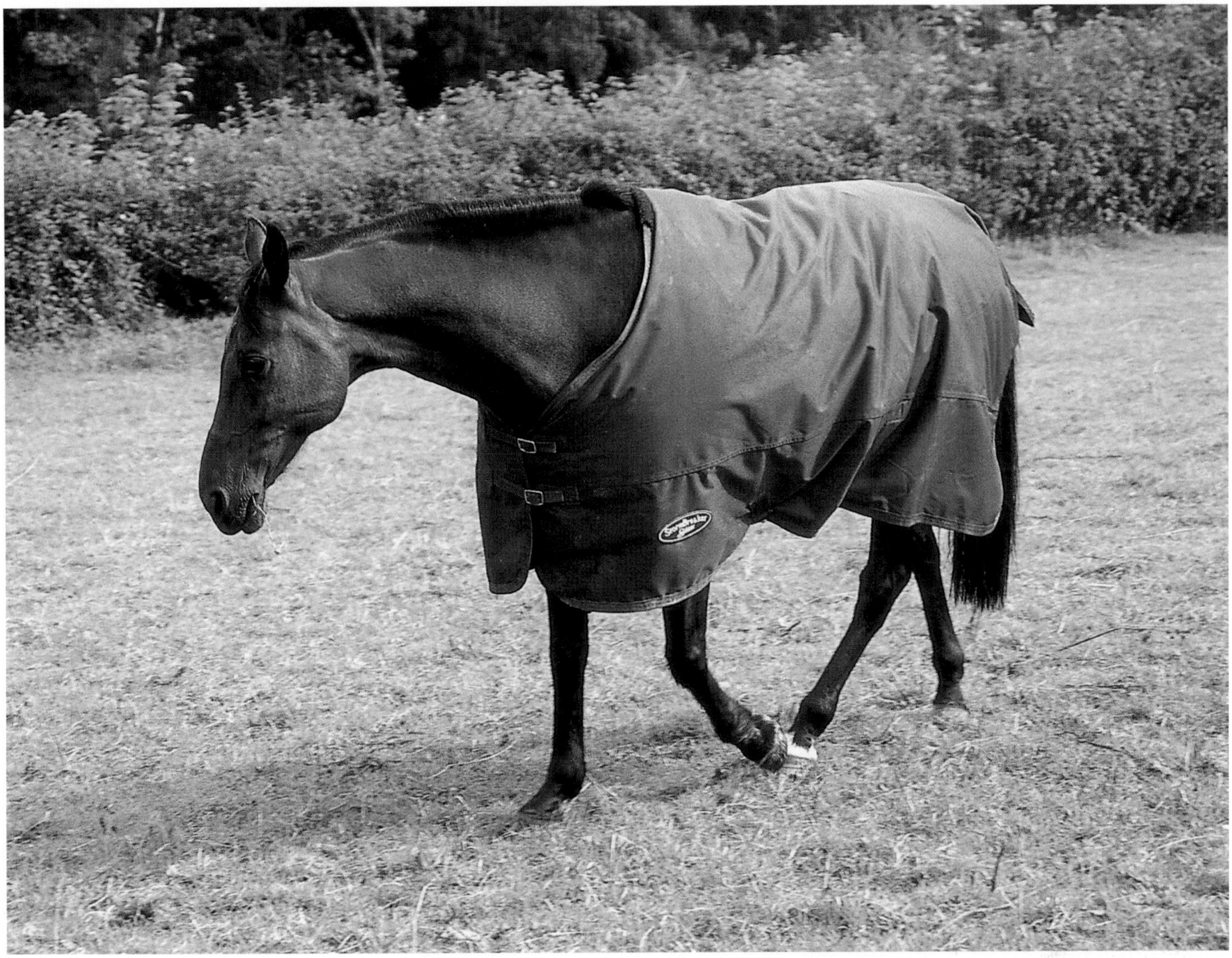

A NEW ZEALAND RUG PROTECTS A HORSE FROM THE COLD AND WET.

RUGS

A stabled pony will need more rugs than a grass-kept one, the latter needing a New Zealand rug or no rugs at all depending on the conditions he lives in through the winter. A stabled pony will need a stable rug, a New Zealand rug for going out in the field and a sweat rug at least. A roller is always useful for securing a blanket under the stable rug during a cool spell in winter. Exercise blankets are useful for stabled horses that have been clipped and will keep them warm while they are doing quiet work. Waterproof exercise sheets are very useful if you are going for a ride and it is likely to rain, as they keep the back and quarters dry so that, on your return, you can put your New Zealand rug or stable rug straight back on without having to dry the pony off first.

NEW ZEALAND RUGS

These rugs are for outside use and are not intended to be worn in the stables. They are made of tough, waterproof fabric – usually nylon or another manmade material – although they used to be made from canvas. Nylon ones tend to be lighter for a pony to wear and dry a lot quicker following a downpour. A rug must fit properly or it will slip and move about when the pony gallops or bucks. Some rugs have a dart in the shoulder, which allows the pony to move more freely, and there are various different straps for holding it in place. A poorly fitting rug will rub and be uncomfortable. Some New Zealand rugs have attachable neck covers and hoods. They protect a horse's newly clipped head and neck from wind, cold and rain. Some rugs also have a flap to cover the top of the tail. New Zealand rugs are available in many forms so ask your saddler to help you choose one that fits well and suits your pony's lifestyle. Sizes usually increase by 5 cm (3 in) at a time. To get an idea of your pony's size, measure from the centre of his chest, along his side and to the point of the buttock. A rug should cover his bottom and be deep enough to cover the belly easily and should fit snugly around the shoulders and chest. New Zealand rugs need to be kept clean and some of them can be washed. Those made of canvas need to be waterproofed every year. A spare New Zealand rug is very handy if one gets torn or very wet.

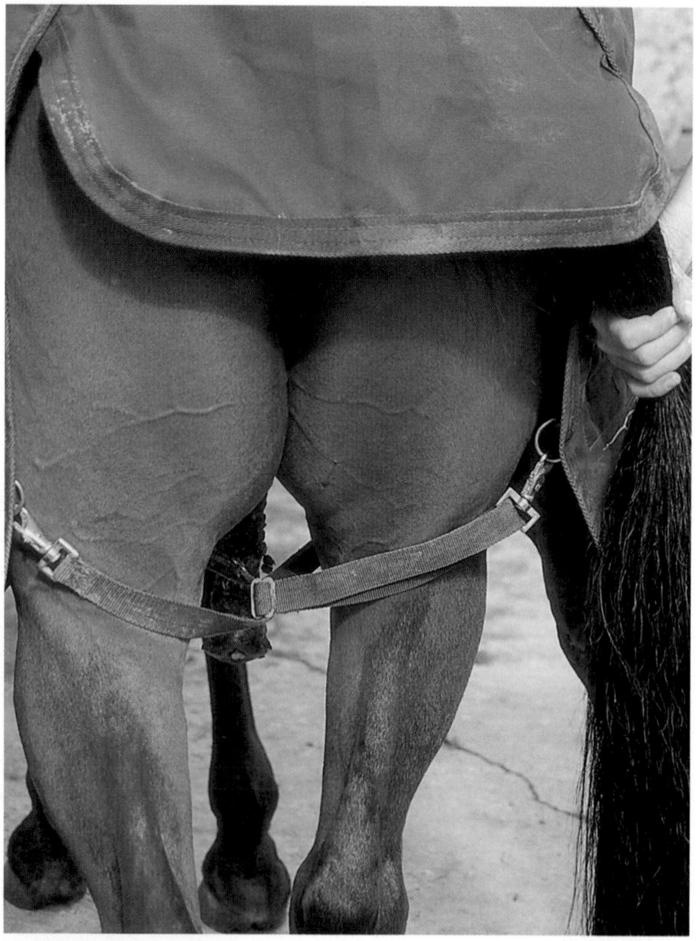

NEW ZEALAND RUGS MUST FIT PROPERLY.

STABLE RUGS PROTECT PONIES AND HORSES FROM DRAUGHTS AND CHILLS IN STABLES.

STABLE RUGS

Use these to keep a pony warm in the stables. They are usually made from manmade fibres and are often quilted. They vary from quite thin to very thick, so select one according to the time of year and whether your pony is clipped. For example, during early spring and autumn you will probably not need a very thick one. Another, thinner rug can be added underneath for extra warmth. As with the New Zealand rug make sure it fits correctly – it is best to ask for advice when buying your first few rugs. Spending a little more on a rug usually gets you better quality and can make a difference to the fit. Many styles and colours are available, but a good fit is of greatest importance.

SUMMER SHEETS

These are light cotton or cotton mix rugs, and are used in the summer to keep a horse free from dust and flies. They are most often used for a stabled pony.

SWEAT RUGS

These are light rugs that can be thrown over a horse if he has been sweating or after a bath. The rug will trap a layer of warm air but also offers ventilation and allows a horse's coat to dry off without him getting cold. Cooler rugs are also available for when a pony is sweating and needs to cool down. They are made of a different material and can act as a summer sheet, be worn under a stable rug, or as a light rug to travel in. These rugs are extremely useful and dry very quickly when washed.

BLANKETS

These can be used under a stable rug during a colder spell in winter, and are made either of a wool mix or of manmade fibres. To put the blanket on under a rug, place it over the pony right up to his ears and fold the two front corners at the withers, making a point at the poll. Put the stable rug on top of the blanket, positioning it a bit further forward than it needs to be. Then fold back the point of the blanket and secure everything with a roller or surcingle. Don't tighten a roller too much, or the pony will be uncomfortable, and make sure it's not twisted anywhere. Ideally, you should use a roller that has a pad on either side of the spine.

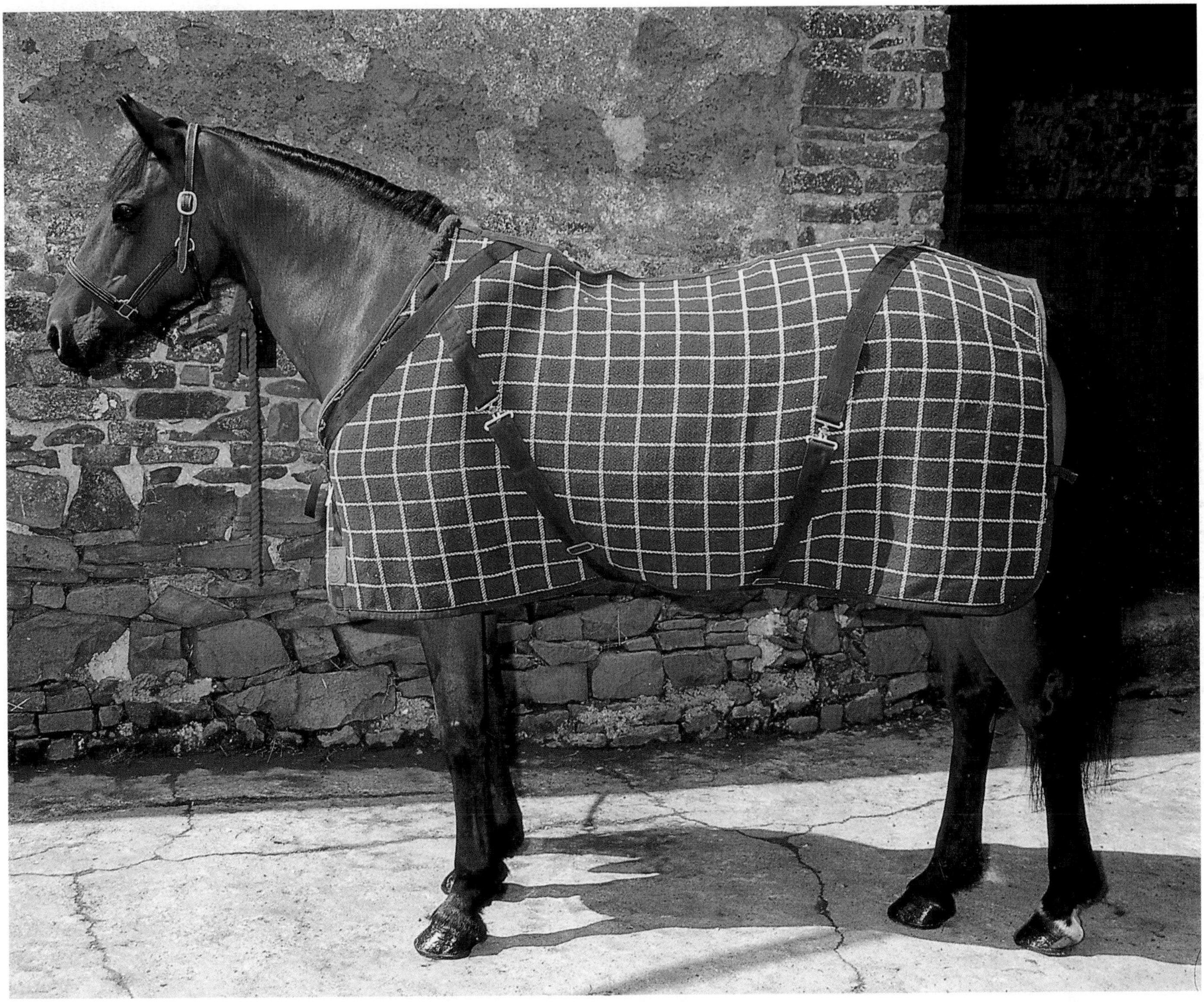

THIS LIGHT THERMAL STABLE RUG IS USEFUL AS A COOLING RUG, OR AS A LIGHT RUG FOR TRAVELLING.

PUTTING ON AND TAKING OFF A RUG

Putting on a rug needs to be done quietly and correctly. It can be a very frightening experience for a pony the first few times, so get an expert to help you get him accustomed to it. Once the pony is used to the process it is very straightforward.

1 Fold the rug in half with the outside of the rug folded inside and place over the pony's withers.

2 Quietly do up the front strap.

3 Now unfold the rug.

4 Place the rug over the quarters.

5 Do up any straps under the belly and any at the back.

6 Pull the rug backwards into place. Never pull it forwards against the lie of the hair. Be careful not to stand where you could get kicked.

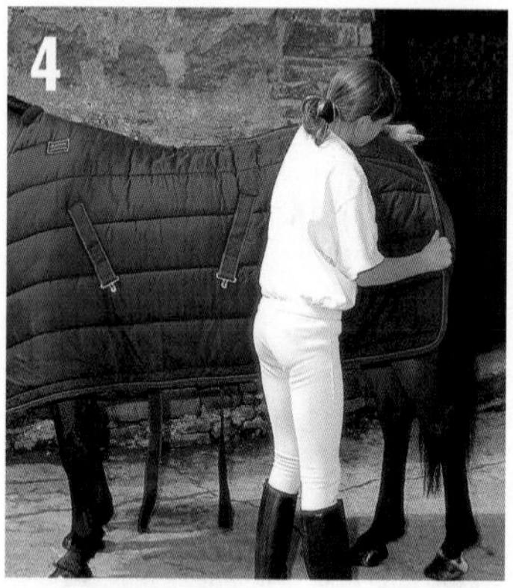

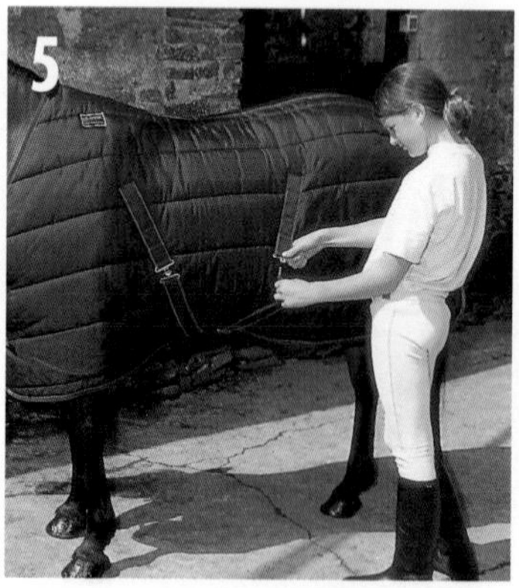

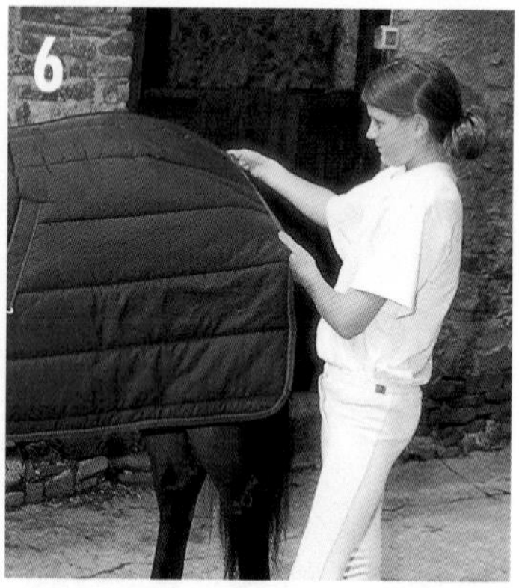

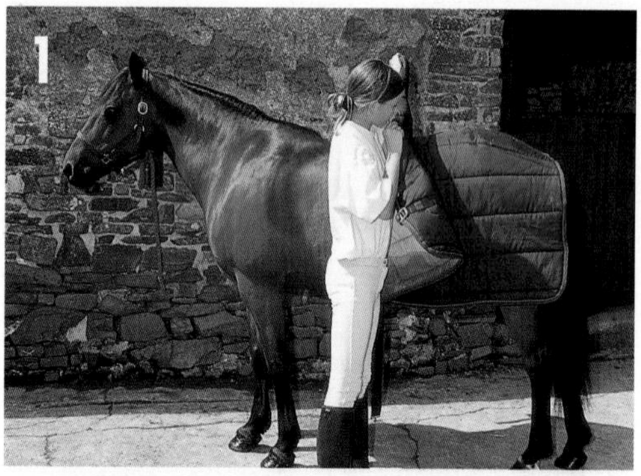

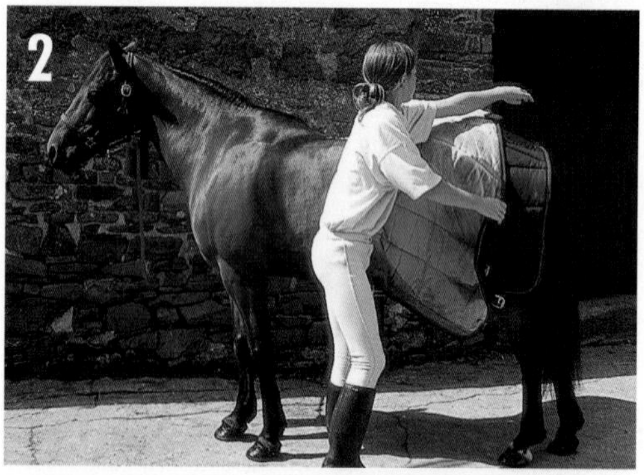

1 Removing a rug correctly is just as important as putting it on properly. Work from the back forwards.

2 Make sure all straps are undone.

3 Fold the rug in half towards the tail.

4 Then slide it off backwards, following the way the hair lies.

BEDDING

Bedding must be provided in a stable to keep your pony warm and comfortable and to protect him from injuries when rolling or lying down. It also provides cushioning for the legs and feet when standing for long periods. Whatever bedding you choose, buy the best quality available and plenty of it. Banks around the edge of a stable will help prevent your pony getting cast. A bed should be deep enough so that a pony will not touch the ground when he rolls. It must be cleaned out daily and fresh bedding added. There are several types of bedding available.

STRAW

The most commonly used and cheapest bedding is straw; wheat straw, easily available locally from merchants and farmers, is the best of them all as it makes a good, warm and comfortable bed. It is baled, which makes it easier to handle and to store, and needs to be kept indoors. It also rots down well and is therefore easy to dispose of.

A deep straw bed that is well banked up around the edges is attractive and inviting to a pony and drains adequately well when mucked out regularly. Barley straw makes an adequate bed, but can be prickly and irritate the skin. Oat straw tends to get wet and sodden quickly and will be readily eaten by most ponies. This is a disadvantage if you are trying to manage your pony's weight.

Be cautious when using straw, as it can be dusty and will contain mould and fungus spores that can irritate a pony's lungs. It can cause coughing and a thick discharge from the nostrils. If this does happen, the pony should not be bedded on straw or eat dry hay. This condition affects a large number of ponies, and there are other types of bedding available.

STRAW IS USUALLY READILY AVAILABLE AND REASONABLY PRICED.

SHAVINGS

These are more expensive than straw, but still quite economical. Only the wet patches and droppings need to be removed daily, so once you have provided a good bed it does not take a lot of shavings to keep it topped up. Shavings make a comfortable, attractive and clean looking bed. They are also free from the spores that cause some ponies problems. Wood shavings come in plastic wrapped bales and, as long as the plastic is not damaged, they can be stored outside or bought as and when you need them. The bales are heavy, however, and are therefore hard to handle. Disposing of shavings is not as easy as straw as they take a long time to rot down.

SHREDDED PAPER

This also comes in plastic wrapped bales and can be stored outside if space is short or bought as and when needed. Paper makes a warm and comfortable bed and is cheaper than shavings but more expensive than straw. It also rots better than shavings. It is dust-free, but does tend to blow around the yard if you are not careful when mucking out.

PEAT MOSS

This is useful where there may be a risk of fire. Wet patches must be removed daily and the bed raked. When you first put peat down it can be dusty, though this will soon settle. When rotted it is good for gardens.

RUBBER MATS

These can be fitted to cover the whole of the floor. Additional bedding is still advisable, but generally you need to use a lot less of it. Rubber mats are expensive to buy but are economical in the long run. They are effective in cushioning the limbs against the ground, but do not always have the appeal of a deep, warm bed.

1 Remove droppings and wet patches from the straw.

2 Add fresh bedding as required.

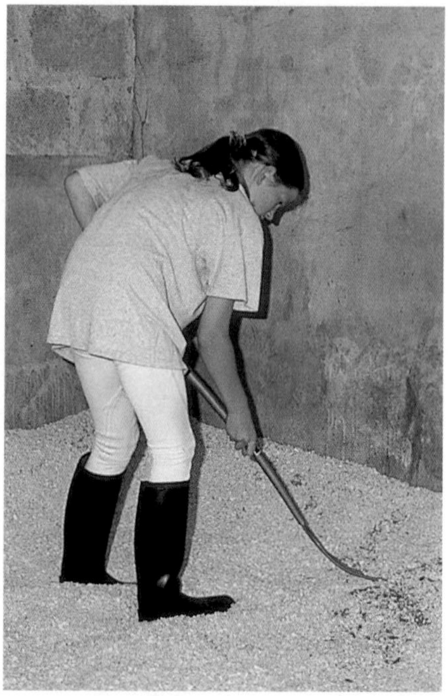

3 Ensure the bed is deep enough and banked up around the sides.

MUCKING OUT

To most pony owners, mucking out is a chore. But, with practice, the amount of time it takes can be reduced to just a few minutes. Mucking out has to be done every day and is essential in maintaining your pony's health. Like you, he will appreciate a warm, clean and comfortable bed. The equipment you will need should include a wheelbarrow, a stable fork, a shovel and a brush for sweeping. Keep the muck heap away from the stables as it will attract flies. Start a new heap every few months, leaving the first one to rot down. Keep all of your equipment tidy, and never leave equipment in the stable with a pony.

HAVE YOUR EQUIPMENT READY FOR MUCKING OUT.

THE MUCK HEAP WILL ATTRACT FLIES, SO KEEP IT WELL AWAY FROM THE STABLES.

MUCKING OUT A STRAW BED

Tie the pony up safely, preferably outside the stable or, if possible, turn him out. Put your water buckets outside. Note that this is a good time to clean the water buckets with a soft brush and to check if the water bowls of the manger needed cleaning out as well. Wheel your wheelbarrow into the stable.

RIGHT: MUCKING OUT IS A DAILY ROUTINE.

1 Start with the fork, and put any droppings in the wheelbarrow. Separate the wet and dirty straw from the clean, and put the soiled straw in the wheelbarrow. Empty the wheelbarrow onto the muck heap.

2 Bank the good straw against the wall and sweep the floor, making sure you get into all the corners. Allow it to dry for a while.

3 When you are ready to spread the straw back over the floor, leave some banked up against three sides of the stable, and add fresh straw as required. The bed should be quite thick, at least the depth of the prongs of the fork.

4 Every two or three weeks you will need to wash and disinfect the floor, leaving it to dry thoroughly before replacing the straw. It is a good idea to bank the straw in a different place each time to ensure that you clean the area underneath the pile.

MUCKING OUT SHAVINGS OR PAPER

If you notice a pony has eaten a lot of his bedding, use a less palatable material. Shavings and paper are more economical if managed slightly differently and, in the short term mucking out takes up less time so may suit you better. Tie up the pony and put the water buckets outside. Use an old washing basket or something similar and a pair of rubber gloves to collect the droppings. Take out any obvious wet patches and sprinkle fresh shavings or paper over the top, banking up around the edges.

Once a week you will need to pull the whole bed up, clean the wet out and disinfect the floor. Allow the ground to dry thoroughly before replacing the bedding and topping it up with fresh shavings or paper. Peat moss can also be mucked out this way.

THE DEEP LITTER METHOD

Some people prefer this method because it saves on both time and bedding, but it does have disadvantages. When deep littering you just pick up the droppings and place fresh bedding on top of old. Then, every few weeks or months, you remove the whole bed. This method works well with shavings because they are very absorbent and the bed does not tend to smell very much. With straw, however, if you are not careful everything can end up getting very soggy and smelly. If you chose this method, make sure that the stable is well ventilated and that the top layer of the bed is always dry, otherwise foot problems such as thrush can develop (see page 104).

CLEAN THE WATER CONTAINER THOROUGHLY.

FINISH BY SWEEPING THE OLD STRAW OUT.

KEEPING A PONY AT GRASS

The amount of space needed for each pony varies depending on the quality of the grazing. As a guide, allow a minimum of between one and a half and two acres (4,000-6,000 sq m /5,000-7,500 sq yd) per pony. Some form of shelter needs to be available, which could be in the form of a thick hedge, trees, walls or a purpose-built open-fronted field shelter. A shelter tends to be used more in the summer than it does in the winter, when a pony will want to get away from the flies. Do not remove any cobwebs as these are useful for trapping flies in summer. Note that shelters with corrugated-iron roofs can get very hot in summer.

Fresh water is vital and can be provided by various means. A freshwater stream should be running constantly and pollution-free. It should not have a sandy bottom as a pony could swallow enough sand to give himself colic.

Stagnant ponds are not a suitable water supply and must be fenced off. A self-filling trough is ideal if checked often for any faults. If you have to carry water to the field then make sure it is in a suitable container with no sharp edges. Belfast sinks can get broken and may result in nasty lacerations to the lower limbs. Some ponies are incredibly accident prone so watch out

PONIES ENJOY GRAZING AS THEY ARE NATURAL FORAGERS.

for other dangerous objects. Remember that water may freeze in the winter and ponies will be unable to break even thin ice.

There are many advantages to keeping ponies at grass. They are natural foragers, so roaming freely to graze as they please is likely to make them much happier than being shut in a stable all day without any company and with nothing to occupy them. A pony at grass will be able to exercise himself to maintain his health. He is less likely to suffer injuries when working, and, he is also less likely to be over-enthusiastic when ridden than a pony that has been shut in a stable all day.

A pony at grass generally costs less to feed because, if the grazing is good quality, then little extra feed is required during the summer months unless the pony is doing a lot of work. You should be aware, however, that too much lush grass can be very bad for ponies, especially the native and more hardy breeds. They can develop a painful condition of the feet called laminitis (see page 102). During the winter months a grass-kept pony will need hay and feed according to the amount of work you require him to do. If you are only doing light hacking at weekends, for example, then hay may be all the additional feed a native pony needs. When feeding hay to several ponies out in the field, place the hay in piles in a circle, with the piles a good distance from each other so that the ponies cannot kick each other. Hay should always be good quality, and as dust free as possible.

A FIELD CONTAINING BROKEN EQUIPMENT OR RUBBISH IS DANGEROUS AND UNSUITABLE FOR A PONY.

TRY TO KEEP YOUR PONY WITH OTHER HORSES, AS SINGLE ANIMALS BECOME LONELY.

Keeping your pony at grass all or most of the year can save a lot of time if you are busy with work or school. However, you will still need to see your pony twice a day to check for general well being, wounds and the condition of his feet. If you only visit once a day and your pony becomes ill or injures himself, is stolen or escapes from the field, it could be a long time until your next visit.

Grooming should not be overdone if a pony is living out all year as this will remove dirt and grease from his coat, which could otherwise help to keep him warm during the colder months. All you should need to do before going for a ride is to remove mud on his legs and body with a dandy brush and to brush out the mane and tail with a body brush. Do not forget to pick out and check his feet too. After a ride always brush off any sweat marks and mud before you turn him back out into the field, although he will probably go straight down and roll. Rolling is a good way for a pony to rub those parts of him that have had the saddle and bridle on, and which may cause itching. Rolling in the winter coats a pony with mud, which helps to keep him warm. Rolling in spring helps to rub out the old winter coat. It appears to be relaxing and fun and so should not be discouraged.

Stabling your pony for part of the time can be useful if you want to restrict grazing, for example, in the case of an overweight pony, or in managing a pony suffering from laminitis. If you are doing a lot of work in the winter you may want to clip your pony and keep him in a stable at night with a rug on, turning him out with a New Zealand rug on during the day. It is really a case of working out a routine that suits both you and your pony.

HORSES NEED PLENTY OF FREE TIME.

ROLLING IS GOOD FOR HORSES AND THEY ALSO SEEM TO ENJOY IT.

A SHELTER WILL HELP PROTECT YOUR PONY FROM BAD WEATHER AND FLIES IN SUMMER.

PASTURE MANAGEMENT

A little time and effort looking after your field will be well invested. It is important that it provides a good quality of grazing, but is not too rich. Neither should it be full of weeds, wet or boggy. A small paddock can quickly become over-grazed and sour. Ponies can be fussy eaters and wasteful when they are grazing. Droppings make parts of the field unpalatable, and, as ponies browse about looking for tasty bits of grass, they tend to trample on the rest. Topping (or mowing) the field will make the grass more attractive and will tidy it up considerably. Sheep and bullocks are useful to graze the field occasionally, as they eat grass that has been rejected by ponies and help to reduce the burden of worm parasites which are not a problem to them, but can be dangerous to your pony. The field will benefit from being divided in two or three sections so that one section can be

DOCK LEAVES INDICATE THAT THE QUALITY OF THE PASTURE IS POOR.

FIELDS NEED MAINTENANCE TO PROVIDE GOOD QUALITY GRAZING. TOO MANY WEEDS CAN CAUSE PROBLEMS.

THICK HEDGES MAKE AN EXCELLENT NATURAL FENCE.

rested to prevent it becoming 'horse-sick'. If the field is large enough, one part could be left to grow to make hay for the winter. If you divide the field up this way, electric fencing is useful, as it is easy to move (see page 40), but make sure the pony still has access to shelter and water.

You will help preserve the condition of the pasture by removing droppings every couple of days, and making sure that stale patches don't develop. If this is not possible, the field can be harrowed at intervals to spread the droppings.

SLACK WIRE IS A HAZARD AS HORSES CAN BECOME ENTANGLED IN IT.

REMOVE DROPPINGS FROM THE FIELD REGULARLY.

FENCING, GATES AND FIELD SAFETY

Whatever method of fencing you choose, it needs to be secure, stable and high enough. The grass is always greener on the other side, and ponies do have a tendency to escape. They need different fencing to other animals because they are more prone to injuring themselves or jumping free. Where fencing has been damaged it must be properly repaired immediately, as some ponies will take every opportunity that arises. Try to remove hazards around the field, including scrap iron, old farm machinery and any large or sharp stones. Stagnant ponds must also be fenced off as they are dangerous.

A STOUT WOODEN FENCE FOR AN EXERCISE RING.

THIS POOR FENCING HAS SHARP EDGES AND IS NOT SECURE.

A WELL-MADE POST AND RAIL FENCE.

POST AND RAIL FENCING

This is the ideal. It is expensive to erect and needs to be well maintained, but it does last a long time if well looked after.

HEDGES

These are suitable if they are thick and well maintained. Regular trimming will help to thicken them and keep them tidy. A good thick hedge will provide shelter from the wind and rain in winter and some shade in the summer. Hedges can become thin in winter so you need to make sure a pony doesn't push through any gaps or weak patches. Watch out for yew and deadly nightshade in a hedge. (see page 41).

STONE WALLS

Common in some parts of the country, these are a good method of fencing if well maintained as they provide a natural wind-break.

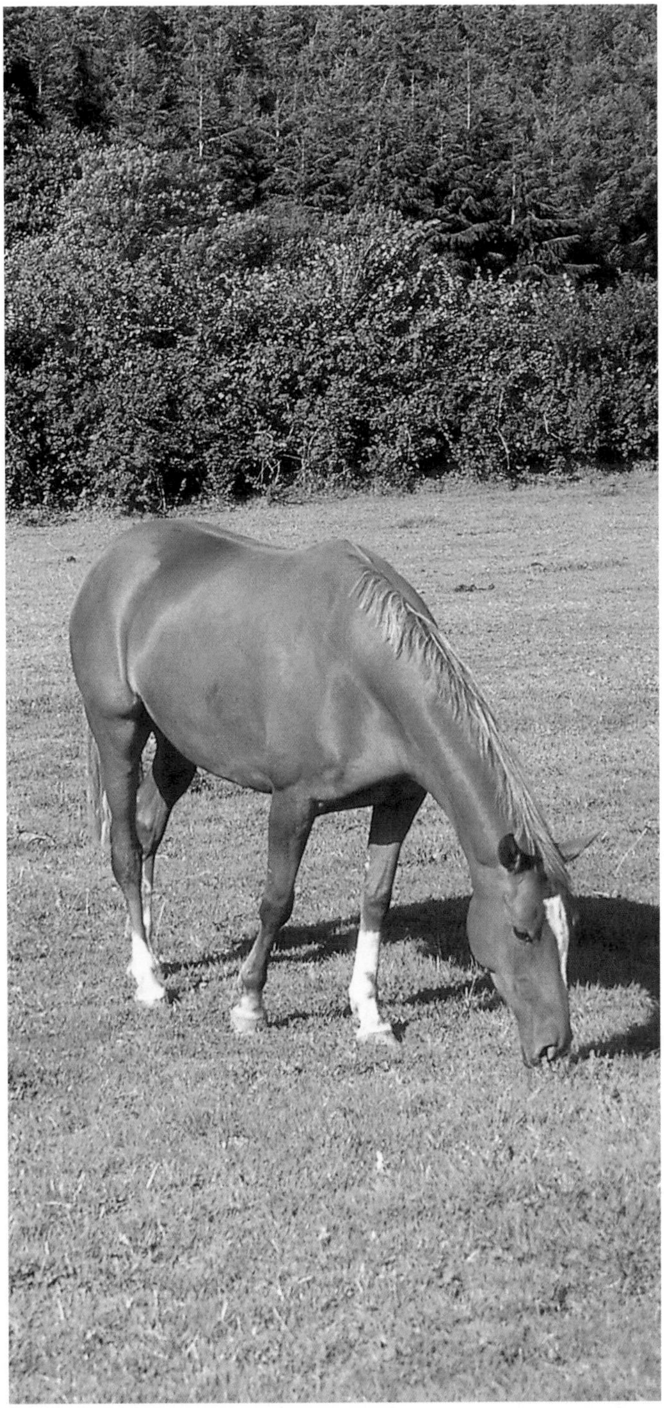

THICK, HIGH HEDGES KEEP THESE PONIES CONTAINED.

BARBED WIRE

This is very dangerous and can be the cause of nasty wounds. It should be avoided at all times. Plain strands of wire are satisfactory if kept tight and if the bottom strand is at least 30 cm (1 ft) off the ground so a pony cannot get a foot over it when grazing close to the fence.

ELECTRIC FENCING

This has its place and ponies soon learn to respect it. It is easy to put up and move around, so it is useful for dividing up a field. Electrified tape is available in various widths from some agricultural merchants. It is much more visible to the pony than just plain wire, and he is less likely to run into it when galloping about.

RIGHT: HORSES SOON LEARN TO RESPECT ELECTRIC FENCING.

BARBED WIRE FENCING.

GATES

All gates should be of strong construction, sturdy and well-hung. Gates are best situated well away from a corner of the field as ponies tend to gather around when a visitor or food are expected, and arguments can develop, ending with one or more ponies getting kicked. If you are creating a new gateway, choose a well-drained part of the field so that it does not get too boggy in winter with all the traffic. For obvious safety reasons, it is best not to have a gate that opens out onto a road. Old iron gates may have sharp edges and are best avoided. The fastenings must be pony-proof so that they cannot undo them.

GATES SHOULD BE STRONG, WELL-MAINTAINED, AND HUNG CORRECTLY.

RAGWORT MUST BE DUG UP (TO COMPLETELY REMOVE THE WHOLE PLANT) AND BURNT — BUT NOT IN THE HORSE'S FIELD.

POISONOUS PLANTS

Some plants are very dangerous to ponies and should be removed from a field immediately. Make sure you dig them up completely (or they may grow back), and burn them. It is worth your while learning to recognise plants that can be a threat. You will find them in the pasture and in the hedgerow and they include:

- Boxwood
- Foxglove
- Green bracken
- Hellebore
- Hemlock
- Henbane
- Horsetail
- Laburnum
- Meadow saffron
- Monkshood
- Nightshade
- Oak
- Poison ivy
- Privet
- Ragwort
- Rhododendron
- Yew

CHAPTER 3

TACK AND EQUIPMENT

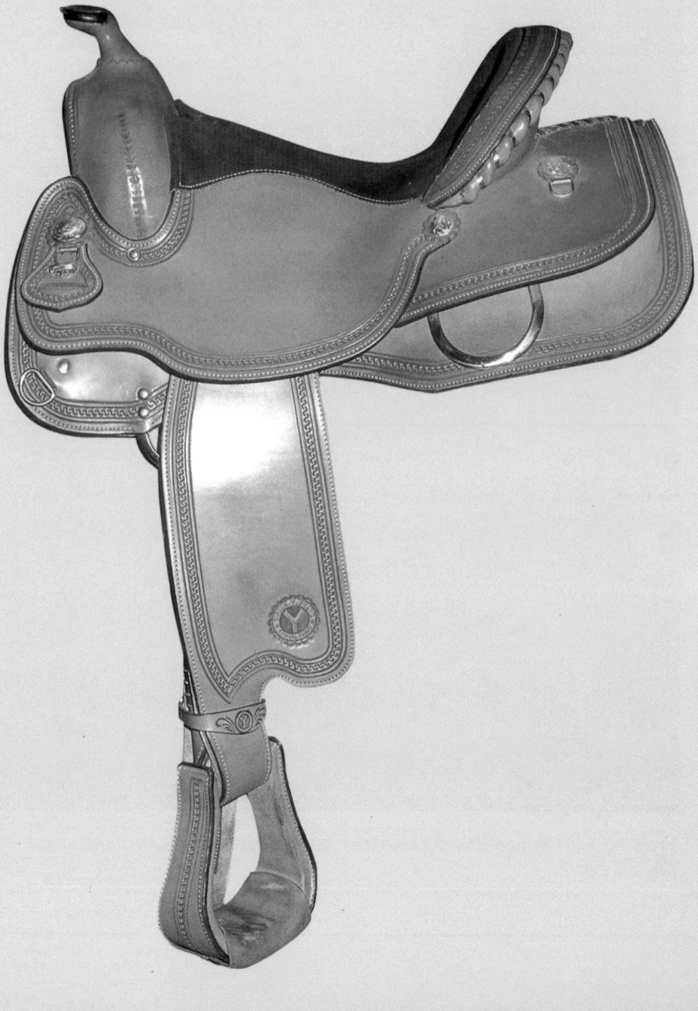

SADDLES AND ACCESSORIES

A saddle helps to keep you secure while riding and helps to remove keep your legs in the proper position. It also helps to spread a rider's weight evenly over a pony's back, keeping pressure away from its spine. Saddles are usually made of leather, although they can also be synthetic. Synthetic saddles are lightweight, which makes them easier to carry, and are easy to clean. Saddles are expensive and you should aim for the best quality saddle you can afford. If you buy a second-hand one be very wary of the stitching and general condition. A good saddle will last a lifetime, unless the pony grows out of it or you change your pony. You should look after it well, checking regularly for signs of wear and tear.

A saddle, even a new one, has to be well fitted or it will damage a pony's back. It should sit evenly and comfortably, and should not wobble about when the pony walks. You should be able to see daylight underneath the gullet when the rider is sitting on it and there should not be any pinching on the pony's body. The underside should not be lumpy and the tree and general condition of the leather and stitching should be checked carefully when buying. A saddler will usually come and check that a saddle fits the pony. Saddles are easily scratched and damaged if not put away correctly. Invest in a purpose-made saddle rack and fix it on the wall of the tack room at a height you can easily reach. Some of them have a hook underneath to hang the bridle on. If you need to stand your saddle against the wall as a temporary measure, use the girth to protect the front arch and cantle from being scratched.

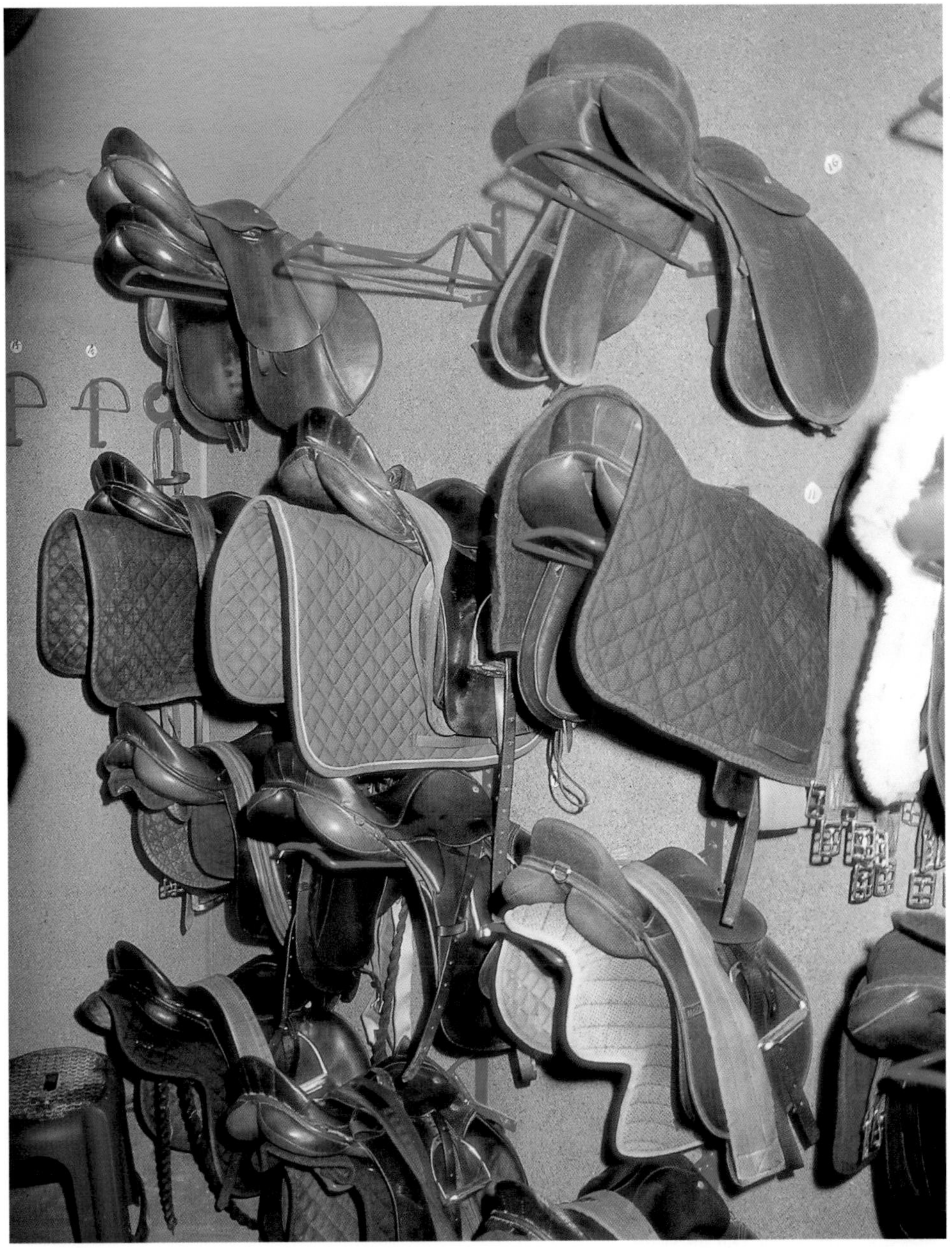

TACK SHOULD BE STORED AND PROPERLY LOOKED AFTER. ALWAYS BUY THE BEST YOU CAN AFFORD.

THE SADDLE

SADDLE TREE

The tree is the frame inside the saddle, usually made of wood or plastic. Different saddles suit different activities, for example, there are western saddles, jumping saddles, dressage saddles and eventing saddles. For general riding, you need a general purpose saddle.

NUMNAH

The numnah is the pad or cloth that goes under the saddle, sometimes cut to the shape of the saddle, which is used to make the pony more comfortable. They can be made of different materials, including sheepskin, which is usually the most expensive. Numnahs have various straps to secure them to a saddle. Make sure a numnah is put on correctly, and never use one to compensate for an ill-fitting saddle.

THE GIRTH NEEDS TO BE CHECKED REGULARLY TO ENSURE IT'S IN GOOD CONDITION.

A SADDLE SHAPED NUMNAH.

GIRTH

This is the strap that goes under the pony's stomach, just behind the forelegs, to keep the saddle in place. It is very important that it is safe and secure. Girths come in a wide variety of size, shape and colour and are commonly made of leather, webbing or nylon. Some are padded. The most important thing is that your girth is safe. Check all parts of it, including stitching, regularly and, if in any doubt, get it checked by an expert or buy a new one. Make sure you keep your girth clean, as dirt and sweat can rub and make the skin sore.

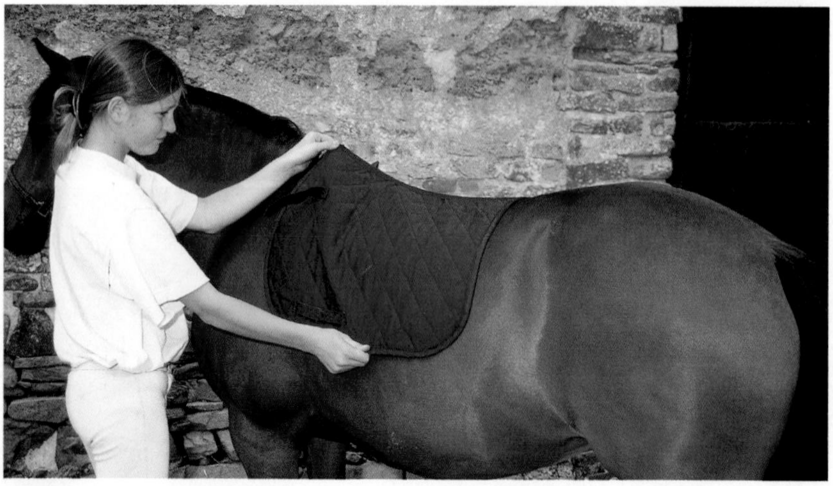

NUMNAHS VARY IN SIZE AND THICKNESS.

STIRRUP BAR

Under the skirt of a saddle is the stirrup bar. The stirrup leathers are attached to this, and the stirrups hang from the leathers. The stirrup bar is open at one end so that, if the rider were to get caught up in something, the stirrup leather would come free, instead of the rider being dragged along with the pony. Some stirrup bars have a device at the end, which can be turned upwards to stop the stirrup leather from coming off when the pony is being led without its rider. You should never ride with the bars in this position.

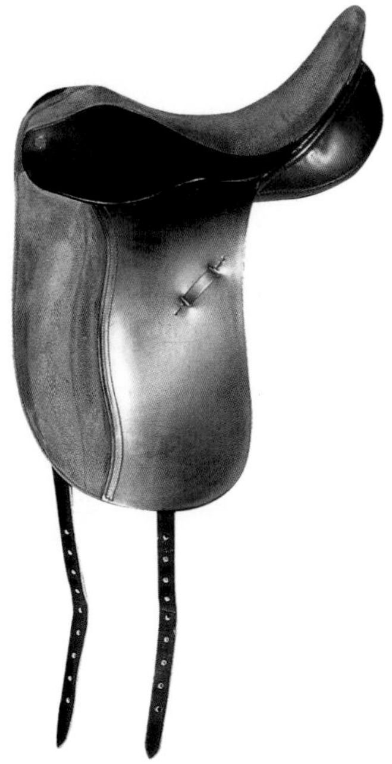

DRESSAGE SADDLE

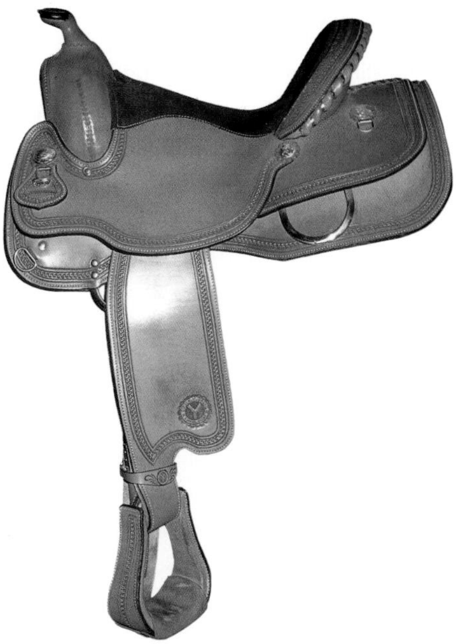

WESTERN SADDLE

SUEDE-EDGED
DRESSAGE SADDLE

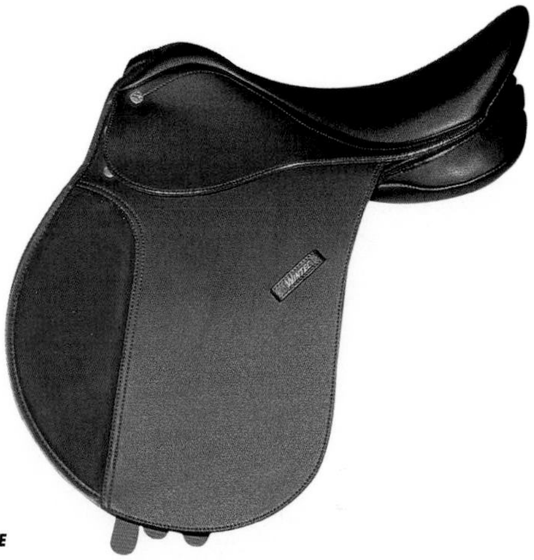

GENERAL
PURPOSE SADDLE

JUMPING SADDLE

SIDE SADDLE

STIRRUP LEATHERS

These hold the stirrup onto the stirrup bar. They are made of ordinary leather or hide, or are synthetic. They tend to stretch a bit, especially when new, so always check that the holes are level or you could be riding with one stirrup longer than the other. Check the leathers regularly for rotten stitching and for signs of wear and tear.

SADDLE HORSE.

STIRRUPS

The stirrup should be approximately 1 cm. (1/2 in.) wider than the widest part of the foot. Rubber treads can be fitted to the irons to stop the feet from slipping. It is important that children do not ride with adult stirrup irons as the whole foot can slip through with frightening consequences. Old stirrup irons made of nickel are dangerous because they may bend around the foot in an accident and crush it.

SAFETY STIRRUPS

If your saddle does not have an open-ended stirrup bar, you should use safety stirrups. These have a rubber band on the side, which allows the foot to be released. Another type of safety stirrup is all metal and hinged at the top. Make sure the hinged side or rubber band is on the outside.

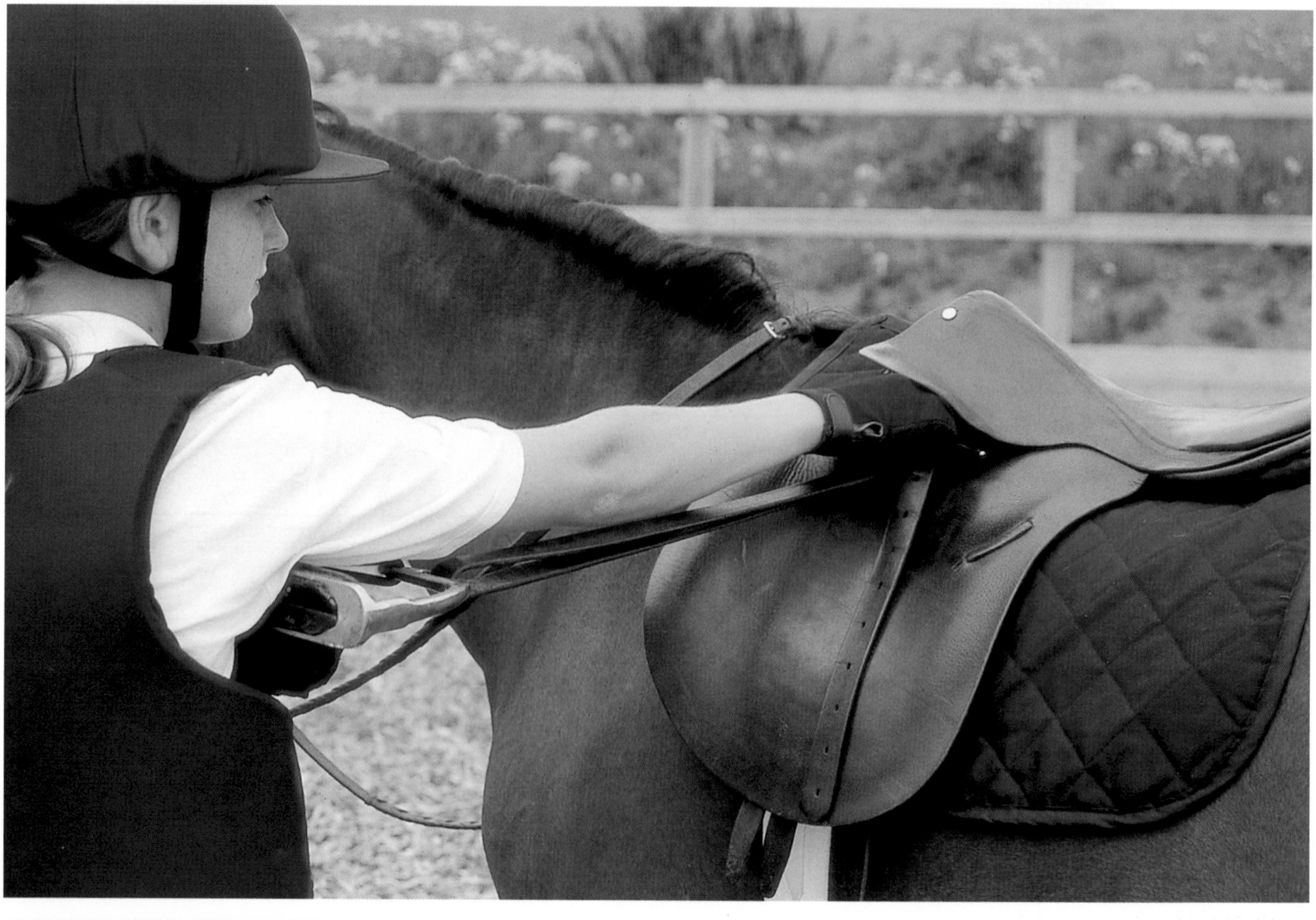

CHECK STIRRUP LEATHERS BEFORE EVERY RIDE, AND CLEAN THEM REGULARLY.

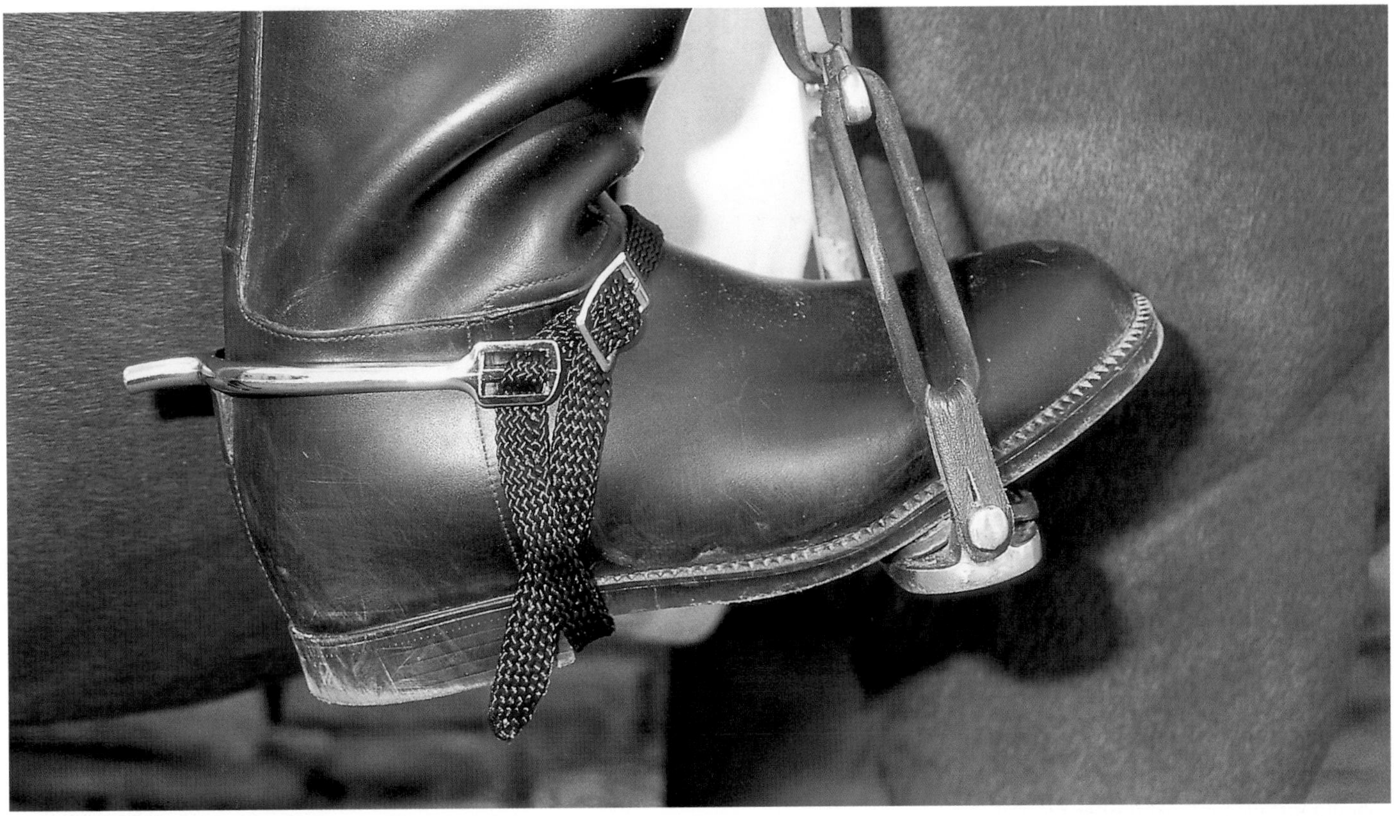

STIRRUPS SHOULD BE A COMFORTABLE FIT FOR YOUR FOOT, AND NOT TOO LOOSE OR TIGHT.

TACK SHOULD BE WELL-MAINTAINED AND REPAIRED PROFESSIONALLY WHEN NECESSARY.

TACK

Tack describes the items that your pony wears for riding. It is essential that all tack fits well, is put on correctly and is looked after to ensure that it is safe to use and is not likely to break – stitching, for example, can rot eventually.

CHECK THE CONDITION OF SECOND-HAND TACK. WITH CAREFUL MAINTENANCE, IT SHOULD LAST WELL.

Basic tack consists mainly of a saddle and a bridle. You need to learn about the different types of tack and why they may or may not be suitable for your pony. If, when you buy your pony he comes with his existing tack, it is wise to check that it is appropriate. Parts of a pony's tack may need to be replaced from time to time. He may need a different noseband or bit, for example. Always buy the best-quality tack that you can afford and, if you buy second-hand tack, take special care over the condition of the stitching and the leather. With a saddle, get the tree checked to make sure it is not broken. Tack is expensive, but should last well if looked after properly.

TACK ROOM

THE BRIDLE

Usually made of leather, this is the set of straps (with buckles) that fit on a pony's head, and which hold the bit in his mouth. The headpiece fits behind the ears so that the throat lash, which is a part of the headpiece, does up on the near side, that is the left side as you are sitting on your pony. The throat lash helps to keep the bridle in place. Other parts of the bridle are the noseband, which fits around the nose, the brow band, which attaches to the headpiece and goes in front of the ears to prevent the headpiece slipping backwards, and the cheek pieces, which attach the bit to the headpiece. Different nosebands are available (see page 50), but most snaffle bridles (see below) have a cavesson noseband. (see picture on page 50). Bridles without bits are used for ponies that, for some reason, are unable to hold a bit in the mouth. Most of them work by using the reins to put pressure on the nose instead of the bit. They are effective, but should only be used in experienced hands.

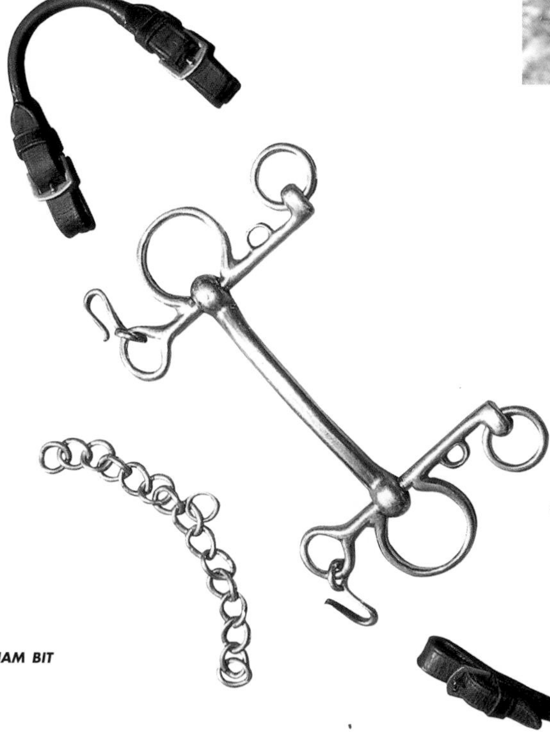

PELHAM BIT

THE BRIDLE

This sits in the pony's mouth, on top of its tongue and between his front and back teeth. There are a huge variety of bits available – all with a different type of action on the pony's mouth. Most bits are made of stainless steel, with the part that actually goes into the mouth varying. Some are made of metal, some of rubber and some of 'vulcanite' – a kind of hardened rubber. Rubber bits are softer on the mouth than metal ones, but don't last as long. You need to check them regularly to make sure they are still in good condition. A poorly fitted bit is very uncomfortable and the mouth can easily be damaged. You can tell when a bit has been fitted correctly because you can see a 1/2cm (1/4in.) gap between the lip and the ring. A bit that does not fit will pinch. The most common type of bit is the snaffle. This may consist of loose rings, which slide through the mouthpiece, or of fixed rings as in the eggbutt snaffle. It can have either a

SNAFFLE BIT

single or double joint in the middle, or a straight bar. Pelham bits are stronger and have a curb chain. They are sometimes used on a pony that tends to be hard to stop. Check with an expert first, though – it may be your riding that needs the attention and not the bit!! Bits should always be rinsed in water after use.

REINS

FOAM AROUND THE MOUTH INDICATES A COMFORTABLE BIT. NOTE THE CAVESSON NOSEBAND.

These are the straps attached to the bit which enable the rider to control a pony. They usually consist of two separate pieces of plain or plaited leather. At one end they are attached to the bit and at the other a buckle fastens them together. Some reins are partly covered with rubber for a better grip. Plain leather reins can be slippery to hold onto in the rain, or if the pony is sweaty, while plaited reins are hard to clean. Wearing gloves will give you a better grip.

NOSEBANDS

Most ordinary snaffle bridles have a cavesson noseband (left). However, if your pony opens his mouth too wide, or crosses his jaw when being ridden, you may be advised to use a drop noseband which is worn lower than a cavesson and does up under the bit. Nosebands need to be fitted by an expert because if they are too low they can interfere with a pony's breathing. They need to be done up firmly to be effective, but not too tightly. A flash noseband is a cavesson noseband with a strap, which can be fastened under the bit to act like a drop noseband. The advantage of a flash noseband is that you can still use a standing martingale if you wish (see below), but make sure you attach it to the cavesson and not to the drop strap.

MARTINGALES

Usually made of leather, a martingale is used to stop a horse or pony from throwing its head too high in the air. Neck straps of all martingales should fasten on the near side and you should be able to get the width of your hand under them and at the withers.

STANDING MARTINGALE

A standing martingale has a strap that goes between the forelegs from the girth to the noseband, and which is attached to either end with a loop. A neck strap supports this strap and a rubber ring keeps it together. Make sure you leave enough slack to allow it to push upwards to touch the throat lash.

RUNNING MARTINGALE

A running martingale attaches to a neck strap and to the girth in the same way as a standing martingale but, as it goes through the forelegs, it divides into two with a ring at each end for the reins to go through. Rubber stops should be fitted between the rings and the bit to keep the martingale in the correct position. Again, the martingale will help prevent a pony from throwing his head too high. Care must be taken to make sure it is not fitted too tightly when attached to the girth. The rings should reach the gullet.

MARTINGALES NEED TO BE CORRECTLY FITTED.

IRISH MARTINGALE

This a small strap of leather about 10 cm (4 in.) long with a ring on each end. The reins pass through the rings and under the neck. This stops the reins being thrown over the pony's head and helps to keep them in place.

CRUPPER

A crupper has a padded loop which goes under the pony's tail and attaches to a ring on the back of the saddle. Its purpose is to stop the saddle from slipping forwards. Keep it clean and make sure that it does not make the tail sore.

BREAST GIRTH

This can be used to stop the saddle slipping backwards. A strap goes across the breast and attaches to the girth straps under the saddle flaps. Another strap then goes over the neck in front of the withers and holds it in place. A breast girth must not be too high or it will interfere with a pony's breathing.

HOW TO PUT TACK ON

It is important that your tack fits your pony properly and that it is well-maintained. It is vital to fasten it correctly every time you put it on and to remove it in the correct manner. A simple mistake such as not tightening the girth sufficiently will make the saddle slip. Not only will the rider fall off, but it may well frighten the pony, too – disaster!

RIGHT: A THIN STRAP UNDER THE BIT HELPS TO PREVENT THE PONY OPENING HIS MOUTH TO AVOID THE BIT.

BELOW: STRECTHING THE LEG FORWARDS HELPS TO SMOOTH OUT ANY UNCOMFORTABLE CREASES UNDER THE GIRTH.

PUTTING ON THE SADDLE

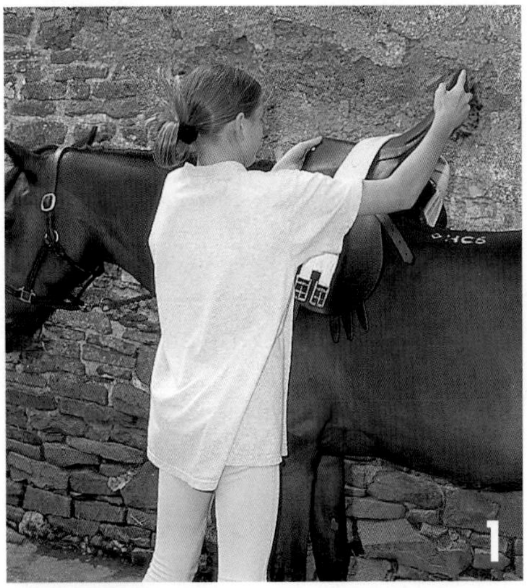

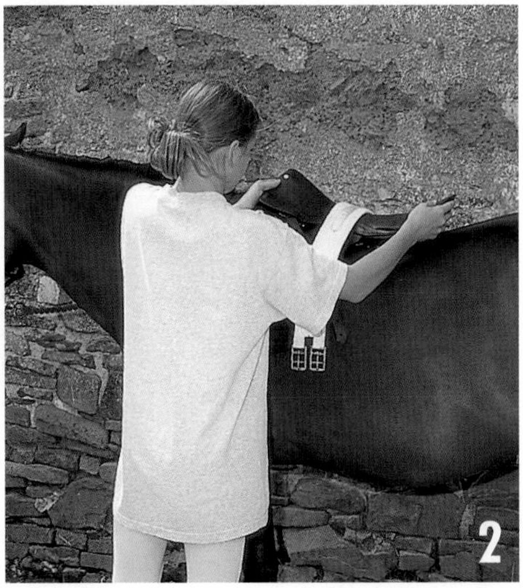

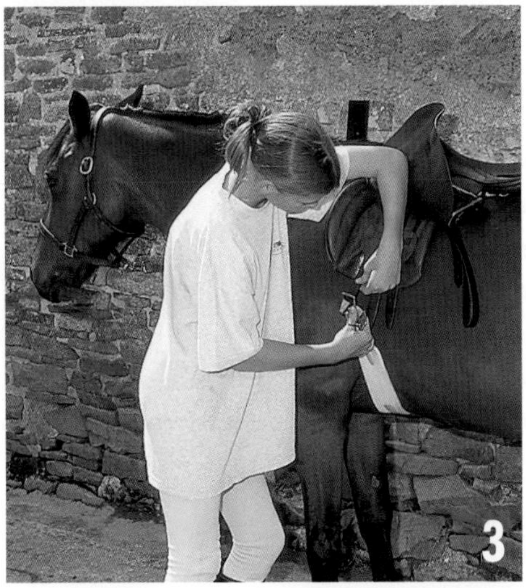

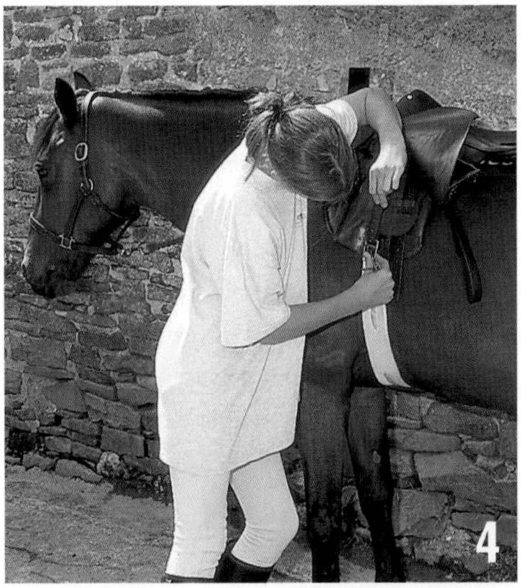

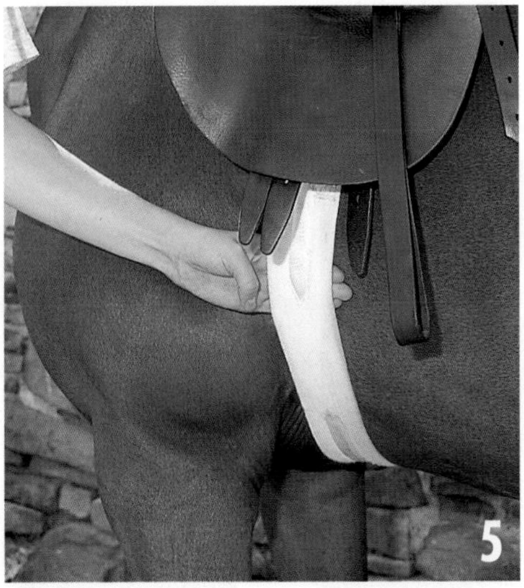

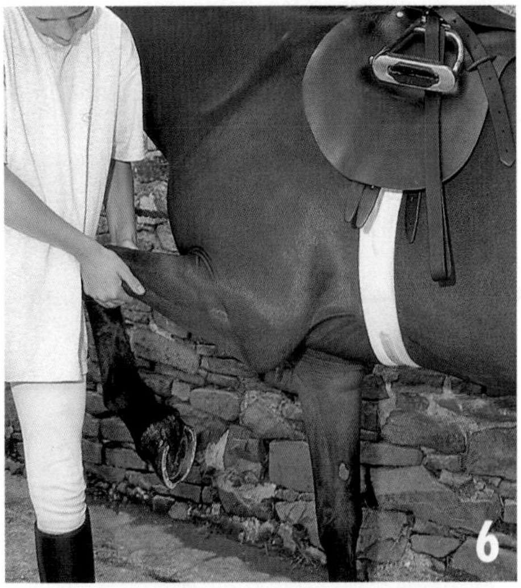

1 Tie your pony up, talking to him as you approach. You usually put a saddle on from the near side (the left side of the pony) so, with your left hand under the front arch and your right hand under the cantle, place the saddle on your pony's back, well forward on the withers.

2 Then gently slide it backwards into the correct position. Go round to the other side to let the girth hang down. Always go in front of your pony and not behind, in case you get kicked.

3 Return to the near side and do up the girth. Make sure the back and girth areas are clean before putting the saddle on, as dirt and sweat will rub and cause sores.

4 The buckles must be level and you should be able to insert your hand under the girth when tightened. Stand close to the shoulder when fastening the girth.

5 Make sure the girth is not twisted and that the numnah is well up into the gullet. Do not fasten the girth too tightly. Many ponies puff out their bellies when you first do up the girth so check it and perhaps tighten it by another hole or two in a couple of minutes.

6 Pull the buckle guards down over the buckles to protect the saddle flap. Remember to check and tighten the girth again before you mount. Leave the stirrup irons run up until you are ready to mount. Stretching the leg forward evens out any creases in the skin under the girth and prevents pinching.

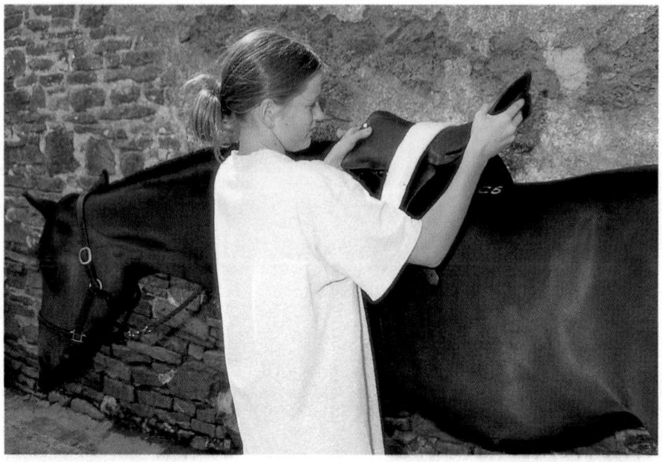

REMOVING SADDLE

A CRUPPER STOPS THE SADDLE SLIPPING FORWARD.

TACKING UP USING A MARTINGALE

If you are using a running or standing martingale, put this on before the saddle and attach the martingale to the girth.

TACKING UP USING A CRUPPER

Put the crupper on after the saddle is on and the girth is done up. Stand by the hind leg on the near side and pass the tail gently through the loop of the crupper. Make sure that all the hairs are flat and comfortable and the crupper is right at the top of the tail. Attach the crupper to the metal ring on the back of the saddle, firmly enough to stop the saddle slipping forwards, but not so tight that it pulls on the tail.

PUTTING ON THE BRIDLE

1 If you are in the stable, remove the head collar and put it away. If you are outside with your pony tied up then slip the head collar off his nose and fasten it around his neck.

2 Standing on the pony's near side, and facing forwards, put the reins over his head.

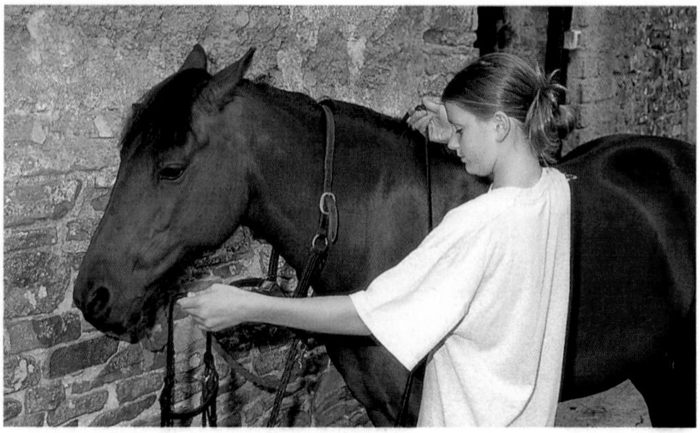

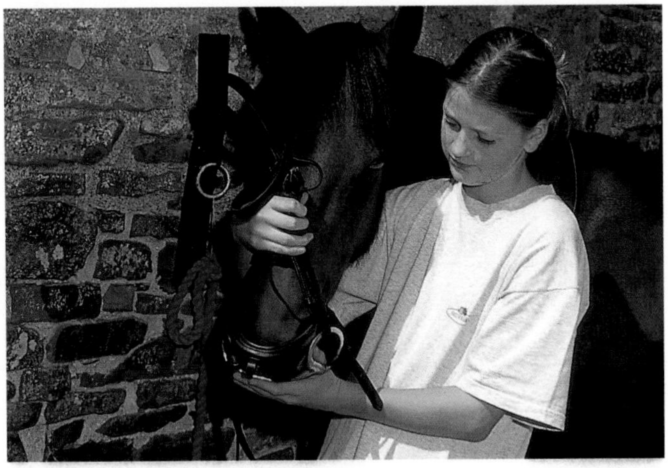

3 Pass your right hand under his chin and back over the top of his nose and hold the bridle as shown.

4 With your left hand, guide the bit into the pony's mouth, raising your right hand slightly to keep the bit in place. .

5 Then put the headpiece over the ears, making sure the mane and forelock are not caught up under the bridle.

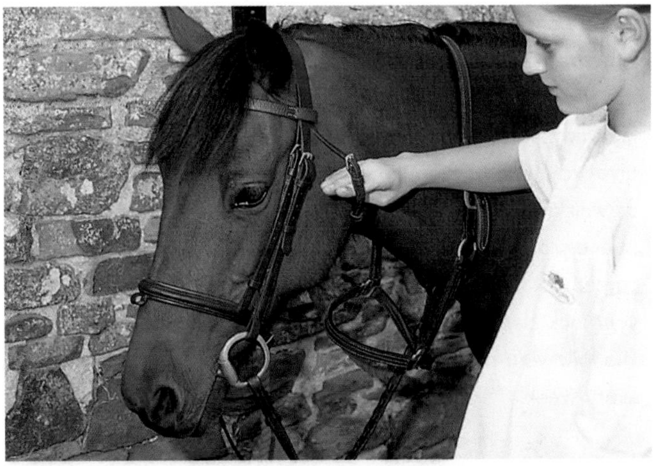

6 Do up the throatlash, so that you can get the width of your hand between the pony's cheek and the strap.

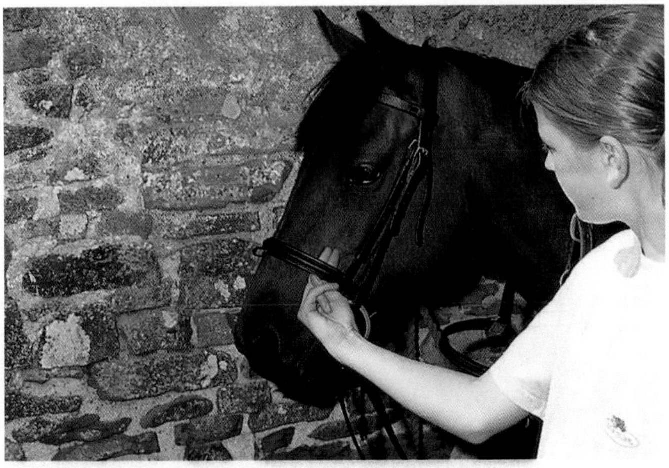

7 Do up the noseband, (attaching the martingale if used) so that you can still get two fingers under it.

8 Make sure all buckles are done up properly and that no straps are left flapping.

If you are using a running martingale or an Irish martingale, unbuckle the reins to pass the rings through and buckle them up again.

Stand in front and check that the noseband, bridle and bit all look level and comfortable.

REMOVING THE BRIDLE

Undo the noseband and throat lash, and slip them over the pony's ears, being careful not to bang his teeth as the bit comes out of the mouth. Put the head collar on and take the reins over the pony's head. Tie up the pony if required.

ALWAYS USE A DAMP CLOTH OR SPONGE TO CLEAN THE BRIDLE AND TACK – NEVER SUBMERGE THEM IN WATER.

CLEANING TACK

Many pony owners do not relish the thought of cleaning tack. However, maintaining your tack correctly is extremely important, and is a good time to check for signs of wear and tear. Pay particular attention to stitching, as this tends to rot and give way quicker than the leather itself. Check stirrup leathers as well and shorten them occasionally to avoid continuous wear in one place. Check the tree of the saddle periodically and be careful not to drop a saddle, which can damage the tree. Wipe your tack clean every time you go for a ride and rinse the bit. The following procedure for cleaning tack should be carried out every week.

YOU WILL NEED:

Old cloths	Metal polish
Sponges	Dandy brush
Saddle soap and oil	Bucket of lukewarm water
Clean rags	A match or a nail

HOW TO CLEAN A BRIDLE

Undo all of the buckles and take the bridle apart. Using a sponge and lukewarm water, clean all parts of the bridle to remove the dirt and grease. Never soak the parts or submerge them in buckets of water. Be careful not to use hot water, which will dry out the leather by removing its natural oils. Wipe over all parts of the bridle with a cloth to remove excess water and leave to dry naturally. You do not need to oil your bridle every time you use it, but be aware that it can dry out and lose its suppleness. When you do oil, use a sponge or small paintbrush and dab oil on the underside of the leather only, which is the absorbent part. Leave the leather to soak in the oil.

Next, apply the saddle soap, making sure you follow the manufacturer's instructions. It usually comes in a bar, a tube or as a spray. If you are using a bar, dip it into the water and rub on a dry sponge. With a tube of saddle soap, apply it with a damp sponge but make sure the sponge does not become too wet. Spray soaps can be sprayed straight onto the leather. Rub soap over both sides of the leather, making sure you clean well around all the buckles and bends. Any holes that still have soap in them can be poked through with a matchstick or a nail. When you have put the bridle back together you can give it a final wipe with saddle soap and a sponge, to remove any fingerprints. To clean the bit, wash with lukewarm water, and clean the rings with metal polish. Be sure to keep the polish away from the mouthpiece, which should only be washed with warm water. Martingales and other leather items can be cleaned in the same way as the bridle.

WIPE OFF EXCESS MOISTURE AND LEAVE TO DRY.

HOW TO CLEAN A LEATHER SADDLE

Put your saddle on a saddle horse. Remove the stirrups and leathers, girth and girth guards, and clean the underneath with lukewarm water. Dry with a cloth and apply oil and soap in the same way as to the bridle. To dry the saddle, stand it up with something soft under the front arch for protection.

Put the saddle back on the saddle horse and clean all of the leather in the same way as you cleaned the bridle. Only apply oil to the rough underside, as oil on the seat or saddle flaps may come off on your clothes. Clean any metal with the metal polish, being very careful not to get any on the leather.

APPLY OIL TO THE UNDERSIDE ONLY – NOT ON THE SEAT OR SADDLE FLAPS.

To clean the stirrup irons, wash them with the treads removed – an old toothbrush is useful for this. Clean the treads separately. Use metal polish on the metal and replace the treads when they are dry.

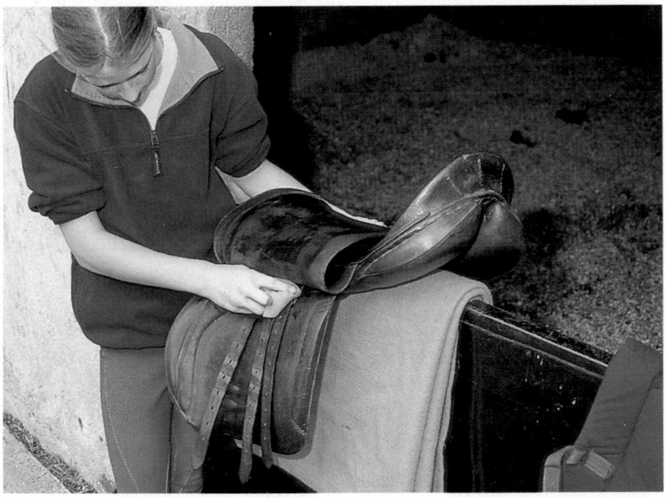

THIS IS A GOOD TIME TO CHECK STITCHING AND SIGNS OF WEAR.

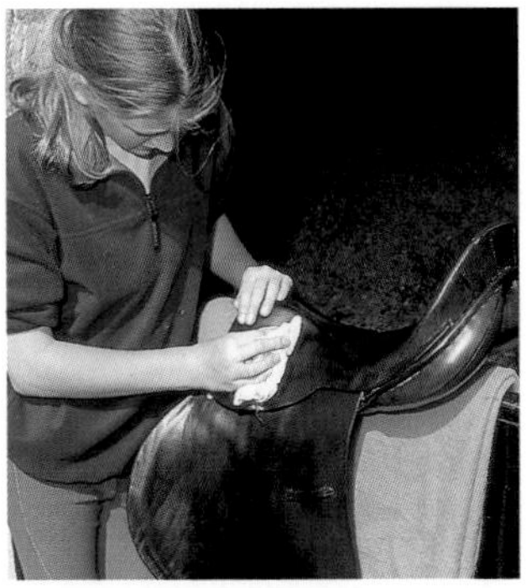

NEVER SOAK YOUR SADDLE WITH WATER.

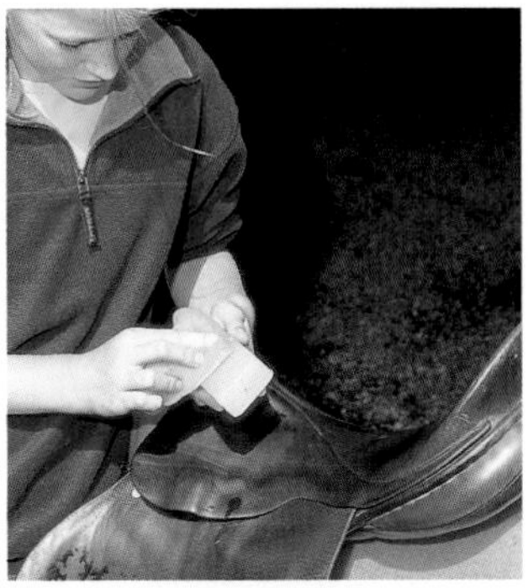

APPLY SADDLE SOAP OVER THE SADDLE.

Stirrup leathers are washed, oiled and soaped in the same way as the bridle. Use a matchstick to remove the soap from any holes and remember to check the stitching. How you clean the girth depends on the material it is made of.

CLEAN THE SADDLE THROUGHLY.

Leather girths can be cleaned in the same way as the bridle. Webbing and padded girths should be vigorously brushed off with a dandy brush after each use and washed regularly. Follow the manufacturer's instructions for cleaning numnahs, and make sure they are kept clean and dry.

Some cotton girths can be machine-washed. Simply place a pillowcase over the buckles. To clean synthetic saddles, wipe them over with lukewarm water and a sponge. Sometimes a mild detergent can be used, but follow the manufacturer's instructions.

BOOTS

A wide range of boots are available to protect a pony's legs from knocks and injuries while being ridden and during travel. Some of the boots used while exercising prevent the pony getting injured, while others, such as brushing boots, for example, prevent him injuring himself, and are used for general riding (see below and picture, right).

ALL-IN-ONE TRAVEL BOOTS

These cover from above the knee or hock down to the coronet band. They are quick and easy to fit and provide good protection. Alternatively, you could use stable bandages with padding underneath (see the picture on page 60).

BRUSHING BOOTS

Fitted below the knee, these protect the pony from any injury should he strike himself with another foot or leg while being ridden. Sometimes a rubber ring with a strap through its centre is fitted just above a pony's fetlock to serve the same purpose. Some people use brushing boots on all four legs, others just on the front legs. Different ponies have different confirmation and action, which makes some of them more prone to injuring themselves than others. Brushing boots should be fitted firmly but not too tightly, and with no mud underneath, which make him sore. Speedycut boots are similar to brushing boots, but are fitted a little higher up.

OVERREACH BOOTS

These are similar to a bell in shape and are made of rubber. They protect the heel and coronet of the fore feet and fit around the pastern. Some have Velcro straps but most are the type you pull over the hoof to fit them, which is not always easy. Turn each boot inside out to pull it over the hoof, then fold it down to cover the coronet and heel. Keep a check on the pasterns to make sure the boots are not rubbing. Overreach boots are used while exercising and travelling to prevent injuries to the coronet and heel should the pony tread on himself with his hind feet. They have a tendency to turn upwards and inside out, especially while riding in muddy conditions, which could trip a pony up.

TENDON BOOTS

Used only on the front legs, these prevent injuries to the tendon area if the horse should strike himself quite high up with his hind foot. They have a thick pad that runs down the back of the leg. Often tendon and brushing boots are combined in one. Tendon boots do not support the tendons.

TRAVELLING BOOTS ARE EASY TO PUT ON.

BRUSHING BOOTS PROTECT THE HORSE FROM SELF-INFLICTED INJURY WHILE BEING RIDDEN.

KNEE BOOTS

These are mostly used to protect the knees while travelling. Knocks can occur while loading and unloading or in an accident. Knee boots are also used during exercise, however these are often referred to as skeleton kneepads. These consist of a hard pad to protect the knee should the horse fall on his knees, particularly on the road. Both types have a padded strap around the top which should be fastened firmly, but not too tight, and strap around the bottom which should be loose enough not to interfere with the movement of the leg.

YORKSHIRE BOOTS

These are very simple and are effective as a brushing boot for some ponies. They are simply a rectangular piece of material, usually felt, with a tape sewn across the middle. It is wrapped around the leg with the tape on the outside, and tied just above the fetlock. You then fold down the top half of the boot giving a double layer of protection.

RIGHT: OVERREACH BOOTS PROTECT THE FRONT LEGS.

HOCK BOOTS

Used to protect the point of the hock, these are usually used against knocks and bumps while travelling. They have a hard pad to cover the point of the hock and a strap above and below the hock to secure them. Fit the boots as you do for the knee boots.

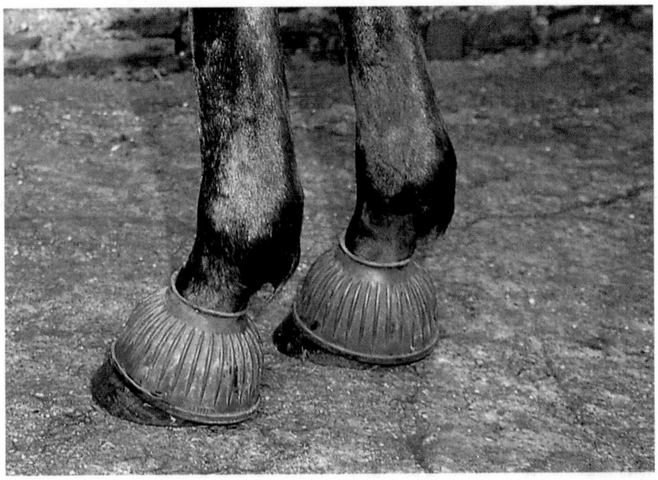

BANDAGES

Used in first aid, during exercise, when travelling or in the stable, bandages have various uses. They must be put on correctly, however. Too loose, and they become ineffective. They could slip and cause an accident. Too tight, and they could actually cause an injury, interfering with a pony's circulation. Never sit on the floor or kneel when fitting a bandage, but squat down. This way you will be able to move away much quicker should you need to.

EXERCISE BANDAGES

Usually about 7 cm (3 in.) wide and approximately 150 cm (6 ft) long these have a cotton tape to secure them. They must be put on correctly and it is probably safer to use brushing boots if you are inexperienced at bandaging. Use padding underneath the bandage for comfort and protection against knocks. Make sure any padding is smooth and without creases when fitted. Exercise bandages are made of slightly stretchy fabric, such as crepe, which is easy to put on too tight. If they get wet during exercise remove them immediately as they tend to tighten even more when wet. These bandages reach from just below the knee or hock to just above the fetlock and must not be allowed to interfere with any of these joints.

STABLE BANDAGES

Made of wool or stockinet, stable bandages are wider and longer than exercise bandages. They are used when travelling and in the stables, and can also be used to bandage ponies' legs when they become wet and muddy. They will help to dry them off and will reduce chapping. They also offer protection from knocks when travelling.

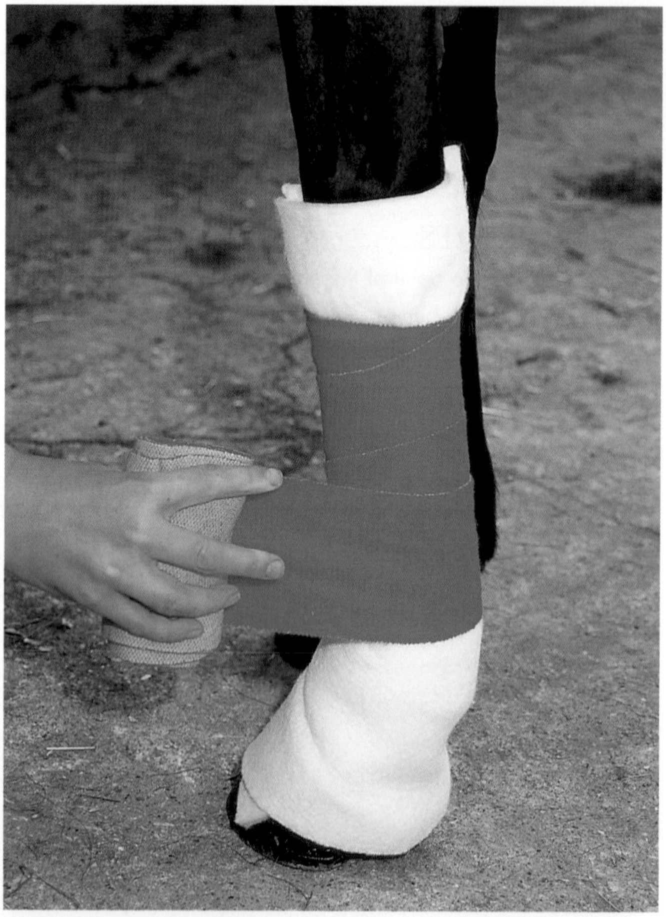

MAKE SURE THE PADDING DOES NOT CREASE UNDER THE BANDAGE APPLY WITH EVEN PRESSURE ALL THE WAY DOWN

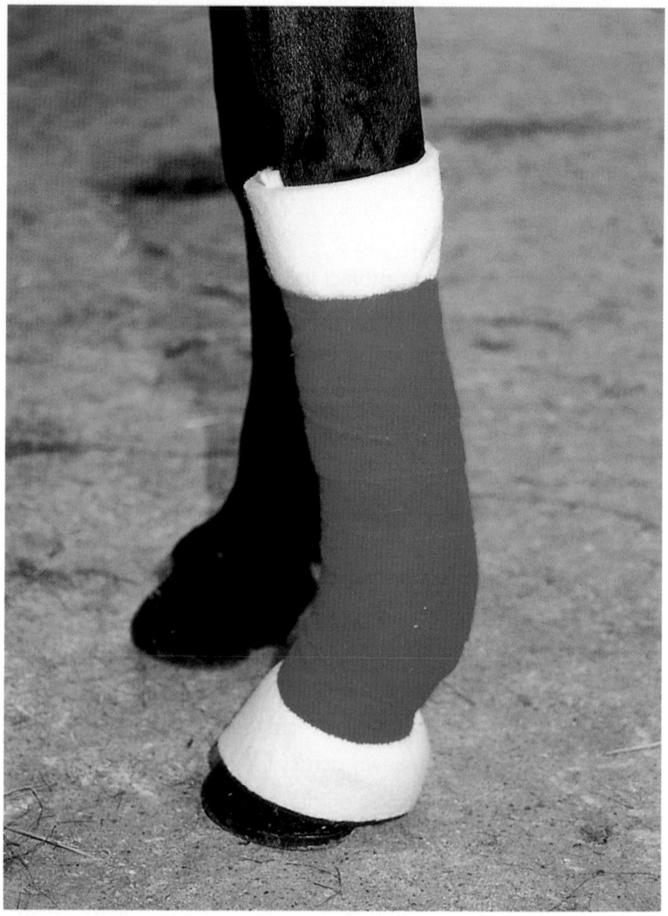

STABLE BANDAGES ARE VERSATILE AND AN ESSENTIAL ITEM FOR YOUR TACK ROOM.

USING A BANDAGE

To put on a stable bandage, wrap the padding around the leg making sure it is not creased anywhere. Then start to bandage just below the knee or hock and wrap around the leg passing the bandage from one hand to the other making sure you keep the tension even until you reach the coronet. Continue back up the leg to the beginning.

Tie a bow on the outside of the leg and tuck the tapes in so they can't get caught on anything. A knot tied at the back of the leg will press on the tendons and should be avoided. When removing bandages, do so quickly and quietly passing from one hand to the other.

Never try to roll the bandage up while you are removing it, do that later. After use, wash and dry the bandage if necessary and put away for the next time. To roll the bandage, fold up the tapes and start with the outside edge upwards.

Roll the bandage up with your hand until you reach the end. If a bandage is not rolled up correctly, you will have to re-roll it before use next time. Practice bandaging when you have spare time and you will soon improve.

When you tie the tape at the end of applying the bandage make sure it is not too tight. You can go over the cotton tape with masking tape if you are worried about it coming undone while you are riding.

TAIL BANDAGES

1 Tail bandages are used while travelling, to prevent a pony from rubbing his tail, and after grooming, to encourage the hair to lie flat. To apply, dampen the top of the tail with a water brush.

2 Pass the end of the bandage under the top of the tail and wind it round once, leaving a small flap sticking up. This gets folded down as you wind around the second time.

3 Wind all the way to the end of the tail bone keeping an even pressure all the way. Then wind back upwards until you run out of bandage, which should be about two-thirds of the way back up.

4 Tie the tapes making sure you keep them flat. Tie a double bow and tuck the ends in. Gently shape the tail.

5 Never put a tail bandage on too tight, as this could injure the bone. If the hairs become severely damaged, they may grow back white.

6 To remove, pull the whole bandage down from the top, and wind up later.

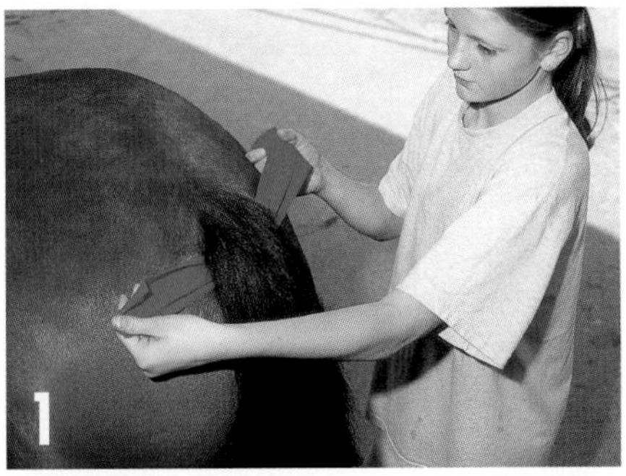
1

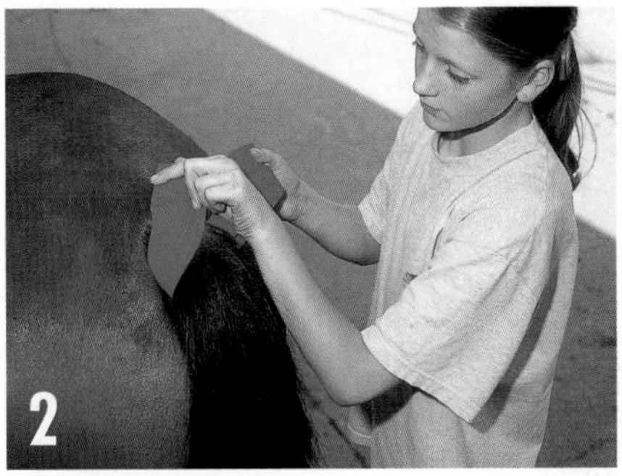
2

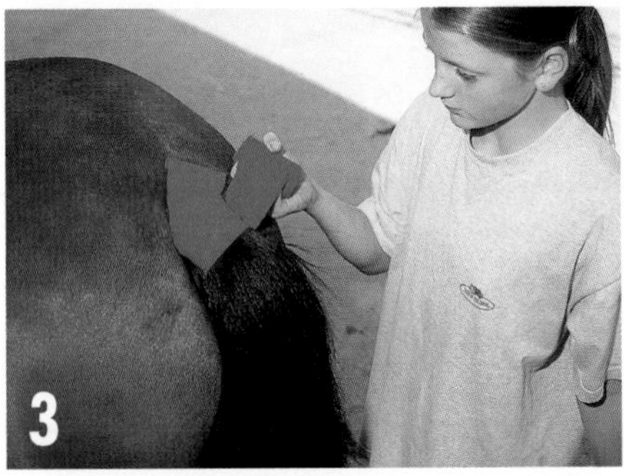
3

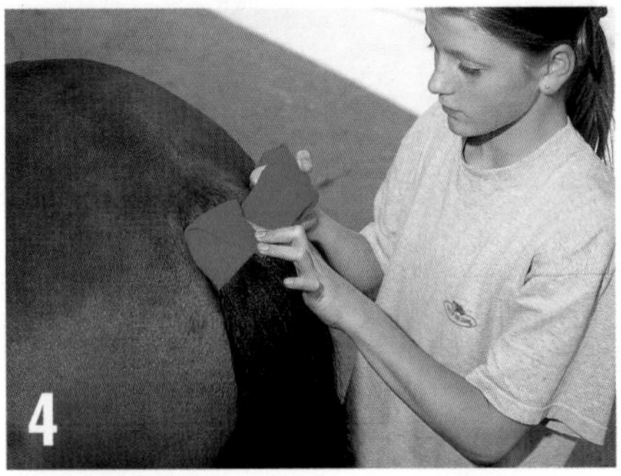
4

5

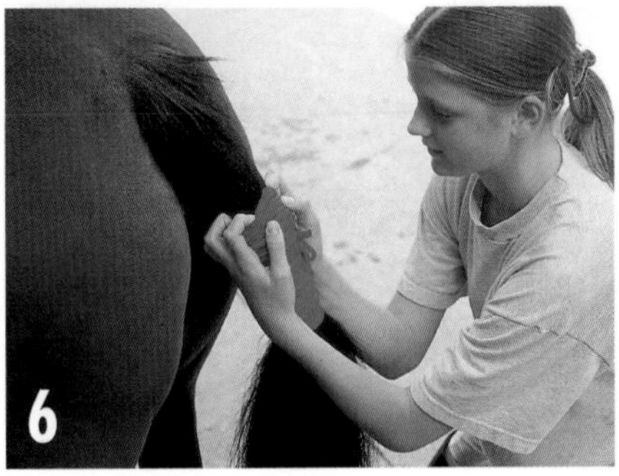
6

CHAPTER 4

HORSECARE

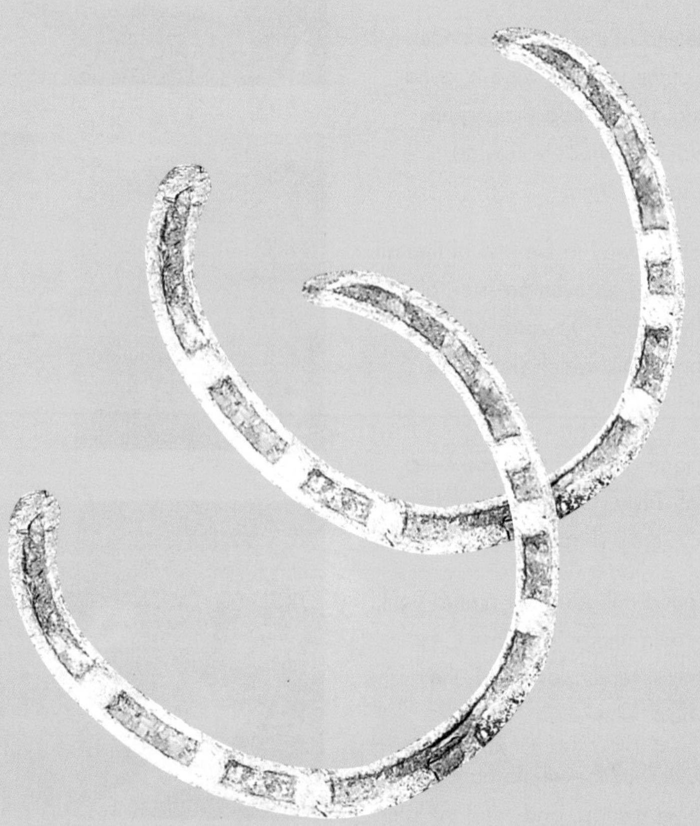

GROOMING

Most ponies enjoy being groomed and it is an ideal time to get to know your pony and check over his general health and condition. Grooming not only makes your pony look neat and tidy, but also helps keep his skin healthy. If you put lots of energy into grooming, you can even improve a pony's muscle tone and circulation. This type of grooming is called 'strapping' and is normally done to stabled horses and ponies. Then, when you want to exercise them, a quick brush over will be adequate. This is called 'quartering'. Ponies at grass will need different grooming routines depending on their lifestyle. A few ponies are ticklish, so try to brush fairly firmly. Grooming machines are used in some large yards, but for most of us, a well-equipped grooming kit and lots of elbow grease will have to do!

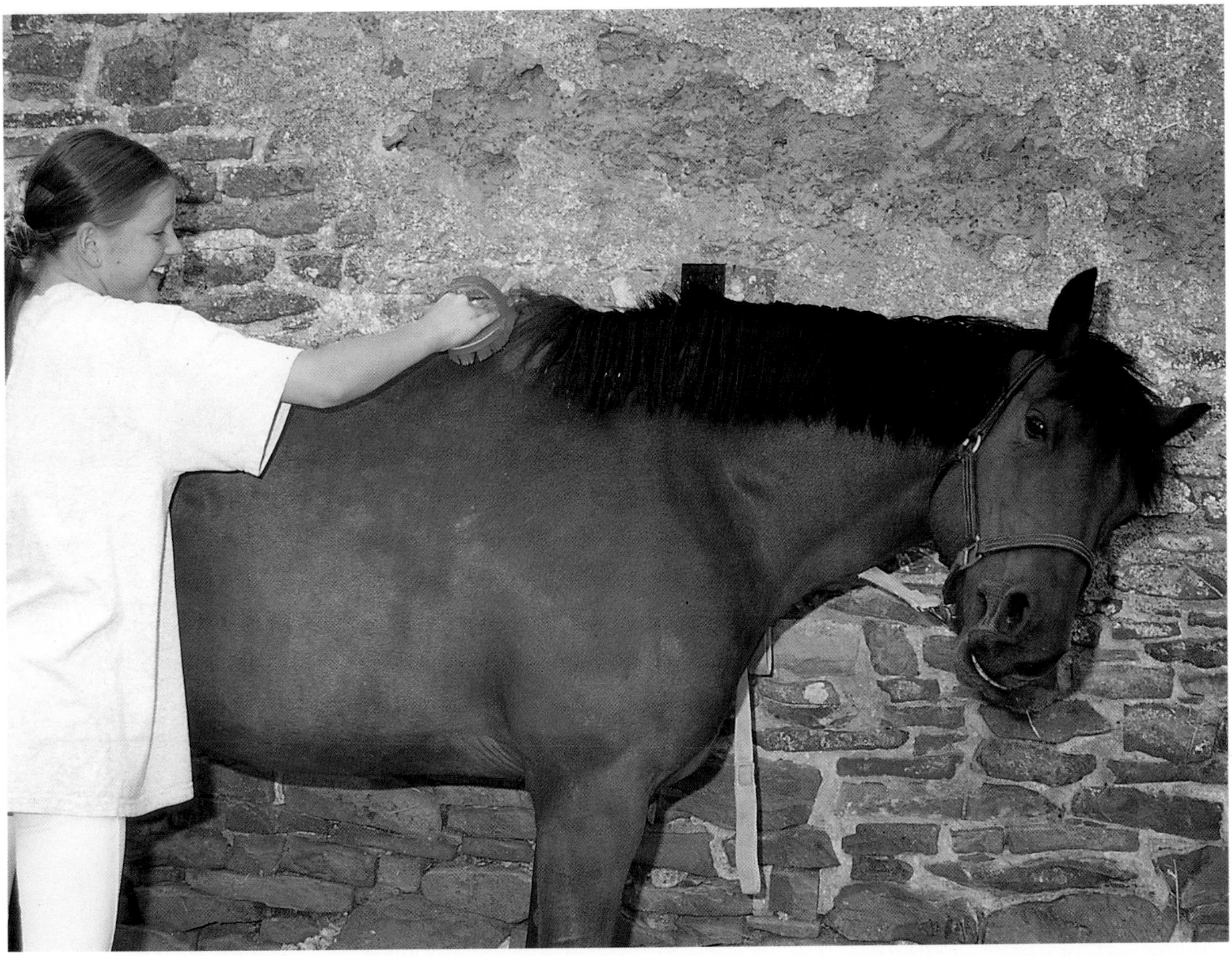

GROOMING IS AN EXCELLENT WAY OF BONDING WITH YOUR PONY.

EQUIPMENT IN A GROOMING KIT

Your grooming kit should be kept in a suitable box – one with a handle is useful. It is important to keep all your equipment clean and tidy or you won't have all your kit together when you need it. Wash your brushes on a sunny day and leave them out to dry.

DANDY BRUSH

A large brush with stiff, long bristles, it is used for caked-on mud, particularly on grass-kept ponies. A dandy brush should not be used on the face or the tail as it is too harsh.

BODY BRUSH

This has shorter, denser bristles and enables you to get deeper into the skin to remove dirt, scurf and grease.

WATER BRUSH

This looks similar to a dandy brush but has softer and shorter hairs. It is used to damp down the mane and tail when plaiting or grooming, and will make the hair lie flat. It is also used to wash and scrub the feet.

CURRY COMB

There are three types of curry comb: a metal one is used to scrape the body brush to get it clean. It has very sharp serrated edges and should never be used on a pony's under body. Rubber and plastic curry combs are good for getting excess hair out of the coat, and for removing caked-on mud. Avoid using curry combs on a pony's face.

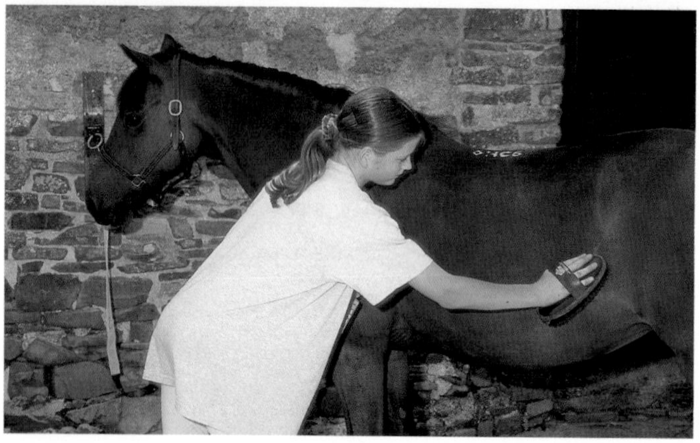

A BODY BRUSH ALLOWS YOU TO REACH DEEPLY INGRAINED DIRT AND GRIME.

MANE COMB

A plastic or metal comb with teeth used to comb manes. It is best avoided on the tail as it tends to pull out hair.

KEEP YOUR GROOMING KIT IN A SPECIAL BOX SO IT'S READY WHEN YOU NEED IT.

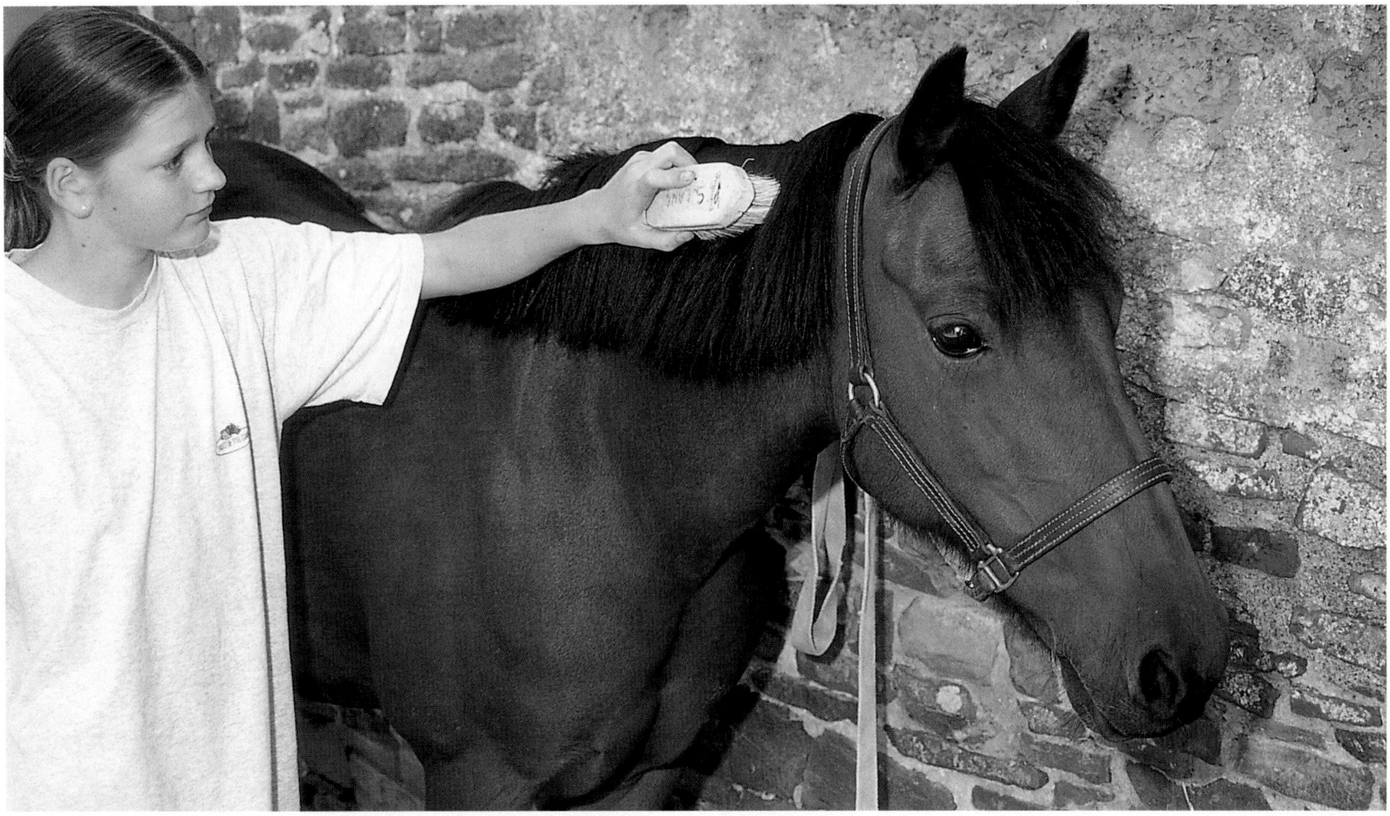

AS A FINISHING TOUCH, USE A DAMP WATER BRUSH ON THE MANE TO ENCOURAGE THE HAIR TO LIE FLAT.

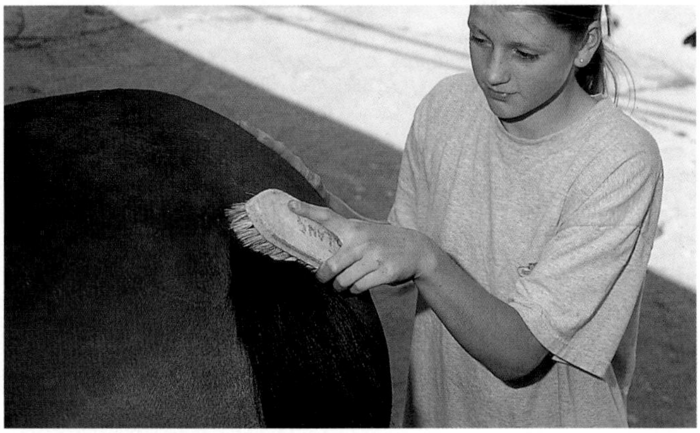

WATER BRUSHING HELPS TO MAKE THE HAIR LIE FLAT.

HOOF OIL AND BRUSH

Use a brush on the hooves. Leave oiling until the end of a grooming session or it will end up with dust and dirt stuck all over it.

STABLE RUBBER

This can simply be a tea towel or a glass cloth, and is used to give a final polish and to remove any surface dust.

SPONGE

You will need three sponges, one for the eyes, one for the nostrils and one for the dock. It is a good idea to label them to avoid confusion.

SWEAT SCRAPER

This has a handle and a semi- circular rubber blade to scrape off excess water.

SHAMPOO

There are a variety of horse shampoos available. Aways use a proper equine shampoo rather than a human variant, as this will avoid irritating your pony's skin.

HOOF PICK

This is used to clean stones and mud out of the feet.

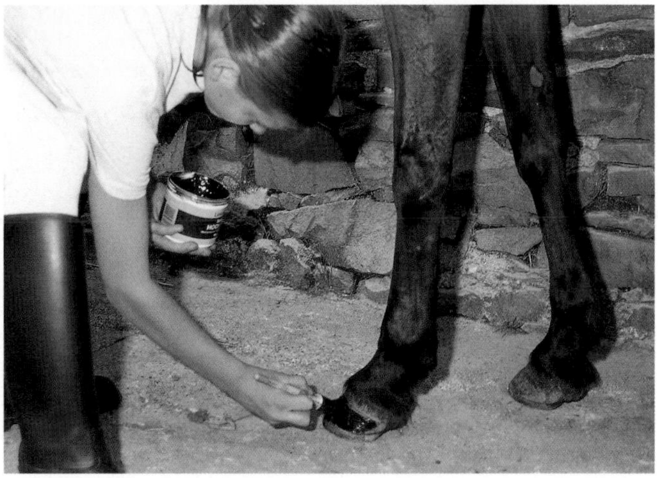

OILING THE HOOVES AT THE END OF A GROOMING SESSION.

GROOMING A STABLED PONY

Take your kit to the stable, put the head collar on your pony, and tie him up. Leave the door open so you have more light. Place the water buckets outside so they don't fill with dirt.
Start by picking out the feet. Facing the tail, lift one foot and, holding the hoof in your inside hand, use your outside hand to scrape the hoof pick from the heel towards the toe. Never scrape in the opposite direction, or you could hurt the frog or the heel. Lower the hoof without dropping it and repeat for the remaining feet. As you go, look out for any bad smell, which could be a sign of thrush (see page 104). This is also a good time to check that the pony's shoes are secure. If you have one, you can save time by picking the feet out over a bowl or bucket.

PICKING OUT THE FEET INTO A BOWL SAVES SWEEPING THE YARD LATER!

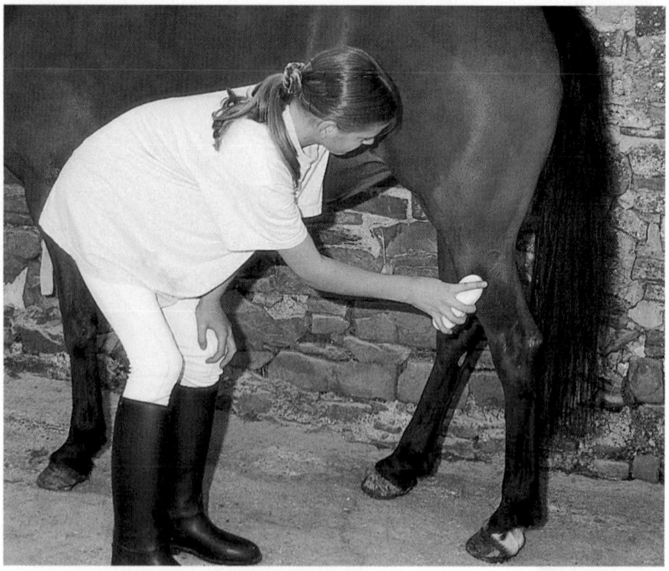

USE A DANDY BRUSH TO REMOVE SWEAT OR MUD.

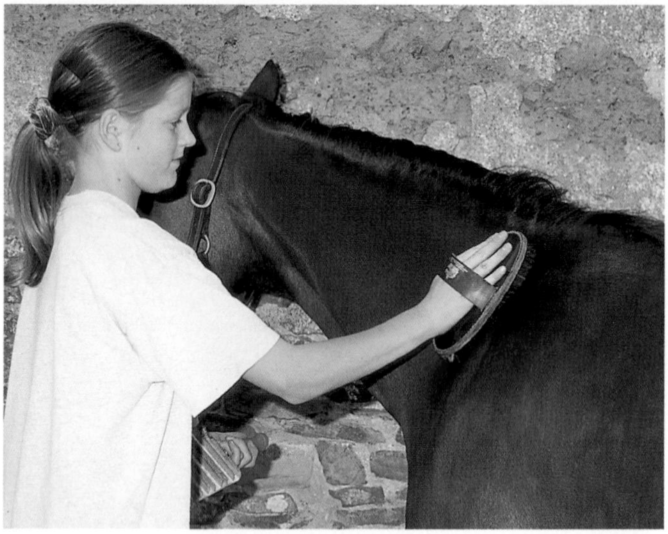

A SOFTER BODY BRUSH REMOVES DEEPER GRIME.

Take the dandy brush and, starting behind the ears, use it to remove any mud or sweat marks. Be careful on sensitive parts of the body and don't use at all on any clipped parts. Pay attention to the hocks, as these tend to get dirty when the pony is lying down in the stable.

Take the body brush and the metal curry comb. You will need to use both hands now. Start behind the ears again and brush down the neck, making sure you get right under the mane. Brush in the direction of the coat and lean into the brush a little as you do so. After about three strokes with the brush, pull it across the metal curry comb to remove mud and grease.

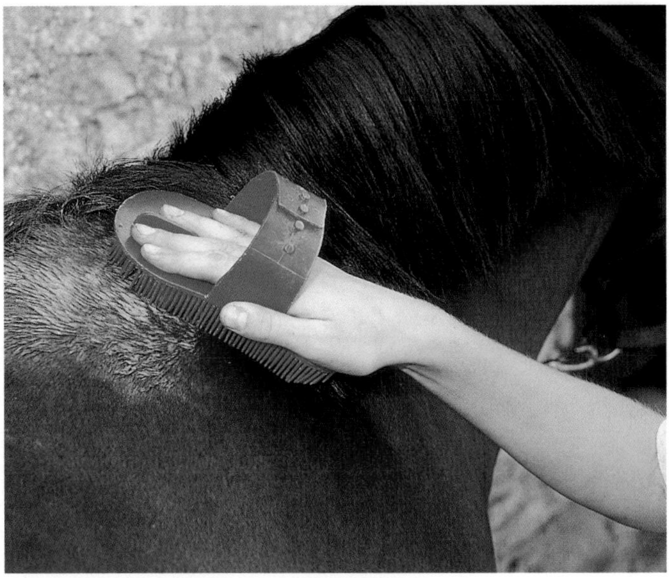

USING A PLASTIC CURRY COMB TO REMOVE DUST.

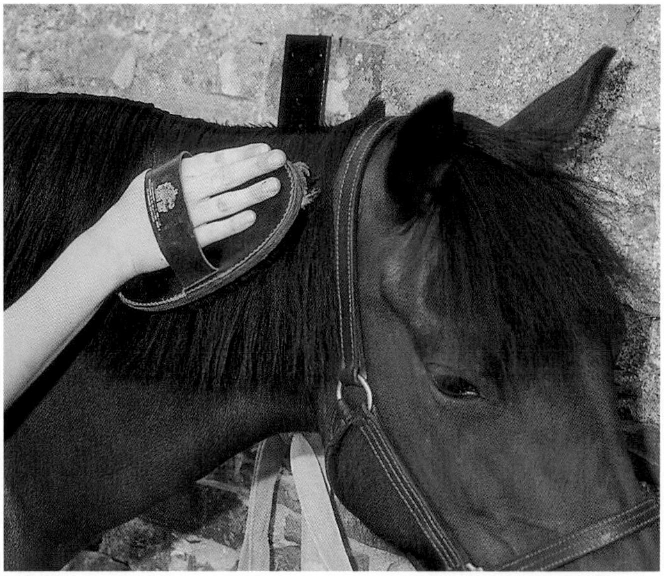

MANE BRUSHING.

To remove dirt and grease from the curry comb, tap it on the stable floor occasionally. You will accumulate quite a pile, even from a pony that looked clean to start with. When you have brushed both sides, move on to the head. Remove the head collar and brush the head very gently. Lastly, run your fingers through the pony's mane to remove any large tangles. Then brush through with the body brush.

Sponge the eyes, nostrils and dock using the different sponges. Always wash the sponges in plain water, and wring each one out well. When wiping the eyes, start in the corner and wipe outwards. When washing the dock, be careful to stand to one side, so that you don't get kicked. Lift the tail and gently sponge the whole area, remembering to clean the underside of the tail as well.

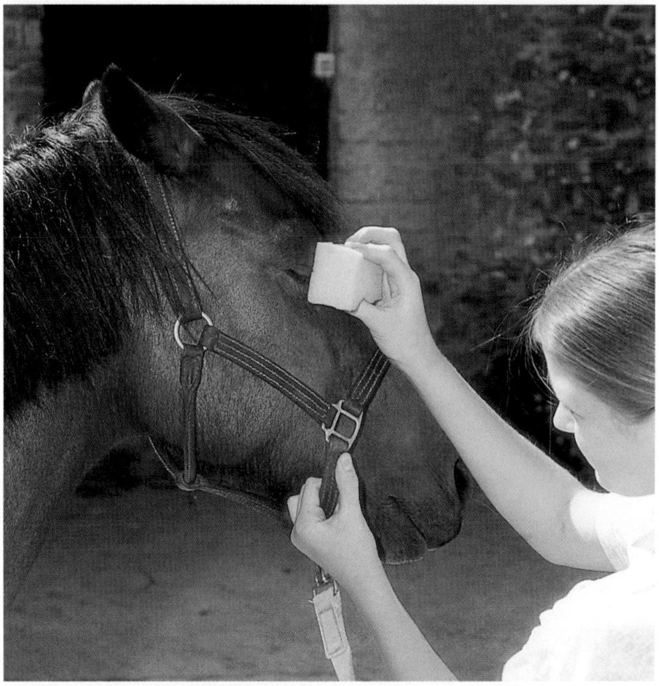

USE SEPARATE SPONGES FOR EYES, NOSE AND DOCK.

Take the body brush again and, after removing the worst of the tangles in the tail with your fingers, brush through the tail, a section at a time. Hold the rest of the tail in one hand and stand to one side to avoid getting kicked or trodden on should the pony take a step backwards. You can use a tail bandage to make the tail hairs stay flat for longer. Dampen the water brush, shake it, and brush the mane and the top of the tail to flatten them.

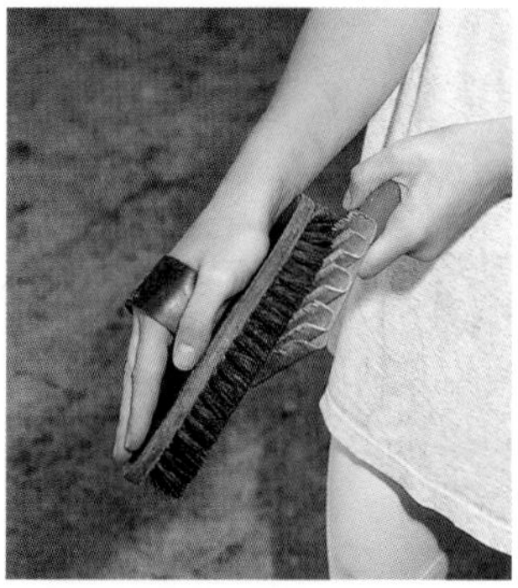

SCRAPE OFF THE BODY BRUSH ON A CURRY COMB.

TAP THE COMB ON THE FLOOR TO REMOVE THE DIRT.

Wipe the whole pony with a slightly damp stable rubber or cloth to remove any last bits of dust. Lastly, using the brush and oil, paint the hooves. Do not use too much oil and be careful not to get any of it on the white hair of the coronet. Opinions vary on whether or not to use oil every day.

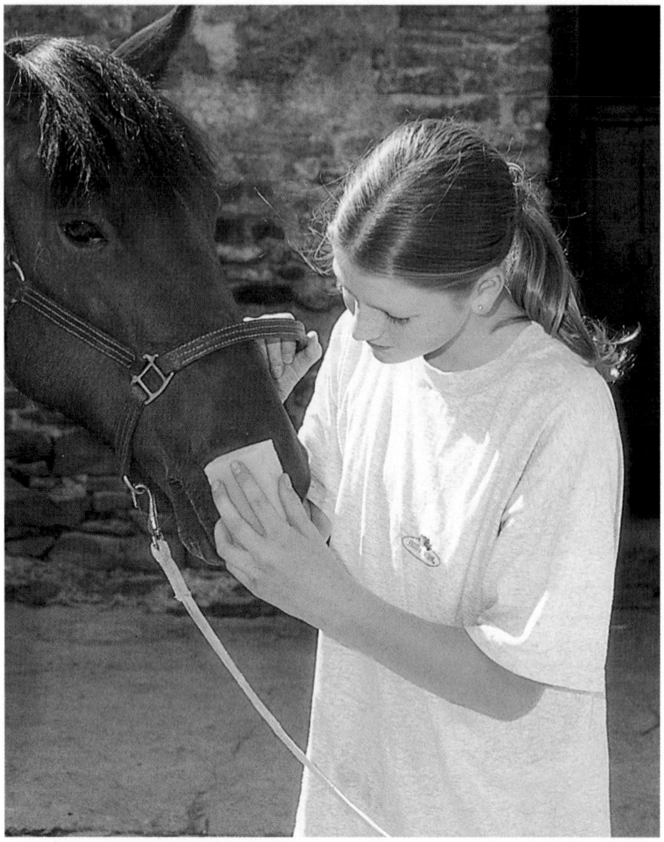

GENTLY SPONGE THE PONY'S FACE.

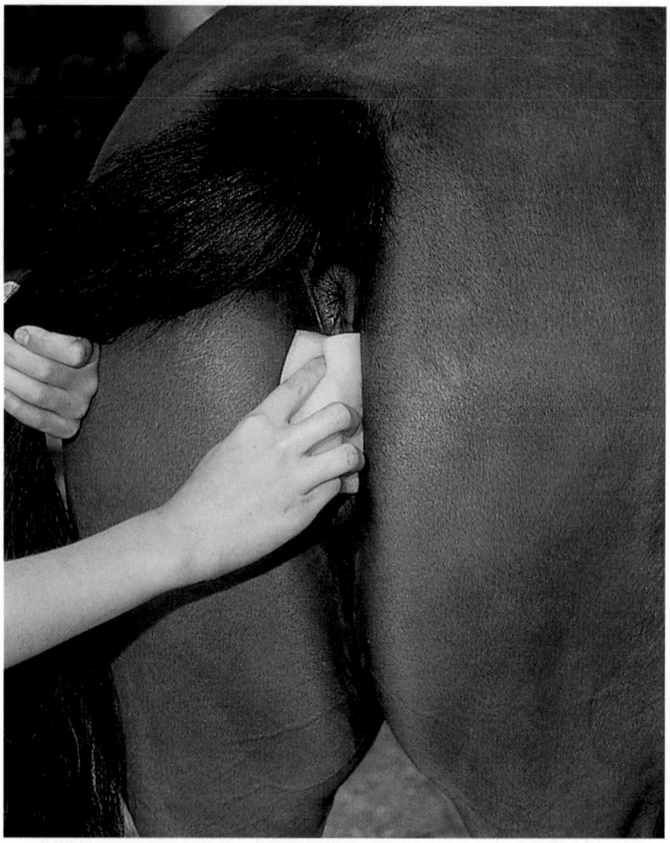

WASH THE DOCK TO MAKE THE PONY COMFORTABLE.

WITH A SOFT BRUSH, COMB A FEW HAIRS AT A TIME.

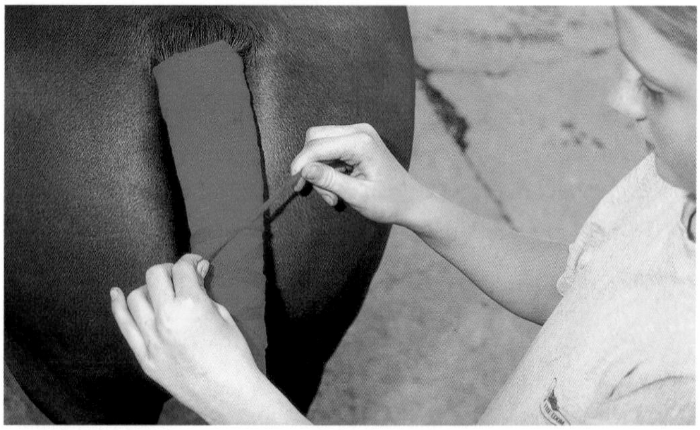

USE A TAIL BANDAGE TO MAKE THE TAIL HAIRS REMAIN FLAT.

QUARTERING

This is a quicker method of grooming and is often used on a stabled horse before exercise, although he will also have a thorough 'strapping' later. Leave the rug on a pony, undoing just the front strap, and brush over the pony quickly to remove any stable stains. Fold the back half of the rug forwards to brush the back half of the pony, and vice versa. Pick out the feet, and sponge eyes, nostrils and dock.

GROOMING A GRASS KEPT PONY

Grooming a pony that is out at grass takes less time, but is still an important part of his day. It is also a good time for you to check him over for any problems. Pick out the feet and sponge the eyes, nostril and dock. Use the dandy brush to remove any mud. If there is mud on the pony's head pick it off with your fingers and then use a body brush on the mane and tail once you have removed the worst of the tangles with your fingers. If the pony has grass or stains where he has rolled over, remove

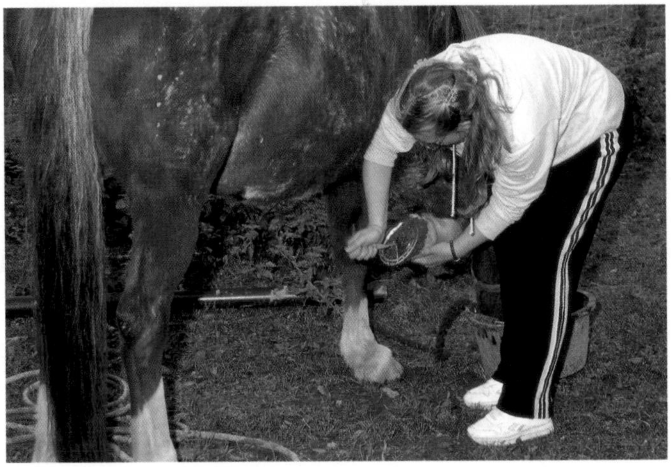

REMOVING MUD FROM A HOOF.

REMOVE THE WORST TANGLES FROM YOUR PONY'S MANE BEFORE BRUSHING.

them with water and a sponge or a water brush. Leave these areas to dry completely before using the dandy brush. If you want to ride when it has been raining and the pony is wet, use a sweat scraper to scrape off all the excess water. Dry the saddle and bridle areas thoroughly with an old towel, and brush the pony over before riding. Even if the rest of your pony is not gleaming, he must be clean and dry under the saddle and bridle or he will become uncomfortable and get sore. Do not forget to dry the girth areas too.

BATHING YOUR PONY

1 When the weather is hot, or if you are off to impress your friends at the local show, bathing your pony will make him look really smart. Some shampoos will help keep the flies away too. It is not sensible to bathe a pony in winter, when he could easily get cold or catch a chill.

2 Some ponies dislike being bathed, while others seem to enjoy the attention. If your pony is not used to being bathed, or is not keen on it, get someone experienced to help you. If a new pony is not used to water being poured over it, do it very gently and avoid getting soap in its eyes.

3 Using a hose pipe tends to frighten ponies, and they can get caught up in it. Use a small bucket or bowl instead and wet the coat with lukewarm water. Shampoo the mane and forelock and rinse thoroughly. Wash the hooves with a water brush.

4 Work over the whole body, making sure you rinse thoroughly with lukewarm water. Use the sweat scraper to remove excess water from the body.

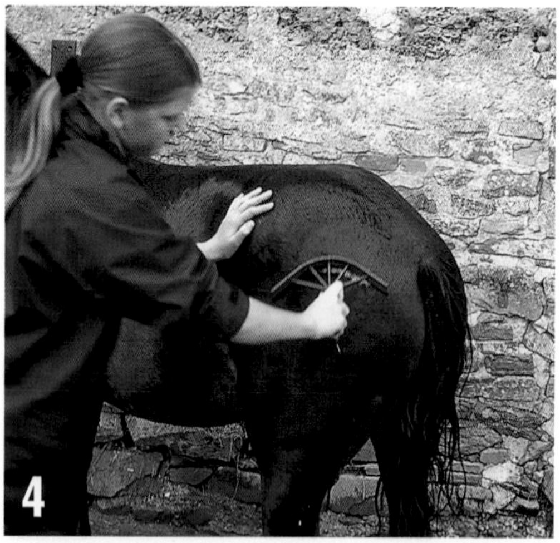

5 To wash the tail, stand to the side as for grooming, then dampen, shampoo and rinse well. Swish the tail around to remove excess water and start to dry it. Never stand directly behind a pony.

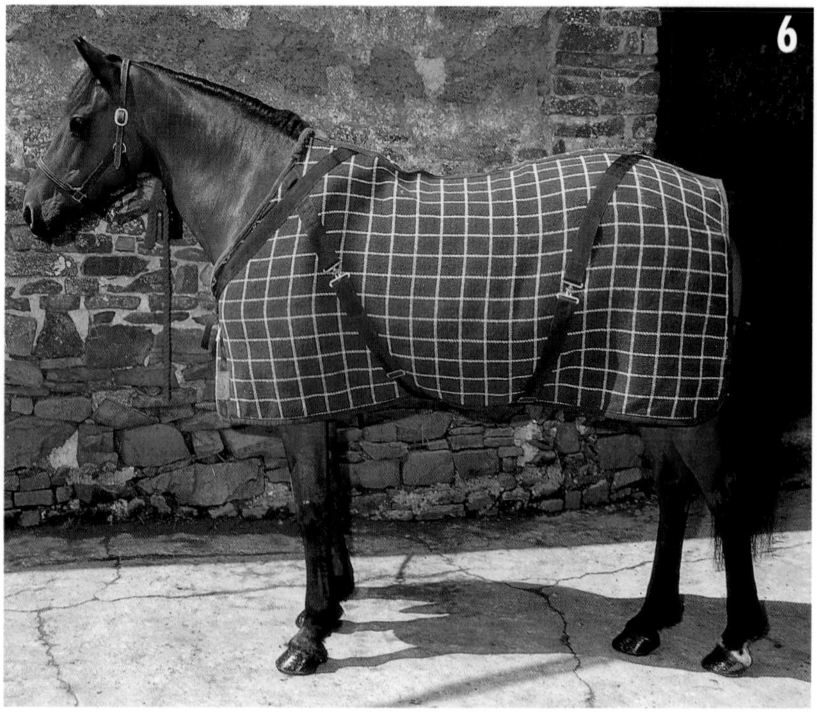

6 When you have bathed the whole pony, you should not let him get cold. Walk him around, rub his legs, heels and head with an old towel and put on a sweat rug with another light rug on top. This will help him to keep warm while drying. Brush all over with a body brush when he is dry.

TRIMMING AND CLIPPING

Horses and ponies need clipping in order to remove their winter coats. Clipped ponies are not only easier to groom, but they also sweat less when working, and then dry more quickly, which helps to avoid chills. Trimming is carried out with scissors or small clippers, and tidies up any unwanted hair.

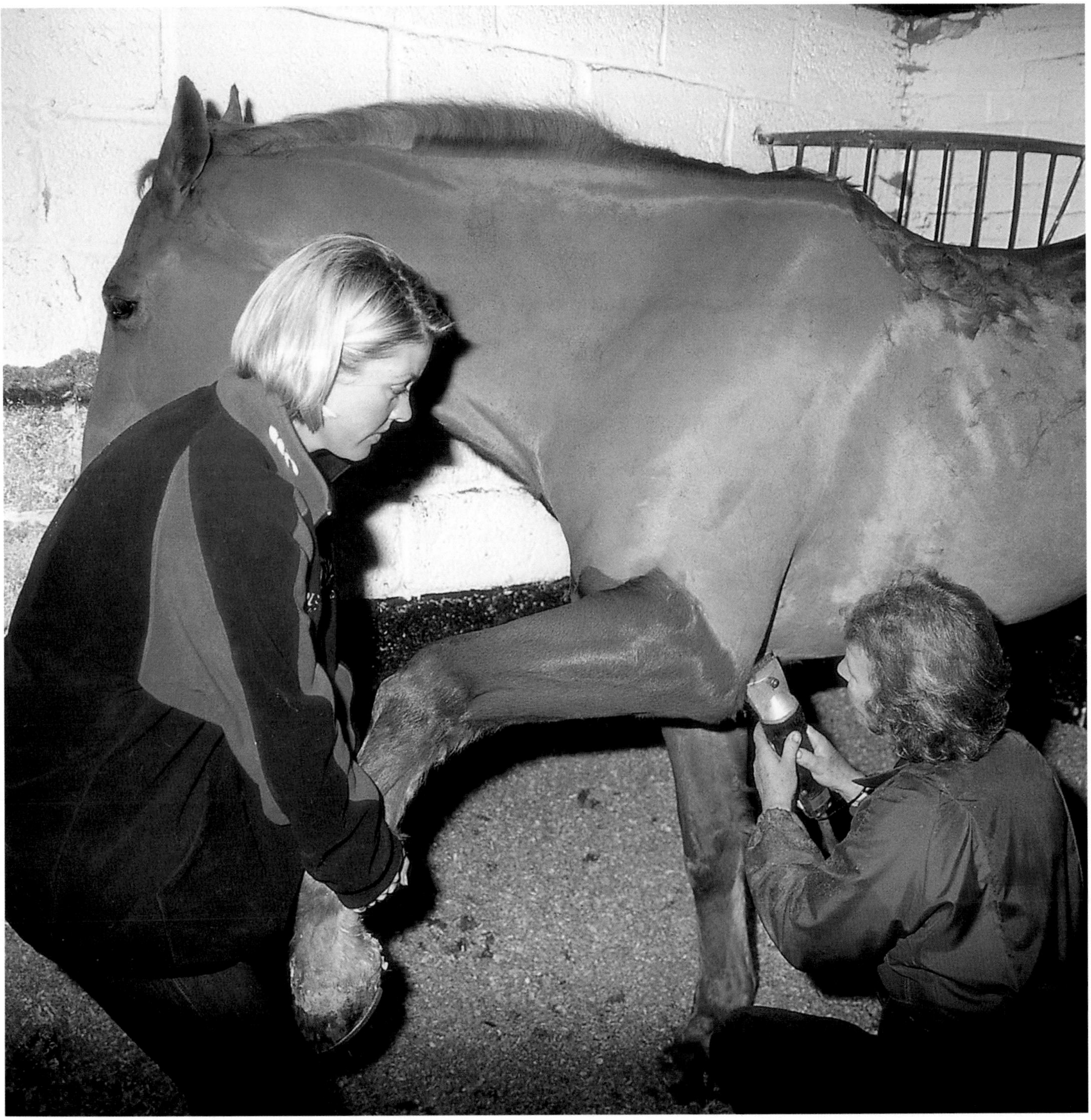

TRIMMING

Trimming your pony helps make him look tidy and smart, although some of the processes such as mane and tail pulling and clipping are best left to the experts. A poorly pulled mane or a bad clip will take a long time to grow out and clipping can be dangerous if you are inexperienced.

Generally, stable-kept ponies need more clipping and trimming than grass-kept ones.

Trimming can be done simply with a pair of scissors in some areas. Ponies tend to get long hairs around the jaw and under the chin, which can be removed. Be very careful with scissors around your pony, particularly near his eyes, and always put them away as soon as you have finished. Ears should be trimmed on the outside only. Never cut any hair from inside the ears. A clever technique is to close the ear together with your hand and trim off any hair left sticking out. Do not cut off a pony's whiskers as they are there to serve a purpose. Without them your pony will not be able to judge some distances and might bump his nose on things.

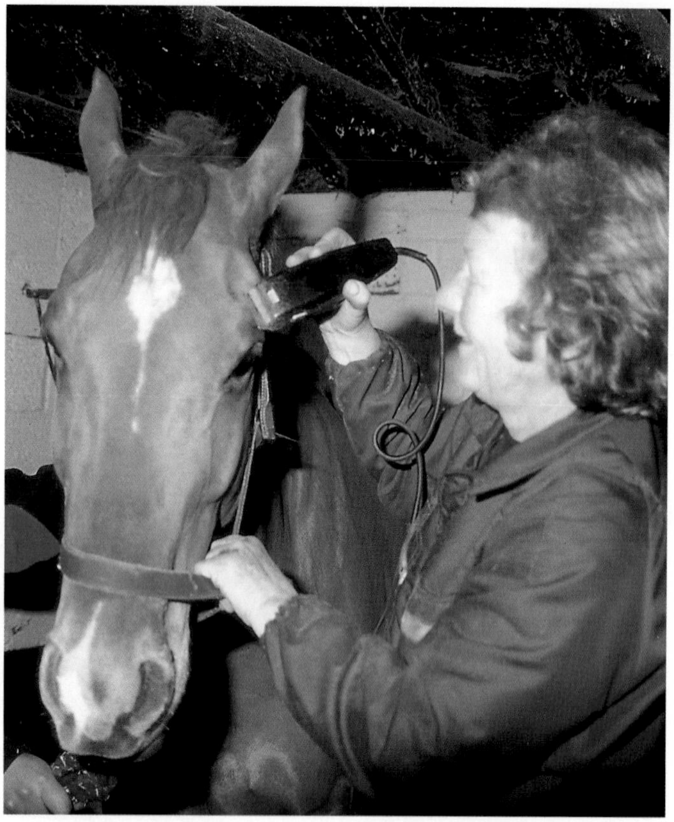

A SMALL SET OF CLIPPERS IS SOMETIMES USED ON DELICATE AREAS SUCH AS THE HEAD.

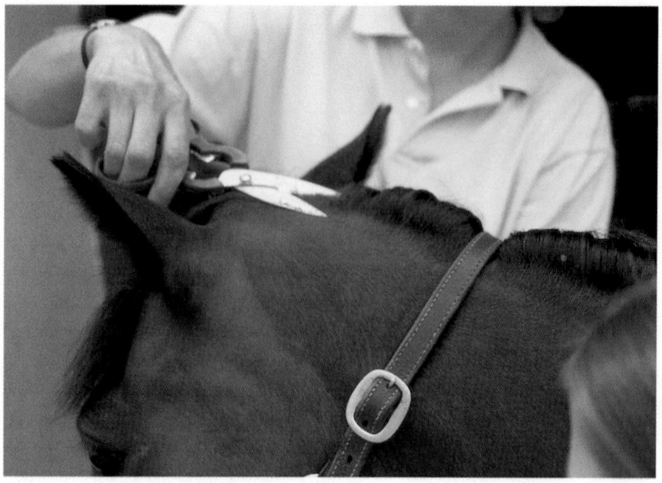

TRIMMING KEEPS YOUR PONY TIDY, BUT IS BEST CARRIED OUT BY EXPERTS.

The heels of a stable-kept pony can be kept trimmed all year. Use a comb to push the hair the wrong way and then cut in an upward direction. The heels of a grass-kept pony should be left untrimmed, particularly in winter when he will need protection from the wet and the mud. The long hairs of the fetlocks act as drain pipes for excess water.

Hair is sometimes removed from behind the ears so that the bridle and head collar sit better (see above). It is not always necessary, but sometimes the mane can be very thick here, so it can help to tidy it up. You will have to keep it trimmed, however, as it will look very untidy when it starts to grow. Some people also trim the mane at the withers but it is not really necessary. 'Hogging' is a term used to describe the cutting off of the whole mane using clippers. This can solve the problem of a patchy or untidy mane, but it will take up to two years to re-grow fully, so be very sure before you do it. The mane is clipped from the withers up to the poll, while the head and neck are gently stretched downwards as much as possible. This needs to be done by an expert and should be repeated every four to six weeks.

'Pulling a mane' is a means of both shortening and thinning it, which tidies up the pony and makes plaiting easier. To pull the mane, you remove the long hairs from underneath, either with your fingers, or by wrapping a few hairs at a time around a mane comb. Pulling should be done after exercise when the skin is warm and the pores are open, making it less uncomfortable for the pony. Keep pulling out the longest hairs, a few at a time along the length of the mane, until the desired length and thickness are achieved. Never take hairs from the top of the mane or it will stick up. Pulling a tail needs practice and it is sensible to watch an experienced person a few times before you attempt it yourself. Remember that the mane of a grass-kept pony helps to keep him warm in the winter, and that he needs a thick tail to protect his dock area from the weather, so it should never be pulled.

To trim the tail you need to cut it straight across the bottom so that when it is carried naturally it is about 12 cm (6 in.) below the point of the hock. A long tail collects mud and looks untidy.

Horses and ponies that do hard or regular work will benefit from being clipped to various degrees. Some only need the belly and under the neck taken off – this is usually the practice on ponies – and others need a full clip where all the hair is removed. The more hair you remove, the more clothing you will need in order to keep him warm when he is not working. Clipping a hard-working horse has several advantages. It removes the winter coat, which would otherwise cause heavy sweating and could affect the animal's condition. It also enables a horse to dry off more quickly after exercise, making him less susceptible to catching a chill.

Grooming becomes much easier too. Clipping is a job for an expert and you should be able to find one by word of mouth or from an advertisement in the local paper. Clipping is usually carried out in late autumn and should be repeated every six to eight weeks until late winter. Do not clip after that time or it will interfere with the summer coat. Ponies that only do a little light hacking at the weekends and don't become too sweaty do not usually need to be clipped. In this case, particularly if he is out at grass, it would be much better to leave his winter coat intact. A New Zealand rug (see page 24) is important if even a little hair has been removed or a pony will quickly catch colds and lose condition. Never leave a clipped pony without a rug on. Once you have removed his natural coat it is your responsibility to keep him warm – anything less would be unkind.

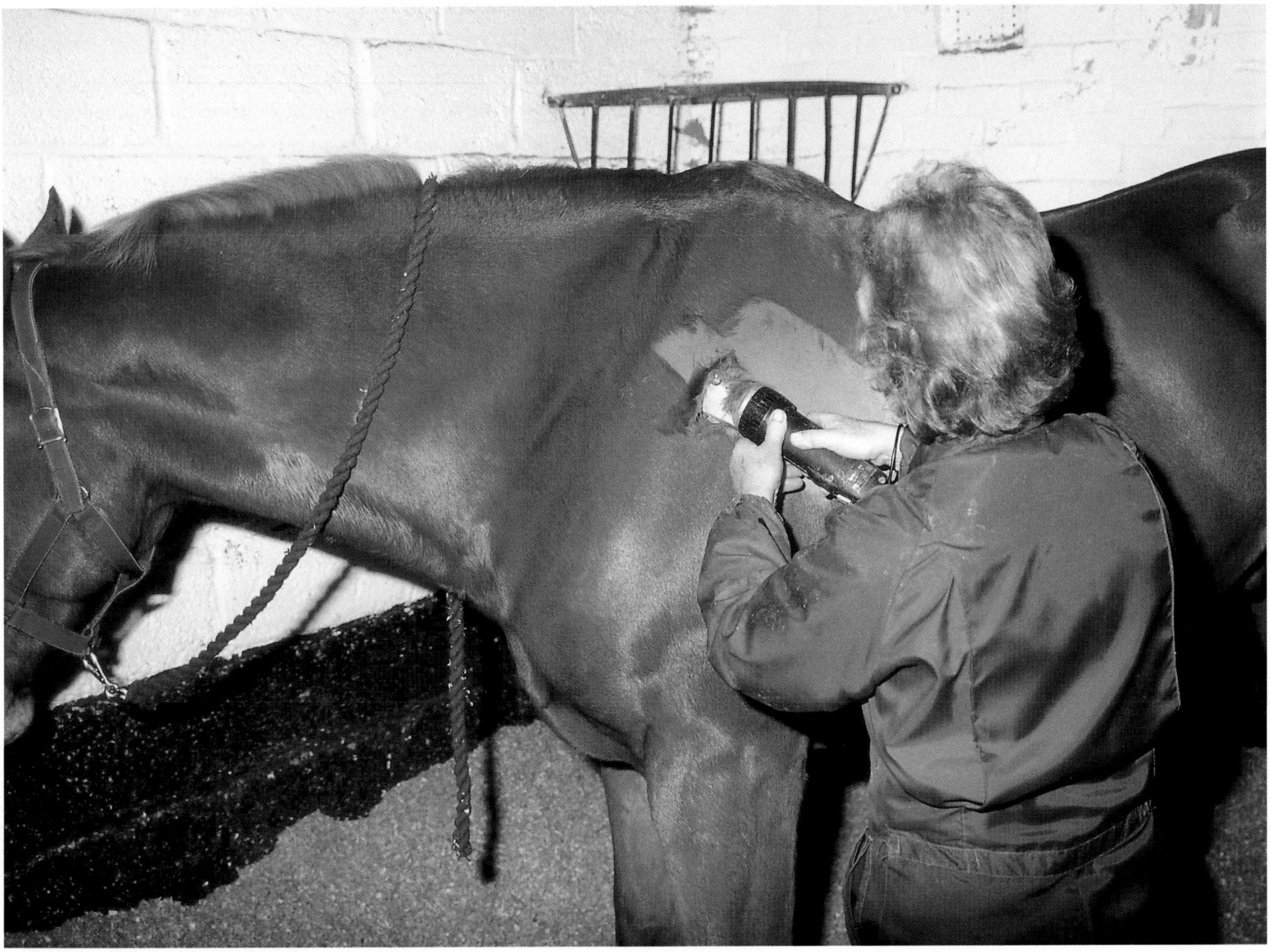

CLIPPING HAS SEVERAL BENEFITS: IT PREVENTS EXCESSIVE SWEATING AND ALLOWS THE HORSE TO DRY QUICKLY.

TYPES OF CLIP

Neck and belly clip:	Suitable for ponies working during weekends and holidays. A pony can live out at grass with this clip if he has a good shelter and a New Zealand rug.
Chaser clip:	As above.
Trace clip:	Suitable for ponies in medium work, this keeps the neck warm but quite a lot of hair is removed. If you put him out in the field often, you will need to make sure he is warm enough. Most ponies would be stabled at night at least with this clip.
Hunter clip:	For horses in hard work. Hair is left on the legs, to protect them from thorns and brambles, and on the saddle patch for comfort. A horse will need to be kept well rugged-up at all times. He would normally be kept stabled and, if turned out during the day, must have a good, thick New Zealand rug.
Blanket clip:	The horse still has hair on the legs, back and quarters. This is best suited to horses and ponies in medium to hard work. They would normally be stabled at night at least.

PREPARING TO CLIP

Some ponies are nervous of clippers. If this is the case, talk to your pony to reassure him and stroke his neck gently. Run the clippers near him for a while to let him get used to the noise before you start. Most will accept being clipped once they are used to it. When you have found an experienced person to do the clip for you, and you have arranged a time for it to be done, you need to groom the pony thoroughly using the body brush to remove as much dirt and grease from the coat as possible. A dirty coat could blunt or overheat the clippers. Never bathe a pony the same day, as he needs to be completely dry. Use a tail bandage to keep the tail out of the way, and be ready with a stable rug (see page 24) as clipping can take a long time and the pony might start to get cold half way through.

MANE PLAITING EQUIPMENT (SEE PAGE 75).

PLAITING YOUR PONY

It's a good idea to practice plaiting so that, when that special occasion arrives, such as a local show, you will be able to make your pony look really smart. The more you practice, the easier it will become, and the end result will be neater each time. You usually plait on the off side of the neck, and the number of plaits down the neck is traditionally odd with the one in the fore lock making it even. I find it best not to plait the night before a show because it rarely looks as neat in the morning.

1 To plait your pony you will need a body brush, a mane comb, a water brush and some plaiting bands. The pony needs to have a short mane that is not too thick. Use the body brush to brush out the mane. You can use a mane comb for the final comb-through once you have removed all the tangles, then use the water brush to dampen the mane.

2 If you don't do this you may end up with stray hairs sticking up all over the place. Divide the mane up into the number of plaits you want to end up with and secure each bunch with a band. Use the mane comb to divide the mane, making sure you get a neat, straight divide between each bunch.

3 You may need to stand on something if you are not tall enough to get a good view of what you are doing. If you use a bucket, be careful that it is strong enough to take your weight and that the handle has been removed. Take the first bunch – it is a good idea to start at the withers' end, as some ponies are sensitive about you pulling on their manes, especially at the poll – and divide it into three equal sections.

4 Pass the right strand over the centre one, then the left strand over the centre one and so on until you reach the end of the hair. It is very important to keep the plait tight all the way down or it will be loose when you come to fold it. Tie a band firmly around the end so that it does not become loose.

5 You can either do all the plaits like this first and then roll them up, or roll up each one as you go along. To fold the plait, bend it in half with the end underneath and then fold in half again. Then, with a band, wind it around the bobble several times until it is tight.

6 Plaiting bands are available in several colours so choose one as close to the colour of your pony's mane as possible. A needle and thread can be used instead of the bands, but I find bands are safer and easier. If you drop the needle, you will waste a lot of time literally searching for a needle in a haystack.

7 Try plaiting as often as possible, as practice makes perfect! And use a little hair wax to smooth and fix down any odd stray hairs for a perfect finish.

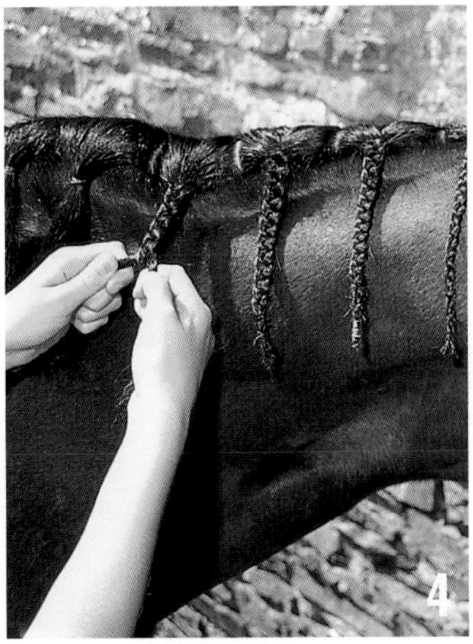

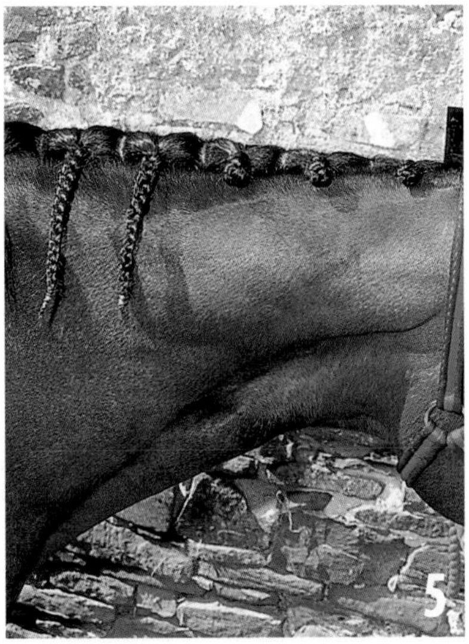

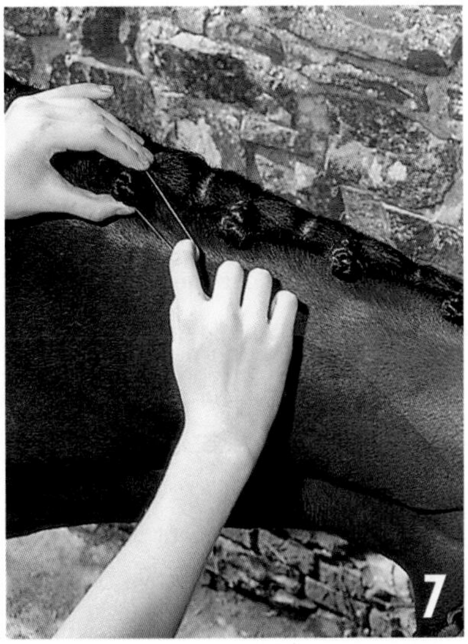

PLAITING A TAIL

1 A well-plaited tail is very smart, but it does take practise. The tail needs to have long hairs at the top and the whole tail needs to be brushed out and clean.

2 A freshly washed tail can be very slippery to plait, so it is better to wash the tail a couple of days before the show if you can. This might not be possible if the tail is very light in colour as it will not stay clean.

3 To plait the tail, take a few hairs from each side and secure them together with a bit of cotton the same colour as the tail. Then take a strand from each side and plait in the normal way until you reach the end of the tail bone.

4 Be careful to keep the plait tight all the way down and keep it centred – it is very easy to drift to one side. When you reach the end of the tail bone continue to plait the three strands you have in your hand until the end of the hair.

5 Secure this with a band, tuck the end under the bottom of the plait and fix with another band. You can use a large needle to sew it in place but be very careful not to loose the needle.

6 A little wax can be used to smooth down any stray hairs or any that were too short to be plaited. Practice will soon make perfect, so have a go at plaiting the tail whenever you have a few spare moments.

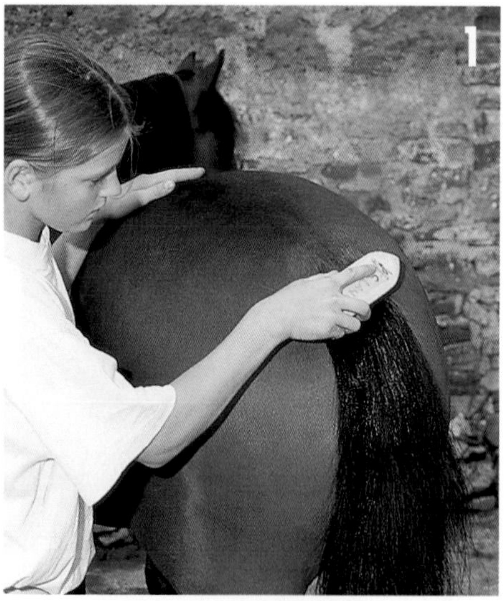

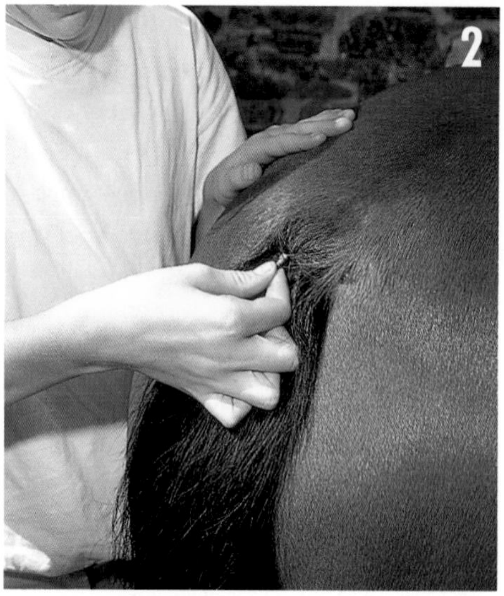

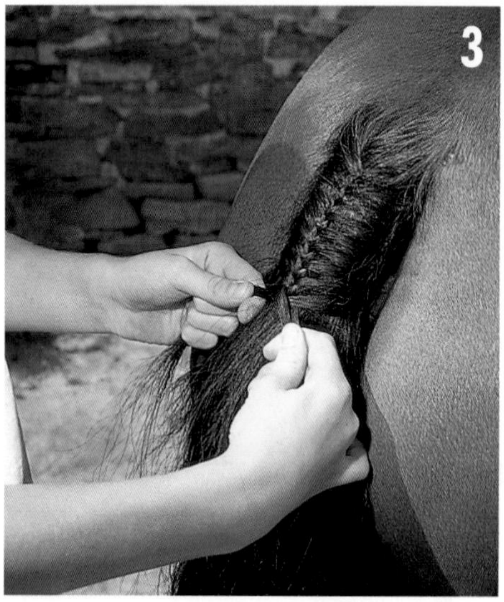

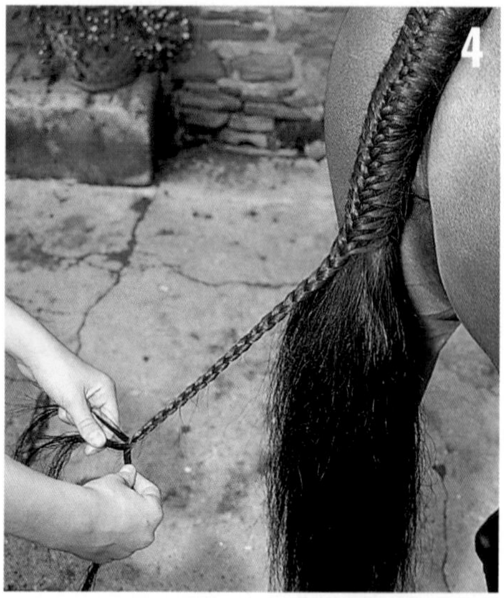

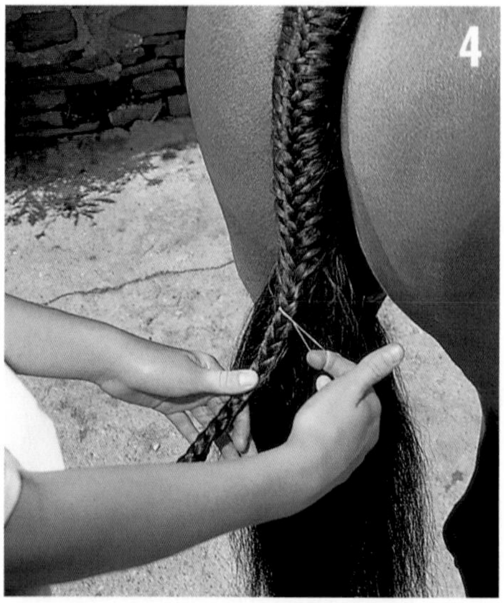

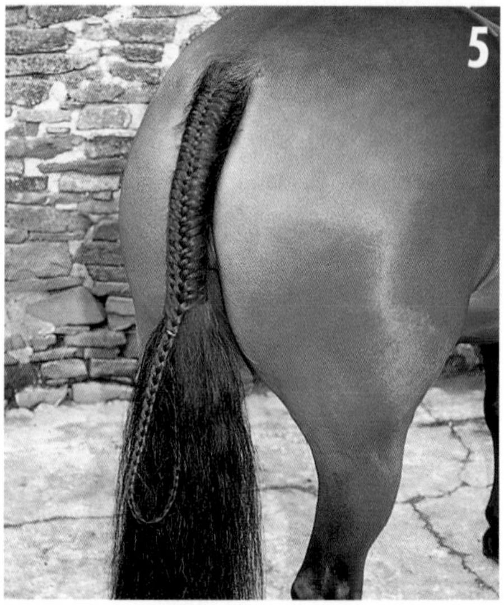

FEET AND SHOEING

The outside of the foot consists of the wall of the hoof, the sole, which is the bottom of the foot and the frog, which is the 'V'-shaped part of the sole. The frog is like a wedge of rubber and helps cushion the foot as it is brought to the ground and prevents the pony from slipping. Together, the parts of the outer foot protect the sensitive internal structures – the nerves and bones – from injury.

Hooves grow throughout a pony's life. In the wild, ponies rely on their feet to make a quick escape if they sense danger, and they wear their feet down naturally on their continual quest for fresh food. By domesticating and riding a horse, you are changing its environment and lifestyle. This means that you also have to change the way that its feet are managed.

Daily care of the hooves must include checking for loose or lost shoes, picking out the hooves and checking for lameness or heat. If a pony is not free to roam over all types of terrain, the feet will not naturally be worn down and so will grow too long and crack. If ridden a lot on the road, on the other hand, the feet will wear down quicker than they grow and will become sore.

THE FROG OF THE FOOT.

Shoes are needed to prevent wear on the hoof. Once shoes have been fitted they must be removed every six to eight weeks, trimmed and replaced. The same shoes can be used again if they are not worn out. Even if a pony does not need new shoes, they must still be replaced and trimmed, because the foot will have grown. Overgrown feet put a lot of strain on the joints and tendons, and can cause a pony to stumble. Other problems that might occur include a shoe becoming loose or being lost altogether, a shoe becoming thin through too much hard work, or the nails that hold the shoe beginning to stick up.

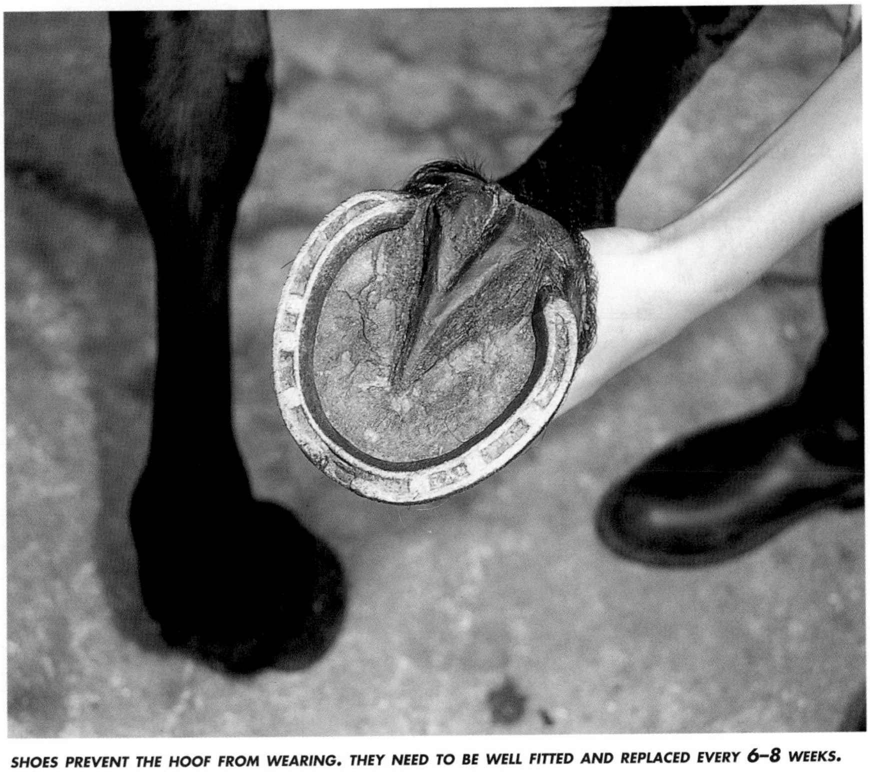

SHOES PREVENT THE HOOF FROM WEARING. THEY NEED TO BE WELL FITTED AND REPLACED EVERY 6–8 WEEKS.

A farrier is very skilled and has to train for a long time before being qualified to trim and shoe ponies. No-one other than a farrier should interfere with or attempt to trim a pony's foot. Most farriers shoe 'hot' which means that they heat the shoe until it is red hot, which makes it easier to shape and enables a better fit. When a pony loses a shoe it is called 'casting a shoe'. When the same shoes are replaced once the feet have been trimmed it is called 'removes'.

First, the farrier removes the old nails.

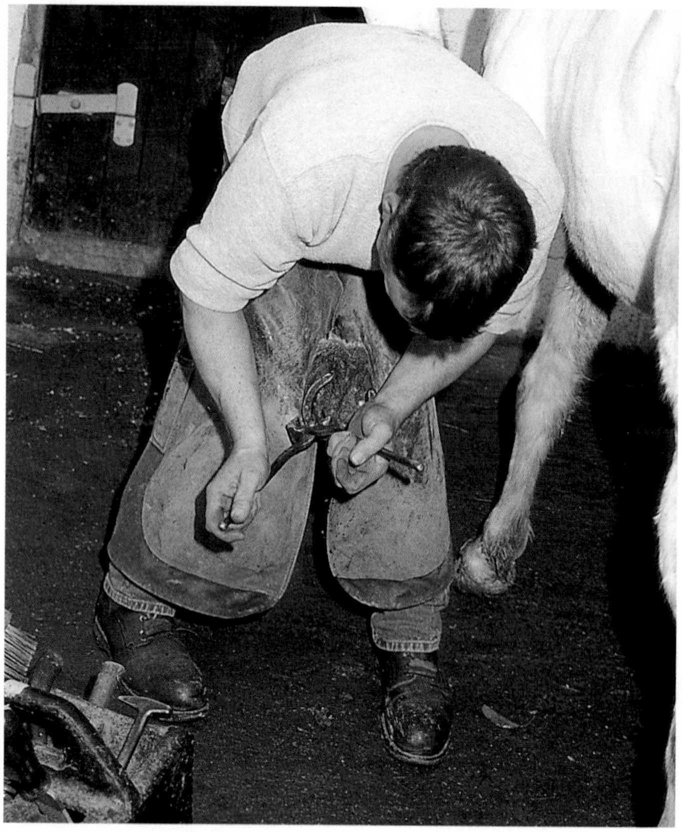

Then he levers off the old shoe.

The horn of the hoof is trimmed.

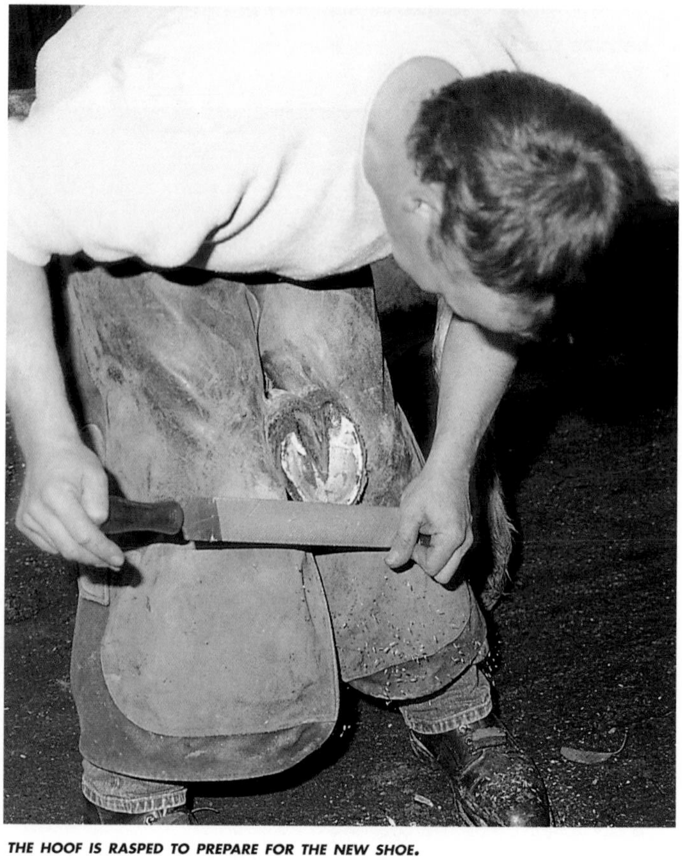

The hoof is rasped to prepare for the new shoe.

A FERRIER BANGING A RED HOT SHOE.

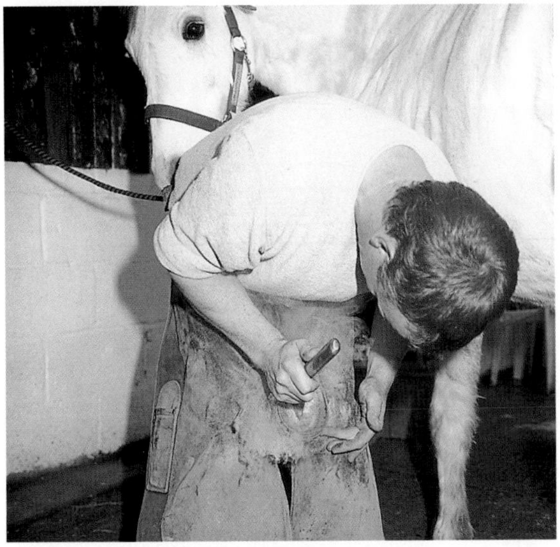

A HOT SHOE IS POSITIONED AMID MUCH SMOKE.

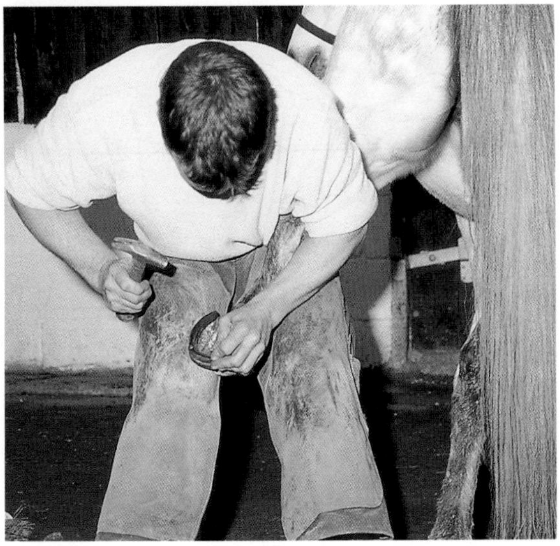

THE NEW SHOE IS NAILED ON.

SHOEING

Hot shoeing is the most common practice these days. First, an old shoe has to be removed. This is done by removing the heads from the nails (clenches) with a buffer and a hammer, and levering the shoe off with pincers.

The long horn then needs to be trimmed back with a knife. A farrier inspects all parts of the foot and rasps it in places to make a level surface ready for the new shoe.

A shoe is then made in the forge, or a ready-made shoe is altered to fit the pony. This is done by shaping the shoe on an anvil using a hammer. The hot shoe is carried to the pony on a 'pritchel' and held against the foot while it is still red hot to measure the fit. This makes a lot of smoke, and smells and looks painful, but does not hurt the pony at all. When the farrier is happy with the shape and size of the shoe it is cooled, usually by dunking it in a bucket of water, and nailed on. The nails are made especially for the job and must be the correct shape and size for the shoe. Great skill is required to make sure that the nails are driven into the correct parts of the hoof and not into the sensitive tissue causing 'pricked foot' (see page 105). There are usually four nails on the outside of the shoe and three on the inside, and the farrier usually begins at the toe. The nails are then bent over and cut off. They are then called clenches, and are then hammered down. The front shoe normally has a clip at the toe and the hind shoe has two – one on either side. These help to keep the shoe in the correct position. The hoof wall and clenches are then tided up using a rasp. Studs are used to prevent a pony from slipping and are screwed into the heel of the shoe or can be a permanent part of the shoe.

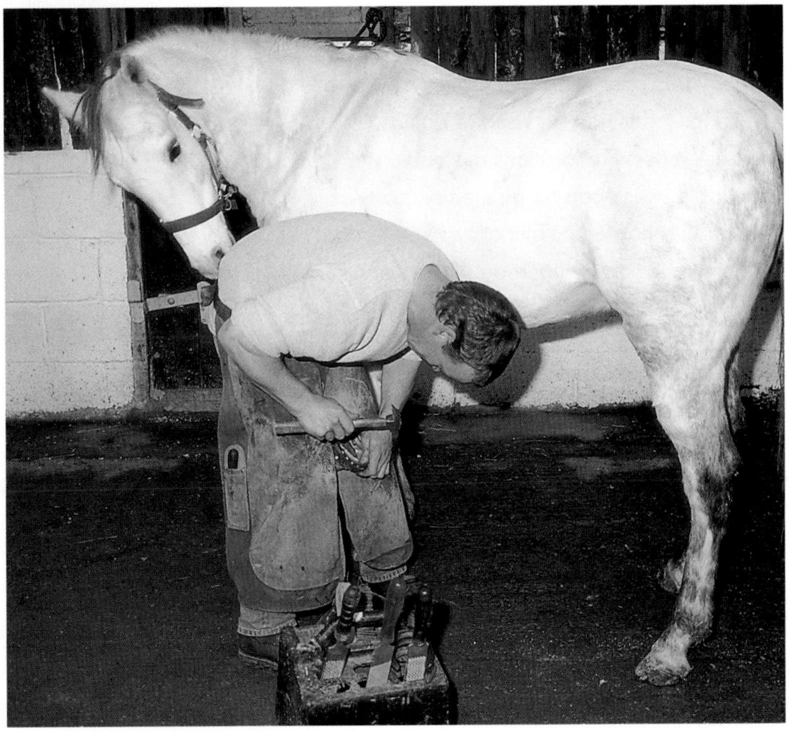

THE CLENCHES ARE HAMMERED DOWN.

MOST FARRIERS ARE MOBILE AND WILL VISIT YOU.

Things to look for in a newly shod foot:

- The shoe must have been made to fit the foot and not the foot made to fit the shape of the shoe.
- The frog should be in contact with the ground.
- The hoof has been trimmed adequately to make it completely level.
- The correct number and sizes of nails have been used.
- The clip is well fitted.
- There are no gaps between the hoof wall and the shoe.
- The clenches are not sticking out and are the correct distance from the shoe.
- The correct type and weight of shoe for your requirements has been fitted.

RIDING WITHOUT SHOES

It is possible to ride without shoes, depending on how much riding you are going to do and on what type of surface you are going to ride. Frequent riding on hard or gritty roads or stony paths will not be possible without causing a pony's feet to become sore and worn down. Riding without shoes obviously saves a lot of money, but the feet still need to be kept trimmed and level. If a pony has been shod in the past, it takes a while for the feet to get used to going out without shoes. Preparations are also available which can be painted on parts of the hoof to harden it. This allows you to do a little more riding on the road than otherwise.

An un-shod pony is less likely to slip on the road and, if you are on the receiving end of a kick, you will fare much better. Some ponies benefit from shoes on the front feet even if they do not need them on the hind feet. You should not be marked down at local shows if your pony does not have shoes as long as the hooves are well trimmed.

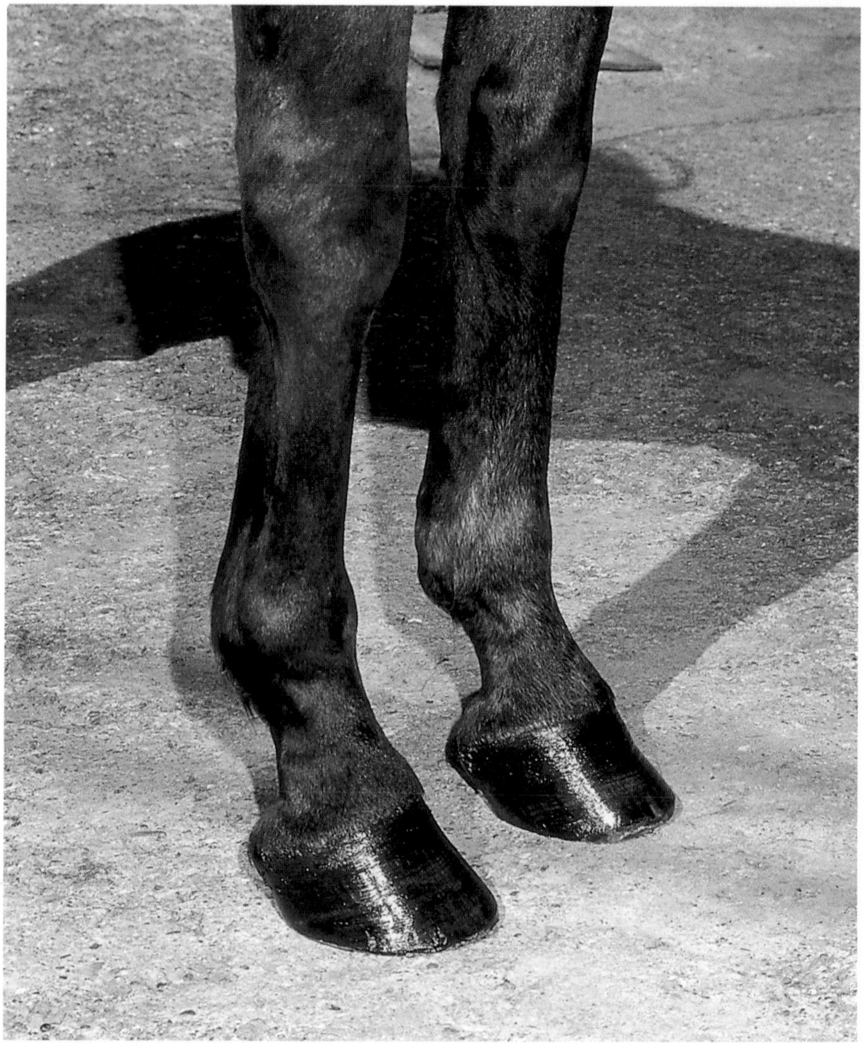

SHOES ARE NOT ALWAYS NECESSARY.

TEETH

Ponies and horses have up to 42 teeth – 12 incisors, 24 molars, 4 tushes and 2 wolf teeth. Some ponies do not develop the wolf teeth at all and mares often do not have tushes. The incisors are at the front of the mouth and are used for grazing. Next there is a gap where the tushes grow, and at the back are the molars. The molars are used to grind the food and it is these that may become sharp as the teeth wear down. If the wolf teeth are present they grow in the top of the jaw, in front of the molars, and may need to be removed as they can cause discomfort.

A pony's teeth need regular attention in order to avoid eating problems and sores in the mouth. They should be checked every six months at least. Unlike our teeth, ponies' teeth grow all the time and natural wearing sometimes leaves them uneven and with sharp edges. Wolf teeth sometimes cause discomfort – especially with a bit in the mouth – and may need to be removed by a vet. Poor teeth are often a cause of loss of condition, as food cannot be chewed properly. The tongue can also be cut by sharp edges, which develop as a pony grinds its food. The teeth grow about 1/4 cm (1/8 in.) a year and are usually worn down at about the same rate. A vet will probably use a rasp to smooth away sharp edges.

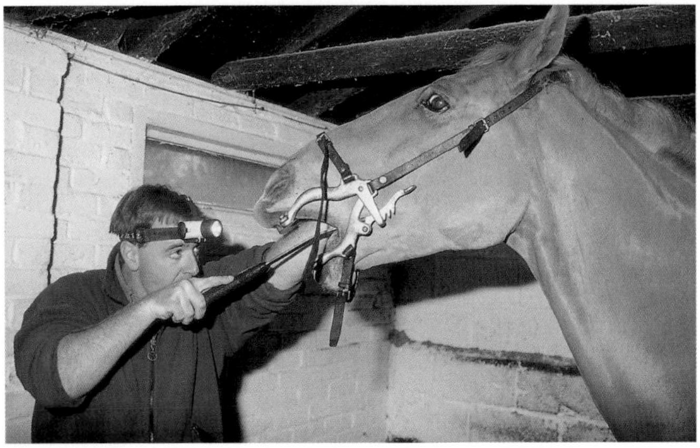

A VET WILL USE A RASP TO SMOOTH AWAY ROUGH EDGES ON TEETH.

TELLING THE AGE BY THE TEETH

The front teeth or incisors can be used to tell the age of a pony, a reasonably accurate estimate if the pony is under 12 years old. The milk teeth tend to be small and white, while the permanent teeth are more yellow in colour and so you can estimate the pony's age as the milk teeth are replaced by permanent teeth. The angles of certain teeth, such as the lower incisors, marks such as the galvayne groove (a groove on certain teeth at a certain age) and the length of the teeth can all be examined together in order to estimate the age of an older pony.

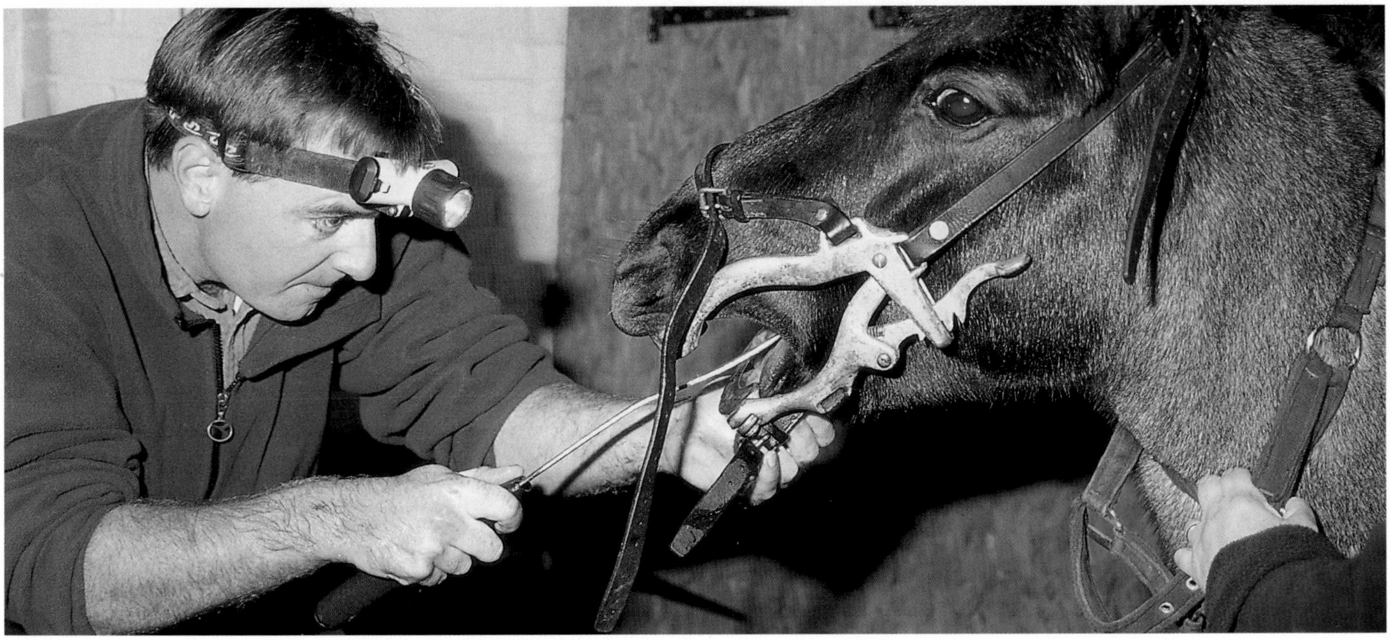

TEETH MUST BE REGULARLY CHECKED TO KEEP THEM IN GOOD CONDITION.

FEEDING

The subject of feeding is one of the most important parts of caring for your pony. Ponies are natural foragers and have very small stomachs for their size. In the wild they would be eating little and often. The feeding requirements for each pony vary, and many different things can influence this. How much work he is doing, for example, his breed, the time of year, the weather conditions, how much time is spent stabled or out at grass, his size and his temperament.

Ponies cannot be sick and so cannot get rid of anything once swallowed. Eating inappropriate foods or the wrong amounts could cause colic (see page 109), which can be painful for the pony and distressing for you. To simplify things, feed is divided into two main groups, fibre and concentrates. Salt should also be available, in the form of a 'lick', so a pony can help himself to it.

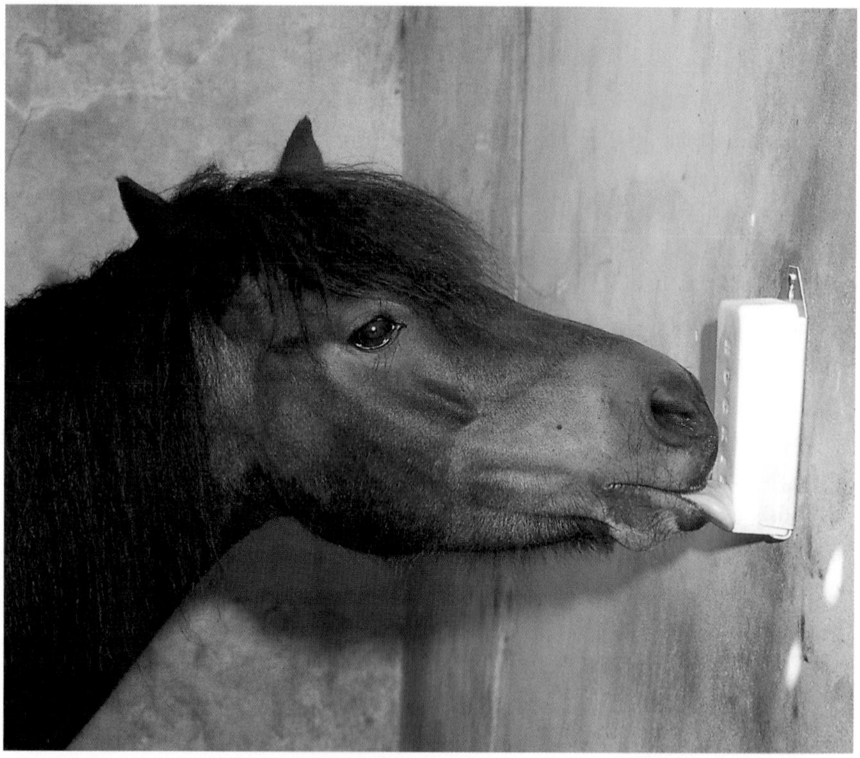

SALY SHOULD BE FREELY AVAILABLE SO THE PONY CAN HAVE IT AS AND WHEN IT NEEDS IT.

GRASS IS THE IDEAL PONY FOOD. A WELL-MAINTAINED PASTURE CAN FULFILL MOST NUTRITIONAL NEEDS.

FIBRE FOOD

GRASS

The perfect food for ponies. A pony on good grazing can maintain himself with the simple addition of hay in winter. You need to be careful not to provide too much lush grass in the spring and summer as this can lead to a condition called laminitis (see page 102).

HAYLAGE

This is grass that has been harvested, treated and sealed in bags or bales. It is free from dust, which makes it good for ponies that are sensitive to the mould and spores in hay which make them cough and could cause long-term damage. It is more expensive than hay. It is a good idea to use a haylage net, which has much smaller holes in it than a hay net and the food will take longer to get eaten. This is better for the digestion and a stabled pony will have less time to get bored. Buy good-quality haylage and store it outside as long as the packaging stays airtight to protect it from the ingress of water.

FEEDING HAYLAGE IS AN IMPORTANT WAY OF REDUCING THE AMOUNT OF DUST OR MOULD SPORES THAT A SENSITIVE PONY IS EXPOSED TO.

HORSE EATING HAYLAGE.

THIS HAYLAGE NET IS POORLY POSITIONED.

CHAFF

Chopped hay or a mix of hay and straw, this can be added to the diet to increase fibre. There are also chaff feeds available, containing alfalfa, which are good for ponies on a high-fibre diet.

HAY

This is made when the grass is cut in the summer and left on the ground to dry out. It is turned a few times and then, after a few days, is baled and stored for feed in the winter. Hay should be made from good-quality pasture and should smell sweet when you pull a handful from the middle of the bale. Meadow hay is cut from a field of permanent pasture that has been allowed to grow long. The quality can vary according to the quality of the pasture. Seed hay is different in that it comes from land that has been re-seeded and therefore contains a variety of good-quality grasses. Seed hay is harder to the touch than meadow hay. There should not be many weeds in the hay and some, such as ragwort, are very poisonous (see page 41). Hay makes the main feed to replace grass in winter or when a pony is stabled. Poor-quality hay is to be avoided at all costs. It is of little nutritional value and the mould and spores can permanently damage a pony's wind, especially if the hay was baled damp. Hay needs to be stored under cover to keep it dry. You need to consider this when deciding how much to buy at a time. Hay is cheaper if you buy it straight from the field, but you cannot use it for six months. Feed hay from a net that is tied at the right height. You can put it on the ground in the field, which is a natural way for a pony to eat it, but there will be some waste. You can also hang it in a net well clear of the ground, but make sure it is not too high or seeds could fall in a pony's eyes when he is eating.

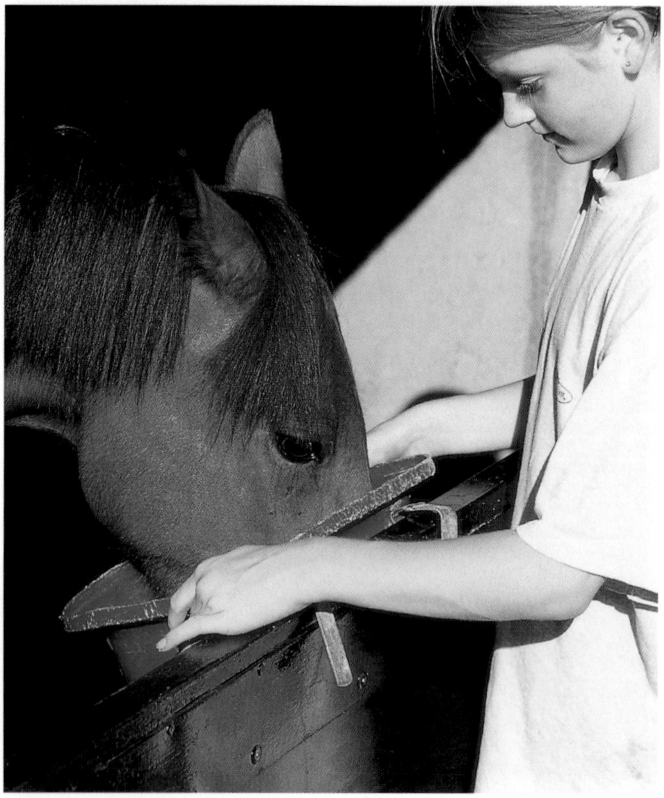

PONIES LOOK FORWARD TO FEEDING TIMES.

CHOP APPLES AND CARROTS TO PREVENT CHOKING.

CHUNKS LIKE THIS CAN BE DANGEROUS.

Silage is best avoided as it can be very high in protein and may cause digestive upsets. Apples and carrots are good, succulent fibre-containing foods. Always chop lengthways to prevent a pony choking.

CONCENTRATES

A native breed of pony doing light hacking may need just grass in the summer with additional hay in the winter. However, those that are stabled or doing harder work will need some concentrates. Cold weather may also have a bearing on this. The simplest way to achieve a balanced diet is to feed a complete feed such as a coarse mix or nuts. This saves you from buying the different ingredients and laboriously mixing them yourself in order to get the balance just right. A variety of mixes and nuts are available to suit most needs, such as low energy nuts, competition mixes, a cool mix (without oats) or a high fibre mix. If you find your pony gets very excitable when you start to feed concentrates, try a low energy mix. Within these mixes are feed stuffs such as oats, barley, maize, molasses, vitamins and minerals. Molasses are a by-product of manufacturing sugar and are very palatable and nutritious to ponies. Chaff can be added to slow down a pony that is bolting his feed. Be careful not to add anything other than carrots and apples or you could upset the balance. Ask your local feed merchant to advise which mix or nut would be appropriate for your pony and always follow the manufacturer's instructions. Remember that the amount needed will be influenced by your pony's energy levels, his current work load, the time of year, the weather, his age, his fitness, breed, condition, and how much grass he is eating. Supplements are not usually necessary, but ask your vet if you think there may be something lacking.

GOLDEN RULES OF FEEDING

- Feed little and often, using the best-quality feeds available.
- Split any concentrate feed into two or three feeds and spread them throughout the day.
- Establish a regular daily feeding routine.
- Provide your pony with a constant supply of fresh, clean water (see below).
- A constant supply of roughage is essential to keep the digestion moving.
- Allow an hour's rest between feeding a pony and working it.
- Each pony's diet must be calculated individually to suit its lifestyle.
- Keep all your feed buckets and utensils clean.
- Feed something succulent every day. If your pony has not been at grass, feed the pony some carrots or apples. Remember to cut the carrots lengthways to avoid choking.
- Do not make any sudden changes to a pony's diet. Introduce new foods gradually, increasing the amounts given over a few days.

PONY NUTS.

A COARSE MIX.

FEED MIXED TO SUIT THE INDIVIDUAL'S NEEDS.

WATERING

A clean and constant water supply is essential for maintaining the health and condition of a pony. Without it, your pony will quickly lose condition.

WATER IN THE FIELD

Streams are a good supply of water as long as they have a stony or gravel bottom and not a sandy one – a pony might swallow enough sand to give him colic. A pony must be able to reach the water easily, without having to climb down a bank, for example. Always check that the stream is not polluted further upstream. Also be sure that it runs constantly all year. If it does dry up you will need to find another means.

STREAMS MAY BE GOOD SOURCES OF WATER, BUT MUST BE ACCESSIBLE AND UNPOLLUTED.

Stagnant ponds are not suitable because water needs to be fresh. They are also dangerous, especially if they have a muddy bottom, and should be fenced off. Automatic troughs are ideal if they are sited away from overhanging trees – which will fill them with leaves – and in a dry, well-drained part of the field, where the ground is less likely to get very muddy in winter. A plug in the bottom makes it easy to empty and scrub out. An automatic trough will probably have a ball cock, which allows the trough to refill as the horse drinks. This must be checked regularly to make sure it is in good working order, especially in the winter when it could be affected by frost. You need to watch for ice in winter, particularly because ponies cannot break it. A plastic ball floating in the water may prevent ice forming.
Buckets must have the handles removed and be regularly

HANDLES SHOULD BE REMOVED FROM BUCKETS.

cleaned and refilled. Remember that ponies drink up to 8 to 10 gallons of water per day, so make sure you provide enough buckets full for the number of ponies in the field. Other containers can be used, but should not have any sharp edges, which can cause injuries.

WATER IN THE STABLES

An automatic drinking bowl ensures a constant supply of fresh, clean water as long as it is regularly cleaned and inspected. Buckets, again, should have the handles removed or be placed in such a way that a pony cannot get its leg caught easily. Make sure you give two full buckets of water at a time to ensure the pony has enough water overnight. Do not place buckets too close to hay, or they will get clogged up.

CHECK AUTOMATIC WATER CONTAINERS REGULARLY.

HANDLING YOUR PONY

Ponies will usually move away from pressure. In order to ask your pony to move over, place a hand on his side and apply a little pressure. Use the same words each time such as 'move over' and he will soon learn what is expected.

You need to be able to lift all of the pony's legs for grooming and for checking the feet. To lift a front leg, face the tail, remembering always to talk to your pony. Starting at the shoulder, run your hand down his leg and tendons to the fetlock joint then put a little upward pressure on the joint and say 'up'. Don't lift the foot too high as this will be uncomfortable for the pony. If he does not pick up his foot straight away, lean on his shoulder a little, which will encourage him to shift the weight to the other leg. To lift a hind leg, stand by the pony's hip facing the tail. Start at the pony's bottom and run your hand down the back of the leg until you reach the hock. Then move your hand round to the front of the leg and down to the fetlock joint. Again, apply a little upward pressure and say 'up'. When you want to put the foot down lower it gently to the floor, never drop it.

One of the areas of handling which is often carried out incorrectly, and which can result in an accident, is turning a pony out in the field. Open the gate wide enough, and make sure that it does not start to close on you and your pony as you walk through. Push the gate open and walk through. Turn the pony away from you in a circle, stand facing the gate, and close it. Never release a pony straight into the field as he may canter off, kicking up his heels as he goes and kicking you in the process. In all aspects of handling a pony you must be patient and well mannered, making everything you do with him a pleasure and safe. Always give him clear instructions and treat him with kindness. You will soon build up mutual respect.

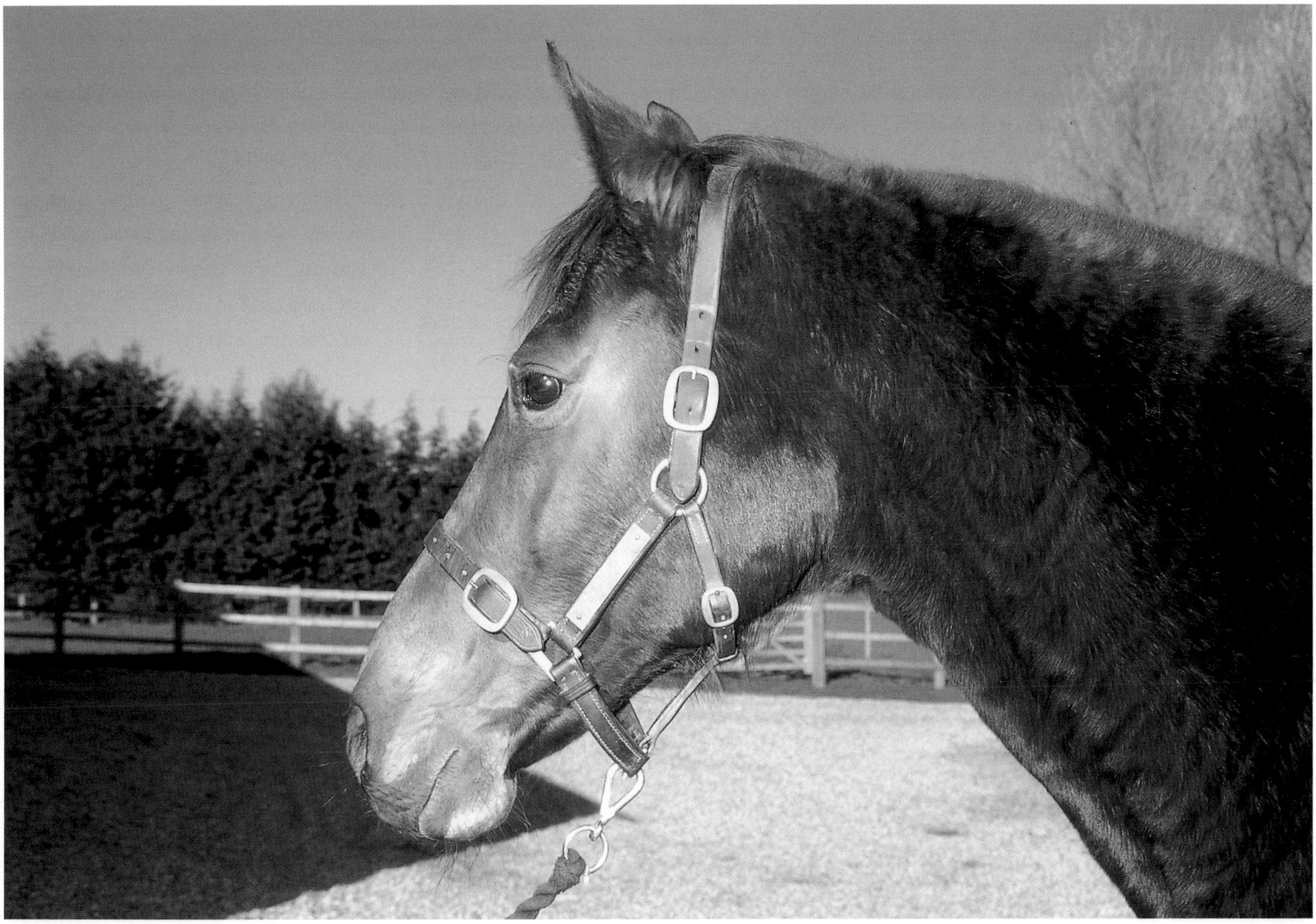

REPETITION OF VERBAL COMMANDS WILL SOON ENABLE YOUR PONY TO UNDERSTAND YOU.

CATCHING YOUR PONY

Whenever you go to catch your pony, whether it is out in the field or in the stable, you must always approach quietly and confidently. He must be aware that you are approaching so that you don't startle him. Always approach by walking up to a pony's shoulder – he cannot see you if you approach from behind – and be careful not to make any sudden or loud noises. Remember that, in the wild, ponies are flight animals, escaping from predators or dangerous situations by running away. It is of the utmost importance to talk to your pony before and during handling him, and your voice will soon become familiar to him. Pat or stroke him on his lower neck or shoulder and slip the rope around his neck quietly. Place the noseband over his muzzle and then put the headpiece quietly behind his ears. Do up the buckle, and pat the pony again. Never try to lead a pony with just a rope around his neck, or lean over a gate from the wrong side to put on the head collar. If you want to reward your pony for being caught easily, take a piece of apple or carrot with you. It is not a good idea to do this every time, however, as he will soon learn to expect it.

ALWAYS TALK TO YOUR PONY WHILE APPROACHING BEFORE CATCHING HIM.

Some ponies can be awkward to catch, usually when you only have a limited amount of time. In such cases you must be patient and keep your cool. Never try to grab the pony or corner him – he is much bigger and stronger than you – and never lose your temper. Never scold him for being awkward. You can try leaving a head collar on in the field but make sure its well fitting. Generally, it is not a good idea to leave them on in case the pony gets caught up in something or gets a leg in it when rolling or scratching. You could also try leaving a short length of rope attached to it, to give you something to get hold of. You could try walking around him in large circles, or walking away from him. Ponies can be very curious to know what you are up to. Some ponies will suddenly become a lot easier to catch if they know you have food, but this could mean having to remove any other ponies from the field first. Never take a bucket of food into a field full of ponies or you will cause a fight and may get stuck in the middle of it. If you begin to lose your temper, go away and come back later. Make sure that your pony always thinks of you coming to the field as something to look forward to. It will earn your pony's respect if you are confident and firm, but always treat him with kindness.

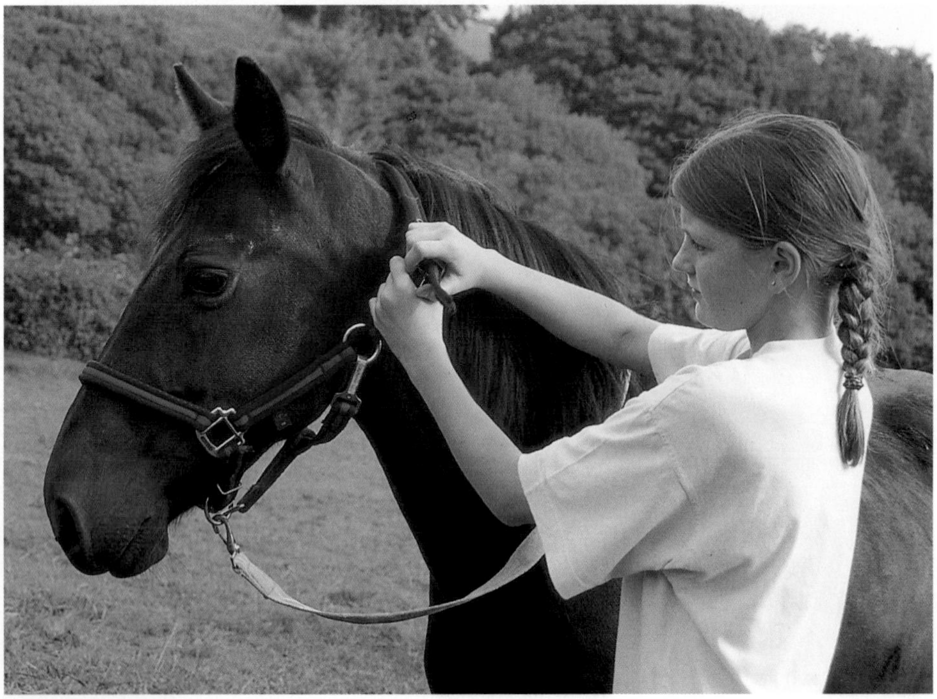

USE A PROPER HEADCOLLAR AND ROPE TO CATCH YOUR PONY IN THE FIELD.

LEADING YOUR PONY

To be safe and to avoid your pony taking you for a walk or treading on your feet, you must learn how to lead him correctly. Always use a proper lead rope rather than a cord or string, which can hurt your hands. It is advisable to wear gloves, and you should never wrap the lead rope around your hand. If your pony is startled and takes off you could end up being dragged. A pony is usually led from the left or near side, but should accept being led from either. To lead a pony in a head collar, hold the rope in your right hand about 30 cm (12 in.) from his chin. Hold the other end of the rope in your left hand, making sure you keep the end well off the ground. Walk beside the pony's head or shoulder and do not get left behind or try to pull him along from in front. To turn him, always push him gently

ALWAYS USE A HEADCOLLAR AND ROPE TO LEAD YOUR PONY.

A PONY COULD GET A LEG CAUGHT IN THIS DANGLING HEAD COLLAR – ALWAYS TIDY UP YOUR EQUIPMENT.

away from you so that you avoid getting trodden on. Do not hold him by the head collar or on too short a rope, as this will make him feel uncomfortable. Too long a rope, however, would mean that you have much less control if the pony makes a sudden movement. If you are leading a pony while it is tacked up, take the reins over his head and lead as before. Do not lead a pony with a very loose girth or with dangling stirrups. If you are leading on the road, it is safer to wear your hat, and lead in a bridle as you will have more control. Walk between the pony and the on-coming traffic. Lightly coloured or fluorescent clothing will make you more visible to motorists.

WALK BESIDE THE PONY: DO NOT PULL HIM FROM THE FRONT OR ALLOW HIM TO DRAG YOU BEHIND.

TYING UP YOUR PONY

Tying up your pony safely is essential. Many accidents occur when ponies are not tied up correctly or are tied to unsuitable objects. Even a pony that is normally very quiet can be startled by something, and it is important that you know how to tie a quick-release knot.

If you are tying your pony to a metal ring on a wall, attach a loop of breakable cord to the ring first and then tie the lead rope to that. The cord should be strong enough not to break with the normal movement of the pony's head, but weak enough to break if the pony was to pull back suddenly.

ALWAYS TIE YOUR PONY SAFELY -- A FRIGHTENED HORSE COULD LIFT THIS GATE OFF ITS HINGES WITH DISASTROUS EFFECT.

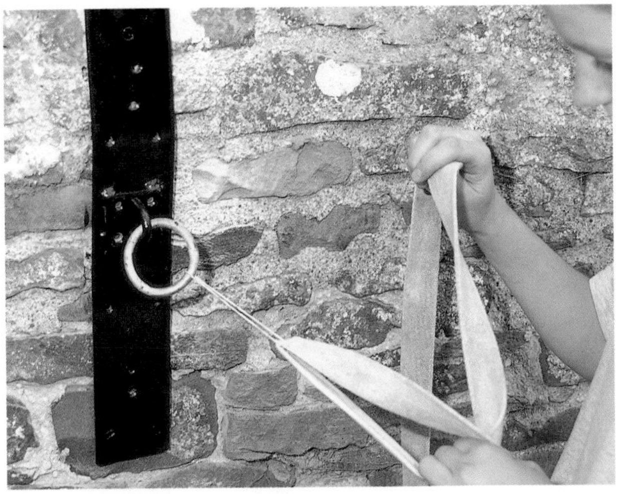

ATTACH A LOOP OF BREAKABLE STRING TO THE WALL RING, THEN TIE THE LEAD ROPE TO IT.

DOS AND DON'TS:

- Never leave your pony alone while tied up in case he gets into trouble.
- Never leave him tied too close to anything that he could get entangled in or kick at.
- Never tie up close to other ponies in case they start a fight.
- Never tie up to a movable object, such as a dustbin or a gate.
- Always use a quick release knot which allows you to free a pony quickly if he gets into trouble.
- Always use a proper head collar and lead rope and do not tie a pony up by its bridle.
- Don't tie up too short as a pony will panic if he cannot move his head.
- Don't tie up too long as a pony could get caught up in the slack rope.

WITH BASIC CARE, MAINTENANCE AND ATTENTION, YOUR PONY WILL BE CONTENT AND COMFORTABLE.

CHAPTER 5

PONY HEALTH

It is important that you learn to tell when a pony is unwell, and once you get to know your pony this will become easier. A knowledgeable person may be able to help you deal with minor problems, but in some cases, or if you are unsure, it is best to call a vet. Some conditions can cause a pony to deteriorate very quickly so it is advisable to get veterinary help as soon as you notice something is wrong. It is better to be safe than sorry, and calling a vet could prevent serious problems before they really get started.

Your pony should have a shiny coat and supple skin in summer. A stable-kept pony will be shiny in winter too. A pony's eyes should be bright and alert with the membranes under the eyelid moist and a salmon-pink colour. A pony's ears should flick back and forth, and he should look interested in his surroundings. He should be neither too fat nor too thin, but well covered. You should be able to feel the ribs underneath the skin, but you should not be able to see them. A pony's legs and feet should be cool to the touch, with no patches of heat or swelling. He should drink regularly and have a good appetite – loss of interest in food is a sign that something is wrong. A pony's weight should be evenly spread on all four legs and he should not be lame, when he walks. Resting a hind leg is normal. Urine should be passed regularly without effort and should be a

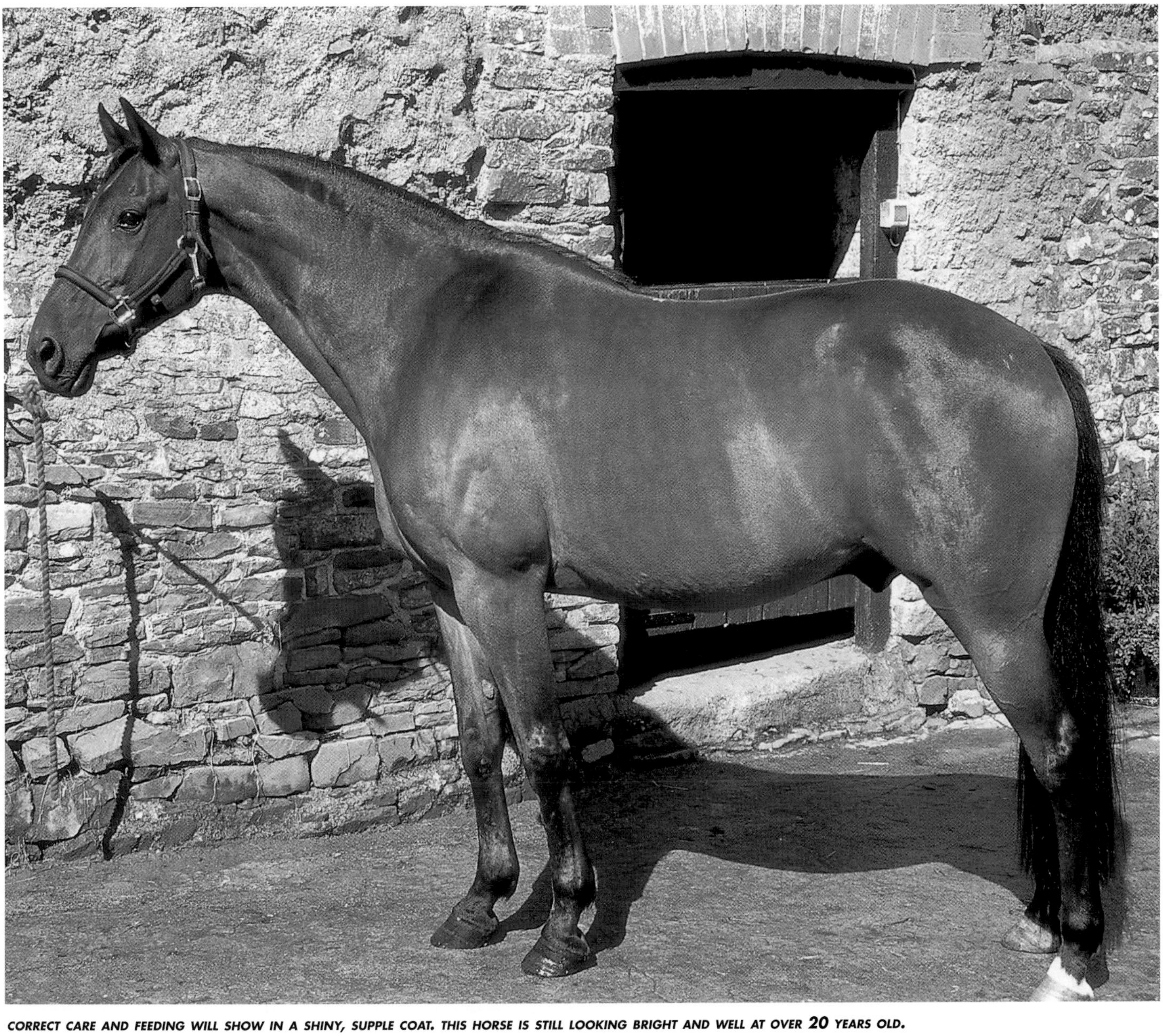

CORRECT CARE AND FEEDING WILL SHOW IN A SHINY, SUPPLE COAT. THIS HORSE IS STILL LOOKING BRIGHT AND WELL AT OVER 20 YEARS OLD.

pale yellow colour or clear. Droppings will vary according to diet, but they should not be too runny. There should not be any discharge from the nostrils or any coughing. Pony's breathe approximately eight to 12 times per minute. This is easier to see when a pony is resting – stand towards the back of him and watch his side moving in and out. You may need to take your pony's temperature. The thermometer should be shaken until it reaches 37.4°C or (100°F). It should be well greased and inserted under the tail into the rectum, get an experienced person to do this. Hold firmly in place for about 30 seconds. The normal temperature for a pony is 38°c (100.5°F). If it is over 1 degree more or less you should call the vet. Pulse rate should be between 36 and 42 beats per minute when the pony is resting. To take a pony's pulse find the artery under his jaw, behind his eye or on the inside of the foreleg, level with the knee where the artery goes over the bone. Press two fingers lightly to feel the pulse. It is wise to keep a note of your pony's normal temperature, pulse rate and breathing rate at rest and compare them with readings you take when you think you pony is unwell. Unless it is a very hot day, your pony should not sweat when resting.

If your pony sustains a serious injury, phone the vet immediately. If your pony has a problem with its feet seek advice from your farrier. Do not ride your pony if you think it is unwell.

CHECK THAT YOUR PONY HAS EATEN ALL HIS FEED.

EXERCISE IS ESSENTIAL TO ENSURE GOOD CONDITION.

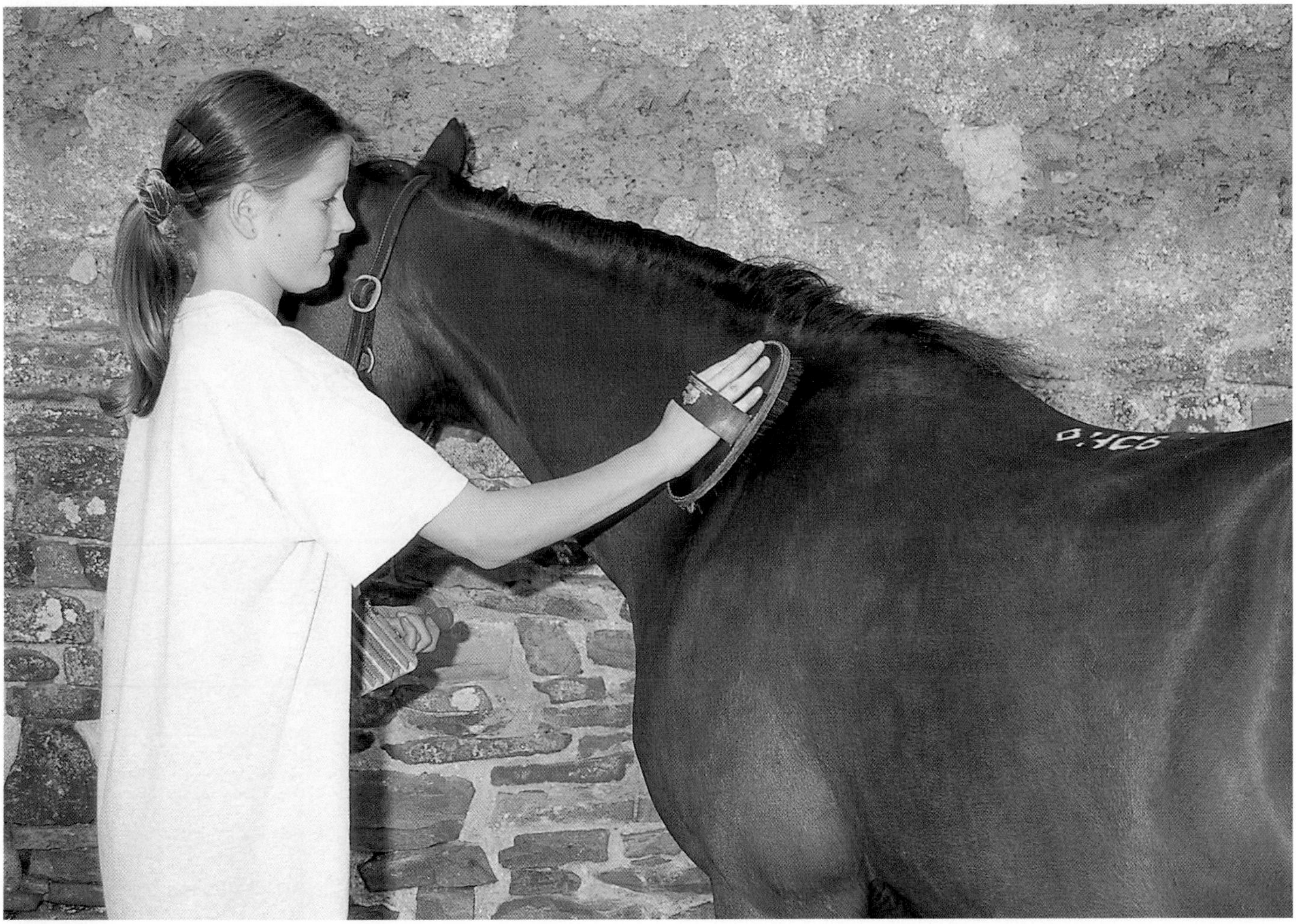

KEEP GROOMING TO A MINIMUM IF YOUR PONY IS SICK.

'Condition' is the term used for the amount of flesh your pony is carrying, basically whether the pony is too fat, too thin or just right. To maintain a good condition a pony must have balanced feed and exercise. Too much feed with not enough exercise will cause a pony to become fat, possibly leading to such problems as laminitis, heart strain and lameness. Not enough feed and a lot of exercise will produce a thin pony. As your experience grows you will learn to maintain good condition by adjusting your pony's diet and management. Until then, seek advice from an expert or a vet if your pony is losing condition.

BELOW: THIS PONY NEEDS A LITTLE LESS FOOD AND MORE EXERCISE.

CAUSES OF POOR CONDITION

- The pony does not have a fresh, clean constant water supply.
- Nutrition is vitally important.
- Your pony may be intimidated by other ponies at feeding time.
- Your pony may lack certain minerals.
- Older ponies find it less easy to keep weight on as a rule, and when over about 16 years, need to be kept warm in winter and may be harder to maintain in condition.
- Sharp teeth may be causing eating difficulties.
- A pony may be suffering from worms.
- A pony may be suffering from disease.
- Ponies kept alone and confined to the stable for long periods may develop compulsive habits and loss of condition.

COMMON CONDITIONS & AILMENTS

Do not be alarmed by this section. Although accidents and illnesses are sometimes difficult to prevent, good stable management and proper care should help reduce the risk of some of them.

A pony that is unwell or injured will need to be kept warm and comfortable. If kept in the stable, he will need a thick comfortable bed, plenty of fresh air, regular attention and, ideally, a companion nearby. Each pony will need individual nursing depending on the condition or injury and his normal lifestyle. Here are some general hints on nursing a sick pony.

Grooming need only be enough to ensure he is kept comfortable. He must be kept warm. Take advice from your vet on what to feed him but as a general rule feed him little and often. If he doesn't eat, take the food away. Do not leave it in the stable, but offer fresh feed a little later. Try to add a chopped or grated apple or carrot to encourage him to eat.

Fresh, clean water must be available at all times, as well as a salt lick. If he is confined to the stable he will appreciate a few handfuls of fresh grass (never feed cut grass or lawn clippings, as these could cause a tummy ache). Do not leave the grass in the stable if he doesn't eat it.

If your pony has a temperature it is essential to keep him warm with light rugs. A sweat rug (see page 25) under a light rug will trap a layer of warm air, which will help if he is sweating. Keep the stable well ventilated but without draughts. Stable bandages (see page 58), will help keep his legs warm if needed. If your pony has something contagious and needs to be kept in isolation, move him to a stable well away from the others and use separate equipment for mucking out and grooming. Do not go near other ponies while you are looking after him, as you risk spreading the disease yourself. Exercise and turning out in the field should be reintroduced gradually if a pony has had a spell of being confined.

STABLE RUGS PROTECT PONIES AND HORSES FROM DRAUGHTS AND CHILLS IN STABLES.

PESTS

WORMS

All ponies carry some worms in their gut, which vary in size from thin threads to the thickness of a pencil and several inches long. Most of them lay eggs in large number in the pony's intestines, having been picked up by the pony while grazing. Good pasture management and regular treatment with a wormer every six to eight weeks helps keep the numbers of worms down. A pony with an excessive amount of worms will have a dull coat, will lose weight and may have a potbelly.

You can treat a pony with worms by putting powder in its feed or by using a syringe to squirt medication down the pony's throat. Be careful to give the correct dose and to follow the manufacturer's instructions. Some preparations don't cover all types of worm so always read the label carefully. If you are unsure, take advice from your vet. If more than one pony shares a field, then all of them must be treated at the same time or the worms will continue to spread between them.

Picking up droppings regularly will help prevent so many worms getting into the pasture. It is best to keep the pony off the pasture for a minimum of 48 hours after worming so as not to re-infect the pasture. If this is not possible, pick up droppings as often as possible over the few days after the treatment.

FEED SOMETHING SUCCULENT DAILY.

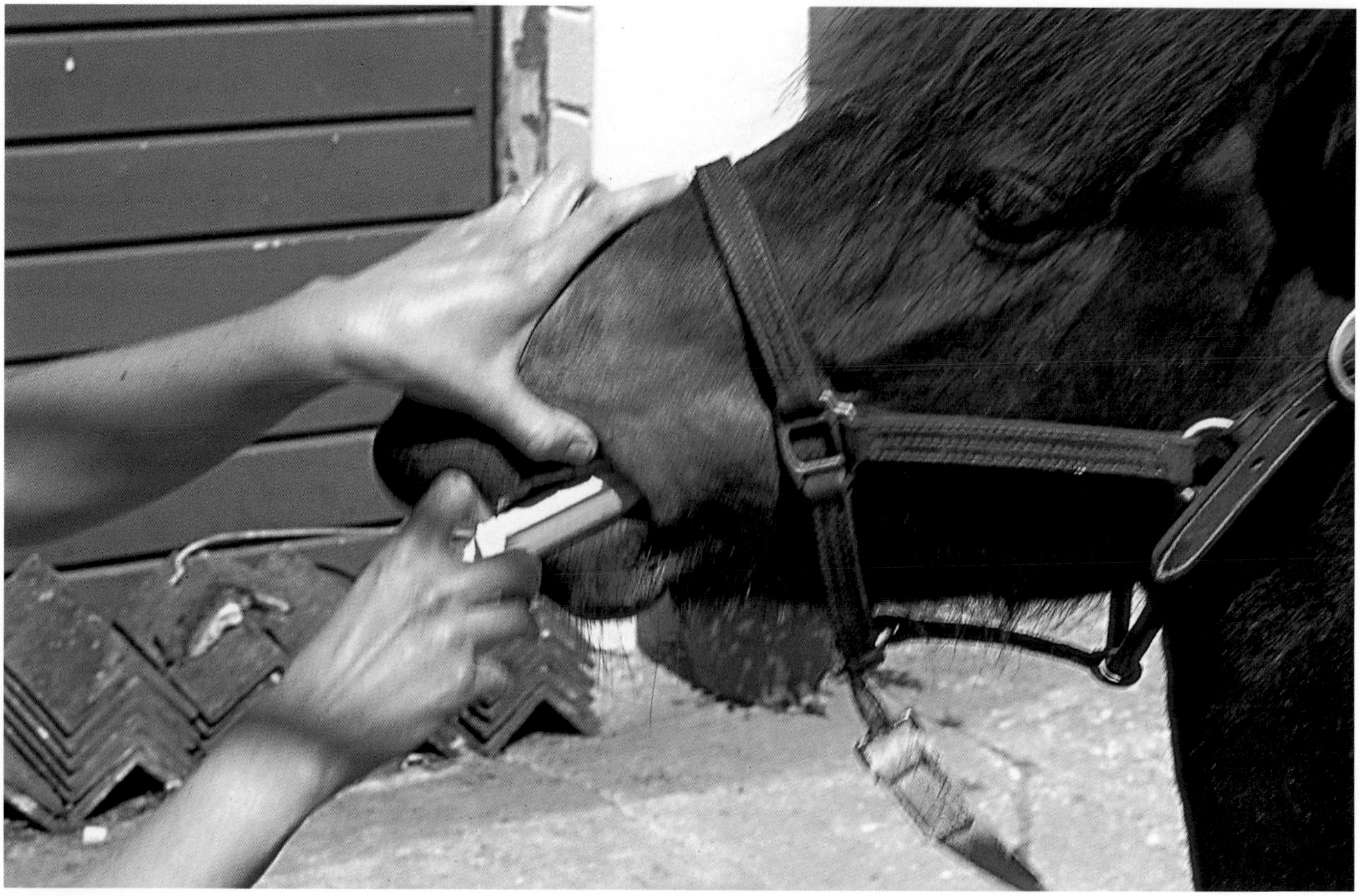

A SYRINGE IS THE QUICKEST AND EASIEST METHOD OF ADMINISTERING A WORMER.

FLY'S CAN IRRITATE A PONIES SENSITIVE EYES AND IN THESE CASES A FLY MASK IS USEFUL.

LICE

These are small pale brown insects. Some types of lice bite, while others suck blood. The blood-sucking lice are normally found in the mane and tail areas and the biting variety are more often found on the legs. Ponies that have been neglected can be badly affected by lice and they will be spread all over the body and head areas. On close examination the lice can be seen amongst the scurf or on the pony's hairs. Lice are less easy to see on a pony at grass with a thick winter coat, so you will need to be more watchful. Ponies rub and scratch the affected areas and this can lead to unsightly bald patches. Seek advice from your vet about how to treat this irritating parasite.

MANGE

This is a condition caused by mites that bite. They live on or burrow into the skin causing severe itching. The hair becomes thin, leaving bald patches with scabs and the skin thickens. Mange is easily spread from one pony to another through close contact, even a shared grooming kit, but is more often seen in ponies that are not very well looked after. Seek advice and treatment from your vet. The stable and all your equipment will need to be disinfected,with all bedding burned to eliminate the pest completely.

WARBLES

Warble flies look like small bees and usually lay their eggs on cattle; they are more commonly found on ponies that share a field with cattle. The larvae hatch after a few days then burrow into the skin. In the spring the grubs accumulate under the skin on the animal's back, where they form a small bump or swelling. They often cause a problem if the swelling is underneath the saddle area. Applying a poultice may encourage the maggots to appear, in which case they can be brushed off. Do not squeeze the swelling as this could lead to a nasty abscess. In the early summer the full-grown grub emerges and falls to the ground to pupate. After about three weeks a warble fly emerges. Seek advice from your vet if your pony is infected with a warble. It is not advisable to ride a pony with any type of sore underneath the saddle.

ABOVE: WARBLE FLIES FROM CATTLE MAY INFECT PONIES.

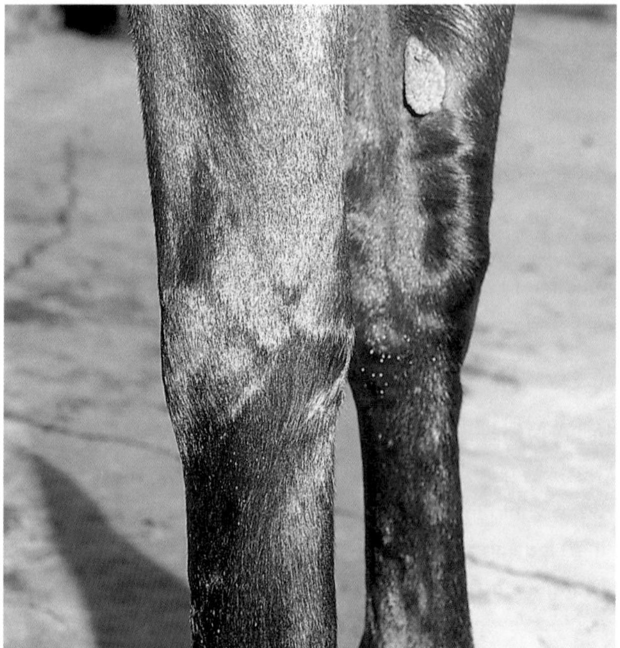

RIGHT: BOT EGGS MUST BE REMOVED TO AVOID INGESTION.

BOTS

Bot eggs are little yellow eggs that attach to the hairs of a pony's legs in summer, and ponies often swallow them as they lick their legs. The grubs attach themselves to the inside of the stomach and feed off the pony until late spring. They are potentially very dangerous and can be fatal. A wormer can rid a pony of bots in the stomach, usually carried out in the autumn, and the yellow eggs can be scraped off a pony's legs with a special knife.

TICKS

Ticks are common and can be found on most domestic animals. They usually attach themselves to a horse's head during grazing and can grow to about 1 cm (1/2 in.) before they drop off. You should never pull a tick off, as part of its body usually remains in the skin and can cause infection. Seek advice from the vet on how to treat a pony with ticks.

LAMENESS

At some time or another, your pony is likely to go lame. This is quite common and can result from a variety of causes, either by injury or disease. In all cases you must consult your vet for diagnosis and treatment.

Lameness could affect any part of the leg, its joints or the foot. Never ride a pony that is lame. If you are out on a hack when he goes lame dismount, and check that there is not simply a stone in his shoe. If not, lead him home quietly. Rest is of great importance when treating lameness, as is a comfortable stable. If a pony is lame on one foreleg the other foreleg may need to be supported with a bandage to ease the extra strain on it.

It is important that you are able to tell when a pony is lame, and helpful if you can tell which leg is causing the trouble. This is not always as easy as it sounds. Severe lameness will be obvious at a walk. If it is not, get someone to trot the pony on a loose rein towards and away from you in a straight line and on hard ground. If the pony is lame on a foreleg he will lower or dip his head when the good leg comes to the ground. If lame in both front legs he will hold his head up and take short strides. If lame in a hind leg his quarters will dip more as the good leg comes to the ground, as the pony tries to keep the weight of the painful leg. When standing still one leg may be rested or one foreleg may be pointed forwards. Common causes of lameness are noted below.

TROT YOUR PONY ALONG HARD AND LEVEL GROUND TO ASSESS WHICH LEG IS LAME.

LAMINITIS

Found more often in ponies than in horses, laminitis is a very painful condition caused by inflammation of the tissues inside the hoof. Because the hoof is enclosed in a solid case that cannot expand, the inflammation causes a pony great pain. Reasons for the swelling might be an inappropriate amount of feed or too much lush green grass. It can also be brought on by a fever and inflammation of the womb in mares. Too much lush grass is the most common cause in ponies, along with too much hard work on a hard surface. Wild ponies are used to managing on moorland, which is sparse with poor-quality grazing. They need to walk a long way to find adequate food. A pony on good pasture will soon have eaten more than he needs to maintain himself, even if he is working, but will tend to carry on eating. This will lead to the pony developing a form of indigestion that poisons the blood stream, in turn resulting in the inflammation of the sensitive tissue in the hoof.

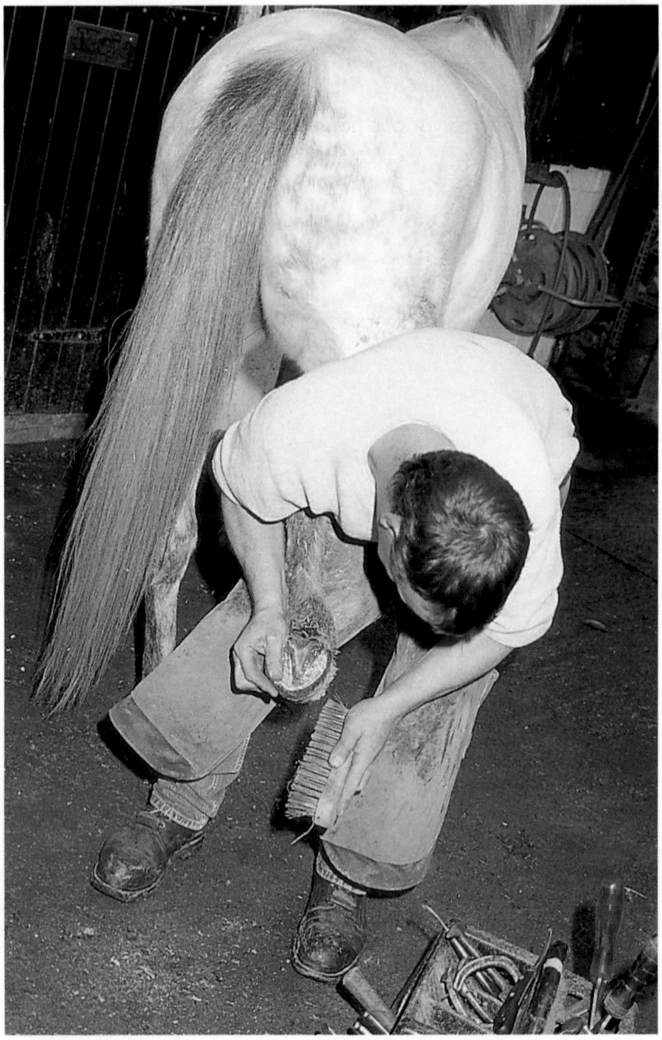

YOUR FARRIER SHOULD BE ABLE TO ADVISE YOU ON FOOT PROBLEMS

A pony with laminitis will stand with his front feet pushed forwards and his hind feet underneath him so as to take the pressure and weight off the toes. The foot will change shape and he will be unwilling to move. The hooves feel warm or hot to the touch and, although the symptoms are more commonly seen in the front feet, all four can be affected. A temperature of up to 41°C (104°F) will probably be present and the pony will obviously be in pain. Veterinary advice should be sought immediately, and painkillers may be given if acute pain is obvious. In the meantime, the pony should be stabled with a nice thick bed to encourage him to lie down. Shavings are best because they help to support the soles of the feet. A farrier will offer advice on footcare, possibly fitting special shoes.

The risk of laminitis can be greatly reduced if you keep your pony off very lush grass. However, some ponies are more prone than others to laminitis and they need to be monitored carefully, particularly in the spring and summer. Poorer quality grazing is often better for these ponies and it may help to stable them for a given time each day, or to use an electric fence to regulate the amount of grazing they have access to each day. You can prevent a laminitis-prone pony from suffering a second time by maintaining a delicate balance between nutrition and exercise.

MUD FEVER

This condition is most often found in ponies kept at grass in the winter, when conditions are wet and muddy. Not all ponies are affected, and the type of soil may be a factor too. Clay soil is particularly irritating. The thin skin around the heels becomes irritated and inflamed, making the heel become sore and cracked. Bacteria are then able to get into the skin resulting in a temperature and lameness. The skin will continue to crack unless a soothing, moist ointment is applied throughout the healing process. Try using a thin layer of petroleum jelly on the heels and pasterns if the skin is becoming inflamed, and do not wash a pony's legs in winter, unless they are exceptionally dry, as leaving them damp in cold conditions contributes to this problem. If a stabled pony comes back from a ride with wet and muddy legs, cover them with stable bandages for a few hours until dry and then remove the bandages and brush off the mud with a soft brush. In very muddy conditions, this condition can also affect the under-belly area.

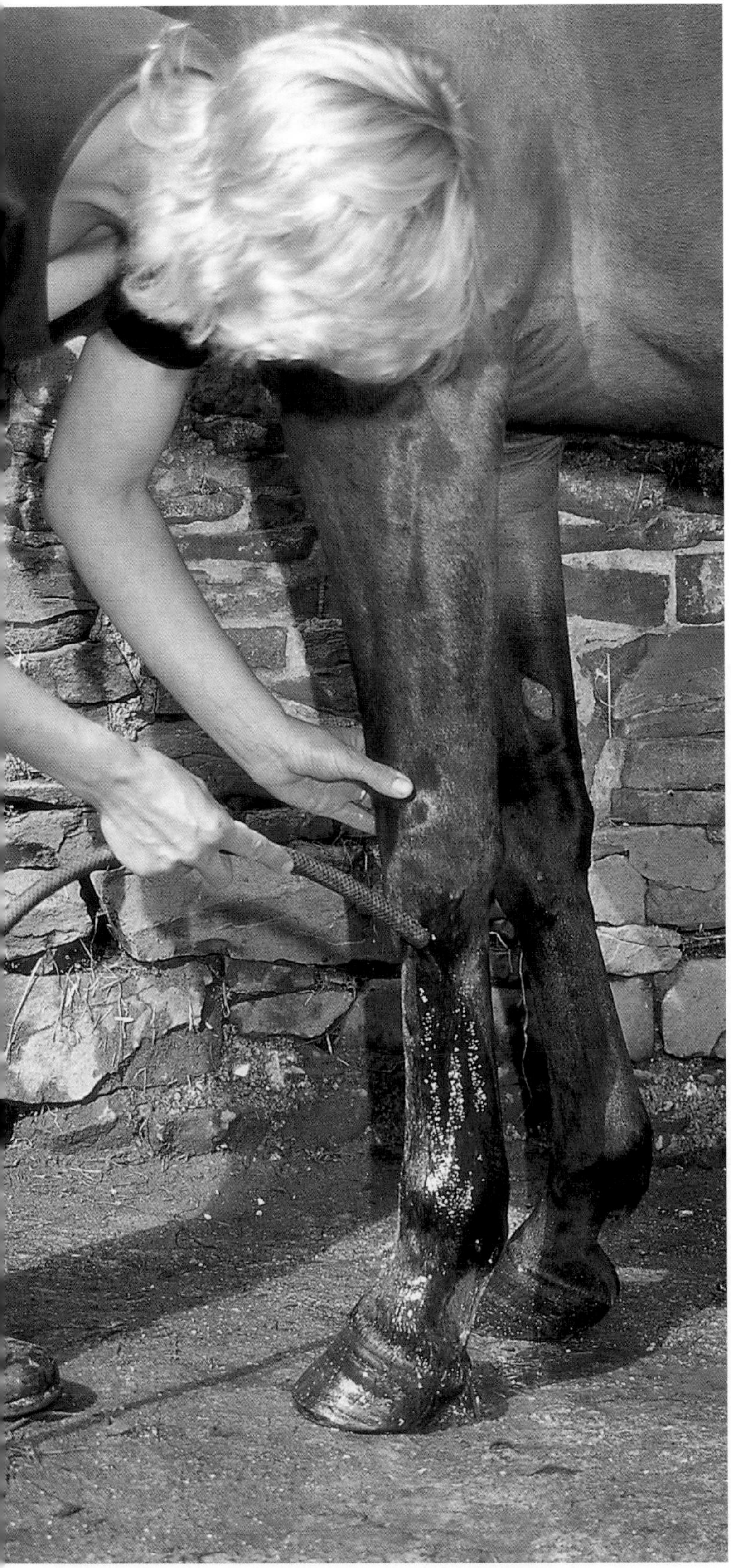

RUNNING COLD WATER OVER A SPRAIN CAN EASE IT AND REDUCE SWELLING.

SPRAINS

These can occur in the muscles, tendons or ligaments. They can be caused during jumping or riding fast in heavy soil, particularly when the pony is tired or unfit. Obvious signs of a sprain are heat and /or swelling in the limbs. Run cold water over the swelling until the vet arrives. This will make the pony more comfortable and will help to reduce the heat and swelling. Tendon and ligament strains are more common in the front legs than in the hind.

CURB

A curb is when the ligament in the hind leg, where the point of the hock meets the top of the cannon bone, becomes strained. It appears to thicken and bulge. When it is forming, it will feel warm to touch and may cause lameness.

SOFT SWELLINGS

Also known as bursal enlargements, these are caused by injuries or strains to the joints, tendons or ligaments. They have various names depending on where they are situated. If you detect any of the following, contact your vet and do not ride your pony in the meantime. Run a cold hose over the affected area to reduce heat and swelling.

A bog spavin is a soft swelling around the inside and to the front of the hock. A wind gall is a soft swelling just above and at the sides of the fetlock. It doesn't usually cause lameness once established, although the swelling often remains. Capped elbow – swelling at the elbow – is often caused when lying down without enough bedding. Capped hock – swelling on the hock – can be caused by lack of bedding or, sometimes, while travelling without enough protection from boots. Thoroughpin is a soft swelling in the dip just in front of the point of the hock.

BONY ENLARGEMENTS

These are bony lumps that form in various parts of the leg, most often the result of concussion. They often cause lameness when they are forming but, once formed, do not cause further problems. Bony enlargements are most likely to occur in young ponies, especially if they do a lot of work on a hard surface.

Heat is often present in the affected area. Veterinary attention will be needed. Ring bone is a bony enlargement on the pastern. Side bones are bony enlargements near the heel. They appear as a hard ridge where the cartilage has gradually changed to form bony lumps. A bone spavin is a bony enlargement on the inside of the hock, which needs to be treated promptly and can cause lameness for quite a while. Splints are bony enlargements on the splint or cannon bone, usually on the inside of the foreleg. Less commonly, they can be found on the hind legs or on the outside of the foreleg. In many cases they have formed by the time the pony is aged seven.

BRUISED SOLE

This is quite common when the pony has had a stone lodged in his shoe, which has caused a bruise to the sensitive sole of the foot. Some ponies are more prone to this than others, especially those ridden on stony ground. If it keeps happening, it is possible to fit a leather pad under the shoe to protect the sole.

NAVICULAR DISEASE

This is caused when the navicular bone in the foot becomes pitted and rough. Pain results as the tendon runs across the bone. A pony with navicular disease will often stand with one leg pointed forwards. Corrective shoeing may help, but this is a serious condition.

THRUSH

This is a smelly condition that affects the frog (the V-shaped part of the sole). It can often result from poor stable management, for example when a pony has been standing in wet muck or if the feet are not picked out regularly. You should consult your vet or farrier if your pony's feet smell.

CRACKS

These can appear in the wall of the hoof with a variety of causes. A sand crack starts at the coronet band at the top of the hoof and heads downwards, often on the hind foot near the toe.

SEEDY TOE IS PARTICULARLY COMMON IN DONKEYS.

A similar crack nearer to the heel is called a quarter crack. They can be painful and need attention.

BROKEN HOOF WALLS

Pieces of hoof can actually break off in chunks when a pony loses a shoe. An unshod pony may get bits breaking off through wear and tear. A farrier will tidy these up.

GRAVEL

This is the name given to describe when a small object such as a piece of grit or gravel has been pushed up into the hoof, causing pain and pressure under the hoof wall. Pain will be felt when the hoof wall is tapped and an abscess may form under the hoof wall. If left untreated, it could travel upwards and eventually break out at the coronet band.

SEEDY TOE

This condition can be caused by poor shoeing, especially where the toe clip is too tight. It can also be caused by an injury to the foot. A hollow forms near the toe, which is actually the separation of the hoof wall from the fleshy tissue underneath. The hollow then becomes filled with a dry crumbly horn. It is common in donkeys and needs attention from the farrier.

PRICKED FOOT

This is caused when the farrier drives a nail into the sensitive part of the foot by mistake while shoeing. It is an accident that occurs from time to time and does not cause too much trouble unless it becomes infected, when it should be treated as a puncture wound.

PUNCTURED SOLE

This is when a foreign body such as a nail or a sharp stone punctures the sole of the foot. The wound tends to heal over quickly, leaving dirt and bacteria inside, which then leads to infection or an abscess. This is very painful as it creates pressure inside the foot. A hole will need to be made to allow the abscess to drain and a poultice will need to be applied. Antibiotics may also be needed. Check that your own tetanus vaccination is up to date.

CORNS

These are bruises that form in the sole, behind the heel on either side of the frog. The sole is quite thin and sensitive here. Corns can be caused by pressure from a shoe. Attention from the farrier is needed, who may cut it out. The wound then needs to be kept clean to prevent an abscess forming. Special shoes can be fitted to ponies that are prone to corns. They transfer the weight to another part of the hoof. Future shoeing must ensure there is no pressure on that part of the sole.

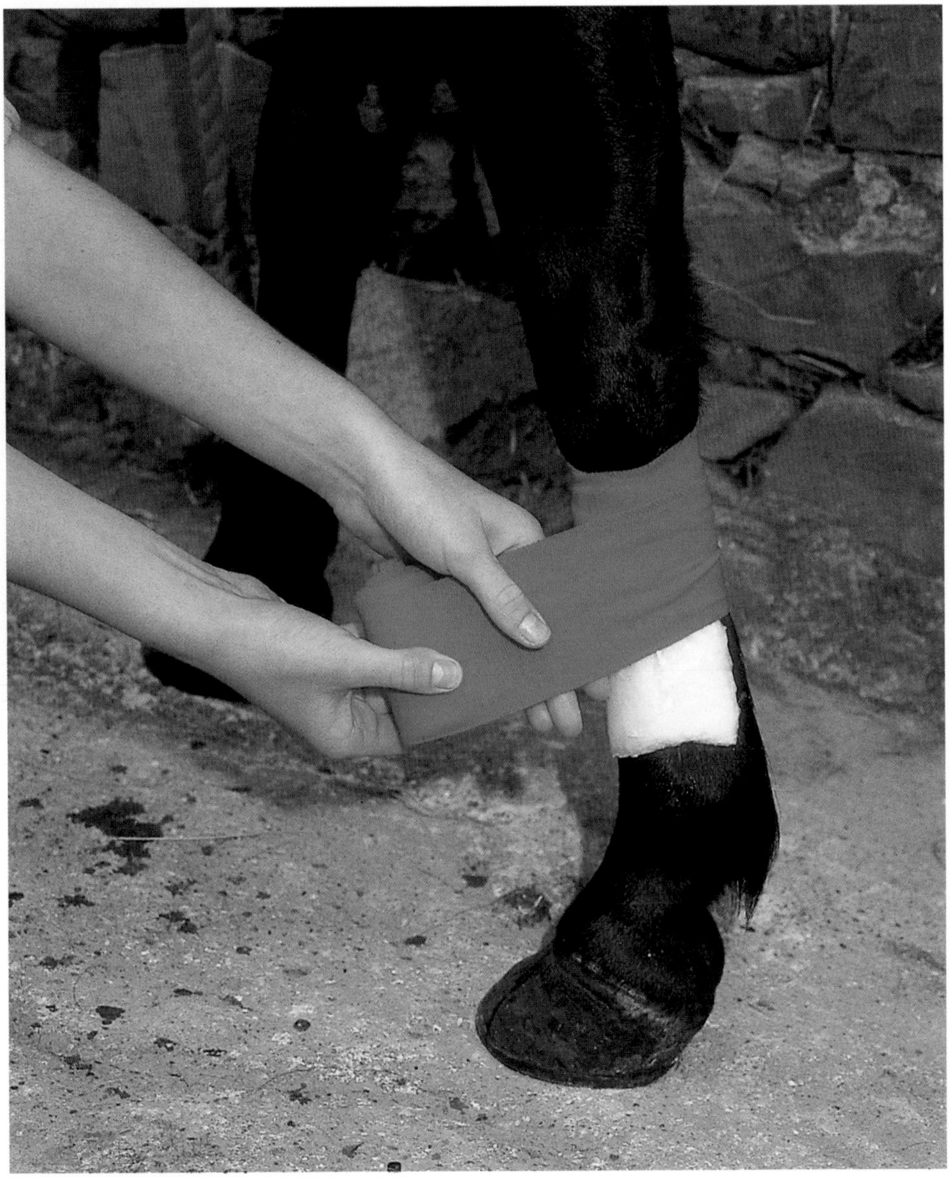

POULTICES ARE USEFUL TO DRAW OUT INFECTION.

SKIN CONDITIONS

SWEET ITCH

Some ponies are particularly sensitive to irritating bites from midges and can rub themselves bald. This usually happens near the mane and anywhere on a line from the poll, (behind the ears) to the top of the tail. This condition is thought to be due to an allergic reaction to midge saliva. A pony with sweet itch will quickly rub out its mane and tail making it sore, difficult to plait and unsightly. A vet can give you a lotion that can be applied to soothe the irritation. Ponies are usually affected from late spring to early autumn, the worst times being a couple of hours before sunset and a couple of hours after sunrise, and they are best brought in at these times. Prevention, by managing the time spent outside and applying lotion twice a day, will help maintain the mane and tail in the summer.

GALLS AND SORES

Most often caused by saddles or rugs that do not fit properly or that have sweat and grease underneath, galls and sores are patches of red, sore and inflamed skin that often appear on the withers or around the girth area. Areas that have been damaged in the past show as white patches where the skin has been damaged. Galls are patches of red, sore and inflamed skin. An anaesthetic powder or cream can be applied to soothe the skin until it is completely healed. If an ill-fitting saddle is the cause of a gall or sore, get the fit checked. The same applies to rugs. A piece of sheepskin can be sewn into the withers area of a rug to prevent rubbing. Vests are also available that help stop the rug rubbing against the shoulders. Girths can also be covered with a sleeve of furry material. Young ponies and those which have not been ridden for a while will gall more easily because their skin is more tender.

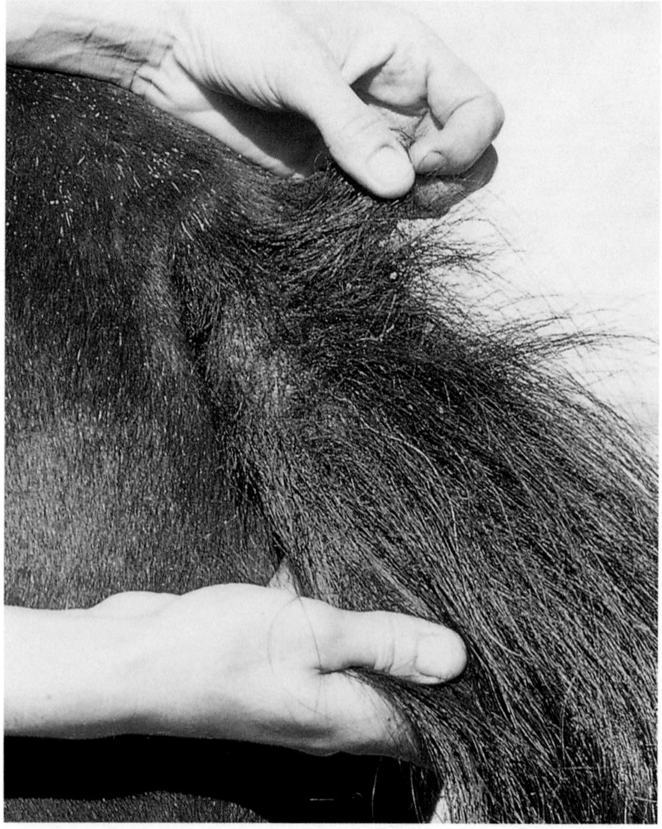

A PONY WILL SOON MESS AND TANGLE ITS MANE OR TAIL IF THEY ITCH IT A GREAT DEAL.

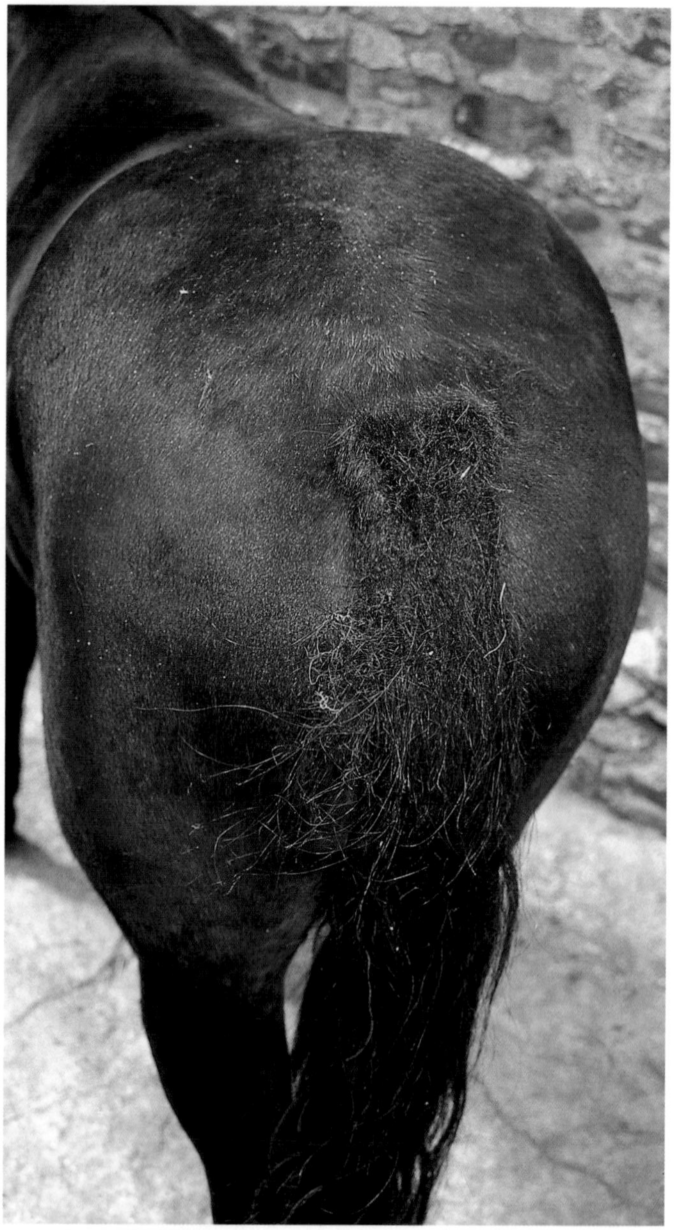

A GOOD TAIL CAN QUICKLY BE RUINED BY SWEET ITCH.

RAIN SCOLD

Caused by spells of heavy rain, this condition is unlikely to occur if your pony is well cared for with adequate shelter and rugs, particularly in the winter. The hair falls out and the skin becomes sore and is susceptible to infection. Seek advice from the vet for treatment, and provide better protection from the weather.

RINGWORM

Ringworm is a very infectious skin condition, caused by a fungus and showing itself as bald, circular patches about 5 cm (2 in.) in diameter. It is easily spread between ponies in a yard, particularly with shared grooming or tack. It does not appear to itch but can be very unsightly resulting in large bald patches. If your vet confirms ringworm, it is best to isolate a pony if possible and keep all equipment separate. Disinfect everything before using on another pony and wash your hands before you touch other animals and people – humans can catch this too. Rubber gloves are recommended when dealing with a pony with ringworm.

LOTIONS ARE AVAILABLE FROM VETS TO TREAT SWEET ITCH. ALWAYS WEAR GLOVE WHEN APPLYING IT.

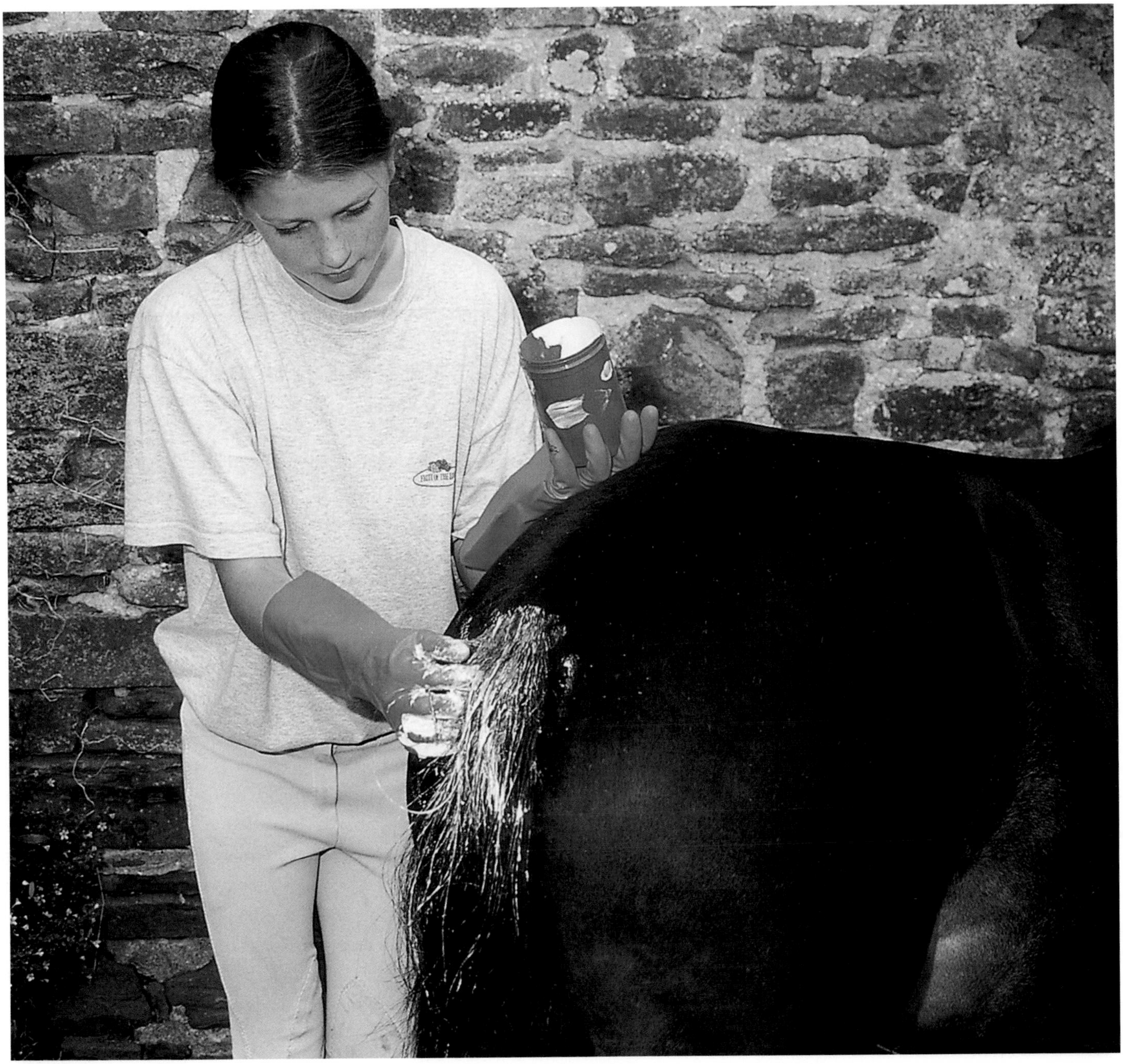

RESPIRATORY PROBLEMS

BROKEN WIND

Several things can cause broken wind, including galloping a pony which is unfit or that has recently had a feed, and constant exposure to the dust and mould found in hay and straw. It may also be the result of pneumonia. Broken wind is a condition of the lungs that causes a double breathing action on exhalation. The pony develops a deep cough and is no longer capable of doing any fast work.

CHRONIC OBSTRUCTIVE PULMONARY DISEASE (COPD)

Dust and mould in hay and straw affects some ponies by irritating the lungs and causing the small air tubes in the lungs to get blocked with discharge. If this is left unattended, the lungs eventually become so damaged that the pony has to force itself to breath to get enough oxygen. It does this by using muscles that it wouldn't normally use, resulting in a double breath on exhalation. This can eventually lead to broken wind (see above). Good management can reduce the number of mould spores. Use an alternative type of bedding, such as shavings and feeding haylage (see page 27) or hay soaked in water for 30 minutes and drained. Ponies affected by this condition will thrive better out in fresh air as long as adequate food and shelter are provided. If they do need to be stabled, ensure good ventilation. Note that it is normal for a pony to cough a couple of times occasionally if followed by a brisk blow through the nostrils.

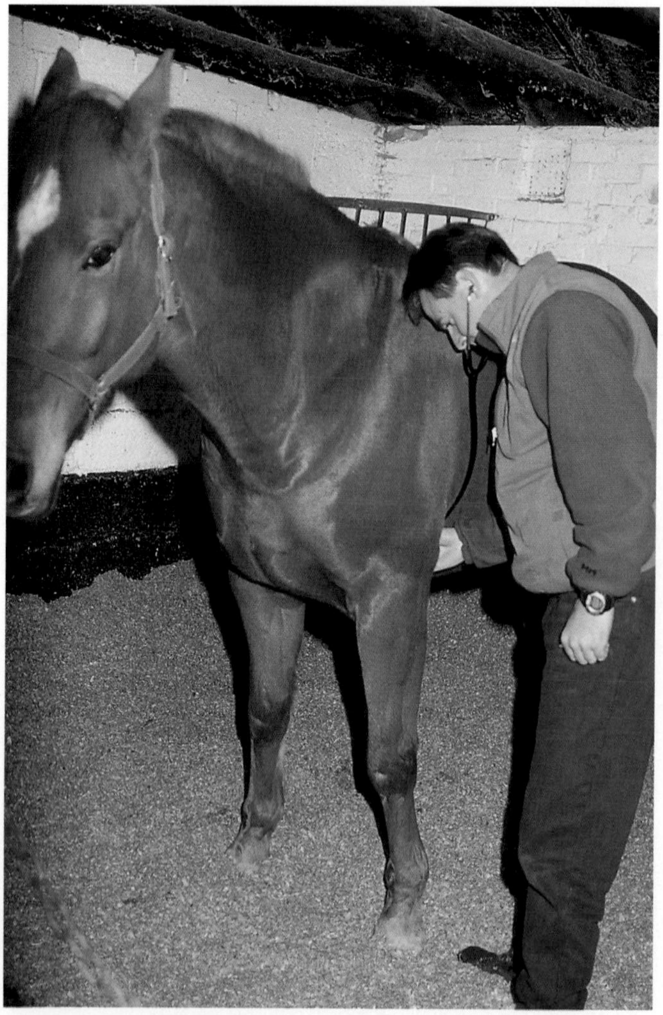

YOUR VET WILL BE ABLE TO ASSESS ANY RESPIRATORY PROBLEMS.

ROARING AND WHISTLING

More common in horses than ponies, this is a condition of the larynx where airflow is restricted, causing the horse to make rasping noises as it breathes when cantering or galloping. The noise is made when a paralysed vocal cord that has become loose in the larynx partly blocks the air passage. Horses with this condition can become short of breath when doing fast work. The condition will not improve on its own, and you must seek advice from a vet.

PNEUMONIA

Pneumonia is inflammation of the lungs. Causes include an infection, virus and fungi. Symptoms are a high temperature, fast breathing and a cough. Discharge can be coughed up from the lungs. A pony with pneumonia must be rested and carefully nursed. Call the vet immediately. Return to work after this condition should be very gradual as the lungs can take a long time to recover.

COUGHS

It is not unusual for a horse to cough, for example if a particle of food becomes stuck, or when he clears his throat when first taken out to exercise, usually followed by a good blow through the nostrils. However, a cough may sometimes be caused by pneumonia (see above) or some other inflammation of the lungs such as COPD (see above), influenza (see page 109), a virus or a cold. In all instances, veterinary advice and treatment should be sought immediately. A cough needs to be investigated, even if the pony seems otherwise well, in order to minimise the risk of permanent damage.

DISEASES

STRANGLES

A very contagious disease, strangles will rapidly spread through an entire yard if infected ponies are not isolated. It can occur at any age but young ponies are particularly vulnerable. Ponies with strangles develop a high temperature and have a thick discharge from the nostrils. Abscesses develop around the throat and under the jaw that cause distress and discomfort when the pony tries to swallow. After about ten days the abscesses burst and discharge pus. This gives a pony some instant relief after which he will gradually return to good health. Bastard strangles is a variant of this condition, when the infection spreads through the blood stream causing abscesses to form in other parts of the body, sometimes the lungs. This is much more dangerous to a pony, and he should be isolated immediately. Treatment will involve eating food that is easy to swallow, a good deal of rest and, sometimes, holding a warm cloth on an abscess to encourage it to ripen, thus speeding recovery. This should not be carried out without the advice of a vet, however.

TETANUS

Easily avoided by vaccination and very difficult to cure, tetanus is extremely serious and can be fatal. A germ that lives in the soil and thrives in droppings, tetanus gets into a pony's body usually via a wound. About ten days later the pony will develop a high temperature and stiffness, and the membranes of the eye will

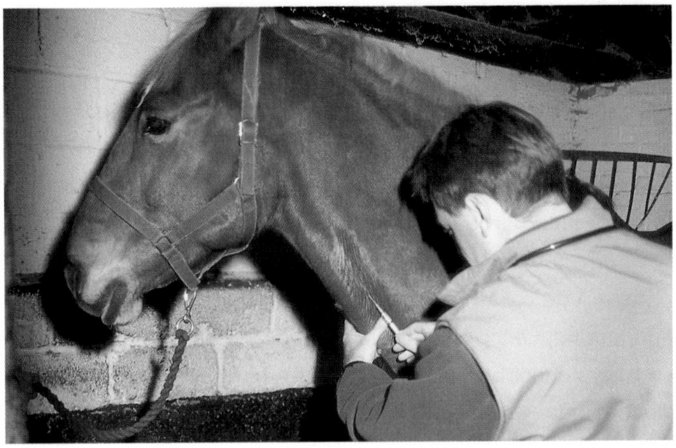

TETANUS IS A SERIOUS AILMENT WHICH IS EASILY PREVENTED BY VACCINATION.

partly cover the eyeball. Later the jaw seizes up making feeding difficult. Keep the pony quiet and call the vet immediately.

EQUINE INFLUENZA

Another complaint that can be largely prevented by vaccination, equine influenza is very contagious and cases must be isolated as soon as possible. It is a virus which shows itself as a high temperature and a general sense of being unwell, There will be a loss of appetite, a cough and discharge from the nostrils. The membranes of the eyes and gums become inflamed and tears fall down the face. The breathing rate is increased due to the inflammation in the lungs. Recovery usually takes about 14 days, but great care should be taken to reintroduce the pony to work gradually because of the damage to the heart and lungs. Veterinary attention and careful nursing will be required.

DIETARY PROBLEMS

COLIC

Colic is generally described as tummy ache and can vary from a mild pain to a fatal twisted gut. Most of the causes are to do with the diet – grass clippings that have heated up, for example. Hay that has not been stored for long enough before use or is mouldy can cause colic, as can too much hard feed immediately before or after work. Other causes may be when ponies eat their food too quickly, a bout of worms, giving a large quantity of cold water to a hot and tired pony, or eating poisonous plants.

There are various symptoms. A pony will turn to look at his flanks or will begin to kick his belly. He may roll or throw himself on the floor. Heart rate is increased and there is obvious pain. The belly may look bloated. A complication of colic is when the pony throws himself down and rolls, while also suffering from trapped wind and muscle spasms. This can cause the bowel to twist which is often fatal. If your pony gets colic you need to call the vet. The pony will need a deep comfortable bed, and leading him around can help to stop him throwing himself down. Try to keep him warm. If he is sweating put a sweat rug underneath a lighter rug to trap a layer of warm air and so helping to keep him warm and dry (see page 25). Colic might pass within a couple of hours, while other bouts can take much longer. Do not feed a pony during an attack and give the pony water in small amounts when he is quieter. To help prevent colic ensure good stable management and follow the rules of feeding together with a regular worming programme.

POISONING

Immediate veterinary help is essential if you suspect your pony may have been poisoned. Causes can include weed killer, rat poison, overdose of medicine, poisonous plants (see page 41), mouldy feed and polluted water. A huge variety of symptoms can be the result of poisoning, depending on the cause, and can include colic, diarrhoea, loss of appetite, weakness, staggering, collapse, trembling and an increased heart rate. As a pony cannot be sick, he will digest and absorb any poison that he has swallowed.

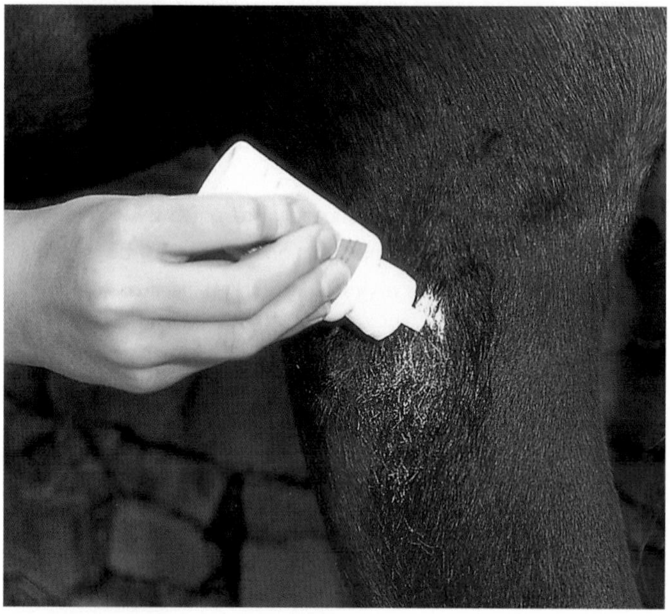

APPLY WOUND POWDER TO PREVENT INFECTION.

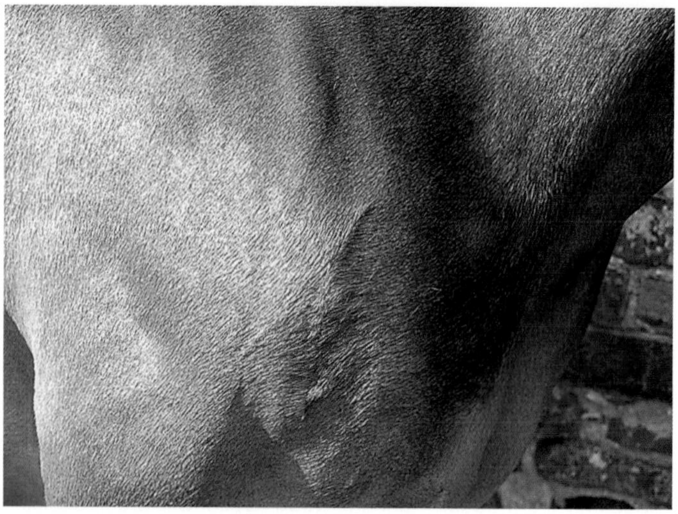

LARGE CUTS OFTEN LEAVE A SCAR.

WOUNDS

A wound could be in the form of a bruise, puncture wound, clean cut or tear.

CLEAN CUT AND TEAR WOUNDS

Anything sharp can cut the skin. If bleeding occurs, place a clean cloth over it and apply a little pressure until it stops. The wound needs to be properly cleaned and any dirt, grit or other foreign bodies must be removed. You can do this either by putting a poultice on or hosing the area with cold water, then carefully wiping away any dirt and grit with a clean cloth. If you cannot stop the bleeding, bandage over the clean cloth to keep it in place and call the vet.

POULTICES

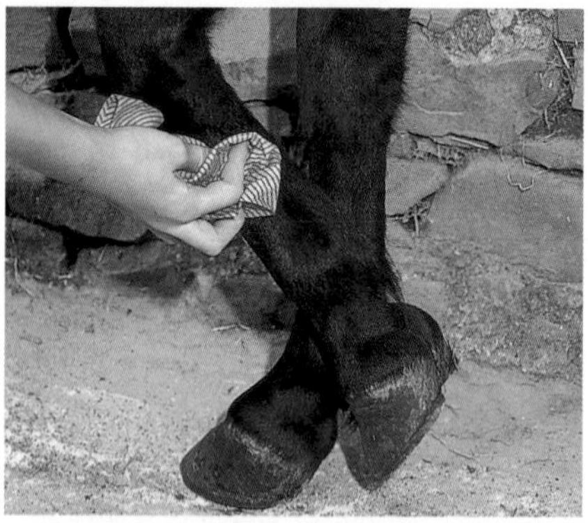

1 Wash and clean the wound thoroughly to remove dirt and foreign bodies.

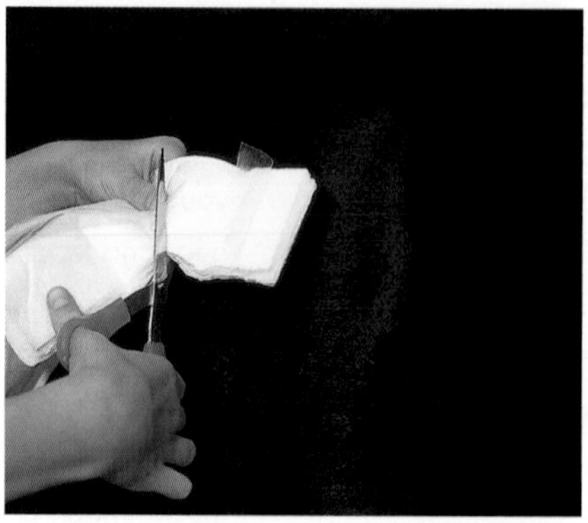

2 Cut the poultice to a size that will generously cover and overlap the wound.

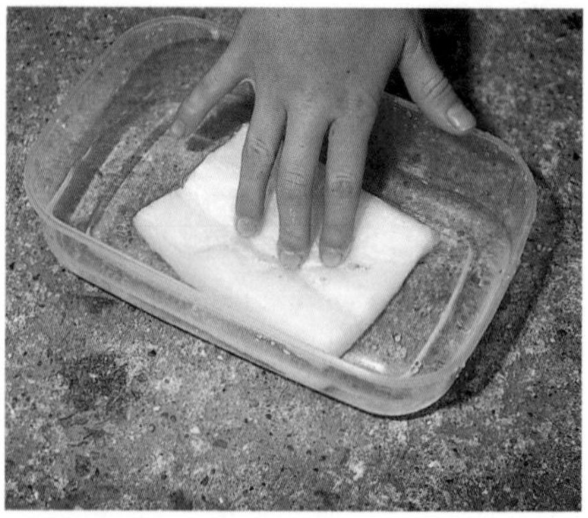

3 Soak the poultice in hot water and allow to cool to body temperature before applying.

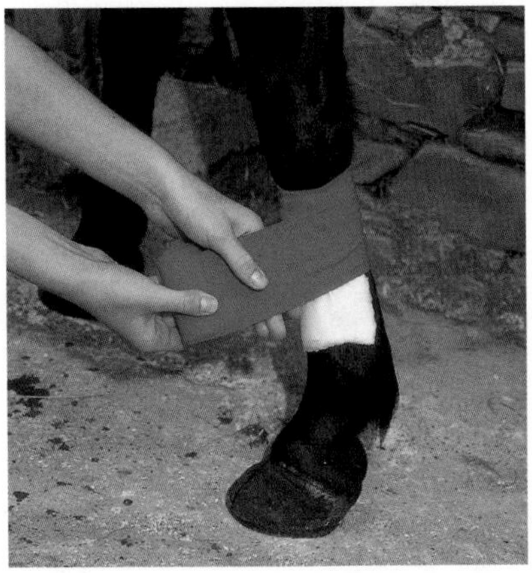

4 Position the poultice over the wound and hold in place with a bandage.

5 Secure the bandage by tying the tapes. Be careful not to tie them too tight or directly over the wound itself.

To test the temperature of a poultice, place it on your elbow and it should feel comfortable. Cut it to the correct size and place it sticky-side-down on the wound. Always follow the manufacturer's instructions. When cooled and held in place with a bandage, the poultice will help to draw out any impurities and will reduce the inflammation. Once clean (if a poultice is not needed), the wound can be sprayed with an antiseptic spray or squirted with wound powder. Call a vet if you think the wound may need stitching. Antibiotics may be needed in some cases, and you should check that the pony's tetanus is up to date. Small scrapes are often best left uncovered and will soon heal.

BANDAGES

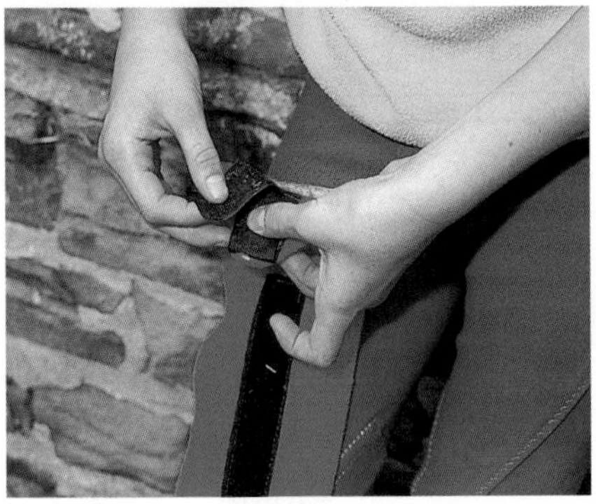

1 Before rolling, fold the bandage so the tapes are on the inside.

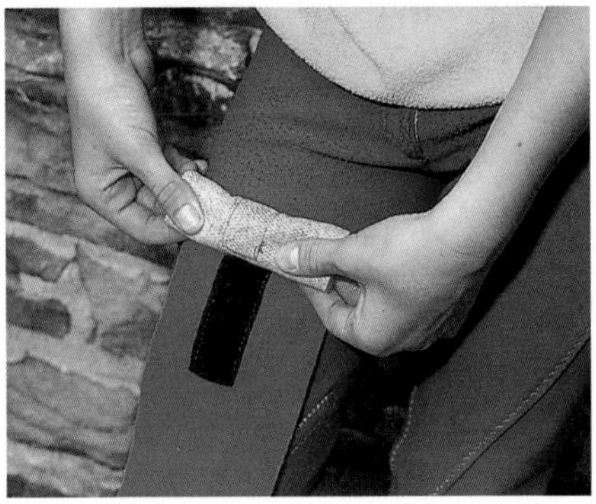

2 Using your leg for support, roll up the whole bandage firmly.

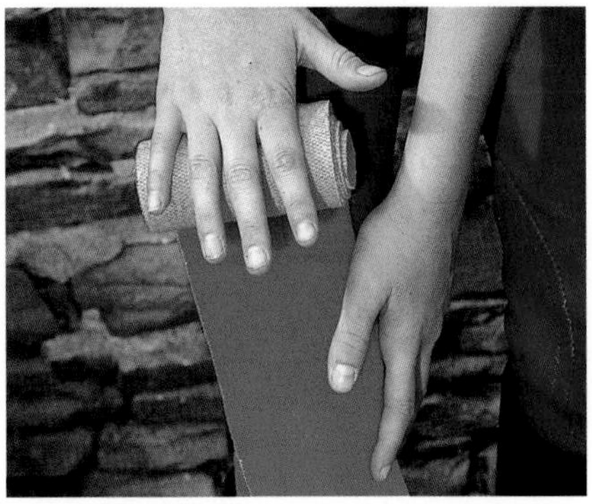

3 Once rolled, secure the bandage with an elastic band to keep it secure.

PUNCTURE WOUNDS

These happen when a nail or other sharp object pierces a pony, usually in the foot, leaving a small but deep wound with a very small entrance site. The wound soon heals over, often leaving dirt and grime behind, and this can cause an infection or abscess. This type of wound often goes unnoticed until the growing infection causes pain. A farrier or vet will locate the point of entry, and will probably open up the wound to allow it to drain. Use the poultice as you would for a clean cut, to draw out the infection. Cover the foot with a poultice, boot or bandage and change the dressing twice daily. When the pony is sound continue for a further 48 hours to ensure that the infection does not flare up again. Antibiotics may be needed and you should check that the pony's tetanus is up to date. The outside of the wound needs to be kept open until the inside is properly healed.

BRUISES

Knocks causing bruising can result from a fall, inadequate bandaging while travelling, kicks from another pony, or from a pony brushing and treading on himself. They do not always break the skin but will cause bleeding, swelling and inflammation under the skin. Running a cold hose over the injury will help reduce the swelling and discomfort during the first 24 hours. After that, applying a warm poultice will soothe it and reduce inflammation. These types of wounds are painful even if the skin is not broken.

CHAPTER 6

READY TO RIDE

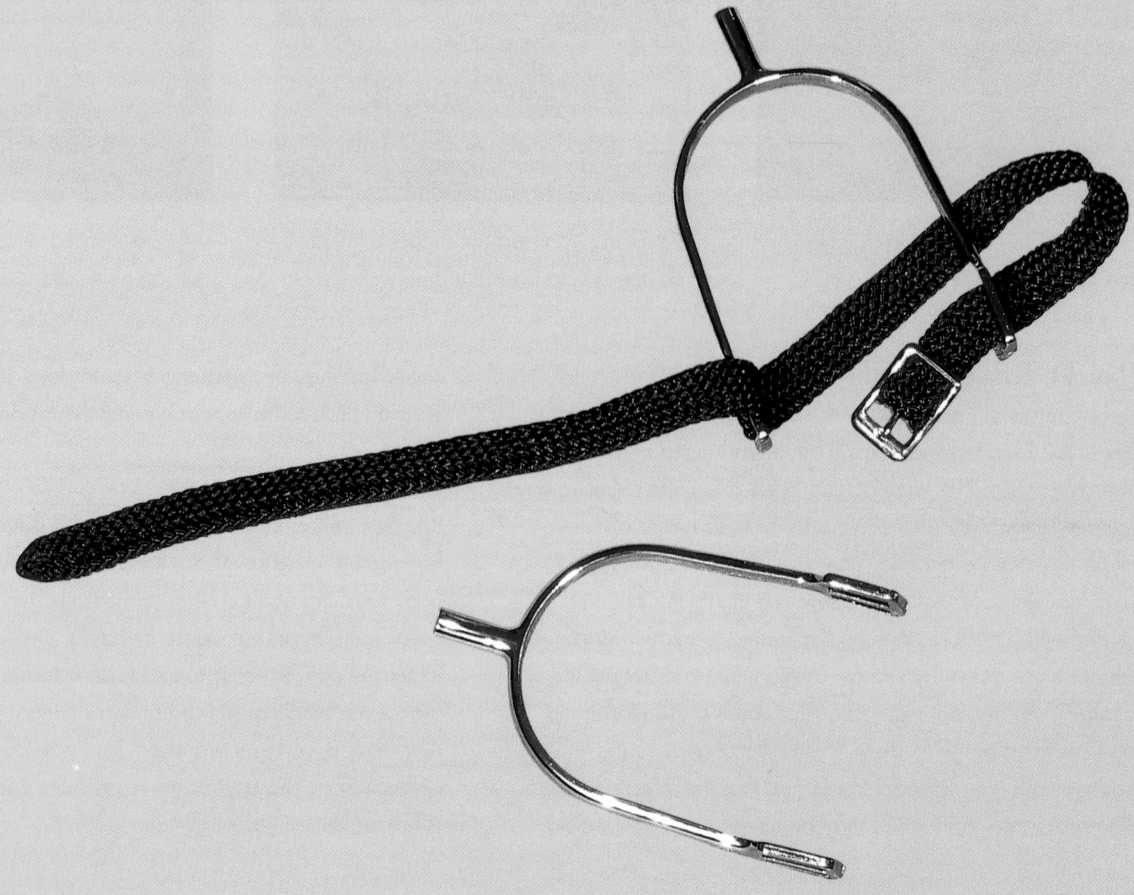

To get the most out of riding, it is essential that you learn to ride properly and take note of all safety precautions. Learning the correct procedures help you gain confidence, understand how to communicate with your horse, read signals your horse is sending you and to deal safely and calmly with any problems that arise. It may seem exciting to simply jump on a horse and gallop away, but this is dangerous, and could lead to injury – both to yourself, and your horse.

WHAT TO WEAR FOR EVERYDAY RIDING

It is not necessary to spend vast amounts of money on clothes when you first start riding, but there are a few things that you will need. The most important factor in deciding what to wear is safety. Around the yard, wear old clothes for mucking out and tack cleaning. If you are handling ponies – loading them into a trailer, for example, you should at least wear your hat and gloves. You might want to wear a body protector as well, just to be on the safe side.

THIS ILL-EQUIPPED RIDER LACKS A HARD HAT AND PROPER BOOTS. TRAINERS CAN EASILY SLIP THROUGH STIRRUPS.

DO NOT BE TEMPTED TO RIDE IF YOU ARE NOT PROPERLY EQUIPPED – LEAD YOUR HORSE INSTEAD.

RIDING HAT

Starting with your head, it is essential to have a riding hat. It must be well fitted and at least up to current safety standards. Never buy a second-hand hat, as it may have been dropped or damaged in such a way that it will not provide maximum protection in the event of an accident. If you do drop your hat you should buy a new one. Skullcaps are used most often for cross-country and jumping. You can wear these on their own or with a brightly coloured silk over the top. Velvet-covered hats have a peak and are a smarter choice for shows. Either hat is fine for general riding as long as it is well fitting and has not been dropped or damaged.

RIDING HAT,

RIDING BOOTS.

FOOTWEAR

When you first start riding, suitable footwear is of the utmost importance. You should have long rubber riding boots or short jodhpur boots. At the very least, use a shoe with a short heel and smooth sole that will stop your foot slipping through the stirrup. Shoes with a heavy tread such as Wellington boots can get caught up on the stirrup, and are not advisable.

TROUSERS

For hacking and general riding jodhpurs are the most comfortable and hard wearing. Jeans and other trousers that have a seam down the inside can rub and be uncomfortable. Jodhpurs are available in a wide range of designs and colours. Cream, beige or white jodhpurs are the most common colour for shows and events but, for everyday wear, you can be as bright as you like!

BODY PROTECTOR

This should be of a good safety standard and well fitted. Your saddler should be able to help make sure that you have the correct size.

A BODY PROTECTOR.

GLOVES

Gloves will help protect your hands from blisters or burns from the reins and ropes. They are also essential for keeping your hands warm in the winter. In the summer thinner gloves can be useful, as sweat from a pony's neck can make the reins slippery and the gloves will give you a better grip. Some of them have rubber bobbles to help with this.

COATS AND JACKETS

Aim for well-fitted garments that are not too loose and baggy. Always keep your coat done up when riding in case the flapping frightens a pony. Lighter colours tend to make you more visible to motorists.

WHAT TO WEAR AT A SHOW

What you wear to a show will depend on what type of event or class you are entering. For local shows, wear your hair in a hair net if you have long hair, with a shirt and tie and a riding or hacking jacket. Wear white, cream or beige jodhpurs and black or brown riding or jodhpur boots and gloves. Everything should be neat, tidy and clean.

READY FOR LOCAL SHOW.

WHERE TO RIDE

Before you get a pony of your own you need to find somewhere to learn to ride. The most common practice is to find a good local riding school and take a course of riding lessons. A national horse society will have a list of recognised and approved establishments in your area. Visit all the riding schools that you are interested in and make a point of noting whether the ponies look happy and well cared for. Check that the yard looks well maintained, clean, tidy and safe and ask to see if your instructor is qualified to teach you. Some stables may let you help out before or after your lesson and you will be able to pick up helpful stable management tips. Others have an indoor school and cross-country jumps. Riding holidays at a good establishment are a great way to spend a fun week riding and generally being around ponies. Always make sure that any stables are covered by the appropriate insurance and licence.

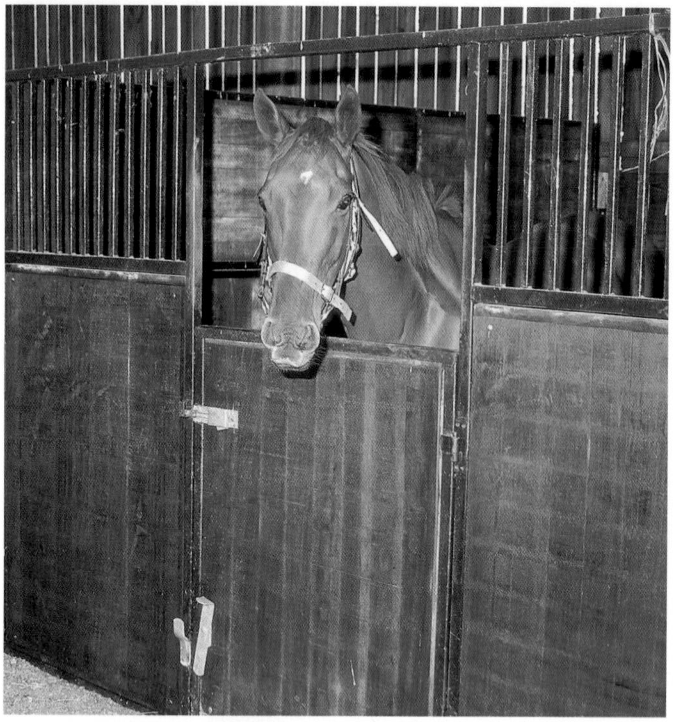

CHECK THAT THE HORSES AT PROSPECTIVE RIDING SCHOOLS APPEAR WELL CARED FOR.

MOUNTING AND DISMOUNTING

MOUNTING

It is important that you know how to mount safely. Your pony should stand quietly while you mount and this is one of the lessons a pony will have already learnt. If he tries to walk off when you are mounting, keep a firm hold on the reins and wait for the pony to stand still again.

Always check that the tack is correctly fitted before you mount a pony, and make sure that the girth is tight enough that the saddle will not slip as you get on, and that the stirrups are down and about the right length. You usually mount from the near side, which is the left side of the pony. When you are experienced enough, practice mounting and dismounting from both sides.

1 Stand by the pony's near-side shoulder and hold both reins in your left hand just in front of the withers. Make sure that the off-side reins are shorter.

2 If you think you might accidentally pull on the pony's mouth as you get on, hold a bunch of mane with the reins.

3 Hold the stirrup with your right hand and place your left foot in it.

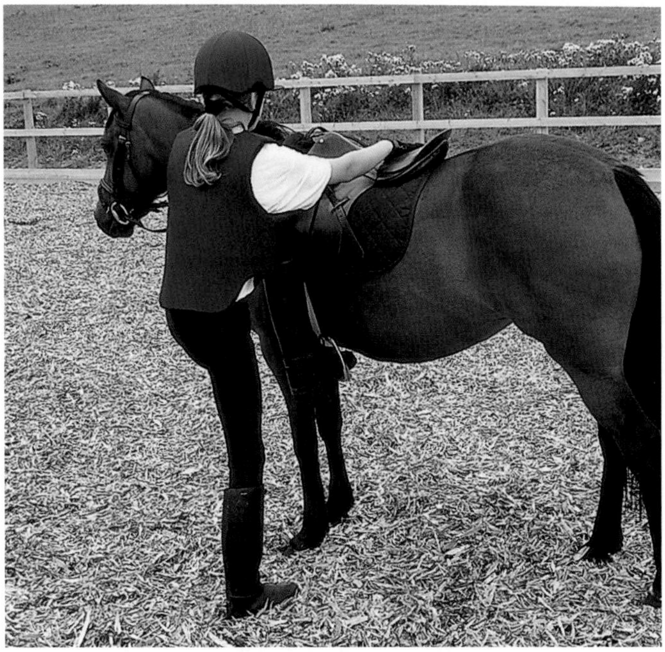

4 Hop round to face the pony's side and, with your toe pushed downwards so that it does not dig into the pony's side, prepare to spring up.

5 Hold the saddle by the waist on the far side, and spring up. As you swing your leg over, move your right hand from the waist of the saddle to the front, right-hand side of the saddle.

6 Sit down gently and place your right foot in the stirrup. Take up the reins ready for riding. Check that safety stirrups have the rubber on the outside. If you need to alter the length of the stirrup, do it now. You can do this by holding the reins in one hand and pulling up the end of the opposite stirrup leather to move the buckle to the required hole. You should practice doing this without looking down, although this is not easy to start with. Keep your foot in the stirrup while altering the length. The correct length of the stirrup can be gauged before you mount by placing your knuckles on the stirrup bar. The stirrup iron should reach to your armpit.

DISMOUNTING

1 Make your pony stand quietly before dismounting. To dismount correctly take both of your feet out of the stirrups, put the reins in your left hand just in front of the withers. Place your right hand on the front of the saddle and lean forwards.

2 Swing your right leg over the pony's hind quarters, being careful not to kick it.

3 Land on your toes, bending your knees and avoiding the pony's foreleg.

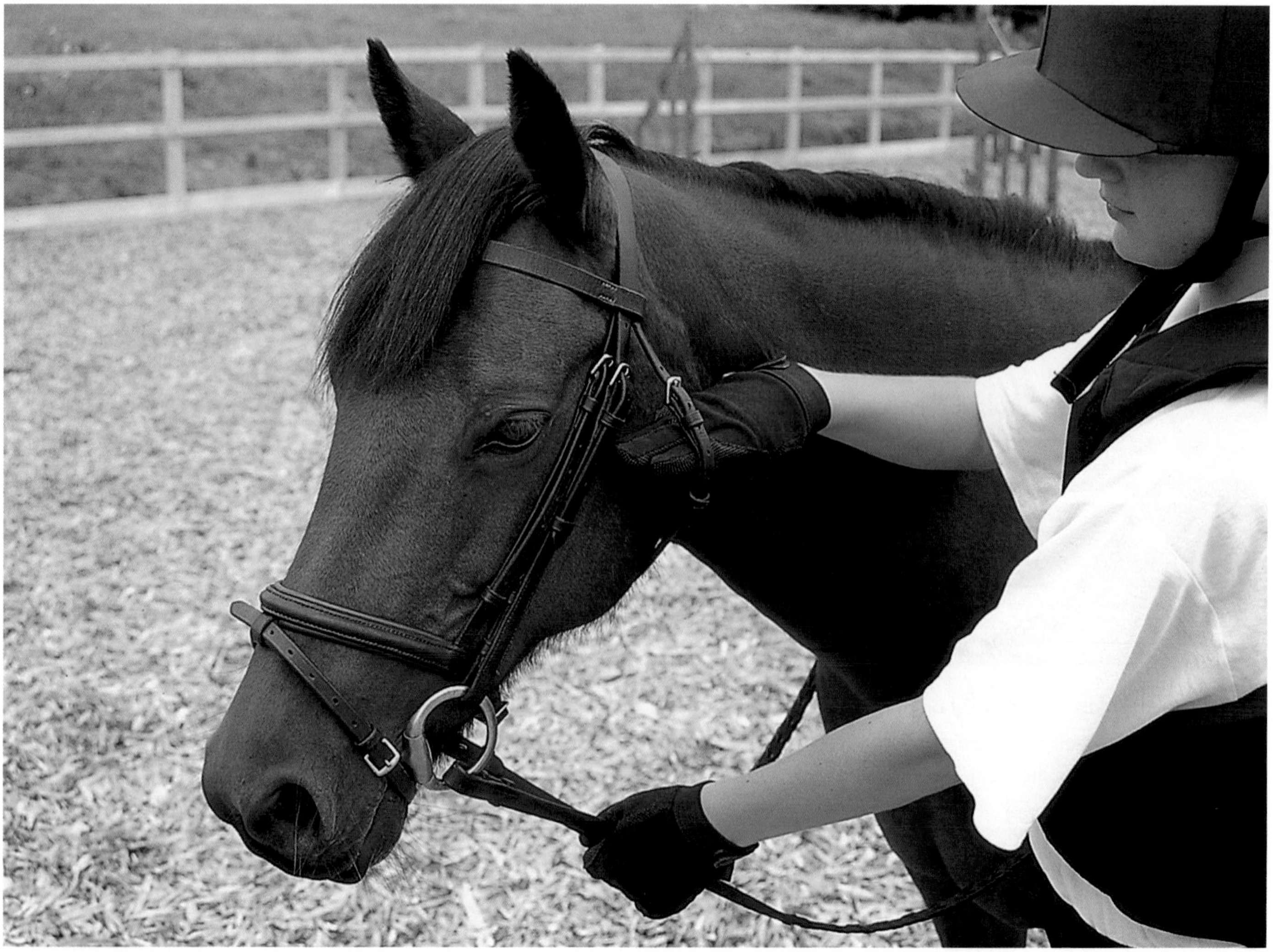

CHECK THE TACK BEFORE RIDING TO ENSURE IT IS FITTED COMFORTABLY AND SAFELY.

STAND IN FRONT OF YOUR PONY TO CHECK THAT THE STIRRUPS ARE THE SAME LENGTH.

SITTING CORRECTLY

It is important that you sit in the saddle correctly and that you are well balanced, otherwise it will be uncomfortable for you and the pony and you won't be able to give the aids correctly. Aids are the signals that you use to communicate with the pony. Your bottom should be relaxed in the saddle with your weight in the lowest part, and evenly spread across the seat bones. Try to stay supple and relaxed. The balls of your feet should be in contact with the stirrups, with your heels slightly lower than your toe.

CORRECT HAND POSITION.

From the side view there should be an imaginary line from your ear, through the shoulder and hip and on down into your heel. Another imaginary line should be seen to go through the pony's mouth, through the reins and your hand and on into your elbow. Your hands should be able to follow the movement of the pony's head, keeping constant and light contact with his mouth, without throwing you off balance.

CORRECT LEG POSITION.

HOLDING THE REINS CORRECTLY

The reins flow from the pony's mouth, between your little and ring fingers, then up through your hand and over the top of your first finger. The thumbs are placed on the reins to help
stop them slipping through your hands. The elbow, shoulder and wrist must remain supple to allow your hands to follow the movement of the horse's head.

Do not bend your wrists inwards and try to keep your thumbs facing the sky.

RIGHT: HOLDING THE REINS CORRECTLY.

AIDS

Aids are used to communicate to a pony. Artificial aids include whips or spurs, and natural aids involve using parts of the body to communicate with the pony, hands, legs and voice, for example. Aids must be given clearly and should be consistent.

SITTING SQUARELY HELPS THE PONY TO BALANCE.

THIS RIDER IS LOPSIDED.

NATURAL AIDS

Your hands, legs, voice and body are natural aids to communicating with your pony. All aids, whether natural or artificial must be quiet, kind and never hurried, rough or sharp. Your voice, for example, can be soothing for a nervous pony, and he will soon learn simple instructions. Never lose your temper and shout. If your pony is not obeying, it probably means he doesn't understand your command. try again making your instructions clearer.

HANDS

Use your hands through the reins and bit to control speed and direction.

LEGS

Use your legs to nudge a pony's side to encourage it to go faster.

VOICE

Your voice should never be underestimated as an aid. Talk to your pony constantly, either to calm him down or as praise. In time a pony will learn to recognise the command given by repeated words or phrases such as 'walk on' and 'whoa'.

YOUR BODY

The way you sit in the saddle and your weight can be used to send signals to the pony when you are more experienced. Ponies tend to be able to tell from your seat if you are nervous.

IN THE CROSS-COUNTRY SEAT RIDER IS LIGHTER IN THE SADDLE. THE WEIGHT OF THE RIDER IS FORWARD, ALLOWING THE HORSE TO BALANCE EASIER AT FASTER PACES.

ARTIFICIAL AIDS

Sometimes a litle extra encouragement is needed to make a pony obey your commands. Use artificial aids sparingly if your horse or pony does not respond to natural aids. Artificial aids can be used to reinforce the messages from natural aids, and in time, your pony may learn to obey the commands from natural aids more quickly.

WHIP

A whip should be used to reinforce a leg aid that the pony has ignored. Use it just behind a pony's leg as you repeat the aid with your leg. When using the whip always take your hand off the reins and place them in the other hand. Never use a whip in anger.

SPURS

Spurs attach to the boots by a strap around the ankle and under the foot. However, they must only be used by an experienced rider who has complete control of their legs at all times.

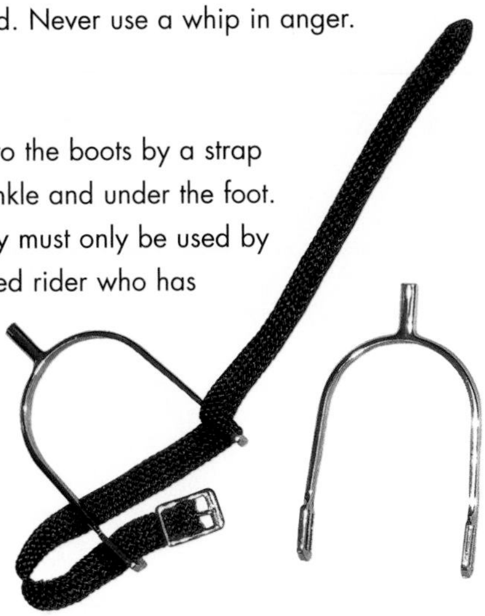

SPURS

SPURS ARE AN ARTIFICIAL AID USED BY EXPERIENCED RIDERS TO ENHANCE NATURAL LEG AIDS.

LEARNING TO RIDE

It is important that novices learn to ride properly with a good instructor and in a standard fashion. For the health and safety of both you and your pony, it is simply not safe to launch yourself on to a horse you do not know, particularly if you only have a vague idea of how to control it. Everyone must learn the basics of riding – how to care for a horse, the equipment needed, how to mount and control the animal at different paces, and how to stop. These fundamentals can be learnt in a series of structured lessons and to do anything less is simply irresponsible. Furthermore, without proper instruction, your first riding experiences may well be unpleasant for both pony and rider.

WALKING

A pony naturally has four paces. The slowest is the walk, where all four feet are brought to the ground at a different time in a certain order, therefore this pace is called 'four–time'.
This is the order in which the feet come to the ground in walk. The pony has at least two feet on the ground at once.

The aids to ask your pony to walk on from a stand still are to shorten your reins to a length at which you have a light feel on the pony's mouth, and to close your lower legs against his sides. As the pony moves off, make sure that you allow your hands to follow the natural movement of the pony's head. When you are giving the aids to 'walk on', sit up straight in the correct basic position and look forward between the pony's ears. If the pony does not move off willingly, give him a nudge with your lower leg. Even though you are sitting up straight, your body should not be tense.

TO HALT

Once you are walking you need to know how to stop again! Use the same aids that you use to steady the pace or to slow down from one pace to another. You must close your legs against the pony's sides and take up a stronger contact on the pony's mouth. Release the pressure once the pony has stopped or slowed as you wished. Do not use too much pressure on the mouth and never be rough or impatient, as it is sensitive and easily hurt.

IN WALK, ALL FOUR FEET COME TO THE GROUND AT SEPARATE TIMES, HENCE A FOUR-TIME' PACE.

TROTTING

The trot is a pace of 'two-time' meaning that the legs are coming to the ground in two diagonal pairs.

The pony springs from one pair of legs to the other as it moves along. There are two ways of 'riding the trot' – sitting or rising. Sitting trot is when you stay sitting in the saddle. Although this is bumpy you should stay in the basic position and allow your body to be relaxed and supple enough to go with the movement of the pony. Always use the sitting trot when changing pace. The rising trot is a way of avoiding the bumping by rising up and down in the saddle with the rhythm of the trot. You sit in the saddle as one pair of feet comes to the ground and rise as the other pair comes to the ground. This takes quite a while to master but is much more comfortable once you get used to it. Make sure that the weight of your body is not in the stirrup, but that you use the inside of your thigh and knee to support you. Keep your back straight and do not tip forward. Do not use the reins to pull yourself up – your hands should not be affected by what the body is doing.

DIAGONALS IN TROTTING.

To slow down from trot to walking pace, close your lower legs against the pony's sides and apply a little bit of pressure on its mouth. When the pony has walked for a few steps repeat this method to stop the pony.

TROTTING.

CANTERING

Canter is a pace of 'three-time', which means the feet come to the ground as a single foot, then a diagonal pair and then on the last foot. The walk, trot and halt must be mastered and well practised before you attempt to canter, as it is obviously a lot faster and you need to be in control.
After the three beats there is a moment when all four legs are off the ground and are suspended in mid air! When you are more experienced you will be able to feel without looking down which leg is leading when you are cantering.)

To ask your pony to canter, sit well down in the saddle and close your lower legs behind the girth. Slowly increase the pressure until the pony strikes off into canter. Do not lean forward as this will encourage the pony to go faster and you will have less control. To decrease the speed of the pony, do as you would when trotting and slow down in stages until you reach a stop. Your first cantering is best done with an instructor in an enclosed area.

CANTERING IS FASTER THAN TROTTING AND REQUIRES GOOD CONTROL.

AT ONE POINT IN MID-CANTER, ALL FOUR LEGS WILL BE OFF THE GROUND.

GALLOPING

Do not attempt to gallop until you are quite a competent rider. To get to gallop from canter is quite easy: you simply close your lower legs and allow the pony more slack on the reins so that he can stretch his neck. Ponies' bodies and strides lengthen when galloping and you must make sure that your hands are free to maintain an even contact with the mouth and be in control at all times. You decrease the pace as with cantering, progressing through all the stages until you come to a halt. Always be sure that the ground you are galloping over is safe without wet, boggy patches or potholes.

GALLOPING REQUIRES A LIGHTER POSITION IN THE SADDLE, WITH THE WEIGHT FURTHER FORWARD.

TURNING

When turning a corner or riding in a circle the pony's body must be bent in the direction you are going with the head looking in that direction.

AIDS TO TURN OR CIRCLE

Keep your body square in the saddle and face the direction that you intend to go in. Your inside hand (on a circle to the left this would be the left hand) steers the pony where you want to go and your outside hand controls the pace, or the speed, keeping the pony's head in the correct direction. Your legs are used slightly differently too. Your inside leg should stay in its normal position, while the outside leg should be a little behind the girth. Use your inside leg to ask for an increase in pace.

STARTING JUMPING

Jumping is great fun, but you must be confident in all other paces before starting to jump. Ponies usually enjoy jumping lessons and jumping the odd log when you are out for a hack. If you are just beginning, try not to interfere with the action of the pony when it is jumping. Shorten your stirrups one or two holes to help keep your weight over the pony's centre of gravity.

TROTTING POLES

There are some things that an instructor may do with you and your pony as an introduction to jumping. Jumping poles laid on the ground are often used to start with. These should be placed about 1 to 1 1/2 m (3 to 5 ft) apart, depending on the size of the pony or horse. The diameter of the poles should be about 10 cm (4 in.). Start by walking over a single pole until the pony gets use to it then move on to a trot. When the pony is happy with this, place two or three poles on the ground about 1 m (3-ft) distance apart and trot over them in a rising trot. These exercises should only be attempted with your instructor. Trotting poles help the rider to develop balance, rhythm and an eye for judging a distance. They have many advantages to the pony as well, helping with balance, rhythm, co-ordination and correct muscle development.

BEND FORWARD FROM THE WAIST AS THE PONY JUMPS.

SMALL JUMPS

A pony's outline changes as it approaches a jump. It lowers its head and stretches its neck to help balance itself. As the pony leaves the ground, he raises his neck and head and places his hind legs underneath them. The pony jumps upwards, lifting its forelegs off the ground and then the hind legs, and is in mid-air over the jump. His head and neck are stretched out and all four legs are tucked beneath him. When landing, the pony stretches out his forelegs and lifts up his head. The hind legs fall just where the forelegs landed and the pony continues to move off.

RIDING POSITION OVER A JUMP

1 You must shorten the stirrups by one or two holes to help keep your weight over the pony's centre of gravity. Keep your lower legs in contact with the sides of the pony, giving a squeeze when you want him to take off. As the pony leaves the ground your bottom should stay in contact with the saddle and you should bend forwards from the waist. Grip with the inside of your thighs and knees to keep you in place. Do not stand in the stirrups, keep looking ahead and let your hands follow the pony's head, maintaining contact all the time.

2 As the pony lands and brings up its head, return gracefully back to your normal position. Do not point your toes downwards at any time or it will be much harder to maintain your correct position. Make sure you 'go with' the pony as it jumps. If your lower legs come back too far you will tip forwards putting you off balance. Always jump under instruction to start with to avoid forming bad habits.

EXERCISES

Exercise will increase your fitness level. You need to achieve a moderate level of fitness to gain the greatest benefits from riding. For those who do not own their own pony, there are some exercises that can be done without using one. Cycling is a good exercise in preparation for riding especially if you stand up to pedal sometimes. It works the same muscles that you use for riding, particularly the thigh and calf muscles. Start slowly and build up gradually. Cycling also helps to make the joints from the hip downwards supple.

Swimming is also an excellent form of exercise. Start slowly and build up the number of lengths you do. Vary the strokes to work as many different muscles as possible. Walking is an essential exercise, with a brisk walk being a very effective way to increase fitness. Start with a short distance, walk energetically and gradually build up distance and pace. Walking can be done almost anywhere and the only expense is a comfortable pair of shoes. Wear loose clothing and walk somewhere safe. Later you can jog for some of the way. Skipping, aerobics and dancing are also all good forms of exercise. Make sure you take advice from a doctor before starting any new exercise.

ALWAYS PRACTICE THESE EXERCISES WITH A QUALIFIED INSTRUCTOR.

EXERCISE WHILE MOUNTED

You must have a very quiet pony to do these exercises and should always have an experienced person to hold the pony still while you do them. Always ensure that you carry out these exercises correctly as injury may result if you get them wrong. A neck strap (see page 50) will give you something to hold if you start to lose your balance at any point.

Shrug your shoulders up as high as you can towards your ears and relax them; do this a few times.

Stretch your arms above your head and then relax them, bringing them down quietly. Rotate your hands from the wrists in both directions and wriggle your fingers to loosen them up.

Remove your feet from the stirrups and cross the stirrups over in front of the saddle. Then turn your feet in a circular motion in both directions to loosen up the ankles.

Hold the front of the saddle and bring your knees up to the front arch. Move your knees out to the side away from the saddle and lower them back down gently. This stretches the muscles on the insides of your legs.

Raise your arms to shoulder height with your fingers stretched out straight. Bring them into your chest one at a time.

ARMS BEHIND BACK.

BACK BEND.

THE AEROPLANE HELPS YOUR SUPPLENESS.

HOLDING PONY FOR LEG STRETCH.

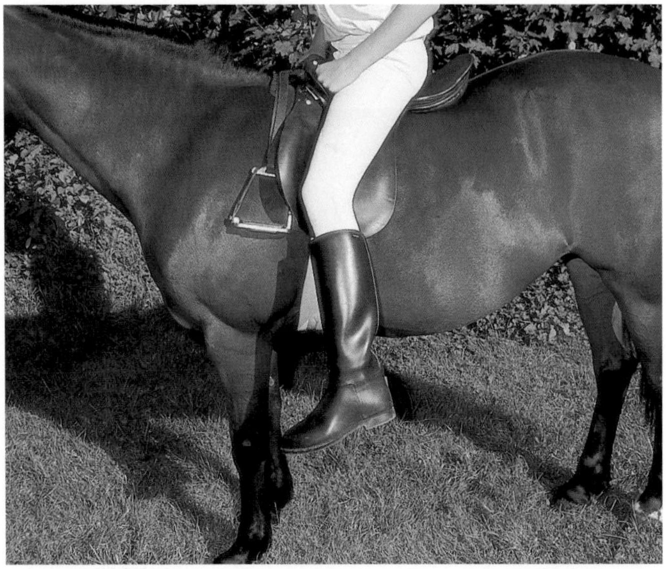

SUPPLE ANKLE EXERCISE.

Hold your arms out straight to the sides at shoulder height and turn your torso so that one arm points towards the tail and the other points towards the ears. Keeping your hips square and your legs still, come back to the front and swing smoothly around to repeat on the other side in the same way. This helps to make the waist more supple.

Raise your arms above your head and bend at the elbow, bringing your fingertips down to touch your shoulders then raise them up again.

To strengthen the stomach, fold your arms and lean backwards gently until the backs of your shoulders touch the pony. Then sit up again. Make sure you keep your leg in the correct position. Only do this a couple of times, as this puts quite a strain on your muscles.

Other exercises might be introduced by an instructor, such as riding without stirrups. Riding bare-back and jumping a row of small jumps without stirrups will help improve your balance but they need to be done under the guidance of an instructor, preferably in an enclosed area such as an arena.

TOUCHING TOES

1 Touching your toes is quite hard and if you cannot get all the way do not push yourself. Raise your right arm above your head and stretch forwards and down to touch your left toe.

2 Do the same on the other side. Only do this a couple of times.

AROUND THE WORLD

1 With the stirrups crossed over in front of the saddle, swing your right leg over the withers to sit on the side.

2 Swing your left leg over the back so you are sitting facing the tail.

3 Swing your right leg over the rump to sit on the right side.

4 Continue around until you are back to your normal riding position.

RIDING SAFELY

Riding on the road is dangerous: riders and ponies are killed every year. Here are a few hints to help maintain proper safety on the road and while hacking. Always ride out with a knowledgeable person or instructor until they consider you to be competent enough to be out on your own.

BRIGHT SAFETY CLOTHING IS ESSENTIAL WHEN ON THE ROAD, ESPECIALLY IF THE LIGHT IS POOR.

FLUORESCENT CLOTHING SHOWS UP WELL AS DARKNESS FALLS.

1 Always listen out for traffic and be aware of the road and its users. Always concentrate on the road and do not stop.

2 You and your pony should wear reflective items of clothing at all times. A large variety of items are available such as fluorescent and reflective hat covers, exercise rugs, tabards for the rider, tail covers, leg and arm bands, whips, jackets, gloves, and boots for your pony.

3 If you are riding out on a hack take a mobile phone, but keep it switched off in case it rings and scares the pony.

4 Wear a watch and keep an eye on the time, particularly in winter when it can get dark very quickly.

5 Always tell someone where you are going and what time you expect to be back.

6 If the road is icy stay near the edge where the horse can get a better grip. Keep your feet out of the stirrups just in case you need to get off the pony quickly. If you come across snow grease the soles of the feet.

7 Take a riding safety course and test in order to learn all of the signals for turning and for asking a vehicle to slow down or pass slowly.

8 Do not canter or gallop on hard or uneven ground.

9 Do not ride on a verge and definitely do not canter on it, as there may be hidden objects, ditches or holes.

10 If your pony goes lame, dismount and lead it home, standing between the pony and the traffic at all times. If you are a long way from home or your pony is very lame then call for help. It is useful to carry a hoof pick with you.

11 Read, learn and always practice the Highway Code.

12 Be polite and considerate to all other road users and always thank someone who is considerate to you.

13 Always wear a well-fitting hat that is up to current safety standards. Keep it done up at all times Riding boots and a body protector are also advisable.

14 Make sure that all your tack and equipment is in good working order before you set out, including any protective boots your pony may need to wear.

RAISING AND LOWERING AN ARM MEANS 'SLOW DOWN PLEASE'.

'I AM TURNING RIGHT'.

'STOP PLEASE'.

TRAVELLING WITH YOUR PONY

Most ponies will travel well in trailers or lorries. However, experience is needed to ensure safety. Protective clothing for the pony and a well-maintained vehicle and trailer or a lorry are essential. Sometimes ponies do not like being locked up in trailers and can resist. Remember that you are asking them to go into a small, confined space which can be frightening, especially if they have had a bad experience in the past.

WHEN TRAVELLING NEVER:

- Use a trailer, vehicle or lorry that is not 100% safe and well maintained.
- Drive fast or brake suddenly.
- Travel with two ponies in the trailer without a partition separating them.
- Let anyone travel with the pony in the trailer.
- Get in between the pony and the partition when in the trailer.
- Travel with a pony that is wearing protective boots and equipment.
- Load a pony without wearing at least a riding hat, boots and gloves.
- Load your pony alone.
- Rush loading your pony.

LOADING

Try to make the trailer as inviting as possible. Put bedding on the floor and leave the doors at the front open to make it light. A haynet hung in one corner or a bucket of feed will help keep the pony busy. Always have experienced help when loading and unloading, and make sure that you wear your riding hat, boots and gloves and a body protector if you have one. Do not drag your pony into the trailer, but gently walk confidently up the ramp with the pony following. Make sure the pony is not too close to the edge of the ramp as he could fall off it. If he is reluctant to go up the ramp, lift a foreleg and place the foot on the ramp. Then do so with the other foreleg. The pony should then just give in and walk up the ramp. Once the pony is in the trailer he should be fastened in securely. If you are loading two ponies, load the easiest one first as this will often give the second one more confidence to go in. Always remain calm and quiet when loading and unloading because a pony will sense if you are nervous.

ALWAYS LEAD YOUR PONY GENTLY TO THE TRAILER RAMP – DO NOT TRY TO DRAG IT.

LEAD YOUR PONY UP THE MIDDLE OF THE RAMP. IF TOO CLOSE TO THE EDGE, HE COULD SLIP OFF.

THE PONY SHOULD NOW WALK QUIETLY AND CONFIDENTLY INTO THE TRAILER.

PROTECTIVE CLOTHING

All-in-one travel boots are the easiest to put on and take off and provide good protection. On the foreleg they reach from the coronet band all the way up to cover the knee, and on the hind legs they reach from the coronet band up over the point of the hock. If you do not have all-in-one travel boots you can use a stable bandage over padding. A light rug will help keep the pony clean and free from flies. A tail bandage or tail guard is used to prevent the tail being rubbed on the journey. If you use a tail guard you will need a roller to secure it. A poll guard attaches to the head collar behind the ears and will protect the pony should he bump his head. Various other items are available including knee, hock and overreach boots, which are most often used with stable bandages (see page 60). Make sure that you use a sturdy head collar and rope.

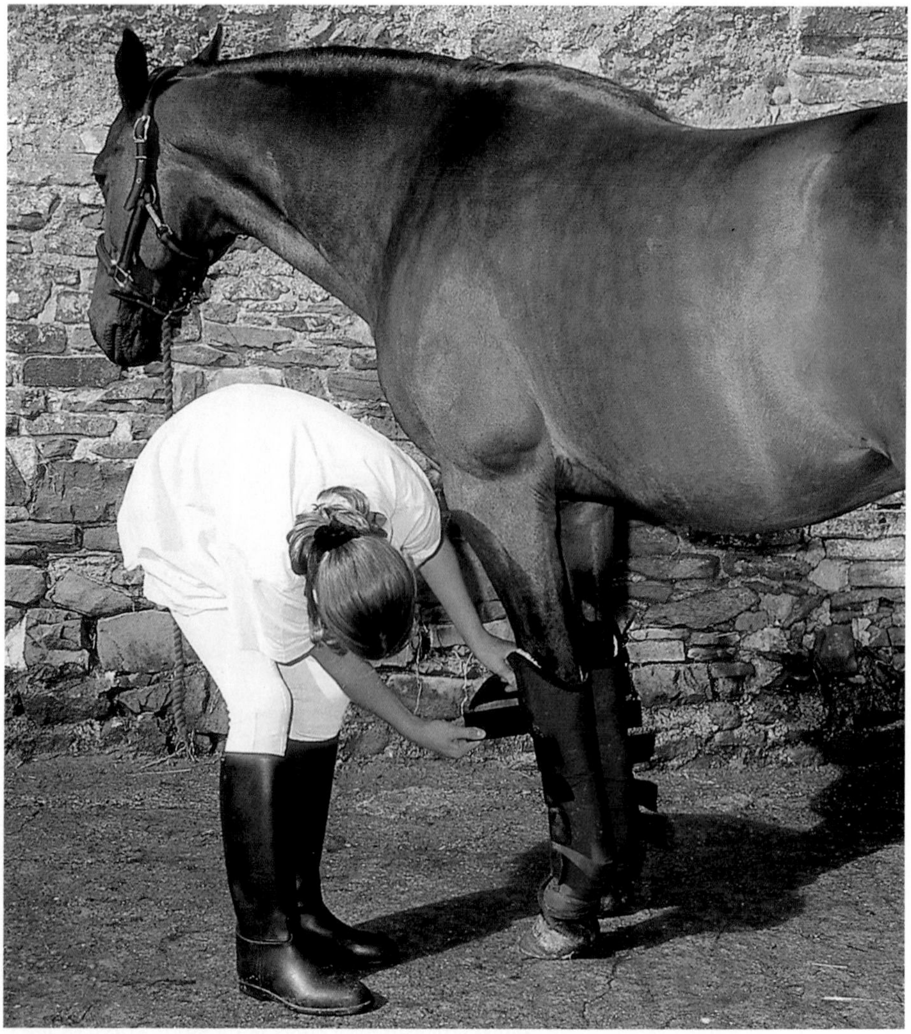

TRAVELLING BOOTS WILL PROTECT THE LEGS.

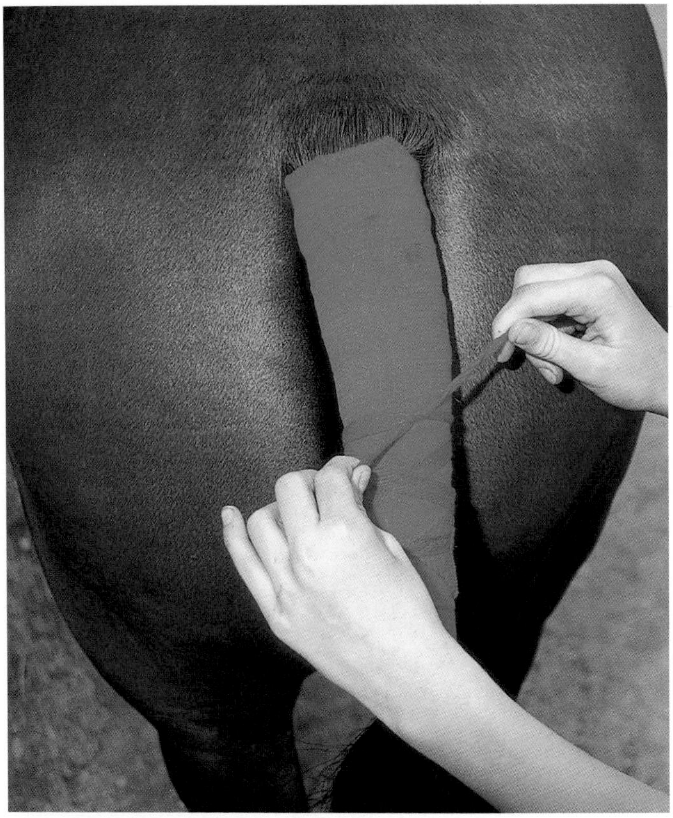

A TAIL BANDAGE WILL STOP THE TAIL BEING RUBBED.

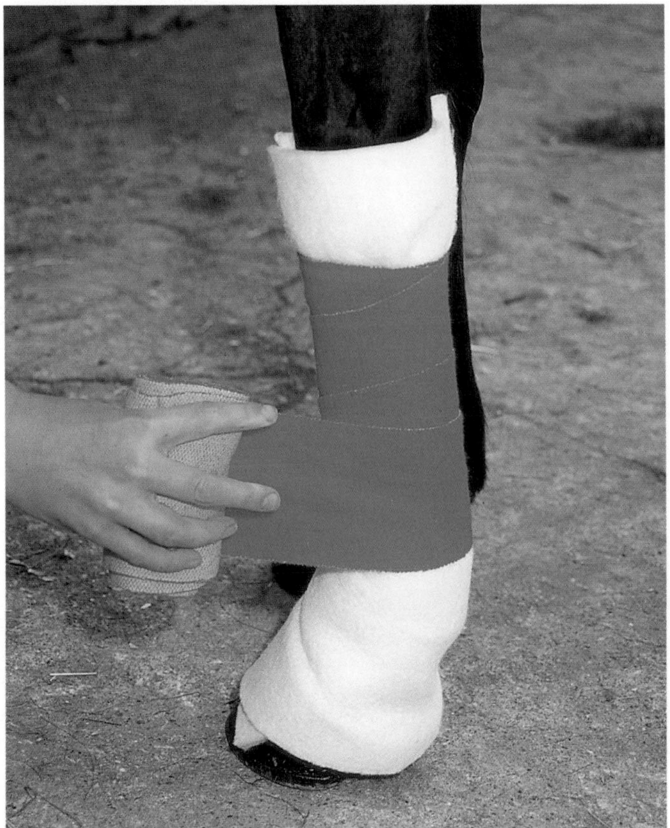

USE BANDAGES IF YOU LACK TRAVEL BOOTS.

UNLOADING

If you are using a trailer with a front ramp, lower the ramp and untie the pony before undoing the breast bar and leading the pony out quietly. If unloading two ponies, unload the one nearest the front ramp first, then move the partition across to allow an easy exit for the second. If a trailer has just a rear ramp, untie the pony and get a helper to lower the ramp. Stand quietly and encourage the pony to go backwards carefully and slowly, but do not let him try to turn round. Always reward a pony with a pat if it has unloaded or loaded quietly and calmly.

TRAILER SAFETY

Always make sure that your trailer or lorry is well maintained and regularly serviced. Pay particular attention to the lights, brakes and hitch, and watch out for the wooden floor, as the boards tend to rot eventually. Make sure all electrics and lights work properly and that you use a safety chain. Check that your ramps are safe and the tyres are the correct pressure.

RIDING FOR THE DISABLED

Ponies are not only therapeutic for disabled people but can have practical uses too. They provide a means of getting around and offer a sense of independence in the way that a guide dog does for a blind person. Mentally or physically disabled people derive a tremendous amount of joy, pleasure and freedom by being able to ride or drive a pony. They often form a deep bond and understanding with a pony. Ponies suitable for the disabled vary, but should always be responsive, well-mannered and kind. Competitions are held for disabled riders and drivers and many are very talented in achieving a high standard despite their disability. Ponies used for driving are often smaller because the cart needs to be low to the ground to allow access for a wheelchair.

CHAPTER 7

HORSE SPORTS

There are many horse sports, and there will be something suitable for almost everyone. Some you can learn yourself with relative ease, while others, like jumping and racing are great spectators sports. You will probably want to try several sports and activities before choosing to concentrate on just one, or you may enjoy them all. You should also bear in mind that not all ponies are suitable for all activities.

LOCAL SHOWS

Shows start at a local level and go all the way up to international competitions. Local shows, held throughout spring, summer and early autumn, are great fun once you have learnt to ride and are completely in control of your pony. They have a large variety of activities and classes, so there should be something for everyone to enter.

Clear-round jumping is when you pay a small fee to enter a ring full of jumps. If you jump them all in the correct order without knocking any down, and without your pony refusing any you will receive a rosette. Another type of jumping class is where, having jumped a clear round, you go through to the next round or enter a 'jump off', usually set against the clock. Competitors are placed in order with the fastest and clear-round jumpers first. Your age, size and pony's ability will decide which classes you are suitable for.

HORSE SHOWS ARE FUN EVENTS AND ARE SUITABLE FOR ALL LEVELS OF RIDER.

There are also showing classes such as 'Best Riding Pony' and 'Best Family Pony'. Some judge the appearance and confirmation of the pony, while others concentrate on the ponies' manners and behaviour. 'Handy pony' is an obstacle course where you have to complete games such as walking over a plastic sheet; hanging washing on a line; posting a letter; dismounting, doing a task, then mounting again; walking past scary things; negotiating obstacles; and walking over and under things. All while managing your pony at the same time!

Gymkhana games are often found at local shows and are great fun as they are a test of how well you can stay in the saddle. Most events involve racing in and out of upright poles. The winner in most gymkana games is the fastest to complete the course. The games are usually run either by the age of the child riding the pony or by the size of the pony. They are good for helping to improve riding.

For some show classes you stand a better chance of winning if you plait your pony's hair, while for others it will not make any difference. Fun classes such include 'Veteran Pony', 'Best Pony Kept Out At Grass' and 'Fancy Dress' competitions. All in all it is a great fun day out.

SIMPLE JUMPS MAKE UP THE MOST BASIC JUMPING COMPETITIONS.

FOR MORE EXPERIENCED RIDERS, SHOWJUMPING IS THE NEXT COMPETITIVE STAGE.

JUMPING EVENTS ARE POPULAR FOR ALL RIDERS.

EVENTS AND SHOWS INCLUDE COMPETITIONS FOR BEST APPEARANCE AND BEHAVIOUR.

POLO

Polo is a popular sport all over the world and has been played for hundreds of years. It was first played in England in about 1800, and is a game where two teams play on a special field with four players in each team. Each player wears a protective helmet and padding and uses a stick with a head made from bamboo. A ball made of willow and bamboo is about 71/2 cm (3 in.) in diameter and weighs between 100-125 g (41/2 and (5 oz). The polo field measures about 274 metres by 183 metres (800 x550 ft). Games last up to an hour and are divided into sections (or 'chukkas') of 71/2 minutes, with 3-minute intervals between them. Half time is about 5 minutes long. Ponies must be agile, fast, responsive and fit. The pony can be of any size. The argentine pony is a popular choice, as it is very agile. Two mounted umpires and a referee oversee the game. To score a goal the ball has to pass between two goal posts. Special training is needed if you want to become a polo player with your pony. Clubs exist in many areas and ponies that are good at gymkana games have been successfully taught how to play polo.

LONG DISTANCE RIDING

Rides can vary from a local pleasure ride of about 10 miles (18 km) to rides of 100 miles (180 km) spread across one or more days. Any fit pony in good condition should be able to manage fairly long rides, although proper conditioning and preparation is required for both horse and rider. Rides often take you over wonderful countryside and participants are friendly and helpful. You will have to travel to the rides, so transport will be a large part of the cost involved. Most rides have inspections by vets to check that a horse is coping with the work and is still sound.

Any breed of horse can be successfully conditioned to complete long rides, although Arabs are most often chosen for the endurance rides. They seem to be less likely to suffer from leg problems and are strong and courageous.

A pony must have a kind temperament and be reasonably sensible and yet forward-going and willing. Attention to the hooves and shoes is of the utmost importance, as a wide variety of grounds will be encountered on a long ride. Make sure that both you and your pony train and are in prime condition before attempting any long rides.

EVENTING

Eventing includes the disciplines of dressage, cross-country and show jumping, and is usually held over one or three days. These events test the all-round ability of a horse and rider, who need to perform well at all three activities to stand a chance of winning.

Dressage involves a written test that has to be followed very accurately and can be done at varying levels of expertise and experience. The horse and rider must perform a particular move at a stated pace in order to gain points. The overall appearance of pony and rider should be smooth and elegant.

Cross-country involves a course of rustic, fairly solid fences over a field or parkland. Obstacles including a water jump and piles of logs for jumping. Usually ridden at a canter or gallop, cross-country tests the strength, skill and stamina of both the pony and the rider.

Show jumping is usually held in an enclosed arena and involves a course of jumps made up of coloured poles and fillers. Faults are gained if a fence is knocked down, if the pony refuses to jump or if you follow the wrong course. If the rider gets a clear round he or she is entered into another round, which is usually shorter but may have higher jumps and is likely to be timed.

You will need to have reached a competent level of riding before you go eventing, and this could give you something positive to aim for. Your instructor will be able to prepare you for your dressage test. Various clothes and items will be needed for each discipline, which could be expensive. The hard hat and boots are the most important safety items for the rider, along with a body protector for jumping. Make sure that your pony is well protected with boots for the jumping section, too. Dressage, show jumping and cross-country events are all also held as separate events, so you may choose to pursue just one discipline.

ABOVE: READY FOR THE OFF!

LEFT: SHOW JUMPING

SHOW JUMPING

DRIVING

Driving is very popular and demands a high level of skill, particularly at competition level. Horses and ponies are driven on their own, in pairs or in a teams. Even if you are used to riding a pony, driving is a very different experience. It is important to be competent and confident before attempting to drive alone.

Good breeds of pony for driving include Fell, Dales, Connemaras, Welsh Cobs, Welsh Ponies, Exmoors, Dartmoors and Shetland ponies. Thoroughbreds, Arabs and Hackneys are not so suitable for the novice driver. Other breeds that are seen are Morgans from the United States and Cleveland Bays.

The harness looks daunting to start with and it is important that it is kept in good condition and correctly fitted. It is traditionally made of leather, but these days it can be made of webbing, canvas, felt, buffalo hide and other manmade materials. Once you are competent you can progress to shows, but get your pony used to being driven in company first.

CHAPTER 8

CONCLUSION

A PONY OF YOUR OWN

Once you have researched the pros and cons of horse ownership, you will realise that the decision to buy a pony should not be taken lightly. Ponies, like other animals, need a lot of attention. You must provide grazing, fresh water and shelter from the weather in winter and from flies in summer. You must have enough knowledge to care for your pony and/or the help of a knowledgeable friend. You must also be sure that you can afford to buy and look after a pony.

There are many things to consider before you buy your first pony. Age and looks are not as important as good behaviour. The pony should be a suitable size for the child and an experienced older pony is likely to be much more patient and usually less flighty than a young one. A more mature, well-mannered, school master will be much safer and more reliable in the long term. A healthy pony is extremely important. A few sores, blemishes or lumps and bumps are acceptable in a first pony, especially one in its teens or older. However, do get any pony checked by a vet before you buy it, even if you know the previous owner.

Prices for ponies can vary enormously, and are usually guided by temperament, safety and suitability for children, rather than looks or talent for leaping huge jumps. Take an experienced horse owner with you if you are buying from someone you do not know. A knowledgeable person should be able to tell you if the pony is suitable for your riding ability and where you intend to keep the pony after you have bought it.

A GOOD STURDY NATIVE PONY IS IDEAL FOR CHILDREN.

THE CHILD ON THE LEFT IS TOO BIG FOR THE PONY, WHILE THE PONY ON THE RIGHT IS TOO BIG FOR THE CHILD.

THIS TYPE OF STURDY PONY OFTEN MAKES A SUITABLE FIRST PONY.

Any pony must be good in traffic. Ask to see the owner of the pony riding it on the road when you come to view it. The pony must be good to shoe and easy to catch. Ponies that are good to travel save a lot of hassle and are much safer.

Be wary of adverts that might bend the truth and take special care when buying from sales and auctions which are sometimes used as a dumping ground for problem ponies. Borrowing or leasing ponies must be accompanied by a legal contract so everyone knows exactly where they stand.

EXERCISING IS FUN IN NICE WEATHER, BUT HAS TO BE DONE ALL YEAR ROUND.

All costs must be considered carefully. Take into account routine veterinary care, and the hidden costs of illness, injury and insurance. It is important to be covered for public liability and other things such as loss of tack and death. Find out how much your local farrier charges for new shoes, and remember he will need to visit you every six to eight weeks. Feed costs will vary with the lifestyle, but find out how much hay and hard feed are locally, and the price of the bedding you want to use. Equipment such as grooming, mucking-out equipment, boots and bandages, rugs, numnahs, girths, saddles, bridles, headcollars, ropes, riding clothes and boots, hat equipment and stable equipment need to be taken into account, and the likelihood that they need to be replaced from time to time. If you are going to shows you will need smart clothes, a trailer (and a vehicle to pull the trailer) and entry fees. You will also need livery or rent fees if you do not own your own land and stables. All of these add up, so be very well prepared and ensure that you can sensibly afford it.

DON'T FORGET – THERE ARE LOTS OF CHORES TO BE DONE – IT'S NOT ALL EXCITING!

YOU WILL SOON PROGRESS TO FUN ACTIVITIES LIKE JUMPING.

CHAPTER 8

BREEDS DIRECTORY

PONIES

Sometime around 6,000 years ago – just before the first horses were being domesticated – it is believed that two separate types of ponies evolved on the plains and steppes of central Eurasia. Pony Type 1 is most likely descended from Tarpan stock, and continued to develop in north–west Europe. Pony Type 2 is probably descended from the Asiatic Wild Horse (Equus caballus przewalskii przewalski Poliakov) and developed in northern Eurasia.

These ponies developed long before the end of the Ice Age, when Britain was still attached by an ice bridge to continental Europe. When the last bridge disappeared around 15,000 bc, the horses and ponies already in Britain were effectively cut off from any further equine influences. It would not be until the Bronze Age, around 1,000 bc when ships were being built that were strong enough to carry livestock and horses, that other types of horses were seen in Britain. Consequently, the ponies 'stranded' at the end of the Ice Age had some 14,000 years to develop their fixed characters. When invaders and traders such as the Romans, Vikings and the Phoenicians, arrived, they brought with them new horses whose genes would influence and mingle with some of the British pony breeds.

SHETLAND PONY

Britain has a number of native pony breeds, often referred to as Moorland or Mountain breeds because of their original habitats. Today there are no truly feral stocks of ponies in Britain: the most 'wild' herds such as the Exmoor ponies are rounded up annually for breed and veterinary inspection, although many owners still keep the ponies in their 'original' environments. These breeds have been 'improved' over the centuries, but nevertheless continue to retain special qualities and characteristics

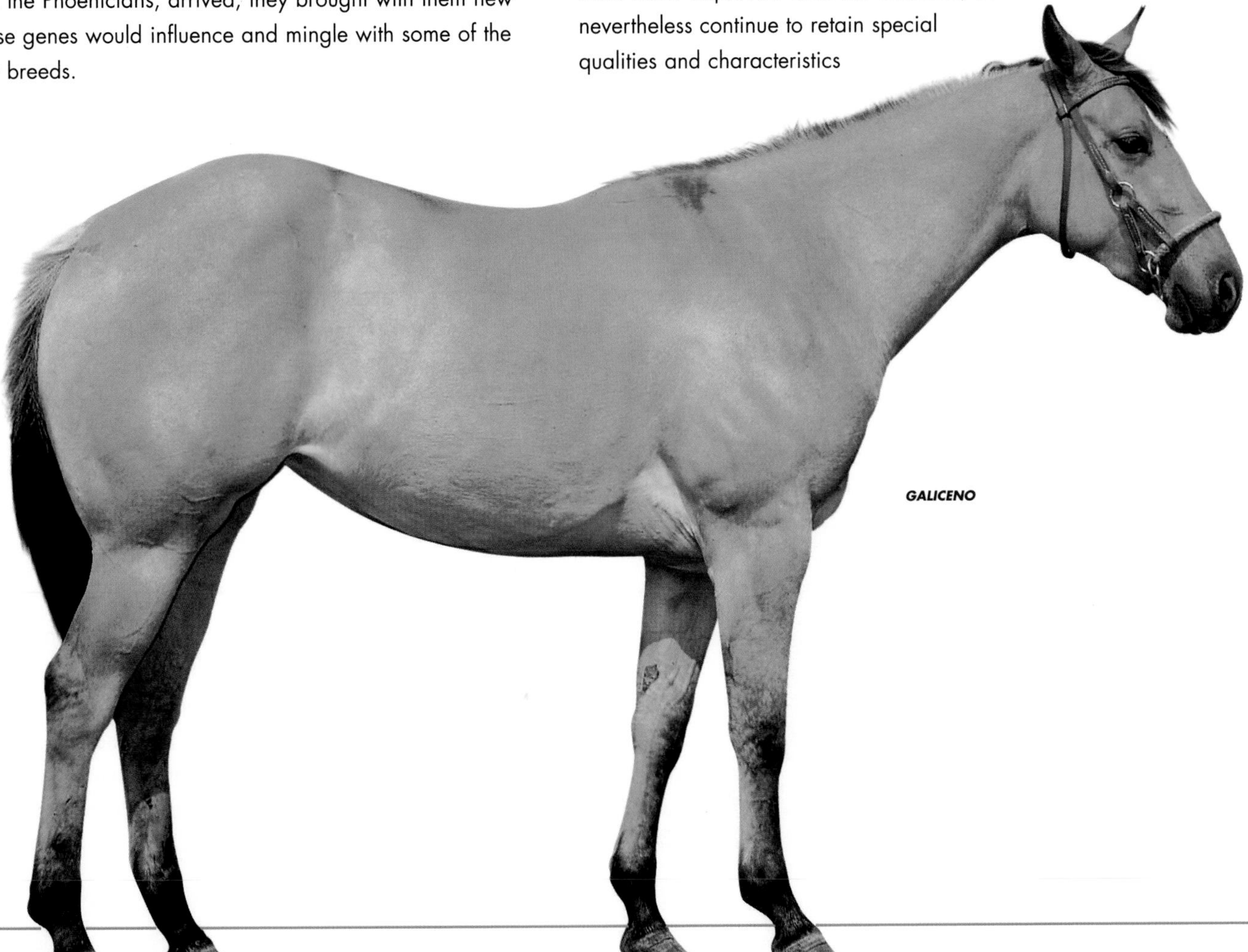

GALICENO

that are the result of particular environmental conditions and their long period of geographical isolation. Breed societies today maintain stud books to ensure that all stock is pure–bred. Another British breed is the Lundy Pony (see page 165) which was established in 1928.

Across mainland Europe and Scandinavia, there are ponies of equally ancient origin. Today many of these ponies are working animals, employed on farms in the rural economies of central and eastern Europe.

In the more industrialised and wealthy western European nations, increasing numbers of ponies of riding quality are being bred to for recreation and leisur pursuits. In North, South, anc Central America, ponies arrivec with the Spanish Conquistadors a were developed later into a wide variety of pony breeds including the Falabella (see page 157), and the Chincoteague (see below). Meanwhile, Asia, the world's largest continent extending from the Arctic Circle in the north to the Equator in the south, there a numerous pony breeds which have developed according to the widely var climates and terrain of the continent.

A POLO PONY

CHINCOTEAGUE PONY

HEIGHT: average 12 hh. (1.22 m)

COLOURS: Any, many are paint or pinto (piebald and skewbald)

USE: Mainly feral, but some under saddle

FEATURES: Short round body, shaggy winter coat, many are light boned with poorly developed joints

These wild ponies have the distinction of being the only indigenous 'pony group' in the USA and are most likely derived from stock that strayed or was abandoned by colonists in the 17 century. The island of Chincoteague, along with neighbouring Assateague, lies off the coasts of Virginia and Maryland, and is among the last remaining habitat for wild equine stock. Conditions on the islands are harsh: there is no shelter from Atlantic storms and there is little sustenance in the vegetation that grows or the sandy, salt marshes. These conditions meant that only the toughest, hardiest and most adaptable ponies survived. These harsh conditions took their toll and by the early 20th century, much of the stock was showing signs of stunted growth, and more serious conformation distortions associated with uncontrolled inbreeding in an isolated ar restricted gene pool.

Around 200 Chincoteague ponies (pronounced shin-ca-teeg), live on the larger Assateague Island and in the 1920s, knowledge of this feral breed became more widespread when the Chincoteague Volunteer Fire Department assumed responsibility for the ponies and improved the stock by introducing Shetland (see page 164), Welsh Pony, and Pinto (see page 229) blood. The Pinto out-crosses have produced part-coloured ponies as well as a more 'horsey' appearance to the Chincoteague's head.

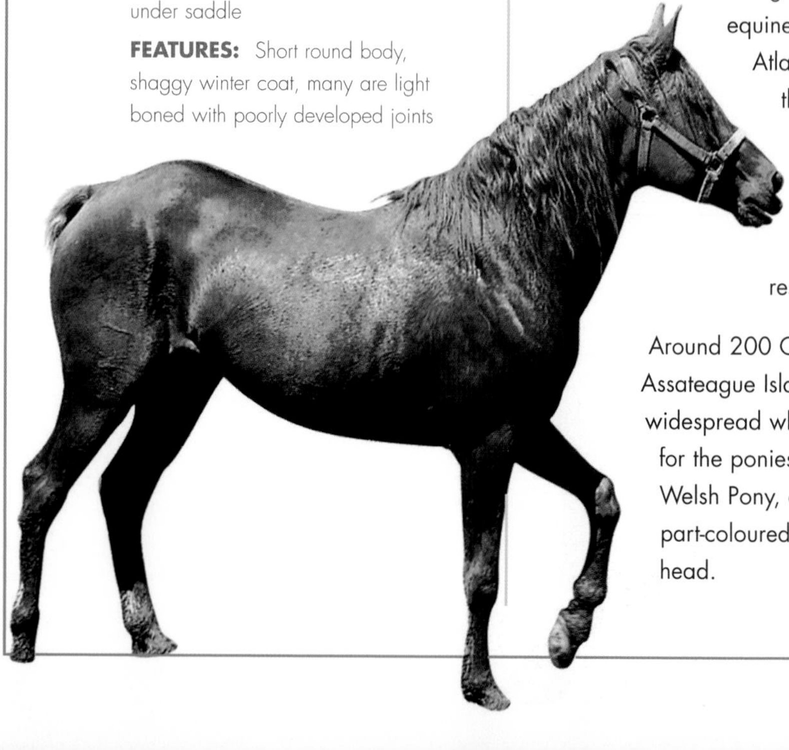

BASHKIR PONY

HEIGHT: 13–14 hh. (1.32–1.42 m)

COLOURS: Chestnut, dun, bay

USE: Saddle, Pack, Draft, Milk and Meat

FEATURES: Thick curly coat, luxurious mane and tail, hard feet (usually unshod), heavy head on thick, strong neck.

The Bashkir, or Bashkirsky, takes its name from Bashkiria, in the southern foothills of the Ural Mountains, close to the steppes of Kirghizia and Kazakhstan. Like most ponies, the Bashkir is naturally hardy, but in its native lands, theses ponies live out all year round – often in deep snow and in temperatures of 30º–40º C below freezing (-22º to -40º F) subsisting on the most frugal of diets.

In spite of these conditions the Bashkir mares are famous for their milk production: in a seven- to eight-month lactation period, an average mare will give upwards of 1,500 litres (330 gallons) of milk. Much of this is used in dairy produce but some is reserved for making Kummis, the 'fire water' of the steppes! Like many horses and ponies, the Bashkir also provided its owners with another valuable source of protein in the form of its meat. The Bashkir also gives freely of its thick, curly coat and its luxurious mane and tail: combings from the pony's hair can be woven to make blankets and clothing. Additionally, the Bashkir can be used under saddle, as a mountain pack pony, and in draft, their endurance is legendary: it is said that a Bashkir troika (a sledge pulled by three horses abreast) can easily cover 120–140 km (75–85 miles) per day through the snow.

Because of the varied and invaluable contribution of the Bashkir to the local economies of the southern Urals, breeding centres were established in 1845 to improve stock, and two types of pony have been developed: the mountain type, suitable for riding, and the heavier steppe variety.

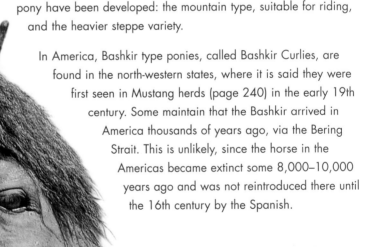

In America, Bashkir type ponies, called Bashkir Curlies, are found in the north-western states, where it is said they were first seen in Mustang herds (page 240) in the early 19th century. Some maintain that the Bashkir arrived in America thousands of years ago, via the Bering Strait. This is unlikely, since the horse in the Americas became extinct some 8,000–10,000 years ago and was not reintroduced there until the 16th century by the Spanish.

CASPIAN PONY

HEIGHT: 10–12 hh. (1–1.22 m)

COLOURS: Bay, chestnut, grey, brown

USE: Saddle, harness

FEATURES: Large, gazelle-like eyes, very short ears (breed standard stipulates no longer than 4 1⁄2 in (11.4 cm). Full flowing mane and tail which is carried high. Strong, small feet which are very rarely shod. Natural jumping ability.

The Caspian pony, a native of the area around the Elburtz Mountains and Caspian Sea in Iran, is one of the world's most ancient horse breeds and represents a link between the early forms of Equus and the hot blooded or 'plateau' horses from which the modern light horses have evolved. Just prior to the domestication of the horse, there were four subspecies in existence: the two pony types and the two horse types. The last of these, Horse Type 4, was the smallest, standing no more than 9 hh, but with regard to its proportions, it was a horse. It native habitat was western Asia, and it is suggested that Horse Type 4 was the prototype of the Arab (see pages 183).

'Miniature' horses of decidedly Arab appearance appear on many examples of art from ancient Egypt and Mesopotamia, and around 500 bc, similar horses were depicted on the seal of the Persian king, Darius the Great (522–486 bc). This seal shows a pair of these horses drawing a chariot from which Darius shoots arrows at an attacking lion– a lion so hug it dwarfs the horses. Miniature horses were also recorded in existence by the ancient Greeks in parts of Medea, the area south of the Caspian Sea, while horse remains have been foun in caves from the Mesolithic period in Kermansh (an area midway between Baghdad in Iraq, and Tehran in Iran). It appears that around 1,000 years ago the tribes from Kermansh moved from the region, and, along with their horses, settled on the northern edge of the Elburtz Mountains.

The Caspian pony is distinguished from other breeds by several unique physical characteristics: there is a marked difference in the shape of the scapula (more like that of a horse than a pony), there is an extra molar in the upper jaw, and, a different formation of the parietal bones of the head which give a 'vaulted' appearance to the skull. Thought to be extinct, these ponies were 'rediscovered pulling carts in Amol, in northern Iran in 1965 by American traveller, Mrs Louise I. Firouz. Subsequently, a selective breeding programme was established to safeguard the Caspian's future and there are now studs in Iran, and Caspian societies in Britain, the USA, Australia and New Zealand.

CONNEMARA PONY

HEIGHT: 13–14.2 hh. (1.33– 1.48 m)

COLOURS: Bay, grey, black, dun, brown

USE: Saddle, harness

FEATURES: Small head on graceful neck, strong legs, sure-footed, natural jumpers. Suitable for child and adult riders.

Ireland's only indigenous pony, the Connemara takes its name from the county in the west of Ireland. The region faces the Atlantic Ocean and is famed for its magnificent landscape of lakes, moors, bog lands, and mountains. The Connemara's ancestors were likely to have been ponies that were similar to the Shetland (see page 164) and Norwegian Fjord (see page 159) but when Celtic raiders arrived in the 5th and 6th centuries, an eastern influence was introduced by the small Celtic pony. Later, when Galway became an important trading centre in the 16th century, Spanish horses were brought in, and it is also said that Spanish blood was introduced from horses saved from the wrecks of the Spanish Armada in 1588.

In the 19th century 'Arab' blood – though more likely to have been the Barb – was brought to Connemara by wealthy landowners. In 1897, in an attempt to halt the deterioration of the breed, a government backed scheme introduced Welsh Cobbs (page 168), Thoroughbreds (see page 188), Hackneys (see page 210) and Clydesdales (see page 176). These crosses marked the beginnings of the modern Connemara which is noted as one of the finest performance ponies: fast and courageous, yet sensible, a natural jumper, and extremely versatile, for the Connemara can be ridden by children and adults alike.

In 1923 the Connemara Pony Breeder Society was established, and in 1926, the stud book was set up. The first stallion to be recorded was Cannon Ball, born in 1906 and still held in awe in the west of Ireland to this day. Cannon Ball won the farmer's Race at Oughterard for 16 years running (locals say he was fed half a barrel of oats the night before the race), and worked in harness his entire life. He was well known for happily trotting home from market with his owner, Harry O'Toole, drunk and snoring on the floor of the cart. Cannon Ball's death was marked with the appropriate Irish traditional ceremonial befitting an admired member of the community: a wake with with plenty of drinking, telling of tales, and singing, that lasted throughout the night – before Cannon Ball was laid to rest in his field at dawn the next morning.

DALES PONY

HEIGHT: 14.2 hh. (1.48 m)

COLOURS: Black, dark brown, occasionally grey

USE: Saddle, harness, farm work

FEATURES: Heavy, very deep shoulders; short back and very strong loins, thick mane and tail; short, flat cannons with no less than 8 in (20 cm) of bone; lower legs are covered in abundant, fine silky feathers.

The Dales pony is one of Britain's heaviest native ponies and hails from the eastern side of th Pennines in the counties of Yorkshire, Northumberland and County Durham. Genetically, the Dales pony is related to the smaller Fell pony (see page 158) whose traditional breeding are is on the western side of the Pennines.

The Dales pony is probably descended from Friesians (see page 207) brought to Britain by th Romans over 2,000 years ago, and the steep terrain and harsh climate of the region have made them both sure-footed and hardy. In the 18th century, Dales ponies provided the power in the lead mines of Allendale and Alston Moor, working both underground and as pack ponies, carrying lead ore across the rugged landscape of the north-east of England to the seaports on the River Tyne. Later, they were also used in coal mines, largely because of their ability to bear loads that are ou of proportion to their weight: the average weight carried by a Dales pony was 100 kg (2 cwt).

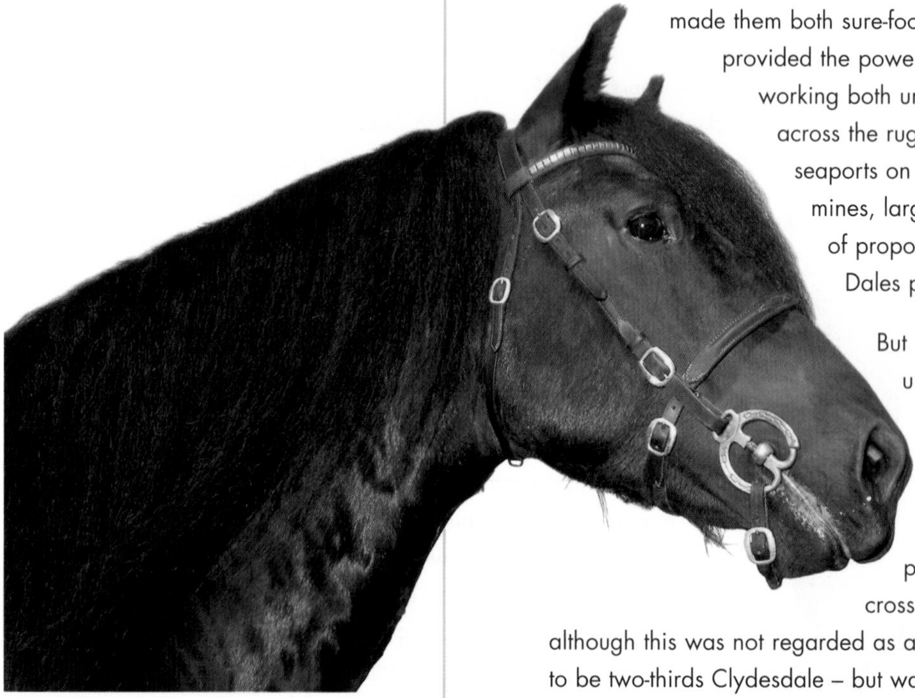

But the Dales pony was also a fine trotter in harness or under saddle and was reputedly able to cover 1 mile (1.6 km) in 3 minutes while carrying a considerable load. In order to improve on this, in the 19th century, Welsh Cob (see page 168) blood was introduced – in particular, that of a trotting stallion par excellence called Comet. In the early 20th century crosses were also made with Clydesdales (see page 176) although this was not regarded as a successful move. By 1917 the Dales was considered to be two-thirds Clydesdale – but was still regarded as the best pack horse for military us during World War One. In more recent times, the influence of the Clydesdale has diminished, leaving the Dales as a pony with great stamina, a calm temperament, and a strong constitution, that is ideally suited to pony trekking. The trotting quality is still prese however, and, this makes the Dales pony a particularly fine harness pony as well.

DARTMOOR PONY

HEIGHT: 12.2 hh. (1.28 m)

COLOURS: Black, bay, brown (only a small amount of white marking is accepted for show and registration purposes.

USE: Saddle

FEATURES: Noted for its sloping shoulders, small head, alert ears, and the lack of knee lift resulting in a long, low action.

In Devon, in the south-west of England, lies a vast, windswept area of wild moorland known as Dartmoor, where, for at least 1, 000 years, sure-footed and hardy wild ponies have roamed free. From the 12th to the 15th centuries the ponies were used to carry tin from local mines.

The type of pony that lived here has varied through the ages: it was influenced by several different breeds such as the Old Devon Pack Horse and the Cornish Goonhilly (now both extinct), as well as eastern or oriental horses which may have been introduced in the 12th century. In the 19th century, Welsh Ponies and Welsh Cobbs pages 168), Arabs page 183) small Thoroughbreds (page 188) and Exmoor Ponies (page 156) were also introduced. In an attempt to produce pit ponies, Shetlands (page 164) were turned out onto the moors: the result was disastrous, with the near disappearance of the tough Dartmoor of good riding type. The breed was saved by the introduction of Welsh Mountain Ponies (see page 168), a Fell Pony (see page 158) and the renowned polo pony stallion, Lord Polo.

In the end, the numerous out-crosses have produced a riding pony with an exceptionally smooth action since the Dartmoor does not lift its knees very high when moving. The ponies were not registered until 1899 when the Dartmoor Section of the Polo Pony Society's (now the National Pony Society) Stud Book was opened and a standard of points drawn up. Interest in the breed gradually rose but during World War Two when Dartmoor was used as a military training area, the breed came close to extinction: only two males and 12 females were registered between 1941 and 1943. Once again, the breed was saved from extinction by a handful of dedicated breeders and today, the majority of Dartmoor ponies are bred on private studs throughout the UK. Sure-footed, kind and sensible, they are ideal riding ponies and are popular in Europe, the USA and Canada, especially as a child's first pony.

EXMOOR PONY

HEIGHT: 12–12.3 hh. (1.22– 1.30 m)

COLOURS: Bay, brown, mousey dun; mealy muzzle and markings around eyes, on underbelly and between thighs. No white markings allowed

USE: Saddle, cross-breeding

FEATURES: Hooded eyes ('toad eyes'); beginnings of a seventh molar tooth; coat almost double–textured; 'ice tail': thick with fanlike growth at top; great powers of endurance.

The Exmoor is Britain's oldest, native breed of pony and retains significant features found in it principal ancestor, Pony Type 1 such as the particular jaw formation with a seventh molar tooth. The Exmoor pony has remained unchanged for centuries, largely because of the isolation of its native high, wild moorlands in north-east Devon, where they have run since the Ice Age. This and the harsh climate of Exmoor has produced a pony that is incredibly strong and exceptionally hardy. On the Rare Breeds Survival Trust's 'critical list', there are now only three principal herds on the moors. The purity and quality of these ponies, which are in a sense 'wild', is carefully safeguarded by the Exmoor Pony Society. Each year in autumn, the herds are rounded up and those foals which pass inspection are branded with a star near the shoulder to indicate that they are pure-bred Exmoors. Beneath the star is the herd number, and on the left hindquarter is the number of the pony in the herd.

Pure-bred Exmoors are instantly recognisable by the mealy-coloured muzzle and markings around the eyes, inside the ears, inside the thighs and under the belly. No white markings are permitted in the breed standard. The prominent eyes are called 'toad eyes' because they are hooded, which provides protection against the weather. The Exmoor's head is also a little larger than other breeds because of the length of its nasal passages: the longer length allows for the air to be warmed up before being inhaled into the lungs! The thick tail hc a natural fanlike growth at the top: this so-called 'ice tail' protects from snow and rain, as does the coat, which is double textured and waterproof. In winter the coat grows thick, harsh and springy in texture; in summer it is dense and hard with a distinctive metallic sheen. Naturally nervous of humans, Exmoor ponies do make exceptionally good riding ponies when properly trained: enormously strong in proportion to the size, they are also noted for their gallop and their jump. Other Exmoor ponies are bred elsewhere in Britain, but ponies which are bred 'off the moors', away from their natural habitat, tend to loose type.

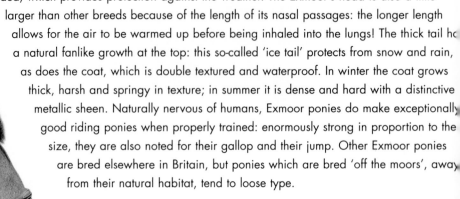

ERISKAY PONY

HEIGHT: 12–13.2 hh. (1.22– 1.38 m)

COLOURS: Grey, with occasional black and bay,

USE: Saddle, harness, croft and deer hunt work

FEATURES: Dense, waterproof coat, and thick tail; fine silky hair on legs.

The harsh and demanding environment of the Western Isles helped to develop a breed of pony over at least 4,000 years that was tough, waterproof and wind resistant. Furthermore, on islands where feed was restricted, the Eriskay pony would frequently supplement its meagre diet by feeding off the mineral-rich seaweed on the shoreline.

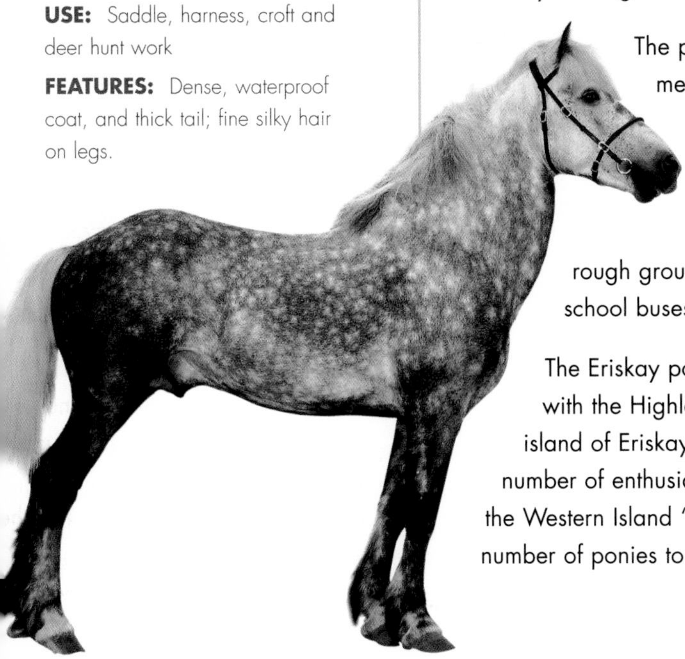

The ponies of Scotland's Western Isles were crofters' ponies: while the islands' menfolk made their livings from the sea, work on the small farmsteads or crofts, was left largely to the women, children and ponies. The ponies carried peat (the only source of fuel of the islands) and seaweed (used in both dyestuffs and as a fertiliser) in vast creels (baskets) fitted to either side of the pony's back. Strong enough to pull loaded carts over rough ground, the ponies were also hitched to harrows for farm work and acted as school buses for the island's children.

The Eriskay pony is related to the larger Highland pony (see page 161): cross-breeding with the Highland resulted in a reduction in the number of pure-bred ponies left on the island of Eriskay and by 1970 the herd was reduced to around 20 ponies. Fortunately, a number of enthusiasts had sought to re-establish the breed which by then was regarded as the Western Island 'type' of Highland pony. The Eriskay Pony Society has successfully risen the number of ponies to around 300, but the Eriskay is still classified as a threatened rare breed.

FALABELLA

HEIGHT: 7hh. (76 cm)

COLOURS: All solid and part colours

USE: Pet, not for riding, sometimes shown in harness in the USA

FEATURES: Miniature horse proportions, luxurious tail and mane, large head in proportion to rest of body.

At various times throughout history miniature horses have been bred as pets and for their 'novelty' value. The Falabella is not really a pony but a miniature horse: it is in fact the smallest horse in the world, and maintains a horse's proportions and character. The very small size of the Falabella makes it completely unsuited to riding, although in the USA it can sometimes be seen in harness.

The basis of the Falabella was the Shetland pony (see page 164) and possibly, at one time, a very small 'freak' Thoroughbred (see page 188). It was first bred by the Falabella family on their ranch in Argentina by deliberately down-sizing with crosses of the smallest animals. In the process, the strength and hardiness of the Shetland has been lost. The smallest Falabella ever bred was Sugar Dumpling, belonging to Smith McCoy of West Virginia, USA, a mere 51 cm (20 in) high and weighed just 13.5 kg (30 lb).

Breeders aim to produce a near-perfect horse in miniature: the preferred height is about 76 cm (30 in) at the withers. But in-breeding often results in poor conformation: some animals have over large and heavy heads, weak quarters and in some instances, misshapen lower limbs. Nevertheless, Falabellas are attractive and appealing and are said to be intelligent, good tempered and friendly horses when kept as pets. Their coat patterns vary, but the spotted Appaloosa-type coat pattern (see page 194) is increasingly sought-after.

FELL PONY

HEIGHT: 13–14 hh. (1.33–1.42 m)

COLOURS: Black, brown bay, occasionally grey. Very few white markings.

USE: Saddle, harness

FEATURES: Small head, broad across forehead and tapering down to muzzle; large open nostrils; luxurious mane and tail, left to grow long; powerful drive in hind legs because of strength and flexibility of hocks; feet are open at heels, with hard, blue horn and heels are feathered.

Smaller and lighter than its close relation the Dales pony, the Fell pony comes from the north-western edges of the Pennines, the rough moorlands of Westmorland and Cumberland. Both the Fell and the Dales ponies are descended from the same black Friesian stock brought to Britain by the Romans over 2,000 years ago, and used as auxiliary cavalry. Each breed, however, would develop slightly differently according to their habitat and to the work to whic they were put.

The greatest influence on the Fell pony was of the swift-footed Galloway, the mount of the border raiders who harassed the Roman Legions, and later, that of the Scottish drovers. Although extinct since the 19th century, the Galloway, which was bred between Nithsdale an the Mull of Galloway, has left its mark in British ponies. It was strong, hardy, and very fast under saddle and harness, and could well have provided some of the 'running horse' stock that would become the basis for the eastern sires in the 17th and 18th century from which would spring the Thoroughbred (see page 188).

At first, however, the Fell pony (like the Dales) was a pack pony, carrying lead ore from the mines: the average load was 95 kg (224 lb) and the ponies travelled around 240 miles (384 km) a week over some of the roughest land in Britain. But, because of its smaller size and better riding shoulders, the Fell pony was soon also used under saddle and harness, especial in local trotting races. In 1900 the Fell Pony Society was formed and the National Pony Society opened a section in its Stud Book: the strict rules and careful selection and line breeding of the strongest lines have ensured that very little 'foreign' blood has been introduce to the breed. Consequently, the Fell is much sought-after in it own right for riding and driving, and, as a cross to produce horses of great competition potential.

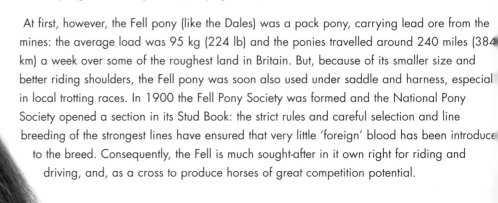

GALICENO

HEIGHT: 12–14 hh. (1.22 –1.42 m)

COLOURS: All solid colours

USE: Saddle, harness, ranch work

FEATURES: Almost pure white tail on palomino coloured horses; Dun coloured horses have black mane, tail and dorsal list and sometimes zebra bars on lower limbs. Smooth gait; swift, running walk.

The Galiceno pony from Mexico derives its name from the Spanish province of Galicia where it was first developed. Galicia is a region famed for its smooth-gaited horses which are distinguished by a very swift running walk. Its ancestors were the Portuguese Garrano (Minho) and Spanish Sorraia, probably brought to America by the Spanish from the island of Hispaniola (Haiti) in the 16th century. Both the Sorraia and Garrano stem from primitive stock such as the Tarpan, which contributed directly to the evolution of the Spanish horse.

Although referred to as a pony, and standing up to 14 hh, in its proportions and character, the Galiceno is really a small horse. Lightly built, the Galiceno has a fine head, large, well spaced eyes, upright shoulders and a short back. Tough, intelligent, agile and versatile, the Galiceno spread out of Mexico into the USA in the 1950s and since 1958, has been recognised as a breed. An attractive riding horse, with its characteristic, smooth gait of a fast running walk, the Galiceno is still widely used in Mexico in harness for farm work. Its hard feet and sound constitution are well adapted to working on hard, sun-baked soil.

NORWEGIAN FJORD PONY

HEIGHT: 13–14.2 hh (1.33–1.48 m)

COLOURS: Dun

USE: Saddle, harness, pack horse

FEATURES: Distinctive upright, coarse mane with black hair at centre and dorsal eel-stripe running from forelock to tip of tail; often zebra bar markings on the legs; tail is often silver, thick and full.

Norway's dun coloured Fjord pony bears a striking resemblance to the Asiatic Wild Horse: it retains the uniform dun coat colour, the dorsal eel-stripe running from forelock to the tip of the tail, and, it sometimes has zebra bar markings on its legs. In conformation the Fjord also retains its ancestor's short, compact form and overall strength and vigour. However, the modern Fjord does not have the convex profile seen in primitive stock.

The Fjord was the horse of the Vikings and accompanied them in their long boats to take part in raids: the first Norse raiders came from Hordaland, the chief habitat of the Fjord pony, and, consequently, its influence can be seen in Scotland's Highland pony (page 161) and in the ancient Icelandic horse.

The most notable feature of the Fjord is its coarse, erect mane – a characteristic of primitive equines. By ancient tradition, the mane is hogged (clipped) so that the black hairs at the centre of the mane stand higher than the rest which are generally lighter, more silver in colour. The mane is cut in a crescent shape from poll to withers, giving the Fjord's neck a pronounced crest.

In Norway and beyond, it is highly regarded for its sure-footedness, stamina and courage, and for its ability to work in hard terrain and in severe weather. It is used for ploughing, as a pack pony, in harness, and under saddle.

HAFLINGER PONY

HEIGHT: up to 13.3 hh (1.40 m)

COLOURS: Palomino, or chestnut with flaxen mane and tail

USE: Saddle, draught work, harness

FEATURES: Characteristic colour with flaxen mane and tail; Edelweiss brand on Halfing bred ponies; exceptionally free action with long striding walk.

The Haflinger is a sturdy mountain breed that originated in the mountainous region of the Austrian Tyrol and which takes its name from the village of Hafling in the Etschlander Mountains where this pony was extensively bred. State studs were also established later at Piber and Ossiach, but today the principal Haflinger stud is at Jenesien where all stallions are owned by the Austrian state and all colt foals are subjected to rigorous inspection before being selected as potential future stallions.

The careful control of the breed and its mountain environment ensures a fixed type of pony, with an unmistakable – and very attractive – appearance: Haflingers are always chestnut or palomino with a beautiful flaxen mane and tail. They are powerfully built, being exceptionally muscular and strong in the loins, and the back. This combination of beauty and strength has led the ponies to be described as 'princes in front, peasants behind'. The Haflinger is sometimes known as the 'Edelweiss pony' as all Haflinger-bred ponies carry the brand mark of Austria's national flower with the letter H in the centre.

The Haflingers breeding can be traced back to cold-blooded, now extinct Alpine heavy horse and related pony breeds on one side, and to Arab (see page 183) origins on the other. Although a cold-blood itself, the modern pure-bred Haflinger can trace back to the Arab stallion El Bedavi XXII. This combination has produced a sure-footed, placid and hardworking pony that is ideal for draught, harness and riding work in rugged terrain. In Austria, young Haflingers are raised on the Alpine pastures – a practice known as 'Alpung' – where the thin but clean air helps to develop their strong lungs and hearts. They are not usually worked until they reach about four years old, but they have been known to work happily until they are 40, a testament to their strong constitutions.

The Italian 'version' of the Haflinger – and which also shares ancestry with El Bedawi XXII – is the Avelignese, bred in the Italian Alps and in the Apennine Mountains. Although the Avelignese is often bigger (around 14.2 hh/1.48 m) and occasionally has white facial markings, in other respects the two breeds are almost identical in appearance.

HIGHLAND PONY

HEIGHT: up to 14.2 hh. (1.48 m)

COLOURS: Variety: duns in grey, yellow, gold, cream and fox; greys, browns, blacks, sometimes bays, sometimes 'bloodstone' (chestnuts with silver manes and tails); piebald also permitted

USE: Saddle, harness, pack

FEATURES: Most have dorsal eel stripe; some have zebra markings on legs. Tails and manes are fine and silky touch. Feather ends in prominent tuft at fetlock.

The largest and strongest of Britain's native ponies, the Highland is native to the north of Scotland and the Western Islands, although the ponies found on the mainland were larger and heavier than those found on the islands. This difference disappeared in the 19th century when Clydesdales (see page 99) were introduced to the islands to produce ponies that were strong enough for forestry work. (See also the Eriskay Pony, page 157).

The origins of the Highland pony appear to be prehistoric: after the Ice Age, ponies living in the far north of Scotland were derived from Pony Type 2 which resembled the Asiatic Wild Horse, and possible crosses with Pony Type 1, which was similar to the Exmoor Pony (see page 1156). Throughout its history however, there have been many outside influences on this original native stock to produce the modern Highland pony. In the Bronze Age, horses were imported from Scandinavia and later from Iceland, but the most significant contributions came in later, in the 16th–18th centuries. Around 1515, Louis XII of France gave King James V of Scotland a gift of horses – which included the ancestors of the Percheron (see page 103). In the late 17th and early 18th centuries, the Clan Chief of Clanranald improved the ponies on Uist by importing Spanish horses. In 1870 century, a Norfolk Roadster type Hackney was brought to the Isles and had a particular influence on the ponies on the Isle of Arran. The MacNeils on the island of Barra introduced Arab blood to their stock, while John Munro-Mackenzie on the island of Mull used the Arab Syrian to develop the famous Calgary strain of ponies on the island.

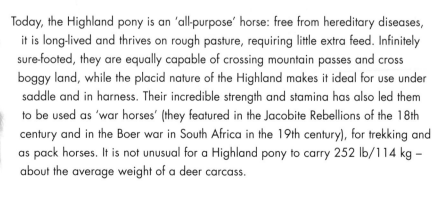

Today, the Highland pony is an 'all-purpose' horse: free from hereditary diseases, it is long-lived and thrives on rough pasture, requiring little extra feed. Infinitely sure-footed, they are equally capable of crossing mountain passes and cross boggy land, while the placid nature of the Highland makes it ideal for use under saddle and in harness. Their incredible strength and stamina has also led them to be used as 'war horses' (they featured in the Jacobite Rebellions of the 18th century and in the Boer war in South Africa in the 19th century), for trekking and as pack horses. It is not unusual for a Highland pony to carry 252 lb/114 kg – about the average weight of a deer carcass.

ICELANDIC HORSE

HEIGHT: 12–13 hh (1.22–1.33 m)

COLOURS: All, but primarily grey or dun

USE: Riding and harness work

FEATURES: Heavy head; short, stocky body; deep girth; short back; very strong limbs with short cannons and strong hocks; peculiarly wedge shaped, sloping quarters but which are very strong and muscular; mane and tail are full; feathering on heels.

Although the Icelandic horse stands no more than 13–13.2 hh, it is never referred to as a pony by the Icelanders. This is one of the toughest of the pony breeds: despite its small size it can easily carry a grown man at speed over great distances and over some of the roughest landscape in the world.

The horse was introduced into Iceland from Scandinavia, notably from Norway around ad 860, brought to the island by the two Norse chieftains Ingolfur and Leifur. These settlers and their horses were soon followed by others from the Norse colonies i the Western Isles of Scotland, Ireland and the Isle of Man. Interbreeding of this early stock gave rise to the Icelandic horse which for 1,000 years has received no outside blood. In ad 930, following a disastrous attempt to introduce eastern blood, the Althing (the world's oldes parliament) banned the import of horses into Iceland.

Even from this early date, selective breeding was being practised, using stallion fights as the basis for that selection. There were four types of Icelandic horse: pack horses and draught horses; riding horses, and horses bred for meat. A more modern selective breeding began in 1879 in Skagafjordur, northern Iceland, which was based largely on the quality of the five gaits that are unique to the Icelandic horse. From this two distinct types emerged: the heavier pony used for draught and pack work, and the lighter type for riding. Both were used extensively in Iceland until the 1920s when they were the only forms of transport available. Because cattle cannot be wintered out in Iceland, horses are still bred for meat. Around half Iceland's horses live out all year round in a semi-wild state with only the occasional supplement of herring to provide extra valuable nutrition.

There are no fewer than 15 basic colour types and combinations of Icelandic horse – including palomino, skewbald and piebald – and some studs concentrate on breeding a preferred coat colour. The Kirkjuber Stud produces the distinctive chestnut colour wit the near white mane and tail, but breeding programmes are based principally on the five gaits.

The five gaits are the fetgangur (walk) which is mostly used by pack animals; the brokk (trot), used when crossing rough country; the stökk (fast gallop), and the tw very ancient gaits, the skeið (pace), a smooth, lateral gait, and the tölt (rack), a four-beat running walk used for crossing broken ground. In pacing races the Icelandic horse changes to the skieð after a 55 yd (50 m) stökk.

NEW FOREST PONY

HEIGHT: 12.2–14 hh (1.22 –1.47 m)

COLOURS: All, except: piebald, skewbald, and blue-eyed cream

USE: Saddle, harness

FEATURES: Good, long sloping riding shoulders; long low action especially evident at the canter.

This British breed, found in the New Forest in Hampshire, has one of the most varied genetic backgrounds – largely because of the accessible nature of their habitat. We know from the Forest Law of 1016 proclaimed by King Canute at Winchester that there were ponies in the forest, decades before the Norman kings exerted their powers over it.

Anyone travelling west through the south of England would pass through the New Forest, giving ample opportunity for the native ponies to cross with domestic stock.

After the Norman Conquest, King William Rufus (1087–1100) made the New Forest a royal hunting ground, preserving the deer and enforcing the Rights of Common Pasture for those people living within the forest. These 'Commoners' had – and continue to have – the right to run their ponies in the forest: today there are around 3,000 ponies running in the forest.

In the 13th century, in the first attempts to upgrade the breed, Welsh mares were turned out in the forest. While there may have been ongoing selective breeding by the Commoners in the following centuries, by the 19th century, the New Forest stock had degenerated so far that immediate action was required. Under the auspices of Lords Arthur Cecil and Lucas, Dartmoors, Exmoors, Highlands, Fells, Dales, Hackneys, Clydesdales, and Arabs were introduced in the New Forest. It was not until the end of World War II, however, that there emerged five stallions that are recognised as the founding sires of the modern breed: Danny Denny, Goodenough, Brooming Slipon, Brookside David, and Knightwood Spitfire.

Some of the varied contributors to the modern breed can be detected in the New Forest pony: the heads are still rather horse-like, and there are often quite substantial variations in height : forest-bred ponies can be small, around 12–12.2 hh (1.22–1.27m) while stud-bred 'Foresters' can reach 14.2 hh (1.47 m).

Nevertheless, the environment of the New Forest itself ensured that a pony of a distinctive 'type' was produced: water, marsh and bog land are a feature of the New Forest moorland where the ponies live, and, while it provides a sufficient diet of coarse grasses, brambles and gorse tips, food is never very plentiful. Consequently, theses conditions have contributed to the creation of a breed of strong-legged, sure-footed and adaptable ponies with excellent riding shoulders and a distinctive, long, low action that is most evident at the canter.

SHETLAND PONY

HEIGHT: Traditionally, the Shetland is measured in inches, not hands: average is 38–40 inches (96 cm –101 cm)

COLOURS: All colours: Black is foundation colour, but brown, bay and grey as well as piebald and skewbald can be found

USE: Saddle, harness

FEATURES: Very thick mane and tail to protect from weather; smooth coat in summer, wiry thick double coat growth in winter. Tough feet of hard, blue horn with pasterns that are sloped.

One of the world's most popular ponies and a favourite as a child's first mount, the Shetland pony has lived in the rugged and isolated Shetland and Orkney Islands situated 185 km off the north-east coast of Scotland, for over 2,000 years. The smallest of Britain's native pony breeds, the Shetland lives on windswept islands with no trees, and where the soil is thin and acid, capable of supporting no more than rough grasses and heathers. These, along with mineral-rich seaweed found on the shoreline, form the staple diet of these little, but incredibly strong, ponies.

The most likely origins of the Shetland pony are in Scandinavia before the ice fields melted and left Britain isolated from continental Europe. The ponies left in the northernmost islands would have been tundra-type ponies: the Shetland in fact retains the extra large nasal cavities which allow for cold air to be warmed up sufficiently before it enters the lungs. Later, the Viking invaders brought their ponies and small, light-boned, active ponies can be seen in stone carvings dating from the 9th century on the islands of Burra and Bressay. These ponies, when compared to the human figures on the carvings, do not seem to have exceeded 40 inches (101 cm) in height.

Crofters on the islands have used the Shetland to work their land, and as a pack ponies, carrying seaweed and peat – the only source of fuel on islands with no wood available from trees – and as a means of transport. In 1847, an Act of Parliament prohibited women and children working down coal mines: consequently, Shetland ponies were in great demand as pit ponies and a heavier, coarser pony was developed alongside the existing Shetland. Today, however, the breed is consistent in type: there has been a movement towards breeding 'miniature' Shetlands, which are even smaller than the general breed standard. With all such attempts at miniaturisation there is the possibility that these Shetlands will loose their type.

The popularity of the Shetland has led to its export across the world: Canada, the United States and Europe all have large populations, and each country operates its own stud books. In Argentina, the Shetland was the basis for the tiny Falabella (see page 157), while in North America, the Shetland has been crossed with the Hackney Pony to create the American Shetland, and, with the Appaloosa (see page 194) to produce the Pony of the Americas.

LUNDY PONY

HEIGHT: Average 13.2 hh. (1.38 m)

COLOURS: Cream, golden and dark dun, bright and dark bay, some black

USE: Saddle

FEATURES: Symmetrical quarters; muscled yet elegant neck; neat head and alert expression.

The granite stone Lundy Island is just 31/2 miles long (5.6 km) by 1/2 mile (0.8 km) wide and is situated off the west coast of England where the Bristol Channel meets the Atlantic Ocean. The west side of the island is exposed to ferocious Atlantic gales, but the east side is more sheltered and supports a diverse range of flora and fauna, including the Lundy pony. The first ponies were brought to Lundy by the island's owner, Martin Coles Harman in 1928; these were New Forest ponies, which after surviving the sea voyage, swam ashore to the island from the transport boat. A thoroughbred stallion was also part of the 'experiment' but he and his stock could not survive the rigours of the landscape and the harsh winters on the island. Subsequently, Welsh ponies (see page 168) and Connemara ponies (see page 153) were taken to the island. The Connemara cross proved to be the most successful and is responsible for the distinctive Lundy pony type although in the 1970s, New Forest stallions were once again used to 'experiment'.

Responsibility for the island herd – which now numbers around 20 ponies – is the Lundy Pony Preservation Society. The society is also responsible for the Lundy herd which is bred on mainland England where only Connemara stallions are used in the breeding programme. On the island itself, the present Lundy stallion is the grandson of the Connemara stallion, Rosenharley Peadar.

The use of different stallions has resulted in a the mainland herd differing from the island herd in type and appearance: the island herd's colours are predominantly cream and golden dun, bright and dark bay, but the use of New Forest stallions led to the principal colours of dark dun and bay. The mainland herd retain the dark dun colour as well as bright bay, but some black coats also appear. In both instances though, the compact body and strong loins, overall conformation and robust constitution have made for a pony ideal for riding and with show-jumping potential.

POLO PONY

HEIGHT: 15–15.3 hh (1.52– 1.60 m)

COLOURS: Any

USE: Sport

FEATURES: Hard, strong feet; hard joints and strong back; fearless and quite aggressive; nimble, very fast and with great stamina.

The Polo pony is not a breed in the strict sense of the word but more a fixed type that evolve with the game itself as it spread westwards into Europe from Asia. The game of polo originated in Persia about 2,500 years ago where it was known as Chaugan, which means 'mallet', but its present name is derived from the Tibetan word pulu meaning 'root', from whi the polo ball was made. Moslem invaders from the north-west and Chinese from the north-ea took the game to India where, in the mid-19th century, English tea planters in Assam discovered the game. Silchar, the capital of the Cacher district became the birthplace of the modern polo game, and the oldest polo club (the Silchar Club, founded in 1859). Originally teams had nine riders, but then these were reduced to seven, and later to four as the ponies became bigger and faster.

The ponies on which the English originally played in India were from Manipur state, betweer Assam and Burma, and which stood no taller than 12.2 hh (1.27 m). By the 1870s, though, the ponies were getting bigger and the height limit was set in 1876 at 13.2 hh (1.37 m) in India and 14.2 hh (1.47 m) in England. In 1916, the height ruling was abolished, largely du to pressure from American players (the game was introduced to the USA in 1878) and from then the height increased to the modern 15–15.3 hh (1.52–1.60 m). The modern polo pon is therefore a small horse – although it is always called a pony.

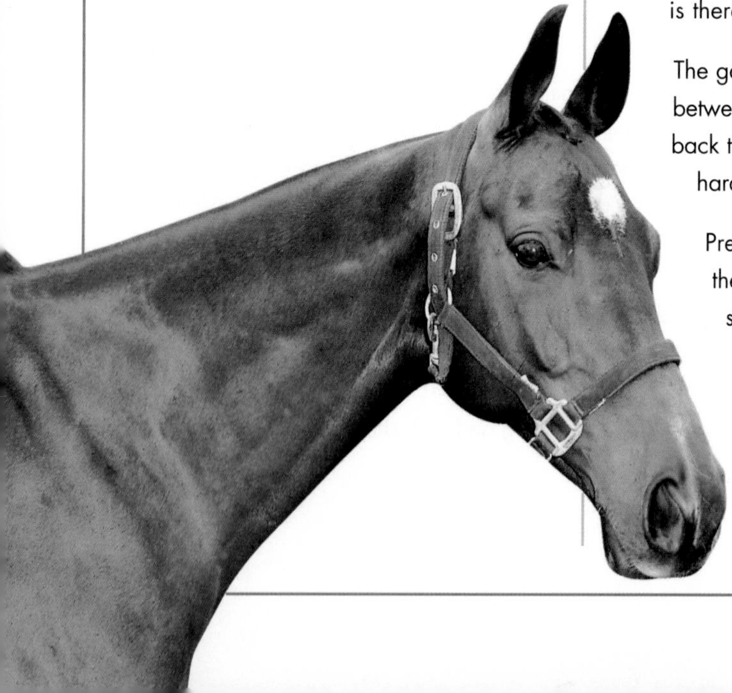

The game is largely dominated by Argentinean ponies, which are the result of crosses between Thoroughbreds and the native Criollo (see page 201) and then putting the progeny back to Thoroughbred. The result is a lean, wiry pony with exceptionally strong limbs and ve hard strong feet – necessary since the game is played at full gallop on very hard ground.

Pre-match preparations for the ponies are meticulous and designed to protect the ponie they involve hogging the mane and plaiting the tail into a neat polo bang so that the stick does not get caught; fitting protective bandage 'boots' onto all four legs, and, extremely careful inspection of the saddlery so that accidents do not occur during play. A draw rein allows the rider to control the pony's head by 'drawing' it inwards while a gag bit raises the head: the degree to which the pony's head ca be raised is governed by a martingale.

BRITISH SPOTTED PONY

HEIGHT: up to 14.2 hh (1.48 m)

COLOURS: Leopard, blanket, snowflake, few spot

USE: Saddle

FEATURES: All British Spotted ponies must display some of the following: white scherla round the eye; mottled skin; striped hooves. Action is low and straight from the shoulder, hocks well flexed with straight action coming well under the body though cob types may display more knee action.

The spotted coat patterns of horses and ponies developed as a form of protective camouflage and are likely to have emerged in prehistoric times. There is very early evidence of spotted horses in the beautiful cave paintings at Lascaux and Pech-Merle in France painted in around 18,000 bc. These are probably the distant relatives of today's spotted breeds. Most spotted breeds share the characteristic of the white sclera round the eyes – similar to that of humans – a mottled skin (particularly evident around the muzzle and genitalia), and distinctive striped feet.

Throughout the centuries, imports of foreign blood into Britain have played their part in shaping the character of native breeds: 2,000 years ago the Roman army brought with them many elegant spotted horses from Spain. Because of their unusual appearance, spotted ponies were highly prized: in a parchment from 1298 listing all the horses purchased for Edward I for use in his campaign at Falkirk, Scotland, a spotted Welsh Cob (see page 168) from Powys, Wales purchased from one Robin Fitzpayne, is the most expensive of all. Later, spotted ponies and horses came to Britain by way of 'diplomatic' gifts between monarchs, and even, in the 20th century, as circus performers.

There are numerous recognised coat patterns of British Spotted Pony,: 'leopard' is spots of any colour on a white or light coloured background; 'blanket' is an area of white over the hips or hindquarters (with or without spots). The base can be any colour and the blanket can extend over the entire back and shoulders. 'Snowflake' consists of white spots on a dark base coat: this colour can appear to be almost roan, but in the British Spotted, there are often varnish marks to distinguish it from 'ordinary' roan. 'Few spot' is distinguished by groupings of dark hairs within an area – usually the nose, cheekbones, stifle, gaskin and knee. In the British Spotted Pony breed standard, piebald and skewbald are not permitted, although solid colours are eligible for entry to a separate breed register so long as they are of proven Spotted breeding and preferably, show some of the other characteristics of the breed mentioned above.

In 1947 the British Spotted Horse and Pony Society was formed to keep a register and to preserve the breed. In 1976, the society split: ponies under 14.2 hh were looked after by the British Spotted Pony Society, while larger ones were entered into the British Appaloosa Society registers. Over the years the British Spotted Pony has regrettably become a rare breed: only 800 or so ponies are currently registered in the society's stud books.

WELSH COB

HEIGHT: No smaller than 14.2 hh (1.48 M)

COLOURS: All solid colours

USE: Saddle, harness

FEATURES: Short muscular legs; high knee action; dished face with large eyes and wide, open nostrils.

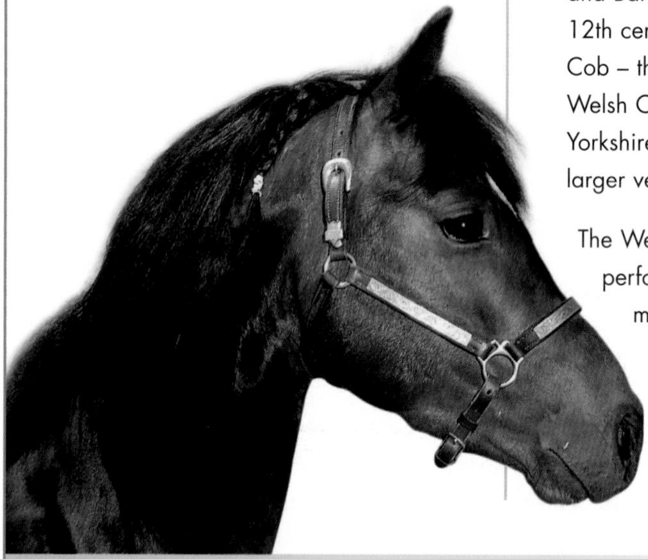

The Welsh Cob is the largest of the Welsh breeds and, uniquely for British ponies, has no upper height limit for showing purposes.

The heartland of the Welsh Cob is Cardiganshire where the breed derived from crosses of Welsh Mountain Ponies with Roman imports and Spanish and Barb-type horses introduced in the 11th and 12th centuries. These resulted in the famous Powys Cob – the mount of the English armies from the 12th century onwards – and the now extinct Welsh Cart Horse. In the 19th century, mixes of Powys Cob stock with Norfolk Roadsters and Yorkshire Coach Horses were also made, but in the end, the Welsh Cob remains essentially a larger version of the Welsh Mountain Pony.

The Welsh Cob is famed for its great powers of endurance, its trotting ability and its performance in harness. In the past it was in great demand as a gun horse and for mounted infantry. A naturally good jumper, the Welsh Cob also makes an excellent hunter, while a Thoroughbred cross – especially a second cross – produces excellent competition horses of size, ability and speed. Before stallion licensing was introduced, breeding stock was selected in the traditional manner in Wales: on the basis of performance over a given distance.

WELSH MOUNTAIN PONY

HEIGHT: 12 hh (1.22 m) max

COLOURS: All except piebald and skewbald

USE: Saddle

FEATURES: Crested neck; tiny, pointed ears; tail high set and carried high; short powerful loin and compact body; exceptionally hard feet of blue horn.

The smallest of Welsh pure breeds, the Welsh Mountain Pony has roamed the mountains and moorlands of Wales for centuries, although over the years, out-crosses have been introduced. Julius Caesar formed an Imperial Roman stud at Bala in Merionethshire and introduced oriental blood to upgrade the stock. In the 19th century there were infusions of Arab blood and from the now extinct Norfolk Roadster (a predecessor of the Hackney, see page 210). The first recorded influence however came from the Thoroughbred Merlin, a direct descendent of the Darley Arabian, who was turned out onto the Ruabon Hills in Clywd in the 18th century: his influence was such that today, such ponies in Wales are still called 'merlins'.

The modern Welsh Mountain Pony, the base from which the Welsh Pony and Welsh Cobbs evolved, is very distinctive in its appearance and is noted for its uniquely powerful action, its intelligence and its hereditary hardiness. The legs are slender and elegant with short cannons and flat, well formed joints and dense bones. The breed should also have what is called a 'bread basket': depth through the girth and a well ribbed middle.

A superb riding pony and exceptional in harness as well, the Welsh Mountain Pony is one of the world's most popular ponies, and, as a foundation in breeding bigger ponies and horses, it passes on its invaluable strengths and qualities.

HEAVY HORSES

More than a century after the invention of the internal combustion engine and two centuries since steam was harnessed as a source of energy, we continue to measure the power of an engine against the horse. This is not surprising when we realise that until the end of the 18th century, the horse was really the only source of motive power available.

Undoubtedly, the first role of the horse was as a pack animal, used to carrying whatever man required to sustain his life. Without such pack horses, local, national and international trade would never have been possible as trading would have been largely confined to coastal regions where ships could safely dock. Pack horses provided the means by which raw materials and manufactured goods produced inland could reach these ships which could then take them across the world.

With the development of the yoke in the Bronze Age (around 5,000 years bc in the Middle East and 2,000 years bc in Europe), a horse could effectively pull more weight than it could carry, and so began the long history of horse-drawn vehicles starting with the chariot and simple carts.

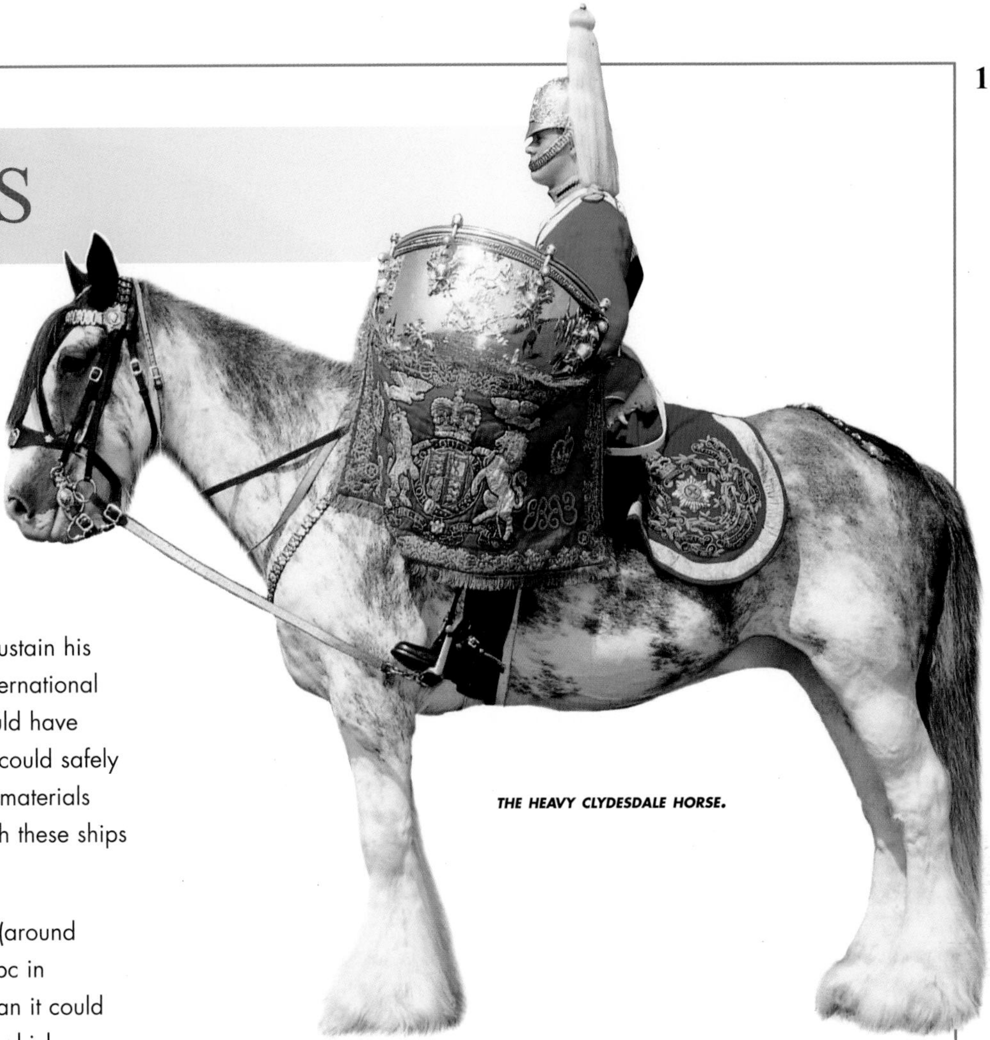

THE HEAVY CLYDESDALE HORSE.

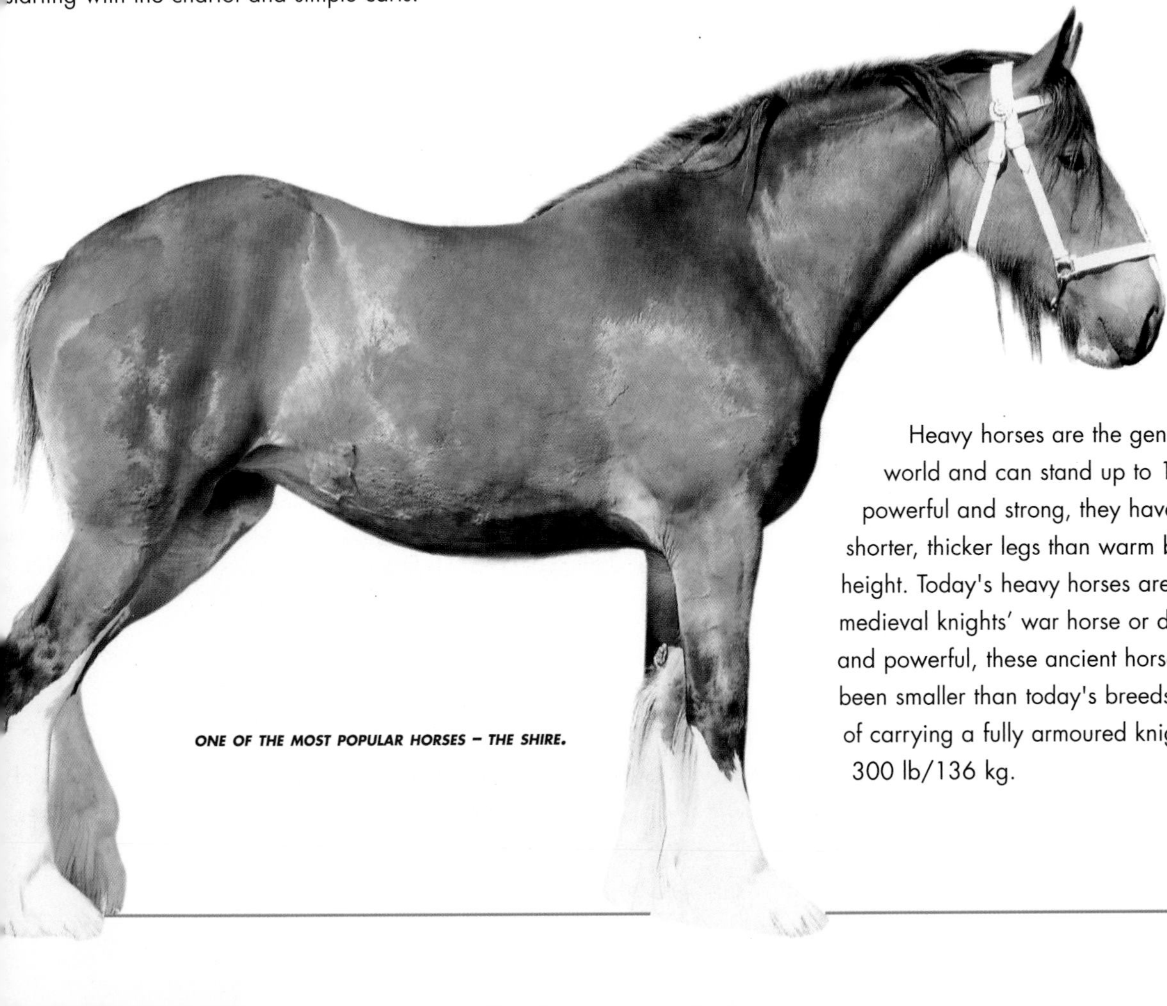

ONE OF THE MOST POPULAR HORSES – THE SHIRE.

Heavy horses are the gentle giants of the equine world and can stand up to 18.2 hh. Immensely powerful and strong, they have deeper chests and shorter, thicker legs than warm bloods of the same height. Today's heavy horses are the descendants of the medieval knights' war horse or destrier. Although large and powerful, these ancient horses would still have been smaller than today's breeds but were capable of carrying a fully armoured knight weighing about 300 lb/136 kg.

A LOVELY CHESTNUT SUFFOLK PUNCH.

Add on the weight of the saddle and the caparison, and the horse still had enough power to provide momentum for the knight's lance which was anything up to 15 ft/4.5 m long.

Since the Middle Ages the destriers' descendants have been bred for their power and size as draught horses. In one way or another, all horses 'work', but a distinction can be made between those horses which are employed for recreational purposes, and those horses which are employed directly in 'industry', in particular, in agriculture. Heavy horses powered the earliest 'mass transit' systems: first, pulling stage coaches up and down the country linking towns and cities together, then, pulling the canal barges, buses and trams. The first railway in Britain opened in 1803 between Croydon and Wandsworth in south London and used horse-drawn carriages; heavy horses continued to be used in railway shunting yards until 1967 when Europe's last shunting horse was retired in Newmarket, Cambridgeshire, England.

The heavy horses also still went to war until World War I but were used as draught horses rather than chargers. Heavy horses pulled the enormous guns into position, hauled supplies and drew ambulances. While many heavy horses continue to work as draught horses, especially those employed by breweries to both pull their dray carts and to advertise their heritage, the military role today of heavy horses is thankfully confined to the purely ceremonial, as regimental drum horses.

The cold bloods, or heavy horses, were part of everyday life on farms and towns all over Europe until quite recently, and indeed, in some parts of northern and eastern Europe, these horses remain essential to effective farming.

The use of heavy horses in agriculture did not occur until the 18th century: only then did the heavy horse supplant teams of oxen in much of the world, and today these continue to provide the main sources of power in Asia and the Far East. But it was the availability of heavy horses that allowed for the development of the sophisticated horse-drawn machinery that encouraged the 'industrialisation' of agriculture from the 18th century onwards until motorisation took over. In the prairies of the United States, the use of horses meant that millions of acres of land could be put to the plough: huge combine harvesters drawn by 40-horse teams controlled by six men were common, while the methods of harnessing were such that one man alone could drive a team of 36 horses to a set of harrows or drills.

A FINE NORIKER STALLION.

SHIRE

HEIGHT: 16–18 hh (1.6– 1.8 m)

COLOURS: Black, bay, brown, grey with white markings

USE: Heavy draught, showing

FEATURES: Average girth of a Shire stallion is 6–8 ft (1.8–2.4 m); short back; powerful loins; legs are clean and muscular with flat bone of 11–12 in (28–30 cm); feet are open and big round the top of coronet; heavy feathers but always straight and silky.

Considered by many as the supreme heavy horse, the Shire takes its name from its traditional breeding ground in the English shire counties of Lincoln, Leicester, Stafford and Derby. The Shire descends from the great medieval war horse, or destrier, (from the Latin word dextrarius, meaning 'right sided' because the knight only mounted his horse just before battle was joined, otherwise it was led from the right, by his squire). This was sometimes called the 'Great Horse', but later became known as the 'English Black Horse' when Oliver Cromwell, Lord Protector of England during the brief period in the 17th century when England was a commonwealth, bestowed the name. Black continues to be the most popular colour of the Shire, but brown, bay and grey, with silky, straight and abundant white feathers, are also to be found.

The main influence on the evolution of the massive Shire – which can weigh between 20 and 22 cwt (2,2240–2,688 lb/1,016– 1,220 kg) – was the Flemish, or Flanders Horse. During the 16th and 17th centuries, large numbers of these were brought to England with Dutch contractors employed to drain the Fenlands in the eastern counties of England in order to increase the amount of available agricultural land, and these Flanders Horses were crossed with native stock. The enormous power of these horses can be seen in the weight-pulling records: in 1924 at the Wembley Exhibition, a pair of Shires pulling against a dynamometer (a device for measuring mechanical power) exceeded the maximum reading and were estimated at pulling equal to a starting load of 50 tonnes. The same pair, driven in tandem on wet granite sets, shifted 18.5 tonnes – with the shaft horse starting the pull before the leader had even got into his collar!

The foundation stallion of the Shire breed is recognised as the Packington Blind Horse, who stood at Ashby-de-la-Zouch, Leicestershire, between 1755 and 1770. He was black and his name appears first in the stud book in 1878 published by the English Cart Horse Society. The name Shire was not used until 1884, however, when the society changed its name to the Shire Horse Society. An indication of their widespread use is born out by the fact that between 1901 and 1914, some 5,000 Shires were registered each year and the breed enjoyed a thriving export market, particularly to the USA. After World War II, there was little need for Shires in either industry or agriculture and their numbers dropped significantly.

Shires were, however, still in employed by many breweries, and their continued existence is largely due to the loyal support of this industry. The Shires can be seen today pulling the brewery drays in many cities and towns where they always turn heads and are real 'traffic stoppers' in their majesty. At the annual Horse of the Year Show in England, the spectacular Drive of the Heavy Horses is one of the most popular events, while the annual Shire Horse Show at Peterborough, Cambridgeshire, attracts an average of 300 entries and over 15,000 spectators. In an age of technology and urban living, hundreds still turn out regularly to country shows to watch and cheer Shires and their handlers in ploughing competitions.

ARDENNAIS

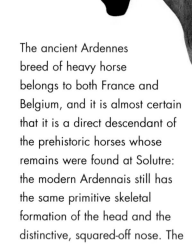

HEIGHT: 15.3 hh (1.57 m) and above

COLOURS: Roan is preferred, accompanied by pale, blonde mane, but also red-roan, grey, dark chestnut, and brown. Light chestnuts and palominos are permitted but black is not.

USE: Heavy draught, also bred for meat

FEATURES: Massive, straight profile head; squared off muzzle; prominent eye sockets; small, pricked ears; broad and unusually short back; unusually for heavy breeds, the withers in line with, or even lower than, the croup; short, very strong legs.

The ancient Ardennes breed of heavy horse belongs to both France and Belgium, and it is almost certain that it is a direct descendant of the prehistoric horses whose remains were found at Solutre: the modern Ardennais still has the same primitive skeletal formation of the head and the distinctive, squared-off nose. The breed was know to the ancient Greek historian Herodotus (c.484-425 bc) who praised them for their hardiness and stamina, and to Julius Caesar. Stocky and compact, with very large bones, the Ardennais was well suited to the Ardennes region, where the severe climate continues to produce excellent horses of medium height ideally suited to farm work.

Before the 19th century, the Ardennais was a less massive horse that was both ridden and used for light draught work. During the French Revolution (1789) and in the Empire years following, they were regarded as the finest artillery horses in Europe. In 1812, during Napoleon's disastrous assault on Moscow, they were the only horses tough enough to withstand the severe Russian winter during the retreat, and were responsible for bringing hom the greater part of the Emperor's wagon train. Descendants of these lighter Ardennes 'Postier or 'post horses' could still be found around Bassigny, in north-east France, until as recently as the 1970s.

The modern Ardennes is the result of 19th century breeding: to increase its speed and stamin crosses were made with Arab (see page 183) blood. Later, crosses were made with Percherc (see page 175), Boulonnais, and Thoroughbred (see page 188). Three types of Ardennes horse emerged: a small, older-type Ardennais of around 15–16 hh (1.52–1.63 m); the bigge and more massive Ardennais du Nord, also known as the Trait du Nord, which resulted from out-crosses with the Brabant or Belgian Heavy Draught Horse, (and which can also be found Belgian as the Belgian Ardennes Horse), and, the Auxois, the larger and most powerful versi of the original Ardennais, found mostly in the Burgundy region in north eastern France.

The Ardennais today is stocky and thick set – more so than any other heavy horse – and has an unusually short back. It has been described as being 'built like a tractor' and as having legs 'like small oak trees'. The feet are surprisingly small, and are lightly feathered and not a thick as many other breeds. The ears are also small and pricked, which is also unusual in a heavy breed. The neck is immensely strong and heavy. Extraordinarily hardy, the Ardennais is also very docile and gentle, to the extent that they can be handled by children. As well as being used for heavy draught work, the Ardennais is also bred for its meat.

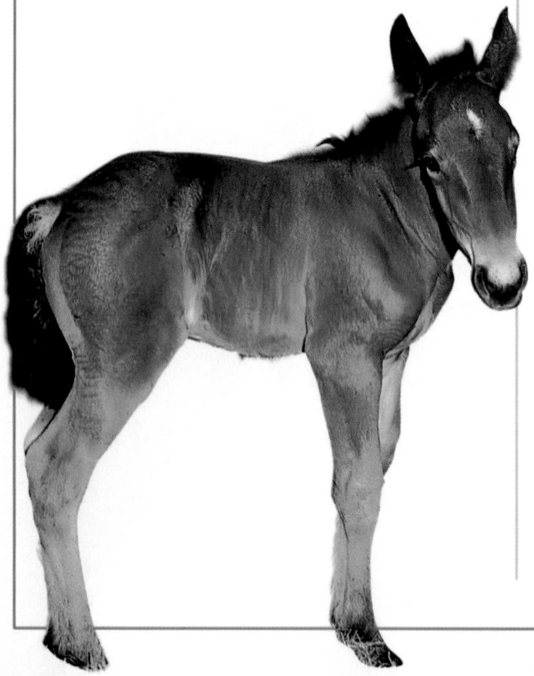

BOULONNAIS

HEIGHT: 16-16.3 hh (1.60-1.67 m)

COLOURS: Usually grey, but bay and chestnuts are also to be found

USE: Draught work

FEATURES: Fine head on short, thick but gracefully arched neck; muscular shoulders and powerful chest; broad, straight back; strong legs; large, solid joints; bushy mane and tail.

A native of north-west France, the Boulonnais, widely held by many to be the 'noblest' of all the draught breeds, is a descendant of the ancient north European heavy horse. These were crossed in the first century bc with horses of eastern origin said to have been from Julius Caesar's Numidian cavalry that invaded Britain in 55-54 bc. Later in the Middle Ages further oriental blood was introduced to the breed during the Crusades.

Crosses with German heavy horses in the 14th century gave greater weight and size to the breed. When the Spanish occupied the Low Countries in the 16th century, Spanish blood was introduced which improved the constitution and action of the horses, and by the 17th century, the breed was established and called the Boulonnais. Two distinct types emerged: the smaller Boulonnais stood between 15.1 and 15.3 hh (1.55-1.57 m) and was known as the mareeur or mareyeur (the 'horse of the tide'). It had an energetic trotting pace which made it ideally suited for the speedy carriage of fish from Boulogne to Paris.

While the smaller 'horse of the tide' no longer exists, the second, heavier type of Boulonnais used for draught work, continues to thrive. The action of the Boulonnais is exceptional in a draught horse: straight, long and swift. The influence of its eastern ancestors is clearly visible in the straight profile of the head, the arched neck, the well-proportioned physique, and the peculiarly bushy tail which is set high in the quarters.

BRETON

HEIGHT: Draught Breton: 16 hh (1.60 m), Breton Postier: 15 hh (1.50 m)

COLOURS: Blue and red roan, chestnut, bay, grey,

USE: Draught work

FEATURES: Square head with straight profile; short, thick arched neck running into short shoulders; broad, strong body; strong quarters; short, very strong and muscular limbs.

Since the Middle Ages, Brittany has been famed for its distinctive types of horse which were derived from a 'hairy' little horse from the Black Mountains in the west of Brittany, possibly a descendent of the Steppe Horse. At one time there were four distinct types, but today, two types of Breton are recognised. The first is the heavy draught horse which is the result of crosses with Boulonnais, Percheron (see page 175) and in the mountain areas, with the massive Ardennes, which produced a stronger and heavier animal. In the mid-19th century, Norfolk Roadster blood was introduced and the result was the second Breton type, the Postier, which was the ideal horse for light draught work. The Postier is a more compact, almost clean legged and lighter version of the Suffolk Punch (see page 178) and its action and constitution is very energetic and extremely sound. In common with the customs of other French draught breeds, the Breton's tail is docked which prevents the reins from becoming caught up under the tail.

Still an immensely popular horse in France, the Breton is exported world-wide both as a working animal and for breeding.

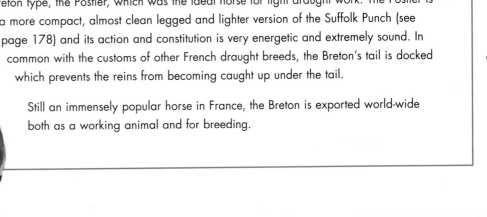

GYPSY VANNER

HEIGHT: 14–15.2 hh (1.43–1.55 m)

COLOURS: Piebald, skewbald, other colours accepted

USE: Draught work, traditionally, hauling gypsy caravans

FEATURES: Long, flowing manes, tails and feathers make horses look as if they are 'flying' when they run.

The relationship between gypsies and their horses is legendary, but the Gypsy Vanner Horse is a 'modern' breed: the registry was created only in 1996 in the United States where Dennis and Cindy Thompson imported the first specimens – two fillies called Bat and Dolly. Gypsy Vanner horses are colourful, compact horses with magnificent flowing manes, tails and feathers. When they run, their hair streams out and it appears as though the horses are flying! On average the horses are between 14 and 15.2 hh and its short neck and back give the horse its power to pull the gypsy caravans.

Developed in eastern Europe over the centuries, the Gypsy Vanner is the result of Friesian (see page 207), Shire (see page 171), Clydesdale (see page 176) and Dales Pony (see page 154) crosses to produce a horse that had plenty of stamina, a calm temperament, and since it was sound and easy to maintain, one that was ideally suited to a travelling lifestyle. Heavy-boned, with flat knees and ample hooves, most Gypsy Vanner Horses are piebald (black and white) or skewbald (brown and white), although the breed society recognises all colours. The mission of the Gypsy Vanner Horse Society is to honour and respect the standards established in the oral tradition of the Gypsy communities in the pursuit of the perfect caravan horse.

COMTOIS

HEIGHT: 14.3-15.3 hh (1.47-1.57 m)

COLOURS: Usually bay or chestnut with a flaxen mane

USE: Light draught work

FEATURES: Square head with a straight profile; small, mobile ears; short muscular neck; moderately well defined withers; straight back; wide, sloping croup; low set tail; deep, wide chest; long, sloping shoulders; slender but strong legs, with a tendency to sickle hocks; ample feathering; solid feet.

The Comtois is an ancient breed of heavy horse form the Franche-Comté region. A medieval war horse, it became renowned as a cavalry and artillery horse, employed by both Louis XIV and Napoleon.

In the 19th century, the Comtois was bred with other draught breeds and since 1905, a much stronger horse with improved legs has been produced using small Ardennais sires. This later influence can also be observed in the free action of the Comtois. Today, the Comtois is bred in the Massif Central, the Pyrenees, and the Alps. Sure-footed, active and very hardy horses, Comtois are still employed for hauling wood or pulling sleighs at ski resorts. The Comtois is also exported to North Africa for agricultural use, and is used for meat production.

A lightly built draught horse, the Comtois can be found in shades of chestnut with a contrasting, light flaxen mane and tail.

NORMAN COB

HEIGHT: 15.3 -16.2 hh (1.60-1.68 m)

COLOURS: Chestnut, bay

USE: Light draught

FEATURES: Powerful and stocky frame without the massiveness of the true heavy breeds. Crested neck; compact body; powerful quarters with tail set high; short legs; medium sized feet.

The Norman Cob is descended from the ancient small Norman and Breton horses known as bidets. The Romans crossed them with their heavy pack mares to produce a strong utility horse, and by the Middle Ages, Norman breeders were famed for their war horses which were ideal as light draught horses. In the 16th and 17th century however, the breed became lighter as a result of out-crosses to Arab and Barb horses. In the 19th century, further crosses with Thoroughbreds, Norfolk Roadsters, and 'half-bred' English 'hunter' stallions led to the development of the Anglo-Norman, which developed into the Selle Français.

At the beginning of the 20th century, a distinction was made between the lighter Norman horses of riding or cavalry type, and the sturdier, heavier horses that could be used as light draught horses. These draught horses retained the energetic paces of their ancestors, in spite of becoming heavier over the years. With docked tails, they were called 'cobs', and were recognised as a breed in their own right.

PERCHERON

HEIGHT: 16–17 hh (1.6–1.7m)

COLOURS: Grey, black

USE: Draught

FEATURES: Feet of hard blue horn, no feathers at heels; straight profile to head with long ears, prominent eyes, and, flat nose with very wide, open nostrils; neck is long and arched.

Owing much to its oriental blood, the elegant Percheron hails from the Le Perche region in Normandy. Only those horses bred in the French Departments of Le Perche (Sarth, Eur et Loire, Loir et Cher, and Orne) are admitted into the Percheron Stud Book, while those bred in other regions have their own stud books.

Percheron ancestors apparently carried the Frankish knights of Charles Martel at the Battle of Poitiers in 732 ad when they defeated the invading Moors. Consequently, the Arab or Barb horses of the enemy influenced the breed, and oriental blood was also imported following the First Crusade.

The Percheron has served as a war horse, as a stage coach horse, as a farm horse and pulled heavy artillery during World War I, and it was also an immensely popular breed overseas: in the 1880s some 5,00 stallions and 2,500 mares were exported to the United States alone, with significant numbers also sent to South Africa and Australia. The percheron has the advantage over many other breeds in that it adapts easily to different climatic conditions, and, it is an excellent base stock for crossing. It is a hardy, even tempered, powerful and versatile horse.

CLYDESDALE

HEIGHT: 16.2–18 hh (1.65– 1.80 m)

COLOURS: Usually bay or brown, but black, grey and roan also appear. Heavy white markings on face and legs, and on underside of body are general.

USE: Heavy draught work, ceremonial

FEATURES: 'Cow hocks' (the hind legs placed close together) are a breed characteristic and hind legs are longer than in many other heavy breeds; straight profile to head; shoulders more sloped and neck proportionately longer than a Shire's.

The Clydesdale is Scotland's only extant heavy horse. It originated in the Clyde Valley in Lanarkshire as a result of crossing local mares with heavier Flemish stallions which were imported at the beginning of the 18th century. The breed was essentially founded between 1715-1720 by the 6th Duke of Hamilton and the breeder John Paterson of Lochlyloch whose interest was in producing strong draught horses suitable for agricultural work and for hauling coal from the newly opened mines in Lanarkshire. Consequently, great emphasis has always been given to breeding individuals with very sound legs and good fee The feet are large, rather flat, but very open with well formed frogs, and are ideally suited tc work on very hard surfaces like city streets. However they are less well suited to ploughing a they can be too large to fit neatly into the furrow! Nevertheless, the Clydesdales worked the prairies of Canada and America and can claim to be the 'breed that built Australia'.

In the 19th century, Shires (see page 171) were also extensively crossed in by notable breeders such as Lawrence Drew, steward to the 11th Duke of Hamilton at Merryton, and David Riddell, who also set up the Select Clydesdale Horse Society in 1883 (in direct opposition to the official Clydesdale Horse Society Stud Book which had been published in 1878). In spite of Shire influence, the Clydesdale has retained its lighter build.

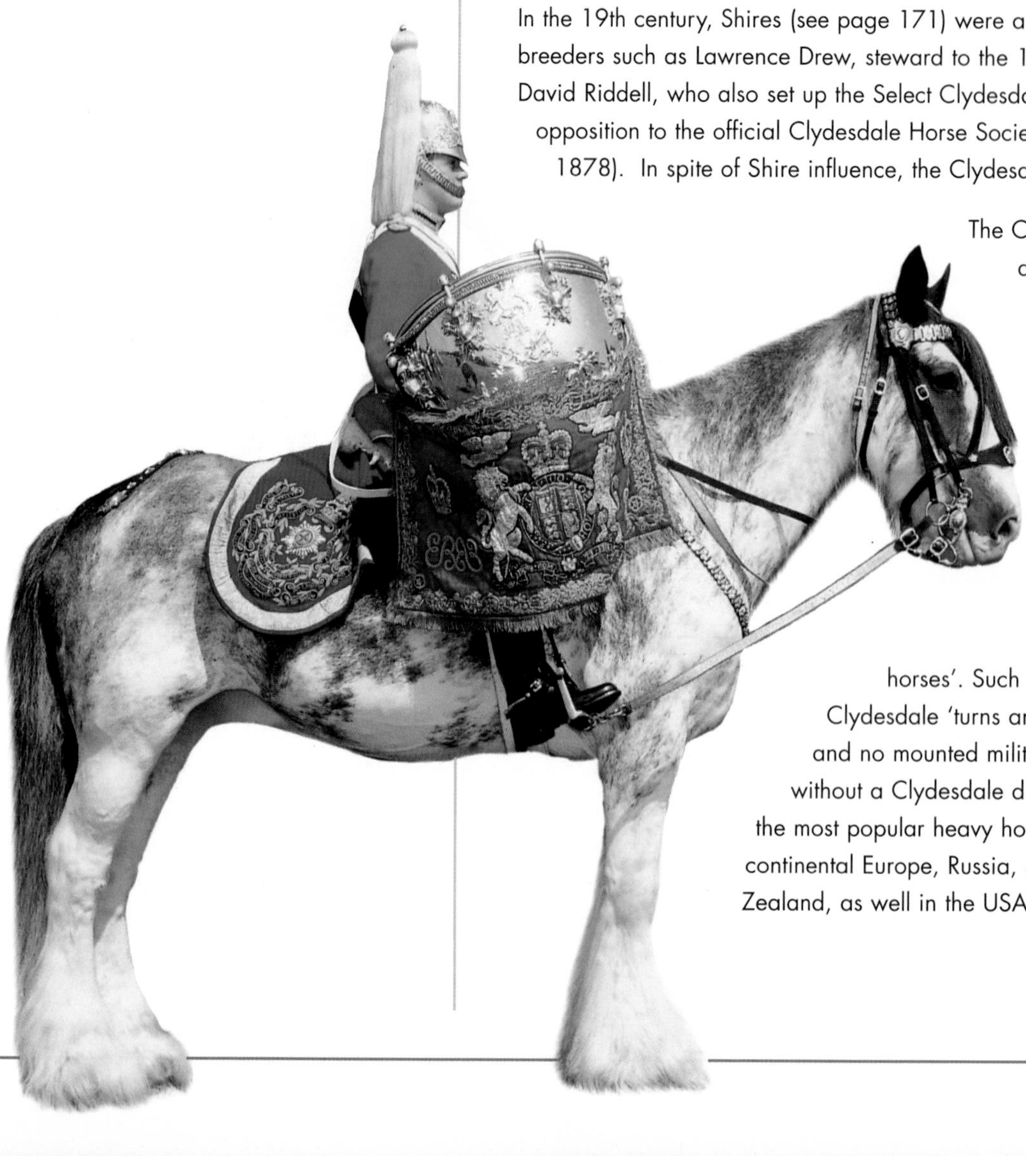

The Clydesdale is now distinctive in both type a appearance: the legs often appear to be lo and carry an abundance of silky feather; the joints are big and the hocks broad, with cow hocks not viewed as a fault but as a characteristic of the breed. T Clydesdale is also famed for its actic described by the Clydesdale Horse Society as 'a flamboyant style, a flashy spirited bearing and a high stepping action that makes him a singularly elegant animal among draugh horses'. Such a delight to watch, it has been said that th Clydesdale 'turns an ordinary beer delivery into a public even and no mounted military parade in Britain would be complete without a Clydesdale drum horse. The Clydesdale is a also one o the most popular heavy horses across the world and can be found in continental Europe, Russia, South Africa, Japan, Australia and New Zealand, as well in the USA and Canada.

NORIKA

HEIGHT: 15–17hh (1.5–1.7 m)

COLOURS: Distinct colour lines recognised include: dapple and brindle coat patterns; black-headed dapple grey; brown; shades of chestnut; Marbach horses have liver-chestnut colour with flaxen mane and tail

USE: Harness, saddle

FEATURES: Hind legs marked by strong second gaskins; great depth at the girth – often exceeds measurement from elbow to ground; heavy squared head tapering to muzzle.

The Noriker takes its name from the ancient kingdom of Noricum which was a vassal state of the Roman Empire. Its borders were about the same as those of modern day Austria, the home of the Noriker. Across the southern borders were the Venetii, who had been established there since 900 bc and were famed for their horse breeding: this would become the native land of the Haflinger (see page 160) and it seems likely that the Noriker owes something to these mountain ponies.

In the mountainous landscape of Austria, the Romans required war horses that could also be used as pack and draught animals.

The Norikers were first bred by the Romans at Juvavum, near Salzburg, but from the Middle Ages onwards, it was the monasteries that were to be the most significant contributors to the formation of the breed, and the finest specimens were to be found in the Gross Glockner area. In 1565 under monastic control, the breed characteristics were regularised and improved and under the Prince-Archbishop of Salzburg, the Salzburg Stud Book was established, new stud farms developed and standards laid down. Later, Spanish, Neapolitan and Burgundian stallions were introduced to improve the breed. This introduction of new blood not only increased the size of the Noriker, but by the 18th century, resulted in the spotted coat pattern that is particularly evident in the horses from the Pinzgau district, called Pinzgauer-Norikers.

In addition to the Pinzgauer, the Salzburg Stud Book recognises four other principal Noriker strains: Kartner (Corinthian), Tiroler (Tyrolean), Steier, and Bavarian – also called the South German Coldblood. At Marbach in Württemberg, is Germany's oldest state-owned stud where the typical strain of Noriker in the traditional liver-chestnut coat colour with flaxen mane and tail is bred. Because of its role in forestry work locally, this Noriker is known as the Black Forest Horse.

All Norikers must meet the strict conformational breed standards and furthermore, are performance tested: stallions are tested before being used at stud, and have to undergo the normal test to prove willingness in harness – the ability to pull a heavy load, to walk 500 meters and to trot 1,000 meters in a given time. Mares, are also subject to testing when they carry their first foals. The resulting breed is a compact, strong, versatile heavy horse suited to working in mountains that is also noted for its gentle and willing temperament.

SUFFOLK PUNCH

HEIGHT: 16–16.3 hh (1.6–1.65 m)

COLOURS: Chestnut

USE: Heavy draught, showing

FEATURES: Longevity; short powerful legs with little feathering; huge, rounded quarters; girth can measure up to 2.03 m (6 ft 8 in); strongly crested neck; broad forehead; ears are relatively small for a heavy horse.

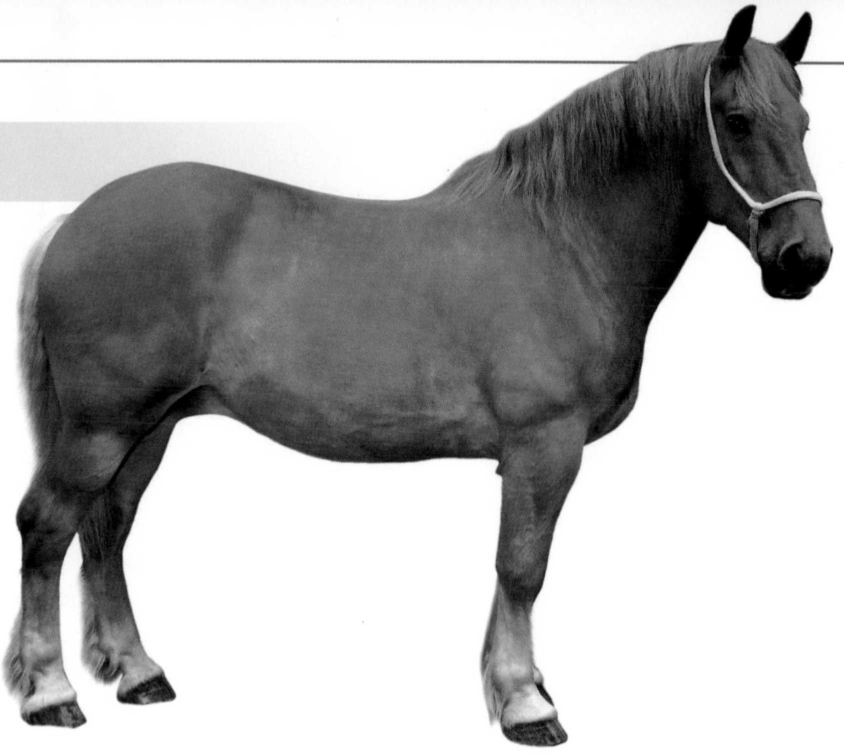

As their name implies, the Suffolk Punch originated in the county of that name, but, for generations they have been regarded as natives of the entire East Anglian region. The Suffol Punch can be traced back to the 16th century: William Camden in his Britannia (published i 1586) refers to the breed as having been in existence since 1505, and, no doubt the trottin Norfolk Roadsters and the heavier Flanders mares imported in the 16th century played a pa in their development: both possessed the same colouring now regarded as characteristic of t Suffolk, and the Flanders Horses were also competent trotters.

The Suffolk Punch is one of the purest of the British heavy breeds: every individual today can trace its descent from one stallion, Thomas Crisp's Horse of Ufford (Orford), stud book numb 404, which was foaled in 1768. This stallion was used in the area around Woodbridge, Saxmundham, and Framlington, where Suffolk Punch breeding is still centred. Crisp's horse was described as large-bodied, short-legged, bright 'chestnut' – spelled then without the 't' – and standing 1.57 m (15.2 hh). All Suffolks today are chestnut, but seven shades are recognised by the Suffolk Horse Society, formed in 1877 by Herman Biddell: these range fro a pale, almost mealy colour, to a dark, almost brown shade, but the most usual shade is the bright reddish chestnut colour.

The Suffolk Punch was developed as a farm horse and is well suited to working the heavy so of East Anglia, for it is both clean-legged and possesses great pulling power and stamina. Th quarters are of great strength, but the hind legs are placed close together to allow the horse walk a 9 inch (23 cm) furrow. The Suffolk also notably thrives on less feed than other heavy horses: typically in East Anglia the horses were fed only once, at 4.30 am and then went to the fields at 6.30 am, where they worked with short rests until 2.30 pm. Other heavy breeds required a mid-morning break and second feed followed by a digestion period.

The success of the Suffolk Punch owes much to careful selective breeding by East Anglian farme and to Biddell's strict rules adopted by the Breed Society for registration and sales: no animal could be shown at any of the leading agricultural shows or sold at the Society's sales without a vet's certification of soundness. At fairs where Punches were offered for sale, they were tested b being hitched to a heavy, fallen tree: the horse did not need to move the tree, but was required get right down on his knees in the typical Suffolk drawing attitude in order to pass the test.

AMERICAN CREAM DRAFT

HEIGHT: 15–16.3 hh (1.52– 1.70 m)

COLOURS: Cream

USE: Draft

FEATURES: Amber eyes, white mane and tail, pink skin

The American Cream Draft horse is the only breed of draft horse to originate in the United States of America. Strictly of draft breeding the American Cream is not to be confused with the American Crème (which is a colour type), Palominos or other 'light' breeds.

Sometime around the beginning of the 20th century, Harry 'Hat' Lakin, from Ellsworth, Hamilton County, Iowa, purchased a cream-coloured mare from a farm sale in nearby Story County, Iowa. This little mare was called 'Old Granny' and she was to become the foundation dam of 98% of all the horses now registered with the American Cream Draft Association. Old Granny's description was also to become the standard by which breeders worked to maintain the breed: a rich, cream colour; white mane and tail, pink skin, and amber-coloured eyes.

Old Granny raised several cream colts on the Lakin farm before being sold to neighbours, the Nelson Brothers. It was Eric Christian, a vet from Jewell who, having noticed one of Old Granny's stallion colts, persuaded the Nelsons to keep him. This stallion was to be called Nelson's Buck No. 2 and is now regarded as the progenitor of the breed: he sired one cream stallion, Yancy No. 3 in 1923, out of a big Percheron (see page 175) mare also owned by the Nelsons.

By 1935, interest in the American Cream Draft was growing and it was due to C.T Rierson, the owner of Ardmore Stock Farm, near Radcliffe, Hardin, Iowa, who had Percherons and Aberdeen Angus cattle, that first thoughts were given to developing this new breed and from then on, accurate records of breeding and subsequent offspring were recorded. Soon other interested breeders were involved: H.L. Bavender and E.E. Reece of New Providence, Iowa; Verner Stromer of Klemme, Iowa; Ray Veldhouse and Gaylord Engle were the founding breeders who set the scene and encouraged new breeders to concentrate their efforts on improving and perfecting the breed they established. In the spring of 1944, at Iowa Falls, Iowa, a group of interested breeders met and formed the American Cream Draft Horse Association; in 1950, the breed was recognised by the Iowa Department of Agriculture.

By carefully selecting and mating the best individuals by line breeding and with the best bloodlines of other draft breeds, the size and quality of these magnificent horses has been improved without loss of their type and characteristics. The ideal American Cream Draft is a rich, medium cream colour, with a white mane and tail and pink skin – which is essential for the cream coat. Some white markings are also highly desirable in the breed, and the beautiful, amber-coloured eyes are also an unusual and distinguishing feature of the breed. Foal are born with nearly white eyes, but they darken soon afterwards. A medium heavy draft horse, the ideal mature size and weight is 15–16 hh and 1,600 lb (for females), and, 16–16.3 hh and 1,800–2,000 lb for stallions.

LIGHT HORSES

AN ANDULUSIAN – GREY

The world's light horses are founded on breeds that are largely 'eastern' in origin: the Arab, the Barb (of North Africa), the Thoroughbred (an Arab derivative) and the Spanish Horse (itself influenced greatly by the Barb). Arabs, Barbs and Thoroughbreds are known as 'hot bloods', a name which reflects the intense 'purity' of their breeding, while other light horses are known as 'warmbloods' and these stand between 15 and 17.2 hh (1.52m–1.75m). Their conformation – a narrow frame, long legs, and sloping shoulders – makes them suitable for riding. Most light horses are fast and agile and many are prized for their qualities of endurance: the so-called 'desert horses' such as the Akhal-Teke (see page 189) are famous for their stamina.

Horse breeds and types originally developed very gradually over time by adapting to both their natural environments and through interrelations with groups of horses sharing the same regional homelands. But when the horse became domesticated, human intervention meant that there was a rapid increase in 'deliberate' breeding to produce specific types and breeds of horses. The practice of gelding male horses meant that breeding could only be carried on from the best stock and this in turn increased the quality and accentuated the characteristics that were most suited to the type of activity in which the horses were engaged. With developments in agricultural techniques and productivity, more nutritious foodstuffs meant that horses became faster, bigger and/or stronger as breeders required.

A POLICE HORSE

From the earliest days of domestication it is likely that horses were used in sport: horse racing, either in harness or under saddle, was well established in ancient Greece and Rome, but many of the modern equestrian sports such as show jumping, dressage, horse trials, and long distance or cross-country riding, in fact have their origins in military practice.

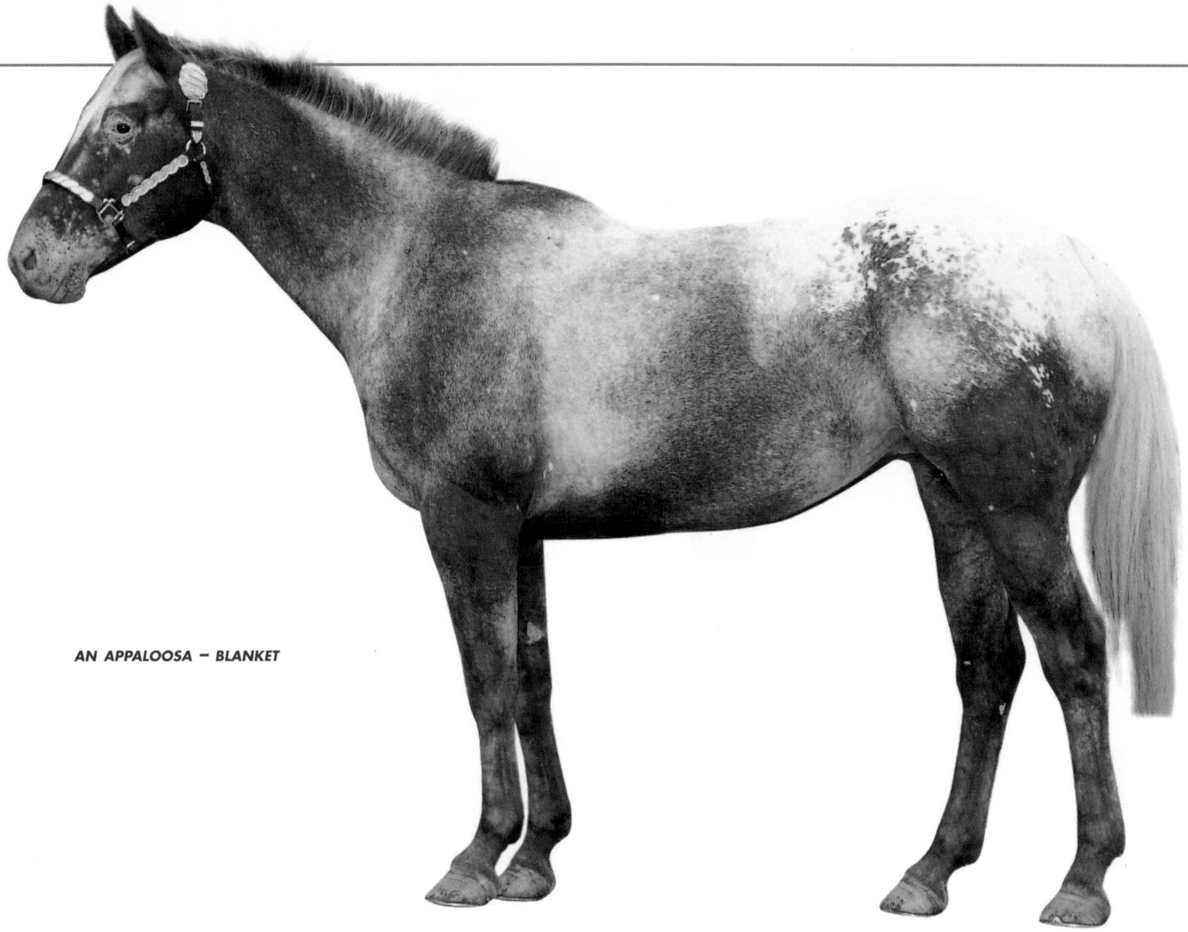

AN APPALOOSA – BLANKET

In the 19th century, the armies of France, Germany, Sweden, and the USA staged 'endurance rides' as part of their cavalry training: rides varied from 30 km (18.5 miles) to a staggering 725 km (350 miles), but no jumping was included: the emphasis was on stamina. The French developed a more comprehensive test, the Championnat du Cheval d'Armes in 1902. A military exercise around Paris, the Championnat comprised a 'dressage' test, a steeplechase, a 50 km (30 mile) race over road and track, and, a jumping competition. This formed the basis for the Three Day Event for military riders, which was included in the Olympic Games in 1912. Post-World War II, civilian riders began to participate, and the sport grew and gained impetus from the establishment in Britain of the Badminton Horse Trials, first staged in 1949.

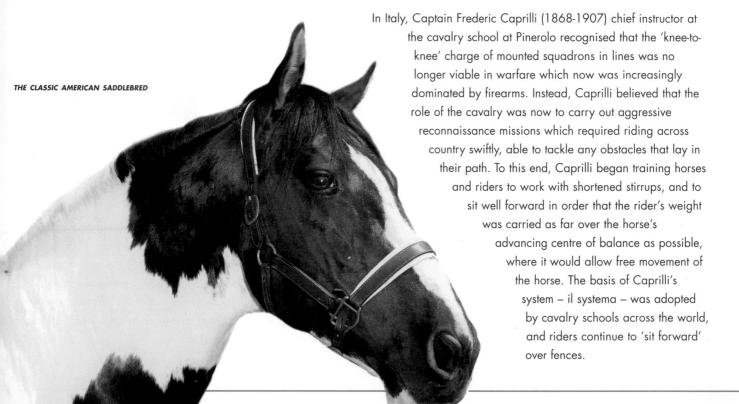

THE CLASSIC AMERICAN SADDLEBRED

In Italy, Captain Frederic Caprilli (1868-1907) chief instructor at the cavalry school at Pinerolo recognised that the 'knee-to-knee' charge of mounted squadrons in lines was no longer viable in warfare which now was increasingly dominated by firearms. Instead, Caprilli believed that the role of the cavalry was now to carry out aggressive reconnaissance missions which required riding across country swiftly, able to tackle any obstacles that lay in their path. To this end, Caprilli began training horses and riders to work with shortened stirrups, and to sit well forward in order that the rider's weight was carried as far over the horse's advancing centre of balance as possible, where it would allow free movement of the horse. The basis of Caprilli's system – il systema – was adopted by cavalry schools across the world, and riders continue to 'sit forward' over fences.

A POLISH ARABIAN

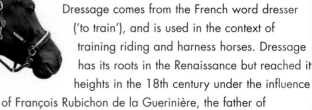

Dressage comes from the French word dresser ('to train'), and is used in the context of training riding and harness horses. Dressage has its roots in the Renaissance but reached it heights in the 18th century under the influence of François Rubichon de la Gueriniére, the father of 'Classical Riding', who published his book École de Cavalerie in 1733 and whose principles are followed today. The cavalry instituted 'best trained charger' tests before dressage became a competitive sport with its first appearance at the Stockholm Olympics in 1912. Competitive dressage includes the very demanding Grand Prix test: advanced movements of passage, piaffe, canter and pirouettes as well as the precise execution of one-time changes at canter. The second leg of the contest, the Grand Prix Special, includes the Kur, the 'equine ballet', a freestyle competition set to music.

Out of a military background, horse riding would eventually develop into a highly sophisticated art form, and today the finest example is perhaps the beautiful Lipizzaner horses of the Spanish Riding School in Vienna (see page 220).

COB

HEIGHT: Ideally, 15 hh (1.52 m); not exceeding 15.1 hh (1.55 m)

COLOURS: All, but many are grey.

USE: Riding

FEATURES: 'Workmanlike' head with an intelligent look; short, strong crested neck; strong, sloped shoulders; short, broad back; well-formed quarters; short powerful limbs; shot cannons, broad open feet.

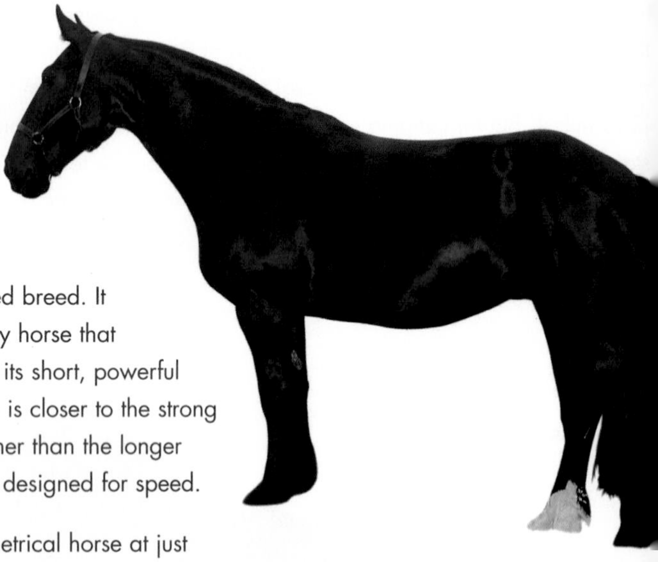

Except for Welsh and Norman Cobs, the cob is a type of horse, not a recognised breed. It is a big-bodied, compact utility horse that stands firmly and squarely on its short, powerful legs. In conformation, the cob is closer to the strong structure of a heavy horse rather than the longer limbed light horses which are designed for speed.

A stocky but completely symmetrical horse at just about 15 hh (1.52 m), the cob is easy to mount and dismount and is expected to give a steady dependable ride. In temperament the cob is endearingly referred to as a 'gentleman's gentleme (a butler) – calm, retiring, but very resourceful!

At one time it was the practice to dock the tails of cobs but this was deemed cruel and unnecessary in 1948 and was made illegal in the UK under the Docking and Nicking Act. Tails are now left full but the mane continues to be hogged, which does suit the neck shape of the cob. In the show ring, classes for cobs are divided into lightweight (capable of carrying up to 8 kg/14 stone with 21 cm/8 1/2 inches of bone), heavyweight (capable of carrying over 89 kg/14 stone and with at least 23 cm/9 inches of bone), and working cobs, which are required to jump. In all classes, cobs must not exceed 15.1 hh (1.55 m).

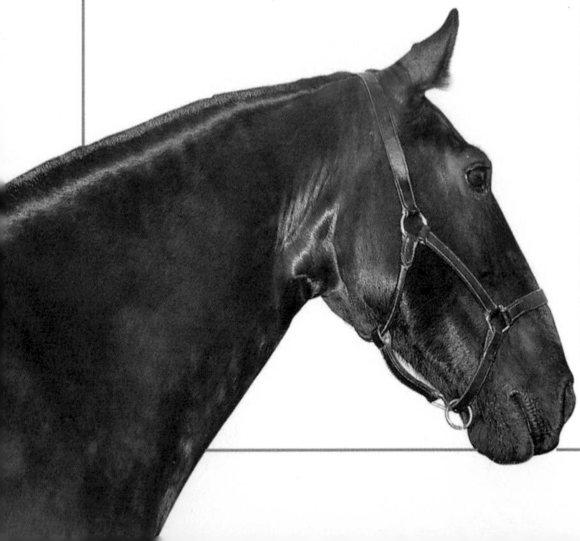

ARAB

HEIGHT: 14.3–15 hh (1.50– 1.52 m)

COLOURS: Grey, chestnut, bay, black

USE: Riding, improving other breeds

FEATURES: Fine silky mane and tail which in movement is carried arched and high; compact body with short, slightly concave back; long level croup; long, slender legs with short canons and clearly defined tendons; head tapers to small muzzle with large, flared nostrils and magnificent, large, expressive eyes.

The debt owed by modern horse breeds to the Arabian, or Arab, cannot be underestimated: the Lipizzaner, the Akhal-Teke, the Thoroughbred, the Orlov Trotter, to name just a few have all been marked by Arab blood. The Arab is recognised as one of the 'fountainheads' of the world's horse breeds and because of its purity, it continues to act as an 'improver' – upgrading and refining other breeds.

It is claimed that the Arab was in existence at the time of the Prophet Muhammad and that it flourished at the courts of the Hashemite Princes in the 7th century. But it is possible that for more than 2,500 years, the Bedouin of Arabia had been breeding these prized horses. The Bedu kept few if any written records, but an oral tradition preserved the horses' pedigrees and maintains that the founding horses were the stallion, Hoshaba, and the mare Baz, who was captured in the Yemen by Bax, the great-great-grandson of Noah.

In ad 786, the historian El Kelbi, wrote the first 'history' and pedigree. Later, in the 19th century, the Emir Abd-el-Kader (1808-83) divided the Arab's history into four eras: from Adam to Ishmael (the outcast son of Abraham and the ancestor of the Bedu tribes); Ishmael to King Solomon (who, in spite of the Israelites' law forbidding keeping horses on the grounds of idolatry, kept 1,200 riding horses and 40,000 chariot horses in the royal stables!); Solomon to the Prophet Muhammad; and from the Prophet onwards. The spread of Islam also ensured the spread of the Arab throughout much of the Old World: it was introduced to Europe by the Moors who invaded Spain in the 7th century, and was instantly desired for its qualities of endurance, courage, gentleness and great beauty. The Emperor Napoleon's horse, Marengo, which was ridden into battle at Waterloo, was a grey Arab.

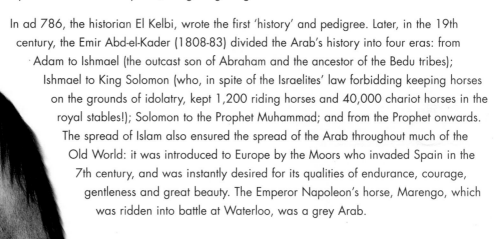

The appearance of the Arab is unique: the most distinctive features are the outline and the head. The outline is governed by the fact that it has a unique skeletal formation: it has 17 ribs, 5 lumbar bones and 16 tail vertebrae where other breeds have an 18–6–18 arrangement. The difference in conformation account for the shape of the Arab's back and quarters and th beautiful high carriage of the tail. The head is very short and fine, with clearly visible veining. In profile it noticeably dished or concave, while the forehead is convex and forms a shield shape bulge between the eyes called the jibbah, which extends from the ears to the nasal bone. A further distinguishing feature is the mitbah, the point where the head joins the neck: the greater the arch here, the greater the degree of mobility in the head in all directions. Additionally, th breed has what has been described as a 'floating action' – as though the horse was moving on invisibl springs! Its stamina is legendary: they can maintain a run for over 100 miles (160 km), and while they can be over 1.52 m (15 hh), on average, t Arab is around 1.50 m (14.3 hh). Regardless of size, the magnificent Arab is always referre to as a horse – never a pony!

POLISH ARABIAN

HEIGHT: 14.3–15 hh (1.50– 1.52 m)

COLOURS: Grey, chestnut, bay, black

USE: Riding, improving other breeds

FEATURES: Arab-type physique

Poland has been a country famous for horse breeding for many centuries, and eastern stallions of all varieties were captured from the Turks during a long series of wars. They undoubtedly had an effect on Polish horses and once a few pure-bred Arabian mares were captured, Arabians were bred pure in Poland. When the Turkish Wars ended at the beginnir of the 18th century, Polish envoys were sent to Asia Minor to purchase stallions from Aleppo, Baghdad and Damascus. In 1845, three pure-bred Arabian mares were imported to the Jarczowce Stud: these three mares were to establish the female line that flourishes today.

Since then, Poland has produced some of the finest Arabian horses in the world, and stallions have been in great demand worldwide: in 1912 the grey stallion Skowronek was exported to Britain where in 1920, he arrived at the Crabbet Stud. His descendants are still prominent in Britain, as well as in South America, Spain, the USA and in the former Soviet Union. In 1926 the Polish Arab Stud Book was introduced under the auspices of the Ministry of Agriculture. Previously, pedigrees had been kept by every stud. Many Polish Arabians have pedigrees that can be traced back for ten generations, and often, many more, extending over periods of 150-200 years. Janow Podlaski, founded in 1817, is now the main Polish stud where both pure-bred Arabs and Anglo-Arabs are produced today.

EGYPTIAN ARABIAN

HEIGHT: 14.3–15 hh (1.50– 1.52 m)

COLOURS: Grey, chestnut, bay, black

USE: Riding, improving other breeds

FEATURES: Fine silky mane and tail which in movement is carried arched and high; compact body with short, slightly concave back; long level croup; long, slender legs with short canons and clearly defined tendons; head tapers to small muzzle with large, flared nostrils and magnificent, large, expressive eyes.

Evidence suggests that the Arab horse was being bred some 2,500 years ago on the Arabian peninsula where it was maintained in its pure form by Bedouin breeders. It was with the Muslim conquests of the 7th century ad that the breed's influence began to spread wider afield: by ad 700, the armies of Islam had conquered and occupied all of modern Turkey, Persia (modern Iran), Palestine, Syria, and North Africa including Libya, Morocco and Northern Egypt. From North Africa, the Moors invaded Spain and so, apart from southern Russia, all the most famous horse-breeding areas in the ancient world were now in their power. The finest stallions and mares were returned to the capital of the Islamic world, Damascus in Syria, where through selective breeding, they were moulded to form the modern Arabians.

The different strains of Arabians in existence today may raise some controversial points, but basically, a strain is a female line descended through the generations from a particular foundation mare owned by a sheikh or a tribe. The dispersion of the Arab began many centuries ago: in 1350 the Rajput Sultan Allah-uh-Din gave 500 Arab horses as gifts on his son's marriage. The Mogul rulers of India, who brought with them the Persian tradition of owning horses of great beauty and size, were among the first to import Arabs sires with the aim of improving Indian breeds. The Egyptian influence is, however, one of the most important and most pervasive: the stud of Ali Pasha Sherif provided the stallions Mahruss II and Mesaoud that were returned to Lady Anne and Sir Wilfred Scawen Blunt's Crabbet stud in England in the late 19th century.

The modern Egyptian Arabs are derived from the herds of Mohammed Ali Pasha and his grandson, Abbas Pasha I, as well as 20 horses from Crabbet which were sent to Lady Blunt's Sheikh Obyed Stud in Egypt. The famous stallion Nazeer passed on his qualities to three sons: Ibn, Halima and Morafic, who went to the United States, while the third son, Aswan, was gifted by President Nasser of Egypt to the Tersk Stud in Russia.

SHAGYA ARABIAN

HEIGHT: 15 hh (1.50 m)

COLOURS: Often grey, but all solid colours can be found.

USE: Riding and harness work.

FEATURES: Arab-type physique, but bigger with more substance and bone than many modern Arabs. Pronounced withers, a more sloping shoulder and notably correct hind legs.

For more than 1,000 years, Hungary has been producing outstanding horses: the climate, and quality vegetation ensured strong animals. Hungarian horses were so highly prized that some 900 years ago, King Laszlo banned further exports from the country to preserve the native stock. Hungary's position at the 'crossroads of Europe' also made it subject to successive invasions and during a century and a half of occupation by the Turkish Ottoman Empire, the horse population was greatly influenced by Arab and Syrian stallions of the Ottoman cavalry.

Two Hungarian breeds are derived from pure Arab: the Shagya Arab and the Gidran Arab. The Gidran Arab originated at Mezohegyes, the first modern stud in Hungary, founded in 1784. This, the oldest of the great Hungarian studs is also famed for the development of the Nonius (page 221) and Furioso breeds (page 208).

The Shagya Arab originated at Babolna, north-western Hungary, a stud founded in 1789, and now the headquarters of pure-bred Arabs in Hungary. The founding sire of the breed was the stallion Shagya, an Arab of the Kehilan/Siglavy strain, who was born in Syria in 1830 and brought to Babolna in 1836 along with seven other stallions and five mares. For an Arab horse, Shagya was large, standing 15.2 1/2 hh (1.58 m) and was said to be a distinctive – and unusual – cream colour. Shagya sired a number of very successful sons who ensured the continuation of the dynasty and his descendants can now be found at stud in Babolna as well as at stud in the Czech Republic, Austria, Poland Germany, Russia and Slovakia.

The Shagya Arab displays all the characteristics of the pure Arab – the good nature, good looks and great intelligence – but rarely stands less than 15 hh (1.52 m), and displays more bone and considerably more substance than pure-breds. The Shagya Arab, once a favourite mount of the Hungarian Hussars, is a very practical horse, used under saddle and in harness.

ANGLO-ARAB

HEIGHT: 16–16.3 hh (1.60–1.67 m)

COLOURS: All solid colours

USE: Riding, racing, competition

FEATURES: A tough, athletic horse with an outline that tends towards the Thoroughbred, with a straight head profile, well sloped shoulders, and prominent withers. The frame is more solid than a Thoroughbred and the croup is longer. Great jumping ability and well suited to dressage.

In England, Anglo-Arab is a cross between a Thoroughbred stallion, the world's greatest racehorse, and an Arab mare – or vice versa – with subsequent re-crossings. There are only two strains in the pedigree and to gain entry into the British stud book, a horse must be able to claim a minimum of 12.5% Arab blood. While the Anglo-Arab originated in Britain, it has also been bred extensively in France. for more than 150 years, where entry into the stud book requires a minimum of 25% Arab blood.

Ideally, the Anglo-Arab should have the Arab's qualities of soundness, endurance and stamina, along with the size and some of the speed of the Thoroughbred – but without the latter's excitable manner. In Britain the popular breeding practice is to use an Arab stallion on a Thoroughbred mare when the offspring are likely to exceed either of the parents in size. (A Thoroughbred stallion on an Arab mare is considered to produce smaller offspring which are less valuable than pure-breds of either breed.)

In France, the principal breeding centres today are the studs at Pau, Pompadour, Tarbes and Gelos. French breeds owes much to the support given by the long established royal – then later, national – studs which were first created by Louis XIV in the 17th century. The systematic breeding of the Anglo-Arab began in 1836 based on two Arab stallions, Massoud and Aslan, and three Thoroughbred mares, Dair, Common Mare, and Selim Mare. A rigorous system of selection based on stamina, performance and conformation was designed into the breeding programme which continues to this day, with the later addition of a racing programme confined to, and designed, to test the breed.

In appearance, the Anglo-Arab tends more towards the Thoroughbred than the Arab: the head is straight (rather than a concave profile), the neck is longer (indicative of greater speeds), the withers are more prominent, and the shoulders more oblique and powerful. The quarters have a tendency to be long and horizontal, but the frame is more 'solid' than a Thoroughbred's. The Anglo's feet are exceptionally sound and strong, and are rarely prone to disease. While the Anglo-Arab may not have the speed of the Thoroughbred, they are very agile and athletic horses: the Anglo-Arabs bred at Pompadour in France are noted not only for their size but also for their excellent jumping abilities.

THOROUGHBRED

HEIGHT: Up to 16.1hh (1.62 m)

COLOURS: All solid colours

USE: Riding, especially racing, cross-breeding

FEATURES: Fine, elegant head on long, arched neck; sloping shoulders and powerful hindquarters; deep chest to allow for maximum lung expansion; large, flat joints, strong legs with plenty of bone.

The Thoroughbred is the fastest and possibly, the most valuable horse in the world, as well as one of the most beautiful: perfectly proportioned and with enormous physical stamina, it is the quintessential racehorse. The Thoroughbred evolved in Britain in the 17th and 18th centuries to satisfy the enthusiasm of the English monarchs – and their subjects – for horse racing. England had long produced 'running horses' like the swift Galloways (the ancestors of the Fell Pony, see page 64), and the Irish Hobby (the forerunner of the Connemara, see page 54). King Henry VIII, the first royal patro of horse racing established the Royal Paddocks at Hampton Court and crossed native 'runnin horses' with horses from Spain and Italy – which were no doubt influenced by the Barb. Later monarchs also continued to maintain a strong interest in 'running horses'. In the 17th and 18 centuries, eastern breeds were introduced – not for their speed, since there was little increase in comparison to the English 'running horses', but in order to breed true to type.

The Thoroughbred has three great founding Arab stallions – none of whom ever raced! The Byerly Turk took part in the Battle of the Boyne in 1690 before standing at stud in County Durham and founding the first of the principle bloodlines which began with Herod (foaled in 1758, the son of Jigg, by the Byerly Turk.)

The Darley Arab, standing at 1.52 m (15 hh) was found at Aleppo in Syria in 1704 and sen to the owner's home in East Yorkshire. He was mated with the mare Betty Leedes and produced the first great racehorse, Flying Childers. His full brother, Bartlett's Childers was the ancestor of Eclipse, who founded the second bloodline and some of the most influential bloodlines of the 20th century stem from him.

The Godolphin Arabian came to England in 1728 to Lord Godolphin's Gog Magog stud in Cambridgeshire and sired the mare Roxanna and produced Lath and Cade, who in turn sire Matchem in 1748 who leads the third line. A fourth bloodline was that of Highflyer, son of Herod. Most – 81% – of Thoroughbred genes are derived from 31 original ancestors, of who the most important are the three founding stallions from whom all modern Thoroughbreds descend in the male line.

The modern Thoroughbred is bred to mature at an early age, with horses raced at two years old. The action is long and low: the hind leg from hip to hock is so long that the hin legs can achieve maximum thrust when galloping while the depth of the girth also allows for maximum lung expansion, both essential features in a racehorse. The clean, clean and very fine head of the Thoroughbred, with a covering of thin skin – thin enough see the veins beneath – has a straight profile unlike its Arab ancestors. The eyes are large and alert, the ears mobile, the nostrils large. The Thoroughbred refinement also extends to the coat which is thin and silky. The principal colour of the breed are brown, bay, chestnut and black. Grey Thoroughbreds are a colour attributed to the 17th century Alcock Arabian and Brownlow's Turk.

AKHAL-TEKE

HEIGHT: 15.2 hh (1.55 m)

COLOURS: Chestnut, Black, Grey, 'Golden-Metallic' Dun

USE: Riding, Endurance, Racing, Competition

FEATURES: Long, thin neck set high and almost vertical to the body; head joins neck at 45 degree angle; line from mouth is often higher than the withers – a feature peculiar to the breed. Coat is exceptionally fine and skin is thin; short, silky tail and sparse forelock and mane. Hard, small feet.

One of the most distinctive and unusual horses in the world, the Akhal-Teke is also one of the oldest breeds and is famous for its stamina and courage. The Akhal-Teke is a descendant of the Tarpan and Horse Type 3: horse skeletons excavated at Anau, near Ashkhabad, the capital city of the Republic of Turkmenistan, in Central Asia, show that 'desert horses' – horses of fine bone and skin – were being bred in this region some 2,500 years ago.

In the later Middle Ages and Renaissance, Akhal-Teke horses were exported to Russia and other European centres where they were used extensively at stud: the Kuban Cossacks were often mounted on Akhal-Tekes. The breed is unique not only for its antiquity, but for the methods of horse breeding traditionally used in the oases of the Central Asian deserts: throughout the year the Turkmeni kept their horses tethered and under blankets, and fed them with a light but highly nutritious mix of food including pellets of mutton fat, barley, eggs and alfalfa as well as quatlame, a fried dough cake. The Akhal-Teke became well suited to the hot environment and is capable of covering great distances in the harshest environments. In 1935, a group of Turkmeni riding Akhal-Teke and Jomud horses rode 4,300 km (2,580 miles) from Ashkhabad to Moscow in 84 days. It became a historic venture, as it included a three day journey with very little water, across 225 miles of the arid Kari-Kum Desert.

Today, the main breeding centre remains the stud at Ashkhabad. The Akhal-Teke is a very distinctive, wiry, horse: by western standards it is not perfect, but this is recognised in the breed description. The body is long and narrow, the rib cage shallow, and often lacks the 'second thigh' prized by western riders. The hind legs are often sickle-shaped and cow-hocked, while the forelegs are usually set 'too close' together. The mane and tail are sparse and fine in texture. A peculiar feature of the breed is for the head to be carried above the level of the rider's hands – a position called 'above the bit', which in the west is a position deemed to reduce the rider's control of the horse.

Nevertheless, the Akhal-Teke is a highly prized horse capable of great speed, of astonishing jumping, and with great qualities of endurance, as well as beauty and grace in movement. The action, like the breed itself, is unique: the Akhal-Teke is described as 'sliding' over the ground in a flowing movement without any swinging of the body. The colours of the fine coat can be chestnut, black, and, grey, but the most striking colour is the dun, which has a gold or silver metallic sheen to it – especially when the horse stands in sunlight.

AMERICAN SADDLEBRED

HEIGHT: 15–16 hh (1.50–1.60 m)

COLOURS: Chestnut, bay, brown, and black. Palominos, greys and roans also appear.

USE: Riding and harness work, pleasure riding

FEATURES: Small, elegant head set high on long, muscular neck; strong back, shoulders, and quarters; except when shown in harness, the feet are grown unnaturally long to enhance action and are shod with heavy shoes. Custom dictates tail is set high by nicking.

A handsome and showy horse with an elevated action, the American Saddlebred was originally known as the Kentucky Saddler, and was developed as an all-round horse for farm work, for riding, and for carriage work, by Kentucky plantation owners in the 19th century. The trotting horses, and the once highly prized ambling and pacing horses, went out of fashion in England in the 17th century when Thoroughbred (see page 188) racing became established, and many of these strains found their way to America where, in a short space o time, they founded the 'American breeds' in which the different gaits were preserved and refined. The American Saddlebred is based on two such gaited breeds: the Canadian Pacer and the Narragansett Pacer (both breeds are now extinct) with the added infusion of Morga (see page 225) and Thoroughbred blood in order to produce this very impressive, speedy a elegant breed.

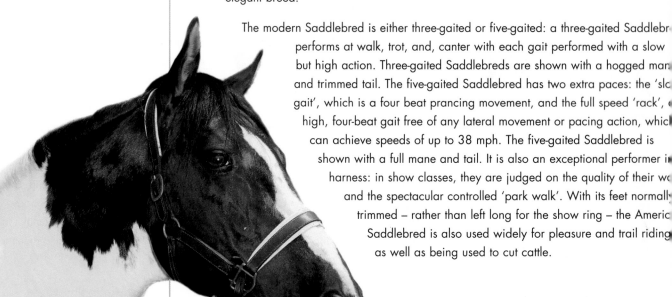

The modern Saddlebred is either three-gaited or five-gaited: a three-gaited Saddlebr performs at walk, trot, and, canter with each gait performed with a slow but high action. Three-gaited Saddlebreds are shown with a hogged man and trimmed tail. The five-gaited Saddlebred has two extra paces: the 'slo gait', which is a four beat prancing movement, and the full speed 'rack', high, four-beat gait free of any lateral movement or pacing action, whic can achieve speeds of up to 38 mph. The five-gaited Saddlebred is shown with a full mane and tail. It is also an exceptional performer i harness: in show classes, they are judged on the quality of their wo and the spectacular controlled 'park walk'. With its feet normally trimmed – rather than left long for the show ring – the Americ Saddlebred is also used widely for pleasure and trail riding as well as being used to cut cattle.

AMERICAN STANDARDBRED

HEIGHT: 15.2-16 hh (1.55-1.60 m)

COLOURS: All solid colours

USE: Racing, driving

FEATURES: A plain head, strong shoulders and perfect relationship to the neck; withers are well defined but may be lower than the croup; longer and lower body than a Thoroughbred, but powerful and deep in the girth; exceptionally powerful quarters; hind legs and hocks must be entirely correct in their construction; sound feet and perfectly straight action are required.

The American Standardbred is undoubtedly the most famous and the fastest trotter in the world and the finest proponent of a style of harness racing which is popular not only in the USA but in Europe, Russia, and Scandinavia. The term Standardbred was first used in 1879 and it refers to the speed standard required for entry into the breed register. Originally the standard was set at three minutes, but later separate harness races were held for conventional, and for diagonal trotters and for pacers employing a lateral gait. The standard was then set at two minutes and 30 seconds for conventional trotters over a mile (1.6 km) and two minutes 25 seconds for pacers over a mile. Today speeds of under two minutes are quite common. The pacer, which is faster and less likely to break the gait, is the preferred horse in the USA, while in Europe, trotters are the more numerous.

The American Standardbred was first established in the eastern states of the USA in the late 18th century. It was founded on an English Thoroughbred called Messenger (a descendent of the Darley Arabian) who was imported from England in 1788. Although Messenger did not race in harness, like all early Thoroughbreds, he had trotting connections via the Norfolk Roadster. Messenger spent 20 years at stud in Pennsylvania, New York and New Jersey, where he was bred to Morgan (see page 195), Canadian and Narragansett Pacers. The foundation sire of the Standardbred was Messenger's inbred descendent, Hambletonian 10, foaled in 1849. He, too, never raced in harness, but he did have a peculiarity of conformation that would contribute to his success as a sire of harness racers. Hambletonian measured 15.3 1⁄4 hh at the croup and 15.1 1⁄4 hh at the withers – a physique that gave enormous propulsive thrust to the quarters. Hambletonian 10 proved himself an equally prolific sire with no fewer than 1,335 offspring between 1851 and 1875.

Standardbred harness racers in the USA compete at over 70 major tracks. Racing is done at the lateral pacing gait with hobbles worn to prevent the gait being broken.

ANDALUCIAN

HEIGHT: 15.2 hh (1.57 m)

COLOURS: Usually bay and shades of grey as well as a very striking mulberry shade

USE: Riding

FEATURES: Hawk-like profile; long, often wavy mane and tail; strong quarters with high degree of articulation makes the breed well suited to the advanced movements of the menage; action described as 'proud' and 'lofty' with a slow, showy, rhythmical walk, a high-stepping trot, and a smooth rocking canter.

In the development of modern horse breeds, the Barb, the Arab and the Spanish horse, play a vital part. The Spanish horse has over the centuries been given a variety of names, most of which derive from the geographical areas in which they were bred: the Andalucian, the Carthusian, the Alter-Real, and the Peninsular. Some maintain that it would be better to know all these 'breeds' simply as the 'Iberian horse', which would then encompass near neighbours such as the Lusitano from Portugal. The Andalucian breed traces back to at least the time of the Moorish occupation of Spain, when Barb horses from North Africa were introduced to the Iberian peninsula. The mingling of Barb blood with native stock – local Sorraira ponies and descendants of the Vandal invasion tribe's tough Germanic horses brought to Spain in ad 40 – was to produce one of the foremost horses of Europe. The Andalucian's 'hawk-like' head owes much to the Barb. In turn, the Andalucian would influence many other European breeds including the Lipizzaner (see page 220), and American breeds such as the Paso Fino and Peruvian Paso (see page 231).

The name Andalucian is also vague: the region encompasses an area in southern Spain around Seville, Cordoba, and Granada, but for centuries, Andalus, in fact meant the whole the southern Spanish peninsula. While many countries still use the appellation Andalucian, since 1912 Spanish breeders have known these horses as Pura Raza Espanol ('Pure Spanish Breed'). The centre for breeding Andalucian horses today remains centred on Cordoba and Seville, and in the Carthusian monastery of Jerez de la Frontera founded in 1476, where for centuries, the monks maintained the purity of the breed by refusing to out-cross with heavy Neapolitan horses in spite of a royal edict which encouraged this practice.

The beautiful and commanding Andalucian has a showy and rhythmical walk, a high-steeping trot, and a smooth, spectacular rocking canter. While not a 'fast' horse, the Andalucian is enormously strong. The innate balance, and agility – coupled with the Andalucian's courageous spirit and spectacular paces – make it well suited to both Haut École and to the bull ring, where it can be seen today. The usual colours of the Andalucian are bay and grey, but there were also strains in the 'old Spanish Horse' that were spotted and parti-coloured: the coat patterns of the American Appaloosa and Pinto are inherited from Spanish horses taken to the New World by the Conquistadors in the 16th century. A most distinctive feature of the Andalucian is the long, luxuriant and frequently wavy mane and tail.

LUSITANO

HEIGHT: 15–16 hh (1.50–1.60 m)

COLOURS: Predominantly grey, bay and the striking mulberry shade also occurring.

USE: Riding and harness work

FEATURES: Head is straight or somewhat convex in profile; small alert ears; widely spaced eyes; short, thick neck; enormously powerful shoulders and quarters; short back and deep chest; long slender legs; full wavy tail and mane; naturally high action.

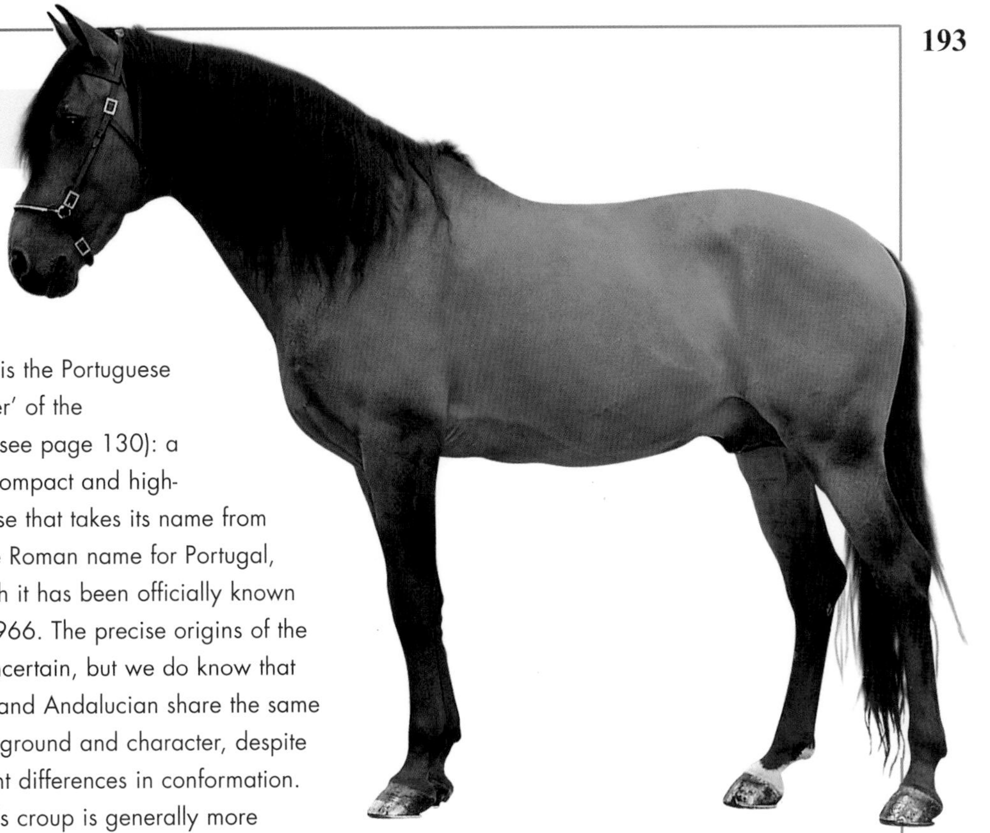

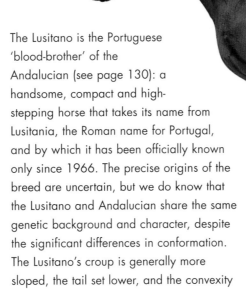

The Lusitano is the Portuguese 'blood-brother' of the Andalucian (see page 130): a handsome, compact and high-stepping horse that takes its name from Lusitania, the Roman name for Portugal, and by which it has been officially known only since 1966. The precise origins of the breed are uncertain, but we do know that the Lusitano and Andalucian share the same genetic background and character, despite the significant differences in conformation. The Lusitano's croup is generally more sloped, the tail set lower, and the convexity in the head is more pronounced, but in both breeds, all shades of bay and grey, as well as the beautiful mulberry shade, are found.

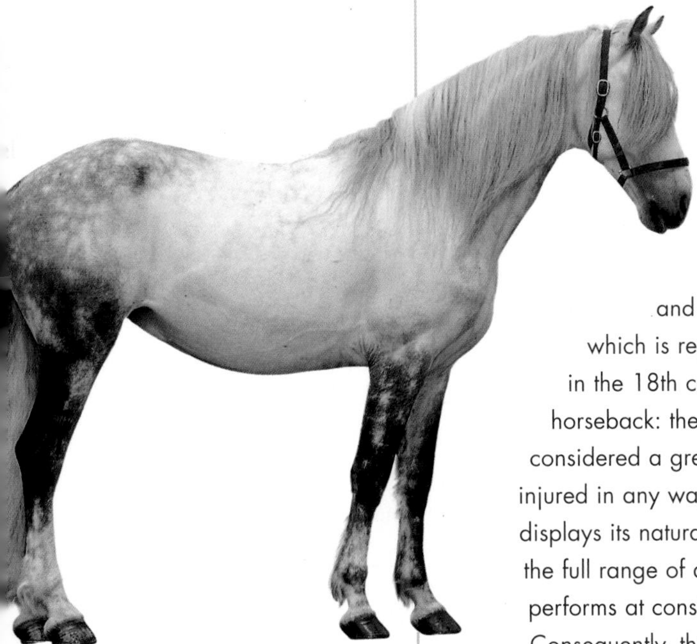

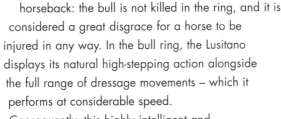

The Lusitano has been bred since the 16th century in Portugal as the 'all-round' work horse: it was used for light agricultural work, as a carriage horse, and, as a cavalry mount. The breeding of Lusitanos is, however, most closely bound to the rearing and fighting of the famous black bulls of Portugal: the agile, intelligent and fearless Lusitano is the favoured mount of the campinos who tend the herds, and of the rejoneadores, the mounted bullfighters. The entire bull fight – which is regarded as an art form in Portugal and the rules of which were laid down in the 18th century by the Marquis de Marialva (1713-99) – is carried out on horseback: the bull is not killed in the ring, and it is considered a great disgrace for a horse to be injured in any way. In the bull ring, the Lusitano displays its natural high-stepping action alongside the full range of dressage movements – which it performs at considerable speed.

Consequently, this highly intelligent and very agile breed is beginning to attract a great deal of attention outside its native Portugal, especially in the USA and the UK.

APPALOOSA

HEIGHT: 14.2–15.2 hh (1.47 –1.57 m)

COLOURS: Spotted – in five basic patterns – usually grey on roan

USE: Riding – including rodeo

FEATURES: Skin on nose, lips and genitals is mottled; sclera (membrane around iris of eye) is white; feet often vertically striped; tail and mane are sparse.

The Appaloosa is an American spotted breed developed by the Nez Perce Indians in the Palouse Valley (Appaloosa is a corruption of Palouse) in north-east Oregon in the 18th century. The Nez Perce excelled at horse breeding and developed animals of such high quality that the merits of their horses were singled out in the journal of Meriwether Lewis, in the Lewis and Clarke expedition to Oregon in 1806.

In October 1877, the Nez Perce were wiped out in a battle with the US Army which lasted for six days, but the legacy of the tribe in the form of the Appaloosa lived on: in 1938 the breed was revived under the auspices of the Appaloosa Horse Club, founded in Moscow, Iowa, and the breed is today one of the most popular in the United States, with ov 65,000 registrations – the third largest breed registry in the world!

Spotted horses have however been around for thousands of years and the Appaloosa's coat the result of a hereditary gene whereby can appear with any other solid body colour, roan being the most common. Spotted horses probably arrived in North America with the Spania in the 16th century, and some of the horses undoubtedly carried the spotting gene and founc their way to the north-eastern states of the USA. Other spotted American horses include the Pony of the Americas, a 'breed' developed from an Appaloosa/Shetland cross, and, the Colorado Ranger Horse (see page 146) based on Arab and Barb foundations.

Unlike the Pinto's broad blotches and randomly shaped forms and shapes which mark its coa (see page 205), the Appaloosa's spots usually assume an organised pattern in which the designs are regular and remarkably precise. There are five basic patterns of spotting in the Appaloosa: leopard, an all-over spotted pattern of dark 'egg-shaped' spots on a white background; snowflake, which consists of light spots on a dark background; blanket, where the coat colour over the hips can be white (white blanket) or when spots occur only on the loins and hindquarters (spotted blanket); marble, which is a mottling all over the body; and, frost, a white speckling on a dark background. The usual ground colour of the Appaloosa is roan; the skin around t nose, lips and genitals is mottled, and the sclera – the membrane around the iris of the eye – is white. Furthermore, the feet are often distinguished by vertical black and white stripes, while the mane and tail are notable sparse and wisp It is said the Nez Perce encouraged this so the hairs didn't g caught up in the thorny shrub they rode through. The moder Appaloosa stands between 14.2–15.2 hh (1.47–1.57 m): while the Nez Perce needed practical, sturdy horses that we suitable for hunting and for defence, today, the Appaloosa is used primarily as a stock and pleasure horse, as well as for racing, jumping, western and long-distance riding.

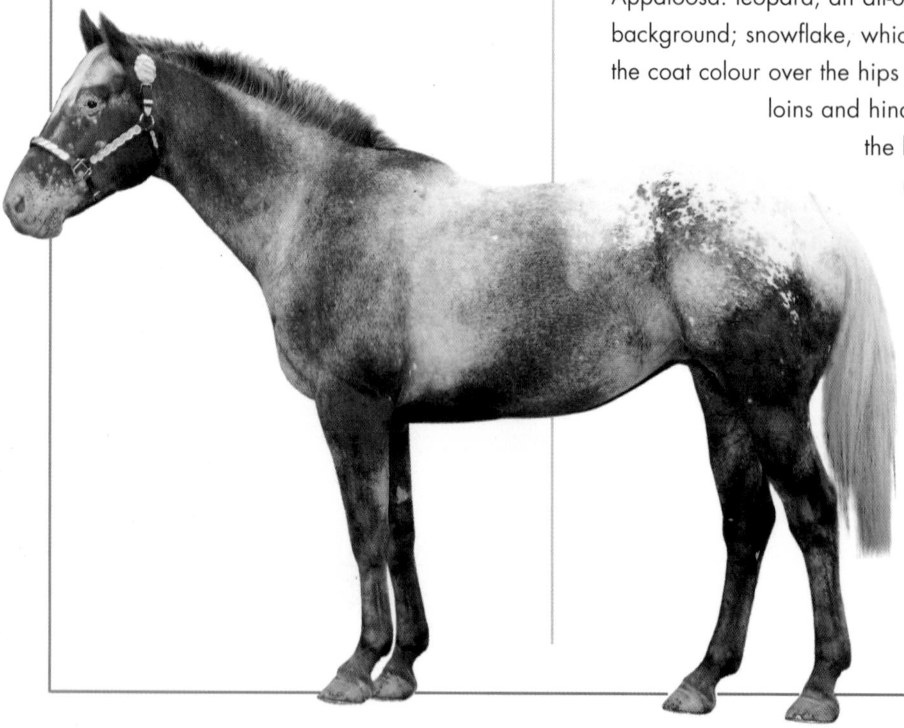

AZTECA

HEIGHT: 14.2–16 hh (1.47–1.60m)

COLOURS: All solid colours, and Tobiano and Overo markings

USE: Riding, trail riding, ranch work

FEATURES: Medium sized head with straight profile (although it can be either slightly convex or concave); broad forehead; slightly arched well-muscled neck; long, sloping shoulders; long flowing tail and mane; knee action can be high and brilliant, or, long and flowing .

The Azteca is often called the 'National Horse of Mexico' and is a recent breed innovation. In 1972, the Charros – the Mexican cowboys – set out to produce a horse with the speed, stamina, agility and 'cow sense' needed to work their ranches. Crossing the Andalucian (see page 192) with their Quarter Horses (see page 233) and Criollo mares (see page 201) they produced an outstandingly versatile and beautiful horse, the Azteca. The Andalucian – the 'Spanish Horse' – gave the new breed its sloping shoulders, sturdy legs and hooves and its stamina, as well as its high stepping action and luxuriant mane and tail. The Andalucian was once the foremost horse of Europe: they were so highly prized that Napoleon stole nearly all of them from Spain during his campaign in the Peninsula War of 1808! Today, the Andalusian, like the Azteca, also works with cattle – but often in the bullrings of Spain. Today, more than three-quarters of all modern breeds – including the Quarter Horse – trace their origins back to the 'Spanish Horse'.

It is from the Quarter Horse that the Azteca gains its strength and speed: the Quarter Horse, developed by the early English colonists in the Virginias and Carolinas, got its name from the three-quarter mile sprints at which it excelled. Azteca breed requirements mean that the Azteca should have no more than three-quarters Andalusian or Quarter Horse blood in the first generations. The aim is for a 'blood balance' between breeds to encourage the best qualities of both. Both Quarter Horses and Paint Horses (see page 229) are used for breeding Aztecas: consequently, all the solid colours of the Quarter Horse, and the Tobiano (a white base overlaid with large patches of solid colour) and Overo (a solid coat colour with irregular patches of white) markings of the Paint Horse are acceptable in the Azteca. They are also distinguished by their long flowing manes and tails, and the varied knee action produces both elevated and suspended gaits, as well as a long and flowing action. This makes the Azteca an ideal horse not only for cow cutting but for haute école as well.

BAVARIAN WARMBLOOD

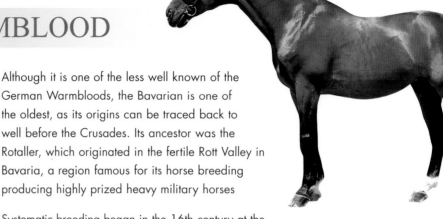

HEIGHT: 15.2–16.2 hh (1.57–1.68 m)

COLOURS: Chestnut, all solid colours

USE: Riding, carriage, light draft

FEATURES: Strong legs; very sound feet; deep girth, steady, reliable temperament; branded with a 'B' in a coat of arms surmounted by a stylised crown.

Although it is one of the less well known of the German Warmbloods, the Bavarian is one of the oldest, as its origins can be traced back to well before the Crusades. Its ancestor was the Rotaller, which originated in the fertile Rott Valley in Bavaria, a region famous for its horse breeding producing highly prized heavy military horses

Systematic breeding began in the 16th century at the monastic studs of Hornbach and Worschweiler in the Zweibrucken region, and in the 18th century the stock was further improved by the introduction of half-bred English stallions, Clevela Bays and Norman Cobs. By the end of the 19th century, Oldenburgers were introduced to give the Rotallers more substance in response to demand for heavily built warmbloods. Thoroughbre blood was also introduced which made the Rotaller a lighter, though still very strongly built hors about 16 hh (1.63m), well-proportioned and with good bone.

In the 1960s, the traditional name of Rotaller was discontinued, and the modern name of Bavarian Warmblood introduced. In spite of the name change, the Bavarian maintains the Rotaller's traditional chestnut colouring. Breeders today concentrate on producing these splendid horses with a quiet temperament: all Bavarians undergo performance testing. As a breed they are well suited to dressage and jumping, but like many other warmbloods, they a not the greatest of gallopers.

BELGIAN WARMBLOOD

HEIGHT: 15.2–16.2 hh **COLOURS:** All solid colours

USE: Riding, jumping

FEATURES: Short, strong neck; deep and wide chest; solid, short limbs with good bones and feet; well rounded body; powerful, sloping quarters; high set tail.

For centuries Belgium has been famous for breeding massive heavy horses such as the Brabant and Ardennes, but more recently, in an effort to meet the demand for competition riding horses, the emphasis has shifted to breeding warmbloods. The Belgian Warmblood is a recent member of the European warmblood family and in a relatively short time, has shown itself to be a breed that excels at competition dressage and show jumping. The Belgian Warmblood, which has an average foal crop of some 4,500 per year is bred all over Belgium, especially in the traditional horse-breeding region of Brabant.

The history of the Belgian Warmblood begins in the 1950s when the lighter and cleaner legged Belgian farm horses were crossed first with Gelderlanders, then later with Holsteiner stallions and the athletic Selle Français – both of which have Thoroughbred backgrounds and are renowned for their straight, rhythmic action. In order to produce the finest possible competition horse, pure Thoroughbred blood was introduced, while to fix the temperament, Anglo-Arab and Dutch Warmblood crosses were added.

The Belgian Warmblood is a powerful, agile and calm horse that is now purpose bred for both dressage and jumping: strong loins, coupled with a short, elevated stride give it a natural advantage.

BUDENNY/BUDYONNY

HEIGHT: Average 16 hh (1.60 m)

COLOURS: All solid colours, but 80% are chestnut.

USE: Originally a cavalry mount, today used in competitive riding: eventing, dressage and long distance events.

FEATURES: Lightly built, but with comparatively heavy body; long straight neck; 'dry' head, veins show through the fine supple skin; the limbs are not the best, but the breed is nevertheless, incredibly tough.

The Budenny, or Budyonny, is one of the breeds developed in the early 20th century in the Soviet Union. The Budenny is named after the Bolshevik cavalry general, Marshal Budenny, a commander in the Russian Civil War (1918-20) and who initiated a breeding programme in the Rostov region on the shores of the Black Sea in the 1920s. This later became the Budenny and First Cavalry Army Studs. The marshall began his programme by crossing selected Don (see page 205) and Chernomor mares with Thoroughbred stallions (see page 188) to produce 'Anglo-Dons' – in essence, a 'Russian Warmblood'. The Chernomor is a Cossack horse very similar to the Don, but smaller, lighter and more active, which was bred originally around Krasnodar, to the north of the Caucasus Mountains.

In a complex crossbreeding programme, the best of the offspring were interbred in order to produce a tough, resilient and strong foundation stock. Special care was taken with the brood mares which were entitled to the finest pastures and winter accommodation. From the beginning of the breeding programme, the young stock aged between two and four years, were performance-tested on the racecourse and in cavalry trials. A total of 657 mares were used to create the fixed type: 359 were Anglo-Dons; 261 were Anglo-Dons crossed with Chernomors, and 37 were Anglo-Chernomors. These mares were mated with Anglo-Don stallions, and subsequently, any mares lacking sufficient Thoroughbred character were put back to Thoroughbred stallions.

Although in 1949, the Budenny breed was officially recognised, in the early days three distinct types were recognised: 'Massive', 'Eastern' and 'Middle'. As demand for an all-purpose competition horse grew, the production of a single type with a greater proportion of Thoroughbred blood was encouraged. The modern Budenny stands on average 16 hh (1.60 m) and the average measurements for a stallion are (ideally): length of barrel: 5 ft 4 in (163 cm), girth: 6 ft 3 in. (190 cm); and bone below the knee: 8 in. (20 cm). This latter measure is described as 'optimistic' since the Budenny's limbs reflect the qualities of the base stock, rather than the Thoroughbred. Nevertheless, the Budenny is a very tough horse. Around 80% are chestnut – often with a beautiful golden sheen which also betrays their Don and Chernomor ancestry. Bay, brown and black horses are also found.

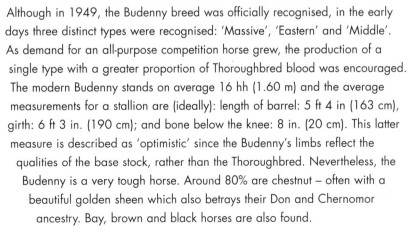

CARMARGUE

HEIGHT: 14–15 hh (1.43 –1.53 m)

COLOURS: Foals are born black, dark grey or brown, lightening to grey or white

USE: Riding

FEATURES: Long, high-stepping walk but short trot; agile and sure-footed; short necks; usually upright shoulders; deep chest; strong and fairly short back; very hard feet which are rarely shod; overall impression is of a 'primitive' horse.

The Camargue area where these horses live is in south-western France, in the Rhône delta between the town of Aigues-Mortes and the sea. This is a harsh region in both landscape and climate: fiercely hot in summer, the rest of the year, the area is covered in cold, salt water through which the icy mistral wind rips. As well as the colour, the most striking thing about the Carmargue horses is that they thrive on a diet of salt water and tough grasses. Although it is only since 1968 that the Camargue has been recognised as a breed, the horses are indigenous to the region and have probably been in existence there since prehistoric times, as these white horses bear a striking resemblance to those painted in the caves at Lascaux and Niaux which date from c.15,000 bc.

Although a large area of the Camargue has been drained and given over to agriculture, manades (herds) still roam free across the lagoon of Étang de Vacares, a 17,000 acre(6,88(hectare) nature reserve where the sight of them galloping through the sea shallows has earne them the nickname of 'the horses of the sea'. They are rounded up annually, branded and selective gelding takes place under the auspices of the Nîmes National Stud. The Camargue horses are also used in their traditional role as the mounts for the guardians, the French cowboys of the south who tend and herd the famous black cattle of the Rhône delta. The guardians use a horsehair lariat and a trident to work their cattle, and employ the deep-seate saddle with a high cantle and caged stirrups that is used throughout the Iberian Peninsula.

The joy of seeing the Camargue horses outweighs the fact that they do not, in fact, have a particularly good conformation: the heads are often coarse and heavy, the necks short, and the shoulders inclined to be upright. But to compensate, they are deep in the girth and have good, strong backs and very tough feet which are seldom shod. The Camargues in short, are incredibly hardy horses with great stamina and an ability to survive on the most meagre of diets.

All foals are born black, dark grey or brown, and lighten as they mature. This can be a slow process: th Camargue does not reach adulthood until it is betwee five and seven years old – but it is exceptionally long lived, often exceeding 25 years. As well as its white coat, the Camargue is also distinguished by its very distinctive action: the walk is long and high-stepping, and it can twist and turn during a gallop. These are th paces at which the Camargue is worked largely because the horse's 'upright' shoulders make for short and stilted trotting action.

CLEVELAND BAY

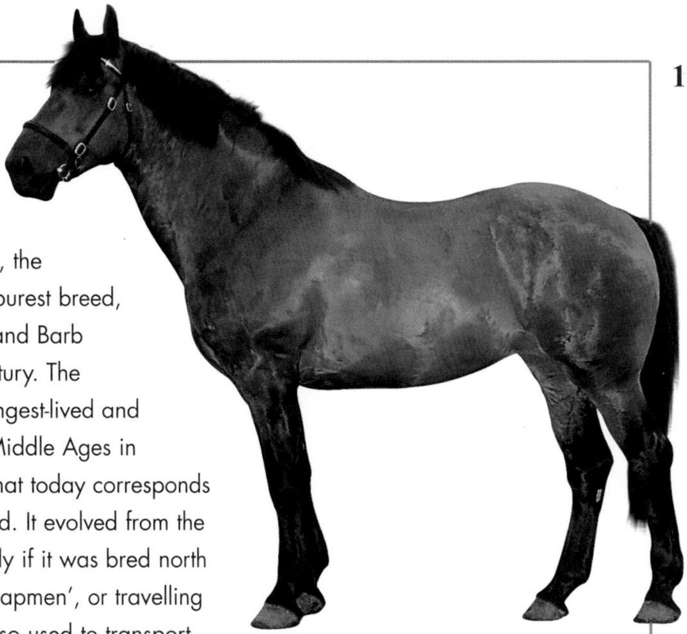

HEIGHT: 16–16.2 hh (1.60–1.65 m)

COLOURS: All are bay with black points

USE: Riding, driving, light draft work

FEATURES: Large convex head; powerful in the neck and shoulders; bone below the knee often 9 in. (22 cm) or more; clean legs, without feathers; open feet with hard, dense horn, large, well-ribbed body; thick black mane and tail.

Apart from Britain's indigenous ponies, the Cleveland Bay is the UK's oldest and purest breed, for it has only a touch of Andalucian and Barb blood that was added in the 17th century. The beautiful Cleveland Bay, one of the longest-lived and most fertile breeds, originated in the Middle Ages in Wapentake of Langbaurgh, an area that today corresponds with north-east Yorkshire and Cleveland. It evolved from the bay-coloured Chapman horse (or Vardy if it was bred north of the River Tees) that was used by 'chapmen', or travelling salesmen. The Chapman horse was also used to transport the region's mining products like ironstone, potash and alum from the hill mines to river or sea ports. The Chapman was, however, a much smaller horse than the modern Cleveland, but even at around 14 hh (1.42 m) it was immensely powerful: the Chapman was known to carry a 100 kg (200 cwt) load over some of the roughest land in Britain.

The proud boast of Cleveland breeders is that their stock has 'No taint of Black nor Blood' – that is, the horse is untouched by either cart horse or Thoroughbred introductions. Two early 'Thoroughbred' sires Jalep (the grandson of the Godolphin Arab) and Manica (a son of the Darley Arabian) do appear in the General Stud Book, but this was long before the Thoroughbred was recognised – and recognisable – in its present form. Of greater influence was the Andalucian (see page 130) and the Barb: in the 16th and 17th centuries there were a great number of these 'Spanish horses' in the north-east of England, and, there was a great deal of traffic between the north-east seaports and the Barbary coast. The marriage of Catherine of Braganza to Charles II in 1661 brought the North African harbour of Tangiers to the British crown and the port constructed there was built by contractors from Yorkshire.

The Cleveland's head still betrays some of the characteristics of the Andalucian – although these are not as evident in the modern breed as they once were in the horses of the Renaissance. The sometimes convex profile – which in earlier times was called 'hawk-like' or 'ram-like' is typical of Spanish stock. After the 18th century, there is no evidence of any infusions of 'foreign' blood and so by then the Cleveland Bay was fixed in type.

Until the reign of George II (r.1727-60) the Cleveland Bay was considered the best and most powerful coach horse in Europe. But new road building technology brought about macadamised roads and the Cleveland was then deemed too slow to maintain the speeds the coaches now required. Consequently it became relegated largely to farm work since it was the only horse that could work the heavy clay in north Yorkshire. The Cleveland went into a steady decline and by 1962, there were only four pure-bred stallions in the country. The breed was saved by H M Queen Elizabeth II, who bought the stallion Mulgrave Supreme and began a breeding programme. In 15 years, there were 36 pure-bred stallions in the UK. The royal Cleveland Bays live in the Royal Mews behind Buckingham Palace in London, and can be seen drawing the royal carriages on ceremonial processions.

There is, however, a shortage of pure-bred mares, and the Cleveland Bay is currently classified as 'critical' by the Rare Breeds Survival Trust.

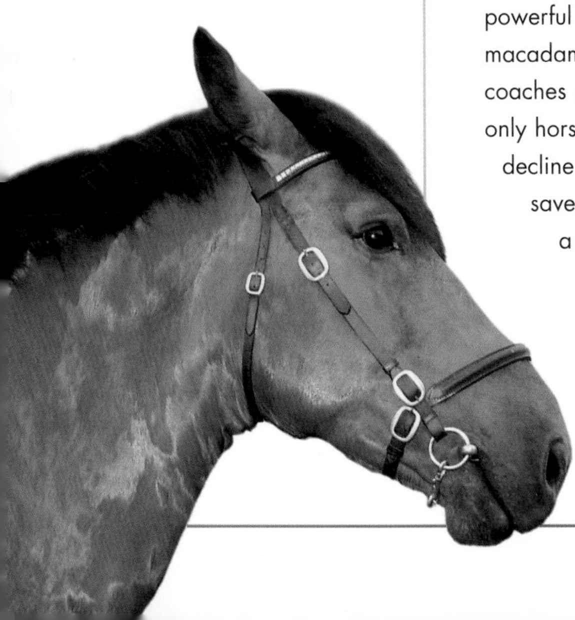

COLORADO RANGER

HEIGHT: Average 15.2 hh (1.55 m)

COLOURS: All Appaloosa colours and patterns (see page 194)

USE: Riding and harness work

FEATURES: Compact with powerful limbs and quarters; small head on strong neck; sound, hard, open feet; spotted coats.

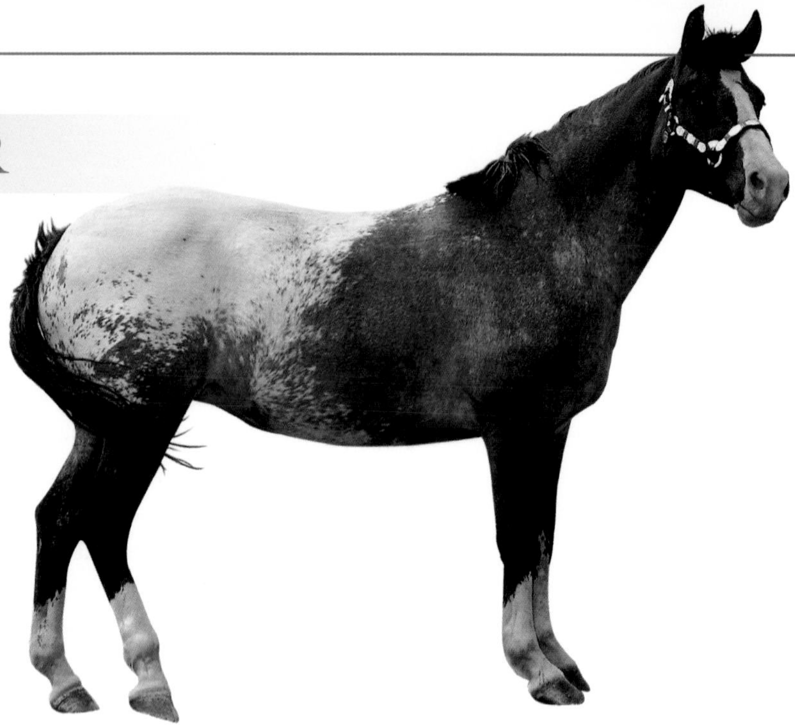

Although the USA has an enormous range of horses and ponies with a wide variety of coat colours, there are only three spotted breeds: the Appaloosa (see page 194), the Pony of the Americas, and the colourful Colorado Ranger Horse. This breed takes its name from the US state in which it was developed, but it did not originate there. In 1878 Ulysses S. Grant was on a visit to Constantinople (now modern Istanbul) to the Sultan Abdul Hamid of Turkey wher he was presented with a gift of two horses: a grey, pure-bred Siglavy-Gidran Arab called Leopard, and a pure blue-grey Barb called Linden Tree. These two horses were taken to Virginia to the stud of Randolph Huntingdon, who proposed using them as the foundation sir for a breed he envisaged as the 'Americo-Arab'.

The two were then 'vacationed' for a season at the Colby Ranch in Nebraska where they sir stock from the native mares, some of which were spotted or coloured, which could have bee inherited from the Barb via the Spanish horses brought to the New World in the 16th century These stunning horses soon attracted attention from Western breeders: A.C Whipple of Kit Carson County, Colorado purchased mares from the Colby ranch, along with a white stallior with black ears called Tony, who was 'double-bred' to Leopard. Consequently, Leopard became the grand sire on both sides of the pedigree and the Whipples continued to extensively line-breed using him and his sons.

But the modern Colorado Ranger breed is essentially the product of Mike Ruby of the Lazy Z Bar Ranch: he bought Patches (son of Tony) and then a Barb called Max who was the son of Waldron Leopard of the original line. Ruby used the two as the foundation sires for the new breed which was now displaying a wide range of unusual colours. In 1934, the breed was named the Colorado Ranger Horse with Ruby as the president of the Association until his death in 1942. The Colorado Rangers were bred as working horses: compact, yet toug and very strong, they have very sound, open feet as a result of hard ground surfaces. All Appaloosa colours and patterns are accepted in the Colorado Ranger: in fact, a Ranger can be registered as an Appaloosa, but an Appaloosa cannot be registered as a Ranger. This is because, entry to the Colorado Ranger Stud Book is governed not by colour (although they must have a patterned coat), but by the possession of the pedigree which must be traceable back to the foundation bloodlines.

CRIOLLO

HEIGHT: 14–15 hh (1.42–1.52 m)

COLOURS: Classically dun with dark dorsal stripe, but roan, chestnut, bay, black, and grey also appear.

USE: Military mounts and pack horses; riding, ranch work, and as a polo pony.

FEATURES: Convex head on elegant, muscular neck; long, sloping shoulders; short limbs with prominent joints and short cannon; strong, compact back and well-muscled loin; well developed second thigh; hard-wearing feet. Some Criollos retain the lateral ambling gait of their Spanish horse ancestry.

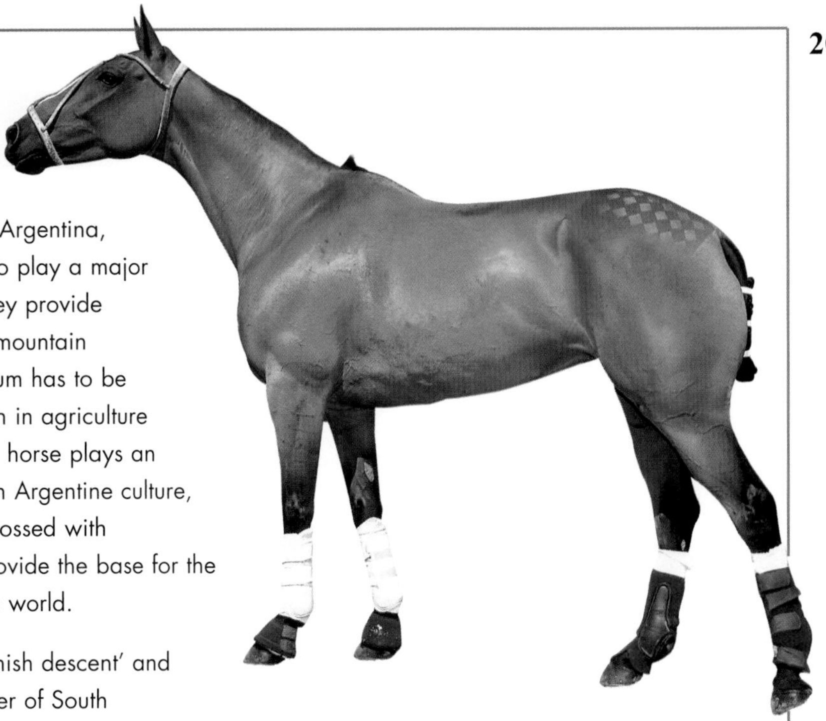

The Criollo comes from Argentina, where horses continue to play a major part in the economy: they provide transport in the remote mountain regions, and as petroleum has to be imported, mechanisation in agriculture has been restricted. The horse plays an equally important role in Argentine culture, for when Criollos are crossed with Thoroughbreds, they provide the base for the finest polo ponies in the world.

'Criollo' means 'of Spanish descent' and the term covers a number of South American horses: in Brazil it is called the Crioulo, in Chile, the Caballo Chileno, in Venezuela it is called the Llnarero, while in Peru, there are three types: the Costerno, the Morochuco, and the Chola. The Argentinean Criollo descends from early Andalucian (see page 130) stock in which Barb blood was pre-eminent. Additionally, there is Sorraia blood. The first significant introduction of horses to Argentina was made in 1535 by Pedro de Mendoza, the founder of Buenos Aires, who brought 100 horses to the Rio de la Plata. Five years later, when the settlement was sacked by the indigenous Charros Indians, the horses escaped and within 50 years had bred so freely that some herds were estimated at 20,000 strong!

Little known outside South America, the Criollo is the mount of the famous gauchos. Tough, sound and capable of carrying the heaviest weights over great distances and the hardest of terrain, the Criollo is well suited to a severe climate, little food and an almost constant shortage of water. Only the hardiest of animals are capable of surviving these conditions. In 1918 a breed society was formed and instituted endurance tests as a means of selection: a 470 mile (756 km) 'march' had to be covered in 15 days with a pack weighing 242 lb (110 kg) – without any extra feed! The most famous 'endurance test' made by Criollo horses was in 1925: Professor Aime Tschiffely travelled with Mancha (aged 15 years) and Gato Cardell (aged 16) from Buenos Aires to Washington D.C: a distance of 10,000 miles (16,090 km) in 2 1/2 years over some of the most inhospitable country in the world, including the Condor Pass at a height of over 18,000 feet in sub-zero temperatures. Gato Cardell lived to be 34, and Mancha, to 37 – and it is claimed that neither had a day's illness in their lives!

The coat colour of the stockily built Criollo is varied: chestnut, bay, black and grey, as well as blue and strawberry roans, skewbald and piebald occur, but dun shades predominate with the most prized colour in the breed being grullo or gateado, a mousey brown-dun shade.

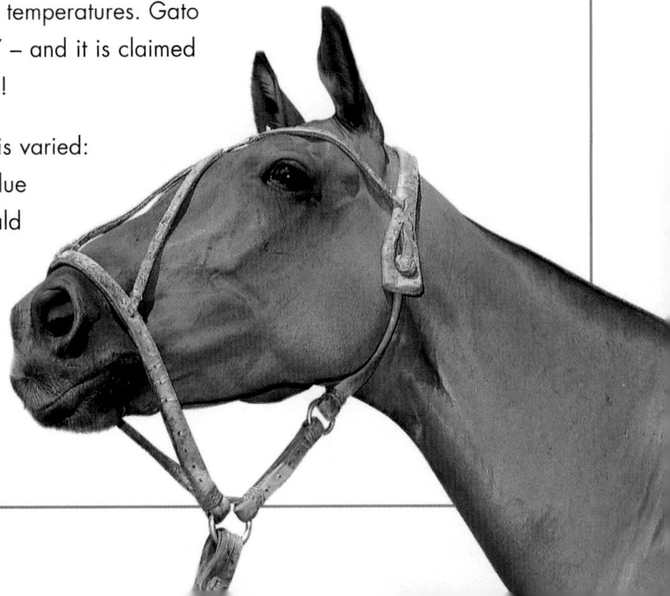

DUTCH WARMBLOOD

HEIGHT: Average 16 hh (1.63 m) and above

COLOURS: All solid colours with bay and brown most common

USE: Riding, competition

FEATURES: Thoroughbred-type head on strong neck and withers; short, strong back; strong shoulders and deep front; strong limbs with short cannons; good feet.

Since the 11th century, horse breeding in Europe was primarily the concern of the agricultur industry and was supported by the great royal and state studs, especially when war horses, cavalry mounts, and coach horses were required. By the end of the 19th century and the ear 20th century, with increased mechanisation in transport, agriculture and warfare, these types of horses had had their heyday. In the 20th century, the emphasis shifted from heavier workir horses to lighter riding horses more suited to sport and recreation.

The Dutch Warmblood is one such horse: first bred in the Netherlands in the early 1900s, it i the product of Holland's two indigenous breeds, the Gelderlander (see page 208), a carriag horse with a strong front, and the heavy, powerfully quartered Groningen. What Dutch breeders did was basically combine the front and back of these two breeds into one, and then adjust the progeny by out-crosses to Thoroughbreds. The result was a more refined horse that still maintained the best qualities of the original Dutch breeds but was improved by the introduction of Thoroughbred blood which also increased their speed, stamina and courage: the carriage horse action and the long, harness back were eliminated, while length was added to the once short, thick neck

Dutch Warmbloods stallions undergo a strict selection process under the auspices of the Warmblood Paardenstamboed Nederland to ensure only horses of excellent conformation, character and temperament are used in breeding. Tests include jumping, cross country trials and occasionally, harness work. More than 14,000 mares are mated each year, and these are als tested for conformation, action and temperament.

DANISH WARMBLOOD

HEIGHT: 16.1–16.2 hh (1.62 –1.68 m)

COLOURS: All solid colours, but bay is most common

USE: Riding, competition

FEATURES: Thoroughbred influence evident in head; clean throat with no fleshiness in the jowls; powerful limbs with good, clean joints; short cannons and good bone below the knee; well placed withers merge with sloping riding shoulders; good quality, even feet.

The Danish Warmblood, formerly known as the Danish Sports Horse, is a recent breed with its Stud Book opened only in the 1960s. Early horse breeding in Denmark occurred at the Cistercian monastery at Holstein where the large German mares were crossed with Spanish stallions to produce horses like the Frederiksborg and the Holsteiner (see page 215).

The basis for the new Danish Warmblood was the old Frederiksborg stock crossed with the Thoroughbred. The half-bred mares were then put to Selle Français to improve conformation and introduce a more athletic character; to Wielkopolski (a Polish warmblood related the Trakehner) which improved stamina and helped to fix the type, and to Thoroughbreds, which gave the Danish horse a further refinement and improved movement, speed and courage. The resulting Danish Warmblood is a handsome horse of Thoroughbred type, but with the substance and strength of its Frederiksborg ancestry.

Standing at an average of 16.2 hh (1.68 m) the modern Danish Warmblood is regarded as one of the finest European-bred competition horses, excelling at dressage and often at cross country events as well. Its limbs are powerful, the joints large and well defined, and there is ample bone to carry the combined weight of both horse and rider.

SWEDISH WARMBLOOD

HEIGHT: 16.2 hh (1.65 m)

COLOURS: All solid colours

USE: Riding, competition

FEATURES: Strong and sound; compact body carried on short, strong legs; good bone and short cannons below large, flat knees.

The Swedish Warmblood – also known as the 'Half-Blood' in deference to the Thoroughbred blood used to refine and develop the breed – was first bred in the 17th century as a cavalry horse at the great studs at Stromsholm.

The Swedish Warmblood is based on a variety of imported horses: from neighbouring Denmark, France, Germany and England, as well as from Russia, Hungary, Spain and Turkey. The result of such a 'cocktail' of influences meant that in the early days, there was no fixed type, but the Spanish and Friesian imports along with the oriental horses, when mated with local mares, produced very strong offspring. Arab, Thoroughbred, Hanoverian, and Trakehner blood was introduced in both the 19th century and again in the 1920s and 1930s and resulted in big and powerful horses that were more fixed in type.

The resulting modern Swedish Warmblood is a strong, sound and very sensible riding horse with an easy temperament and straight paces. With Trakehner ancestry, it is not surprising that the Swedish Warmblood is an excellent dressage horse, as well as being good show jumpers and event horses. They are also highly regarded as driving horses. Before being accepted for breeding, individuals are subjected to rigorous performance and temperament testing to ensure the finest qualities which are embodied in the breed are maintained.

DON

HEIGHT: 15.3–16.2 hh (1.57–1.68 m)

COLOURS: Chestnut and brown, often with a golden sheen

USE: Riding, light agricultural work

FEATURES: Medium head with straight profile; straight neck; short straight shoulders; well developed chest; rounded croup with quarters tending to slope away; hind legs have tendency to be sickle-hocked; forelegs are generally straight, but there is tendency to 'calf knees' – an inward curve below the knee; tail and mane usually short and thin.

One of the best known of the Russian breeds, the Don is the horse of the famous Cossacks: when most of Napoleon's horses died during the harsh winter of the French retreat from Moscow in 1812, the tough Don endured. The breed evolved in the 18th and 19th centuries from the horses reared by the nomadic tribes on the pastures of the Don steppes. Early influences were undoubtedly the Mongolian Nagai, horses of northern Iran, Persian Arabs, the Turkmene, a desert horse closely related to the Akhal-Teke (see page 189), and the Karabakh a horse from the mountains of Azerbaijan. The influence of these last two horses is evident in the golden sheen of the Don's chestnut or brown coat colour. In the 19th century, Dons were improved by the Cossacks using Orlovs (see page 228), Thoroughbreds, and Anglo-Arabs, but from the beginning of the 20th century, the breed has been kept pure and no outside blood has been introduced.

The Don horses are never 'pampered' but instead, fend largely for themselves, in winter, feeding off frozen grass under snow which was cleared by scraping with their hooves. While not the most elegant equine, the Don is nonetheless tough and versatile, able to adapt to a range of climatic conditions with apparent ease. Famous for their endurance, the Don is an all-purpose horse worked under saddle and in harness, and is used by the shepherds of the steppes and in the semi-desert regions of Kazakhstan and Kirghizstan. Many Dons are today also bred in the Budenny (see page 197) and Zimovnikov Studs in the Rostov region of the Black Sea.

In spite of its rather restricted and stilted action caused by the straight, short shoulders, 'calf knees' (an inward curve below the knees), a tendency towards sickle-hocks and upright pasterns, the Don also excels at long distance races! A standard test under saddle is a ride of 275 km (170 miles) – to be covered in under 24 hours.

FLORIDA CRACKER

HEIGHT: 13.5–15.2 hh (1.38 –1.55 m)

COLOURS: Solid colours and greys predominate

USE: Riding, ranch work

FEATURES: Refined head; grey, blue, or dark eyes with white sclera; well-defined, narrow neck without excessive crest; short, strong back, well-sprung rib cage; sloping croup and medium-set tail; natural ability to gait.

The Florida Cracker traces its origins back to the Spanish horses brought to the New World by the Conquistadors in the 16th century. Their mixed ancestry includes North African Barb, Spanish Sorraia and Jennet, and Andalucian blood, which makes the Florida Cracker similar to the Spanish Mustang (see page 241), the Argentine Criollo (see page 201) and the Peruvian Paso and Paso Fino, which are also descendants of the horses introduced by the Spanish to the Caribbean Islands and the Americas. The Cracker was to become a distinct part of this breed family because of its isolation in Florida, where the herds roamed freely. Their natural herding instinct combined with their Spanish ancestry accounts for the Florida Cracker's naturally fast walk. While not all Crackers are considered as 'gaited', most do however perform a gait called the 'Coon Rack'. Other gaits performed by the Cracker include the flatfoot walk, running walk, trot, and ambling or 'Paso-type' gait.

Because of its ability to survive in, and adapt to, its isolated environment, the Florida Cracker became an essential part of the state's cattle-based economy. Florida cowboys were nicknamed 'crackers' because of the sound made by their whips as they cracked in the air. This became the name given to both the cattle they tended, and eventually to the small, very agile horses they rode. The Florida Cracker has also been known as the Chickasaw Pony, Seminole Pony, March Tackie, Grass Gut and Florida Cow Pony.

In the 1930s however, the breed suffered a reversal of fortune: the Great Depression led to a number of government-sponsored relief programmes, and one of these was to encourage moving cattle from the Dust Bowl of the Midwest states to Florida. With these cattle came the screw worm parasite which was to change the practice of cattle raising. Before screw worm, cowboys were able to use the small, fleet footed Crackers to herd and drive cattle. Screw worm-infected cattle required roping so they could be held for veterinary treatment and a larger and stronger horse like the Quarterhorse (see page 233) was needed for this task. As a result, the Cracker went into decline.

The Cracker is now rare (but lucky!) There is an estimated population worldwide of just 2,000 or so horses with fewer than 100 new registrations each year. Nevertheless, the breed has survived, thanks to the efforts of a few dedicated families who kept the distinct bloodlines alive in their herds, and numbers are increasing slowly, but steadily. These families include the Ayers, Harvey, Bronson, Partin, Matchetts and Whaley families. Furthermore, in 1984 John Ayers donated a group of horses to the Florida State Department of Agriculture and Consumer Services to begin the Withlacoochee State Forest Cracker herd. This was followed by the purchase of further Crackers which were released on the Paynes Prairie State Preserve, and the establishment in 1989 of the Florida Cracker Horse Association which united owners and breeders in one organisation. In 1991 the Florida Cracker Horse Registry began registering horses under strict guidelines in order to protect purity of the bloodlines: horses may be registered under the Foundation Series or the Cracker Series (the descendants of the Foundation horses).

FRENCH TROTTER

HEIGHT: Average 16.2 hh (1.65 m)

COLOURS: Black, brown, grey and chestnut

USE: Trotting, both in harness and ridden

FEATURES: Alert head on strong, straight neck; flat withers; strong trotting shoulders that are sufficiently sloped to give a long action; muscular quarters; long, hard legs with short cannons and strong feet.

Taller and more powerful than other trotters, the French Trotter, was developed in the 19th century in Normandy, France. Breeders who had produced tough, all-round foundation horses for breeding both riding and light draft military use, began to specialise in horses of both types. Supported by the Administration of National Studs, the French began importing English Thoroughbreds (see page 188), half-bred or Hunter stallions (see page 212) and th greatest trotting horse in Europe under saddle or in harness, the incomparable Norfolk Roadster. Two of the most important English horses to contribute to the breed were the half-bred Young Ratler – often called the 'French Messenger' because his influence on the French Trotter was comparable to that of Messenger, the foundation sire of the American Standardbred – and the Thoroughbred Heir of the Linne. Ultimately, five important bloodlines were established to which most modern French Trotters can trace back: these lines were Conquerant, Lavater, Normand, Phaeton, and, Fuschia. Later American Standardbred blood was introduced to give the French Trotter more speed but without loosing its larger size and diagonal trotting gait.

The sport of trotting, both in harness and under saddle was stabilised in the 19th century in France: the first trotting races for ridden horses were staged on the Champs de Mars in Paris in 1806 and the first purpose-built racewa was constructed at Cherbourg in 1836. Today, 10% of all French trotting races are for horses under saddle which has encourage a more substantially built horse able to carry a relatively heavy weight that is level in its action. The premier ridden race in France is the Prix de Cornulier; and the harness equivalent is the Prix d'Amerique, both staged at the Hippodrome de Vincennes. This track is considered the supreme test for both saddle and harness trotter: it begins downhill, then levels out until the last 900 m (1,000 yd) of the 1 1⁄4 mile km) track when it turns steeply uphill. In n1989, the qualification time for ent in races for horses of four years old and over was 1 minute 22 seconds over 3⁄5 mile (1 km).

Recognised as a breed in 1922, the French Trotter has also contributed to the development of the Selle Français (see page 239) and is also noted as a sire of jumpers.

FRIESIAN

HEIGHT: Average 15 hh (1.52 m)

COLOURS: Always black, with no white markings

USE: Harness work

FEATURES: Small in stature, it is compact yet strong and muscular; fine head, short legs with some feathering on the heels; hard feet of blue horn; tail and mane is thick and luxuriant and are rarely pulled or plaited.

The Friesian is one of Europe's oldest breeds, and, like the famous Friesian cattle, takes its name from its native Friesland, off the north coast of the Netherlands where a heavy horse is known to have existed as far back as 1,000 bc. The Roman historian Tacitus (ad 55-120) recorded the Friesian's existence and noted its value as an all-round, powerful utility horse. Descended from the primitive Forest Horse, and influential in many breeds, especially in British breeds such as the Fell (see page 158) and Dales (see page 154) ponies, and Shire horses (see page 90), during the Middle Ages, the Friesian carried Friesian and German knights to the Crusades. Today, magnificent black Friesians continue to maintain their qualities of strength, endurance and gentle nature that has been prized for over a thousand years. As a result of contact with eastern horses during the Crusades, and later through crosses with Andalucians (see page 192) and Barbs when the Netherlands became part of the Spanish dominions during the 16th and 17th centuries, the breed was further improved in stamina and movement.

Not surprisingly, the Friesian was in great demand to improve other breeds and to act as foundation stock. The German State Stud at Marbach used Friesians in the 17th century, while the Oldenberger (see page 227) was founded on Friesian stock. Despite its profound influences on British and European breeds, during the early part of the 20th century, the Friesian nearly became extinct. This was largely due to the popularity of trotting horses in the 19th century: the Friesian had a trotting ability but the demand for lighter, faster horses meant that it became less suited to the agricultural work that it had hitherto performed. By 1913 only three Friesian stallions were left in their native Friesland: paradoxically, the breed was to be saved by the Second World War, when fuel shortages encouraged many Dutch farmers to return to horse power. A new breeding programme was started using imported Oldenberger stallions, and the breed was revived. A new society was formed and in 1954 this was given a royal charter.

Today's Friesians are always black: incredibly versatile and willing, they are used for farming, are driven in harness, and are prized as dressage horses. In London a magnificent team of Friesians is still employed by the famous Knightsbridge department store Harrods where they make deliveries and promotional 'excursions' through the London streets. Furthermore, in England the fashion for traditional funerals requiring horse-drawn hearses, sees the Friesian very elegantly attired in black mourning feathers.

FURIOSO

HEIGHT: 15.2–16 hh (1.55–1.63 m)

COLOURS: Black, dark brown and dark bay are most common.

USE: Riding, harness, competition

FEATURES: Thoroughbred-type head although the ears are more prominent; squared muzzle and large nostrils; hind legs are strong and hocks are low; quarters slope down from croup.

The Furioso, also known as the Furioso-North Star Breed, was first bred in Hungary in the 19th century and is one of the many breeds developed at the time when the Austro-Hungarian Empire was a dominant force – both politically and in equine terms – in Europe.

The studs at Mezohegyes, founded in 1785 by the Hapsburg Emperor Joseph II became the centre for breeding first the Nonius (see page 221) and then later, the Furioso, which used Nonius mares as its base. The breed derives its name from two English horses, a Thoroughbred (see page 188) called Furioso, who had been imported to Hungary by Count Karolyi in around 1840, and, North Star, who had Norfolk Roadster ancestry and who arrived in Hungary about three years later.

Furioso produced no fewer than 95 stallions at Mezohegyes, while North Star, sired a great number of harness racers. At first, the Furioso and North Star lines were kept separate, but in 1885 they were inter-crossed, and from then on, the Furioso strain became predominant. Infusions of Thoroughbred blood continued to be introduced to upgrade the breed and the resulting Furioso was a horse of quality that could take part in all equestrian sports.

Hardy and intelligent, the Furioso is bred today across central and eastern Europe. In Hungary, Furioso breeding is centred on the Apajpuszta Stud situated between the rivers Danube and Tisza. Strong and willing, the Furioso, like its relative the Nonius, is not built for speed, but it does excel at harness racing and at steeple chasing, where courage and strength are more prized than velocity.

GELDERLANDER

HEIGHT: 15.2–16.2 hh (1.55–1.65 m)

COLOURS: Solid colours, usually chestnut, sometimes grey, often with white markings on legs and face

USE: Riding, harness, and light draught work

FEATURES: Plain head on long, strong, slightly curved neck; good shoulders set on low, broad withers as appropriate for a harness horse; compact body; strong, long back; strong quarters short, strong legs; energetic action and proud carriage.

The Gelderlander is one of the most popular carriage horses in the Netherlands where it originated in the province of Gelder, and, along with the Groningen, is the chief influence on the make up of the Dutch Warmblood (see page 202).

The Gelderlander was first bred in the 19th century with the aim of producing a first class carriage horse that had both presence and action, and that was capable of light draught work and being ridden. Great emphasis was placed on producing a horse with a very equitable temperament, so local mares were crossed with Cleveland Bays and Norfolk Roadsters; Nonius and Furiosos; East Prussians; Orlov Trotters, and, Arabs. Later, Oldenbergers and East Friesians were introduced into the breed and in 1900, Hackney blood was infused.

The modern Gelderlander is a very impressive carriage horse with an eye-catching rhythmic and lofty action and a tail carried high on strong quarters. While a few have become above-average show jumpers, it is in competition driving that these bright chestnut coloured horses have really excelled.

HACK

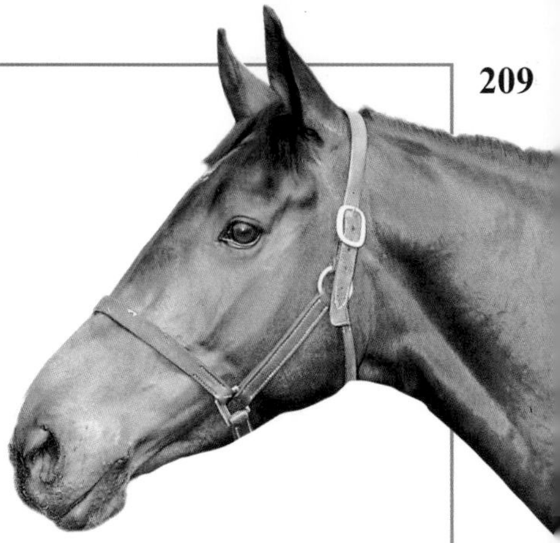

HEIGHT: Between 14.2 and 15.3 hh (1.47–1.60 m) depending on class

COLOURS: Any solid colour

USE: Riding, competition

FEATURES: A neat head, without any concavity, tapering to the muzzle; long, elegant neck running smoothly into prominent withers; sloped shoulders; rounded quarters; long, graceful legs with 20 cm (8 in) of bone expected below the knee; overall shape is that of a Thoroughbred.

The Hack is something of a British phenomenon, although it has been adopted by show ring exhibitors elsewhere in the world. It is also a breed that is easy to define on paper, but in practice, it is more difficult: what 'makes' a Hack is one of the most hotly debated ringside topics. The word Hack (like Hackney, see page 210) comes from the Norman-French word haquenée which was used to describe a horse for general riding purposes – as distinct from a war horse. In the 19th century, two types of Hack were recognised in Britain: the Covert Hack and the Park Hack. The Covert Hack was a good looking and elegant, even 'showy' Thoroughbred riding horse which carried its owner at a smooth 'hack canter' to the meet on hunting days. His Hunter (see page 212) would have been ridden by his groom in advance and was ready waiting at the meet. Since the Hack was not required to carry the rider's weight for the full day's hunt, it was lighter in build than the Hunter: bone, strength and stamina were of less importance than elegance, presence and smoothness of action. Covert Hacks no longer exist in either the hunting field (where motorised transport made them redundant) or in the show ring. The closest equivalent are to be seen in the show classes for riding horses.

The Park Hack was an even more elegant and refined horse on which riders paraded before admiring ladies – and critical gentlemen! In London's Hyde Park, Rotten Row was the place for showing off both one's clothes and the skill and beauty of the Hack: this horse needed to be very well mannered in order that the fashionable beau could strike just the right 'casual' pose by controlling his mount with one hand in a light, single curb bit.

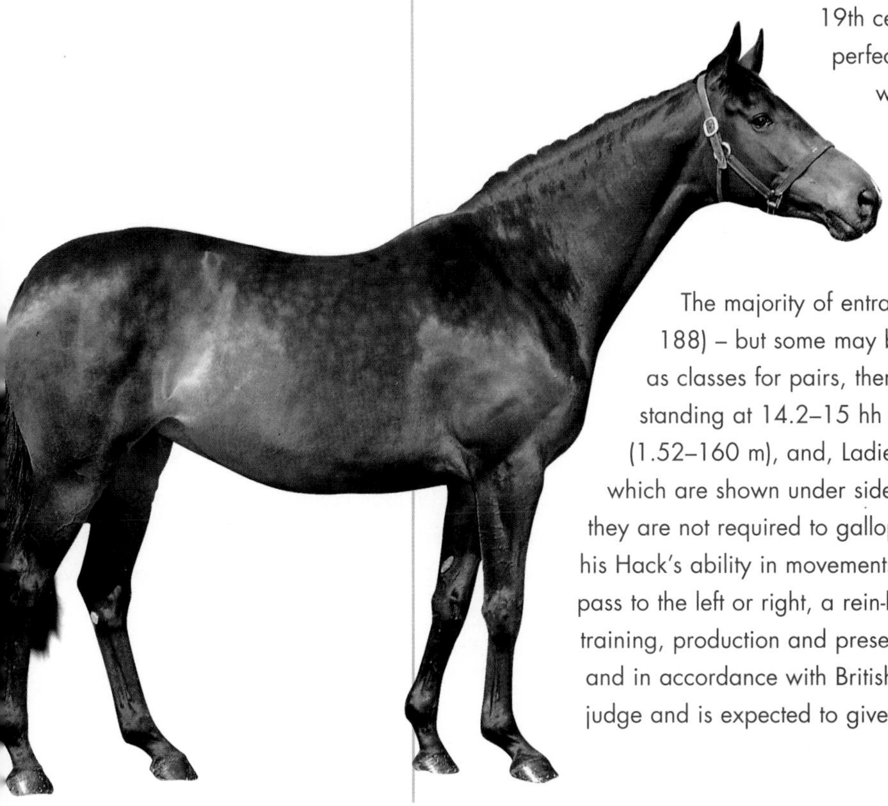

The modern Hack is expected to have all the attributes of the 19th century Hack: lightness, grace and an example of perfect proportions. In action it must be straight and true, with the hind legs consistently 'tracking up' – falling into the imprints left by the forefeet. At the trot, the movement should be low and 'floating', with the toes extended without any 'dishing' or lifting of the knees.

The majority of entrants into Hack classes are Thoroughbreds (see page 188) – but some may be part-Arab or Anglo-Arabs (see page 187). As well as classes for pairs, there are three classes for single Hacks: Small Hacks standing at 14.2–15 hh (1.47–1.52 m); Large Hacks of 15–15.3 hh (1.52–160 m), and, Ladies' Hacks between 14.2–15.3 hh (1.47–1.60 m) which are shown under side-saddle. Hacks are shown at walk, trot and canter – they are not required to gallop – and each rider must give an individual display of his Hack's ability in movements such as simple leg changes, a change of rein, a half pass to the left or right, a rein-back, and a halt with complete immobility. The training, production and presentation of the show Hack is nothing less than an art, and in accordance with British conventions, the Hack is also 'test ridden' by the judge and is expected to give him or her an equally smooth and elegant ride.

HACKNEY HORSE

HEIGHT: Hackney Horse: 14–15.3 hh (1.42–1.60 m) Hackney Pony: up to 14 hh (1.42m)

COLOURS: Bay, brown, black and chestnut

USE: Driving

FEATURES: Head is slightly convex in profile; small, neat ears; fine muzzle; large eyes; long neck rising almost vertically out of shoulders which are exceptionally strong; withers are quite low; compact body, but great depth to chest; feet are allowed to grow longer than usual to give 'snap' to action; fine, silky coat.

The high-stepping Hackney horse – and the related Hackney pony – are perhaps the world's most impressive harness horses. Both horse and pony have their base in the tradition of English trotting horses of the 18th and 19th centuries (although the pony also has Fell influence) The name was chosen as the breed appellation when a Society was formed at Norwich in 1883 in order to compile a stud book for English trotting horses.

The best of the trotting horses – from both Norfolk and Yorkshire – traced their descent from Shales . Born in 1755, he was the son of the Thoroughbred Blaze (the great-grandson of the Darley Arabian, one of the three founding sires of the Thoroughbred and who was also related to Messenger, founder of the American Standardbred harness racer). From the middle of the 19th century, Hackney stallions were in great demand as improvers of native stock in many countries and for producing military and carriage horses. By the end of the century, the popularity of horse shows led to a demand for stylish, high-stepping carriage horses, and in this role, with its lofty gait, the Hackney was supreme. With the advent of motor transport, demand for the Hackney went into decline.

Today, the original regional variations are gone, but the finest qualities of the trotting horses are combined in the modern Hackney which has both Arab and Thoroughbred blood. It is mostly seen in the show ring – where its extravagant and elevated trot is ideally suited.

While the Hackney horse shares the same common ancestry and indeed, the same stud book as its 'cousin', the Hackney pony, the latter is a real pony, not exceeding 14 hh (1.42 m), not just a small horse. The Hackney pony was essentially created by Christopher Wilson of Cumbria, who, in the 1880s, had created a distinct type based on trotting lines crossed with Fell Ponies (see page 64). The 'Wilson Ponies', as they were called, were restricted to their required height by being wintered on the fells where they were left to fend for themselves – a practice which also ensured a very hardy constitution.

HANOVERIAN

HEIGHT: 15.3– 16.2 (1.60–1.68 m)

COLOURS: All solid colours

USE: Riding, competition

FEATURES: Light, medium sized head; long neck running into big, sloping shoulders with pronounced withers; broad, powerful loins; muscular quarters with a flattening at the croup; powerful, symmetrical limbs with well-pronounced joints with good bone length below the knee on forelimbs.

One of the most successful European warmbloods, the Hanoverian has a worldwide reputation as an excellent show jumper and dressage horse. The breed traces its origins back to the 17th century when Spanish, oriental and Neapolitan stallions were imported into Germany and crossed with local mares to create the Holsteiner (see page 215). In 1714, George, Elector of Hanover became George I of England. He exported early 'Thoroughbreds' from England to upgrade the German stocks.

In 1735, George II founded the Stallion Depot at Celle where the aim was to create a core stock of strong stallions that when mated with local mares, would produce an all-purpose agricultural horse. The breeding programme started by using 14 powerful coach horses, the black Holsteiners. The Thoroughbred was introduced to produce a lighter, better quality horse that could be used in harness or as a cavalry remount, as well as for agricultural work. From the outset, all the horses at Celle were registered, and branded with the distinctive stylised letter 'H', and by the end of the 18th century, detailed pedigrees were being kept.

During the Napoleonic Wars, the stock at Celle was depleted. When the stud reopened in 1816, there were only 30 stallions remaining from the 100 that had been kept there before the war. Numbers were rebuilt using more English Thoroughbred imports and horses from Mecklenburg (the stud to which the Celle horses had been evacuated for safety). Thoroughbred blood, had always been strictly monitored and kept to a mere 2-3 % to avoid producing horses that were 'too-light'. By the mid 19th century, however, Thoroughbred influence had risen to around 35% and the Hanoverian was now too light for the agricultural work for which it was first intended.

By the end of the First World War, Celle had 350 stallions, and by 1924, it had 500. But after the Second World War, the role of the horse in agriculture went into a decline and this would affect many breeds as many breeders turned to producing competition riding horses. Some 'refugee' Trakehners (see page 234) from East Prussia found their way to Celle and were added to the stock, along with Thoroughbreds. These acted as a 'refining agent' on the Hanoverian: they lightened the still heavy-bodied horse and gave it a greater degree of movement – at the expense of some of its power. Today the Hanoverian shows no trace of the high knee movement that characterised the old Hanoverian carriage horse and they are renowned as show jumpers and dressage performers.

The breeding of Hanoverians is conducted under the auspices of the Society of Hanoverian Warmblood Breeders in Hanover, while the stallion depot at Celle, along with the affiliated stallion testing centre at Westercelle, is maintained by the federal government of Niedesachsen.

MALAPOLSKI

HEIGHT: 15.3–16.2 hh (1.57–1.65 m)

COLOURS: All solid colours

USE: Riding, larger version used for light draught work

FEATURES: Strong, muscular body; wide, deep chest; tendency towards a concave face; eyes wide set; longish neck; prominent withers; long, straight back; slightly sloping croup; long, sloping shoulders and well-muscled legs; good joints; feet of tough horn.

The Malapolski, also known as the Polish Anglo-Arab, is a relatively recent breed which contains a good deal of oriental blood. It was developed from primitive local horses, with infusions of Furioso-Northstar, Thoroughbred, and Gidran Arabian blood.

There are two distinct 'versions' of the Malapolski: the differences are the result of the regions in which they are bred. The Sadecki has been greatly influenced by the Furioso, and while it makes a fine riding horse, it is often bigger and therefore used extensively in south-western Poland on farms. The smaller Malapolski, the Darbowsko-Tarnowski, is also bred in the south west of Poland but has received more influence from the Hungarian Gidran Arabian. All the Polish Warmbloods are also known as Wielkopolskis, but those horses, like the Malapolski, which are bred in certain areas of Poland, are still regarded as being of specific types.

The Malapolski is a quality riding horse with exceptional jumping abilities. Its calm and level character coupled with its great stamina make it a fine performer in sporting competitions.

HUNTER

HEIGHT: Variable, from 15–18 hh (1.52–1.83 m) but on average, 16–16.2 hh (1.60–1.65 m)

COLOURS: All colours

USE: Riding, hunting, show ring

FEATURES: All the qualities of a riding horse with substance, strength and good bone: well slopped shoulders, compact body, deep girth, powerful quarters, cannon bones aligned with hocks, clean joints. No set pattern for head but should be of quality and have an alert, intelligent expression.

A Hunter is any horse used for the purpose of riding to hounds. It is a type of horse and, depending on the country in which it is used and the terrain which it has to cross, Hunters may vary. Consequently, Hunters do not have 'shared' characteristics – for example, colour – and so the Hunter is not a breed. Nevertheless, a good Hunter is one that is sound, well-proportioned and with all the conformational attributes of a top-class riding horse. These qualities are further combined with courage, agility, jumping ability, stamina and a robust constitution.

The finest Hunter horses are bred in countries which themselves have a long tradition of the sport, such as the UK and Ireland. Increasingly though, Hunters bred in countries such as the United States where Thoroughbred influence is important, are producing Hunters of great quality. In general, the greater the amount of Thoroughbred blood, the greater the

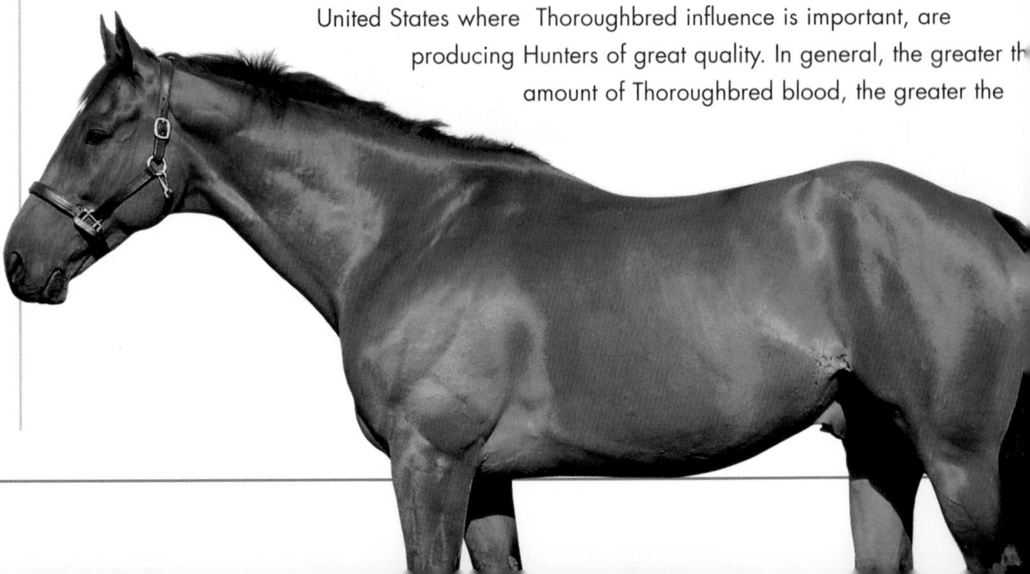

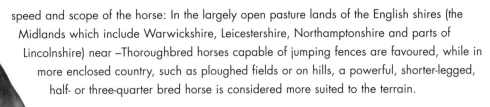

speed and scope of the horse: In the largely open pasture lands of the English shires (the Midlands which include Warwickshire, Leicestershire, Northamptonshire and parts of Lincolnshire) near –Thoroughbred horses capable of jumping fences are favoured, while in more enclosed country, such as ploughed fields or on hills, a powerful, shorter-legged, half- or three-quarter bred horse is considered more suited to the terrain.

Thoroughbred crosses with Cleveland Bays (see page 199) – a hunter in its own right – results in fast horses that can still carry a very substantial rider (up to 252 lb/114 kg) for a full days hunting across heavy clay soils and over large obstacles. Other heavyweight Hunters are the result of Thoroughbred and English heavy horse crosses, such as the Clydesdale (see page 99), but equally good horses are also produced from crosses and second crosses with British native pony breeds. Some of the larger British ponies themselves, such as the Welsh Cob (see page 89) are also at home in the hunt where they can easily carry a lighter adult in most hunting countries. Irish Hunters, considered by many as the finest cross-country horses in the world are based on a Thoroughbred/Irish Draught (see page 218) cross. These horses are hunted as three- and four-year-olds, and almost always in a plain, snaffle bridle.

A profound influence on the breeding of Hunters, encouraging the breeding of a particular type, are the Hunter showing classes which are among the most prestigious of all in the show ring. Ridden Hunter classes are divided into eight categories: in each category the horses are galloped, shown stripped (without tack), and in Britain and Ireland – though not in the USA and Canada – are ridden by the judge. Weight classes are divided into light, middle, and, heavy weight. This does not refer to the size of the horse, but to the weight it is capable of carrying, which is linked to the amount of bone it possesses. This is measured around the cannon bone. There are also classes for small Hunters of 15.2 hh (1.55 m) or under; ladies' Hunters, which are ridden side-saddle; novice, for horses that have not yet won a certain level of prize money; four-year-old classes, and, classes for working Hunters, which are expected to jump a course of between eight and 12 natural fences. Conformation and manners are all assessed by the Hunter judge, who is also looking for quality and substance in the right proportions. But a champion Hunter must not only be as perfect as possible when standing still: movement and ride are also assessed by the Hunter judge.

WESTPHALIAN

HEIGHT: 16– 17.2 hh (1.65–1.75 m)

COLOURS: All colours

USE: Riding, competition

FEATURES: Noble head on a long neck; sloping shoulders and high withers; well muscled back and croup; strong legs with large joints.

Warmblood breeding in Germany is largely dominated by the Hanoverian Horse (see page 169): more than 7,000 mares are served annually by selected stallions and the type has become a guiding factor in warmblood breeding. Consequently, many other breeding regions in Germany use Hanoverian stallions to produce Hanoverian horses, but, there can be some differences in type. One such example is the Westphalian Horse.

Horses have been bred in Westphalia since Roman times and through the course of the centuries, wild horses survived in the marshy parts of the region that were not put to the plough. Until the 19th century, five herds of wild horses existed; the last marshy area in existence is the Merfelder-Bruch near Duelmen, which is home to the last herd of semi-wild horses in Germany.

The Westphalian was bred at the state stud in Warendorf in Westphalia, which was founded in 1826. In the early stages of its development, the Westphalian was based on Oldenburger (see page 201) blood with the addition of Anglo-Norman stallions, but these were not suited working the Westphalian soil. Since the 1920s, the Westphalian breeding programme has been based on Hanoverian blood with some Trakehner and Thoroughbred influence, with the aim of producing a large riding horse with a quiet temperament that could excel at shows and be used for pleasure riding.

The Westphalian is, in effect, a Hanoverian, but, they are also called Westfalisches Pferd. They can also sometimes be a little coarser in build: the Westphalian is more of a 'coaching type', although it can also be used for riding. At the hacienda of La Escondida, in north-east Mexico, 15 Westphalians were imported by Guillermo Zambrano in 1978, and since then, the ranch has produced many outstanding show jumpers and dressage horses, including Romanow II.

The breeding of Westphalians is conducted under the auspices of the Westphalian Stud Book in Munster, while the federal government of Northrhine-Westphalia maintains the Warendorf stud of Westfalisches Pferd stallions, and where each year there is a spectacular parade.

HOLSTEINER

HEIGHT: 16–17 hh (1.63–1.73 m)

COLOURS: All solid colours

USE: Riding, driving, competition

FEATURES: Thoroughbred-type head, although of the plainer type; large, bright eyes; long, slightly arched neck; pronounced withers; powerful quarters and strongly muscled stifles, thighs and gaskins; short cannons; large, flat knees; forelegs set well apart with elbows clear of the body.

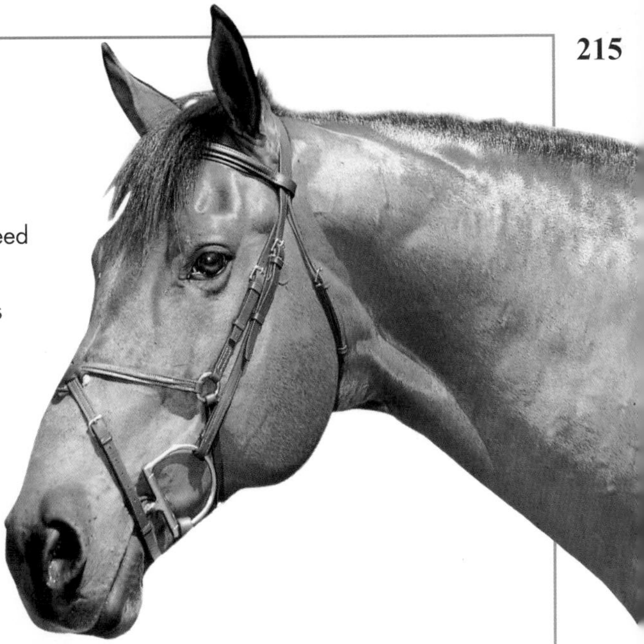

The oldest of the German warmbloods, this breed takes its name from the Elmshorn district of Holstein, where the breeding of horses reaches back into the mists of time. By the 14th century, horse breeding in the region was largely the concern of the monasteries, in particular, the monastery at Uetersen which used the nearby marshes of Haseldorf on the River Elbe as its stud. The monastery was dedicated to producing war horses and 'tourney' (tournament) horses for which they received noble patronage from the Kings of Denmark and the Dukes of Schleswig-Holstein. Later, the local horses received an infusion of Spanish, Eastern and Neapolitan blood which made them lighter in build, and from the 16th to the 18th century, the Holsteiner was in great demand across Europe as a tough, carriage or coach horse.

Holsteiners were also being used to improve other German warmblood breeds such as the Hanoverian (see page 211) and the Westphalian (see page 214). In 1680 at the Holstein royal stud at Esserom, the Holsteiner stallion Mignon was used to begin breeding the famous cream horses that became the pride of the Electors of Hanover. When the English crown passed to the House of Hanover in 1714, these cream horses formed part of the stable of the Royal Mews in London until the 1920s.

In the 19th century, two imported bloodlines were introduced: the English Thoroughbred (see page 188) and Yorkshire Coach Horses. The Thoroughbred would make the Holsteiner more compact and shorter legged, and the prevailing 'Roman nose' was straightened out, while the galloping ability was also improved. The Yorkshire Coach Horse brought the characteristic high and wide gait and the even temperament to the Holsteiner, so it now had a reputation as a fine dual-purpose carriage and riding horse. The breed continued to be developed along these lines at the Traventhal Stud founded by the Prussians in 1867, but, when this closed down, the Society of Breeders of Holstein Horses in Elmshorn assumed responsibility for the breed, which, like all European warmbloods, is subject to rigorous performance testing.

Since World War II additional Thoroughbred blood has been introduced to produce a lighter, multipurpose riding and competition horse, who can gallop and jump extremely well: Meteor and Tora are just two examples of the fine German show jumpers which have achieved international fame. Powerfully built, the Holsteiner is a good-tempered, intelligent, willing and very handsome horse.

KARBARDIN

HEIGHT: 15–15.2 hh (1.52–1.57 m)

COLOURS: Dark Bay, Bay, and Black predominate

USE: Riding, trekking, harness, and light draught work

FEATURES: Considered to be a 'perfect mountain horse' its features include those often considered defects in other mounts: straight shoulders, flat withers, narrow poll, ear turn slightly inwards, hind legs are sickle-shaped, but forelegs are a good feature being clearly defined with short cannons. Unbelievably hard hooves make shoeing a problem, but most Kabardins go unshod on even the hardest ground. Luxurious mane and tail.

The Kabardin is a little mountain horse from the Caucasus which has been regarded as a breed since the 16th century. In the 17th century, these horses became more widely famous and were considered the finest mountain horse in the whole of central Asia. Bred by mountai tribesmen, using indigenous mountain breeds with infusions of Turkmene and Karabakh bloo (both of which are 'southern' Russian breeds), along with Arab genes in the 19th century, the Karbadin is the product of centuries of selective breeding for survival under the harshest conditions. Later the Kabardin was crossed with neighbouring Karabakh horses, and with Thoroughbred (see page 188) mares to produce the bigger – and faster – Anglo-Kabardins.

Today, the finest Kabardin horses are bred at the Malokarachayev and the Malkin Studs whe in spring, breeders form kosyaks, small herds of around 20 mares in the charge of a sire wh protects them from wolves and other sires. Early in May the herds begin to move uphill, and the snow line recedes they climb higher and higher until they reach their summer pastures where the only supplement to their diet is salt. Early in August, the stallions are separated fro their herds and all the mares are brought together; in September, with the first snows, the herds begin their migration downhill to spend the winters outdoors in enclosures where they receive additional hay. Weaning takes place in November and yearlings are divided according to sex and grazed and trained separately.

The Kabardin has developed characteristics that are suited to its terrain and to the rigours of the climate – characteristics which in other mounts would be considered defects. The blood o the Kabardin has a heightened oxidising capacity which makes them supreme performers at very high altitudes: they can climb – with a rider – to heights of more than 5,000 m (16, 50 ft) and unlike other breeds, do not need to recover from their exertions. Their hearts, lungs, tendons, ligaments and muscles are immensely strong and efficient!

To compensate for their often meagre diets, when there is food, Kabardins quickly accumulate body fat to keep them going. Their bodies are dense, massive and elongated, their backs are well-muscled, short and straight, and the quarters slope away from the rounded croup. The loins, while very strong, are often slightly concave. By Western standards the withers are flat and the shoulders are straight – which accounts for their high action. Some Kabardin pace naturally: it is said that this gait was passed on to all horses of Mongol blood by the favourite mount of the mighty Genghiz Khan. The head profile is 'Roman-nosed' and between the ears the poll is particularly narrow and the occiput ill-defined. The hind legs are often sickle-shaped – which in a mountain horse is a great advantage. The hooves are also unbelievably hard: most Kabardin are left unshod, even in the hardest of mountain terrains.

Kabardins have the most remarkable abilities and thrive in the most difficult terrains, often at extremely high altitudes. They will happily cross steep mountain passes, travel through deep snows and icy rivers, for they are seemingly impervious to cold. They rarely stumble, even when trotting or cantering downhill, are undeterred by falling rocks and they have an unerring sense of direction: the mountain tribesman know their mounts will find their herds within two kilometres – even through the darkness of night or heavy mountain mists. While they are not particularly impressive on the race course, over distances they are rarely beaten. In 1946 a major test of the performance of Russian breeds was organised in Moscow: a 250 km ride – with the final 2 km to be covered at a trot – was won by the Kabardin stallion Ali-Kadym in just 25 hours.

IRISH DRAFT

HEIGHT: 15–17 hh (1.50–1.70 m)

COLOURS: All solid colours

USE: Hunting, light draught work

FEATURES: Small head in relation to size of body; deep-chested, though body may be a little long; distinctive oval ribcage – horses should not be 'slab-sided'; long, arching neck and sloping shoulders; withers set well back; quarters slope downwards from the croup to meet the tail which is carried high in movement; strong, powerfully muscled hind thighs and large hock joints; minimal feathers.

Without doubt one of the finest cross-country horses in the world (and the foundation of the great Irish Hunter) the Irish Draught's development started in the 12th century when native Irish horses were upgraded by heavy French and Flemish horses which were imported to the country following the Anglo-Norman invasion of 1172. The strong mares that resulted were further improved by introducing Andalucian (see page 192) blood which produced draught horses that were used for every kind of work on small Irish farms, but were also versatile enough to be used under saddle. Once common all over rural Ireland, the breed declined during the famines of 1847.

Attempts were made to improve the remaining stock through crosses with Clydesdale (see page 176) and Shires (see page 171), but these added a coarseness to the Irish and also were responsible for the breed becoming somewhat 'tied-in' below the knee, a fault that has taken some time to eradicate. By this time the 'old' Irish Draught was a low built animal standing no more than 15.2–15.3 (1.52–1.53 m), with upright shoulders, dropping quarters and a goose-rump. Nonetheless, these horses could trot in harness and canter and gallop under saddle, and they were said to be fine jumpers who were fearless of even the greatest obstacles.

The introduction of Thoroughbred (see page 188) blood in the 19th century gave the Irish Draught quality and speed, without removing any of its innate hunting abilities. The breed was also substantially improved when stallion subsidies were made in 1904 and breeding encouraged. In 1917 a Book for Horses of Irish Draught Type was opened with 375 mares and 44 stallions entered.

However, the breed declined with the advent of mechanisation in farming, and numbers suffered further during World War I when many of the finest mares were requisitioned by the army for military use as 'Gunners'. Clean-legged, they did not develop the 'grassy heels' suffered by many horses in the wet of the Flanders mud and because of their ability to thrive on meagre army rations, many Irish Draughts which left their homeland as gun teams in 1914 entered Brussels in the Ceremonial Parade in 1918. In the 1960s, exports to Europe for slaughter led to near extinction in its homeland until legislation was introduced in 1964 to curb the trade.

Fortunately, Ireland regards their horses as part of their national treasures and in 1976 the Irish Draught Society was formed and which operates a grading system to ensure quality animals are produced for registration. When crossed with Thoroughbred mares, the Irish Draught passes on to its progeny its bone, substance, size and athleticism. Today, the Irish Draught is a bigger horse than a century ago, with most standing 16 hh (1.63 m) – while stallions easily reach 17 hh (1.70 m).

KNABSTRUP

HEIGHT: 15.2– 15.3 hh (1.55–1.57 m)

COLOURS: Spotted

USE: Riding

FEATURES: Conformation varies and is closer in character to that of the Appaloosa (the line of the back from the wither is peculiar to Knabstrup and some Appaloosa strains);the neck is strong and well-muscled, but tending to shortness; sparse mane and tail; spotting extends down legs to feet; cannons are short, knees are flat and wide; horn of feet often has vertical stripes.

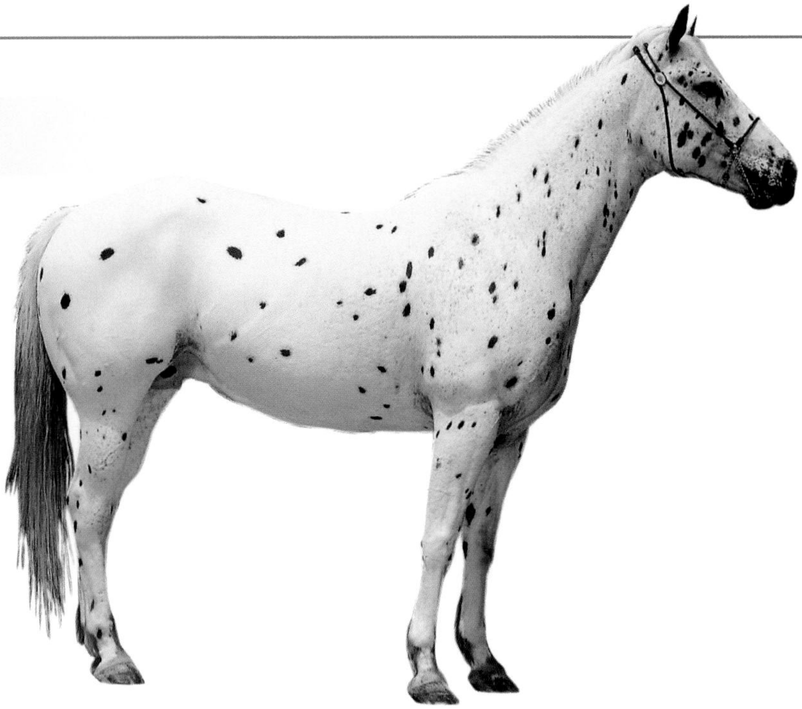

The Knabstrup traces back to a spotted Spanish mare called Flaebehoppen which translates as 'Flaebe's horse'. She was bought by a butcher in 1808 (who was called Flaebe) from a Spanish officer during the Napoleonic Wars and who was then sold on to the founder of the breed, Judge Lunn. Flaebehoppen was renowned for her speed and endurance, and at his estate in Knabstrup, Denmark, Judge Lunn bred her with Frederiksborg stallions and produced a line of spotted horses that were not as substantial as the Frederiksborg, but were very much in demand for their colour and ability. These were the 'Old Knabstrups': they had more of a harness conformation which was evident in the shoulders and short neck. They were also stronger and more raw-boned than the modern horse, but they were equally tough and quick to learn.

These qualities, coupled with their colour (which was originally white with brown or black spots of varying size covering the whole body) made them popular as circus horses. Injudicious breeding for colour rather than conformation led to the deterioration of the breed and it nearly died out. The 'Old Knabstrup' is now rare but over the past 50 years, improvements to the breed have been made, and the modern Knabstrup is a much more substantial, better quality horse than the 'Old Knabstrup' of the 19th century: the best examples of the breed have well-rounded quarters with good muscular development. To a large extent, the conformation defects that occurred in the limbs have also been corrected and today they also occur in a greater range of colours. The sparse mane and tail appears to be a characteristic accompaniment of spotted coats: they are found in both the 'Old' and modern Knabstrup as well as in the Appaloosa (see page 194).

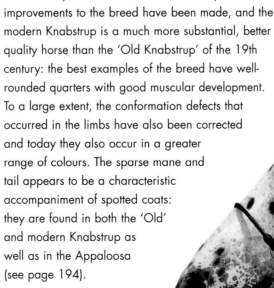

LIPIZZANA

HEIGHT: 15–16 hh (1.50–1–60 m)

COLOURS: White, but solid colours including black, bay and chestnut can also be found

USE: Haute école dressage; harness

FEATURES: Arab influence in head is often apparent, but the 'ram-like' profile of the Spanish horse can also be seen; body is compact and deep with considerable depth through the girth; short neck; withers are not pronounced and shoulders are well suited to both riding and harness; action tends to be high rather than low and long; powerful quarters; short, powerful limbs with flat joints; hard feet; silky mane and tail.

The Lipizzaner is to the equine world what Rudolph Nureyev was to ballet: even those who have never been on a horse could probably name this, one of the world's most beautiful horses. Indeed, the Lipizzaners at the famous Spanish Riding School in Vienna perform the most beautiful of 'dances' including the famous leaps called 'airs above the ground'.

This ancient breed takes its name from the Lipizza (Lipica) Stud, in Slovenia, where it originated and is still bred. Once part of the great Austro-Hungarian Empire, the Lipizza Stu was founded in 1580 by the Archduke Charles II. The formation stock of the breed were nin Spanish stallions and 24 mares which were imported from the Iberian Peninsula with the ain of providing suitably grand horses for the ducal stables in Graz and the court stables in Vienna. Other studs were also founded, the most important of which were at Piber, near Grc in Austria and Kladruby in the Czech Republic. Founded in 1572 this stud is the oldest in Europe, and is the home of the Kladruber carriage horse. Also bas on Spanish stock, the Kladruber was to influence the Lipizzaner quite considerably.

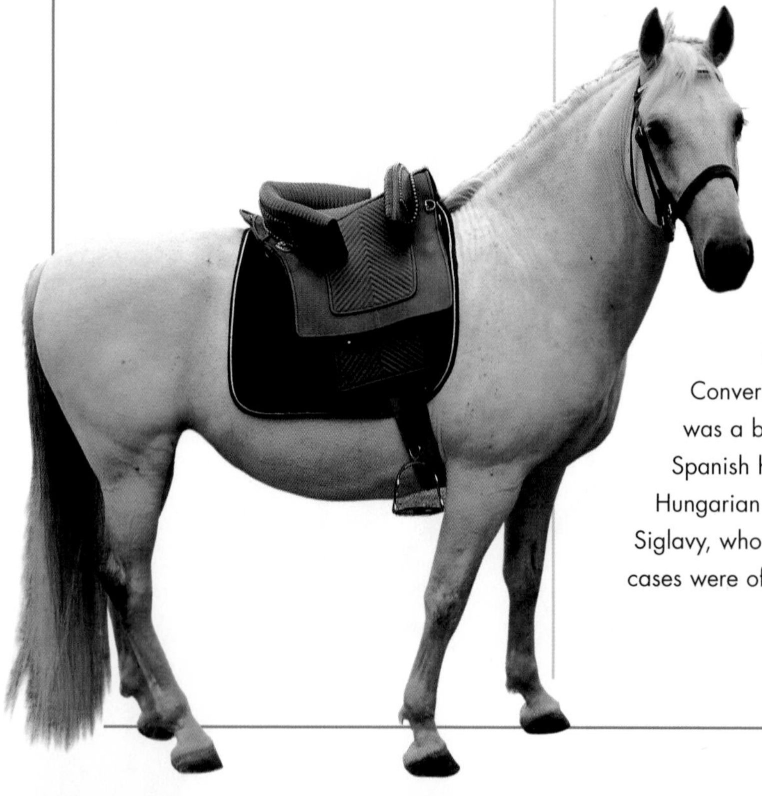

The Spanish Riding School in Vienna – so called because it had used Spanish horses from the outset – had been established eight years earlier a wooden arena located next to the Imperial Palace. Today the school is housed in the Winter Riding Hall, built on the orders of Charles VI and completed in 1735. The horses that can be seen there today can trace back to six principal foundation stallions: Pluto (born 1765) was a white horse of Spanish descent obtained form the Royal Danish Court Stud; Conversano (born 1767) was a black Neapolitan, while Neapolitano (born 1790) was a bay Neapolitan from Polesina, both of which were said to have been bred fro Spanish horses. Maestoso (born 1819) was a white Kladruber horse bred at the famo Hungarian stud at Mezohegyes; Favory, a dun born at the Kaldruby Stud in 1779; and Siglavy, who is believed to have been an Arab born in 1810. The foundation mares in mc cases were of Spanish origin.

Over the years, stallions were frequently exchanged between the studs at Lipizza, Piber and Kladruby, but when the Spanish Riding School opened 'for the education of the nobility in the art of horsemanship' horses from the Lipizza stud were found to be more amenable to training in the haute école and they began to be regarded as a separate breed. Although the Lipizza Stud's policy was always to breed white horses until the 18th century – considered to be the most suitably dignified colour for the Imperial house – other colours including black, bays and duns, as well as magnificently spotted, piebald and skewbald did exist.

The modern Lipizzaners, which appear at the Riding School in Vienna, have since 1920 been bred at Piber. Fewer than ten are selected each year and their training takes between four and six years. They are white, although the foals are born black or brown. There are also occasional bays, and while these are not kept for breeding, by tradition, one bay is kept at the Riding School. The 'Piber Lipizzaner' generally stands a little over 15 hh (1.52 m) and is a compact, very strongly limbed horse, powerful in the quarters and neck and often featuring the 'ram-like' profile of its Spanish ancestors.

As well as the Spanish Riding School's Piber Lipizzaners, Lipizzaners are bred throughout Hungary, Romania, Slovakia and the Czech Republic. While all of the studs maintain the six stallion lines on which the breed was founded, variations in type do occur and the Piber type is by no means predominant. All Lipizzaners are used under saddle, but outside the 'hot- house' Piber stud, they are also used for harness work and some can still be seen working on farms.

NONIUS

HEIGHT: 15.3–16.2 hh (1.53–1.62 m)

COLOURS: Bay and brown predominate but blacks and chestnut shades occur

USE: Riding, carriage

FEATURES: Head is that of an honest, half-bred horse; neck is well formed, though not long or elegant; sloped shoulders and well defined withers; strong back and quarters, sometimes inclined to slope away from the croup; short legs but very strong.

The founder of the breed, Nonius Senior, was foaled at Calvados in northern France in 1810, said to be from an English half-bred stallion out of a Norman mare. During the Napoleonic Wars, Nonius was captured by the Hungarian cavalry following Napoleon's defeat at Leipzig in 1813 and taken to the Mezohhegyes Stud, where he produced 15 outstanding stallions out of a variety of mares.

Nonius was not apparently the most attractive of horses: he stood at just over 16.1 hh (1.64 m), had a coarse, heavy head with small eyes and 'mule' ears. He also had a short neck, long back, narrow pelvis and a low set tail. Nevertheless he proved to be a prolific sire, consistently producing offspring that were far superior to himself in both conformation and action.

In the 1860s Thoroughbred blood was introduced and the breed was divided into two types: large carriage or light farm horses, and the smaller Nonius type which carries a little more Arab blood, for riding and light harness work. By this time the breed had also established its tendency to mature late – at six years old – but also to be commensurately long-lived.

MANGALARGA

HEIGHT: 14–16 hh (1.43–1.60 m)

COLOURS: Chestnut, bay, roan, and grey

USE: Riding, stock work, endurance riding

FEATURES: Long head; short, strong back; powerful quarters; low set tail; long legs.

In 1541, Alvar Nuñez landed near Santa Caterina on the Brazilian coast with a fleet carryi a number of horses – Alter-Reals from Portugal. Some –or all –of these horses either escaped were set free, spreading out and breeding in the same way as the descendants of the Spani horses that landed in and near the Argentine. The modern descendants of these Portuguese horses are similar to their cousins the Criollo (see page 201), but are smaller, and throughou the different parts of Brazil, different types appear. The Brazilian Crioulo can be found in north-east Brazil where it is known as the Nordestino and in Goias State, as the Courraleiro. These two varieties are very hardy horses and able to survive on minimal rations. A further – and better – variety of the Crioulo is bred in the Rio Grande do Sul region, from which it tak its name.

The Mangalarga is a 'cousin' of the Crioulo: in the 19th century, Brazil imported selected stallions from Spain and Portugal which were used to upgrade the native stocks. One of the best stallions, called Sublime, was sent to stud in the Minas Gerais, where he founded the Mangalarga breed which is known locally as the Junquiera. The Mangalarga is a larger hor than the Crioulo and has longer legs. It is also distinguished by its peculiar gait, the marcha which is described as being halfway between a trot and a canter. Attempts have been made to improve the Mangalargas with warmblood stallions, and the most successful crossbreeds f riding purposes have come from Arab (see page 183) Anglo-Arab (see page 187), Thoroughbred (see page 188) and Trakehner (see page 244) stallions.

In 1840, Cassiano Campolino also set out to improve the Mangalarga by selective breeding this was so successful that a new variety, the slightly heavier Campolino came into existence and now flourishes in and around the state of Rio de Janeiro where they make excellent ridin horses and are known for their great endurance which far exceeds that of imported horses.

MISSOURI FOX TROTTER

HEIGHT: 14–16 hh (1.42–1.63 m)

COLOURS: All solid colours, but chestnut predominates.

USE: Riding

FEATURES: A strong, compact horse with an attractive, tapered head with flared nostrils; arched neck; short strong back; deep in girth; muscular quarters; good length from hip to hock; hind legs are quite heavily built but well spaced: shanks are longer than normal; good feet are a feature of the breed.

The Missouri Fox Trotter is one of America's oldest and least known breeds. It is one of the trio of American gaited horses – the other two being the American Saddlebred (see page 190) and the Tennessee Walking Horse (see page 243). The breed was established in around 1820 when settlers moving westwards across the Mississippi River from the hills and plantations of Tennessee, Kentucky and Virginia made their homes in the Ozark Mountains of Missouri and Arkansas.

The most famous of the breeding families were the Alsups who bred the Brimmer line of horses descended from racehorses of the same name; the Kissees, who established the Diamond and Fox strains, and the Dunns, who produced Old Skip.

These families took with them their Thoroughbred horses (see page 188), Arabs (see page 183) and Morgans (see page 225) and the mares were then bred to the fastest sires. Originally, the horses were bred to race, but Puritan religious zeal put an end to such a frivolous pastime. The Ozark breeders instead turned their efforts to producing a fixed type of utility horse that would comfortably carry a rider at a steady speed over rough terrain. Following infusions of Saddlebred and Tennessee Walking Horse blood, the result was a very sure-footed, smooth-moving horse with a unique gait, the fox trot.

The fox trot gait is a 'broken gait performed': this means that it performs an active walk in front, while trotting behind, and the hind feet step down and slide over the track of the forefeet. The sliding action – which should be perfectly straight – reduces concussion in the lower limbs and reduces the amount of movement in the back which means it stays very level. The only things that 'bobs' up and down rhythmically are the head and the tail. The result is that the rider sits comfortably in the saddle without feeling any of the action. The Missouri Fox Trotter can maintain this gait for long distances at around 5-8 mph (8-13 km/h) and for short distances at a speedy 10 mph (16 km/h). Other gaits performed are a walk in strict four-time beat where the hind feet distinctly over-stride the front track, and the canter.

The Breed Society is very strict in overseeing the breed and its training: artificial training aids or 'appliances' such as false tails or tail sets (which give a high upright carriage to the tail) are not permitted to accentuate the natural gait. Excessive weighting of the feet with specially designed shoes is also forbidden, and any marks or sores around the coronets which indicate the use of chains mean that horses and riders are immediately disqualified. In show classes, where the Missouri Fox Trotter is ridden in western gear, 40% of marks are awarded for the fox trot and 20% each for the walk, canter and for general conformation. Outside the show ring, the Missouri Fox Trotter is equally sure-footed which makes it an ideal and very popular trail riding horse.

MORAB

HEIGHT: 14.3–15.3 hh (1.47– 1.57 m)

COLOURS: Solid colours

USE: Riding, ranch work

FEATURES: Full, silky mane; 'Arab' shoulders; broad chest; withers are not defined; strong back; straight croup; tail set high; wide across hips; good feet but in most cases, hocks are a little too far off the ground; forearms long and muscular.

The Arab has long been acknowledged as a pre-eminent upgrading influence in the breed structure of the world's horses. When crossed with the Thoroughbred (see page 188) it creates the Anglo-Arab. The equivalent horse in America, which uses the Morgan (see page 225) in place of the Thoroughbred, is the Morab.

Although history's first Morab was Golddust, born in 1855 and registered in the Morgan Registry as No. 70, the name Morab is said to have been coined by the American newspaper magnate, William Randolph Hearst. In the 1920s, Hearst used two Arab (see page 183) stallions on his Morgan mares to produce horses to work on his San Simeon Ranch in California.

The most hotly debated Morab issue is their status as a breed: some say they are part-bred, other term them half-breeds. But to others, Morabs which are the progeny or Morgan-Arabian breeding, are neither half-Morgans or half-Arabs but a very distinct breed. The Morab Horse Association (MHA) in the United States has claimed full breed status for the horses of Arab-Morgan cross: it seeks the acceptance of 25%Morgan-75% Arab breed standard for registrable Morabs.

The MHA and the International Morab Registry (IMR) maintain detailed registries and archives. There is an also a breed standard, and although this really consists of generalisations that are applicable to all 'well-bred' horses, it does state that the shape of the hindquarters and the angle of the pelvis in the Morab are significantly different to other breeds.

Today's Morabs, with a century of breeding behind them, combine the strength of the Morgan with the refinement of the Arab. They have a shorter back than most other breeds, but this is combined with the longer croup of the Morgan which gives the Morab great strength and a smooth gait which combine to allow it to excel at competitive and endurance events.

Owners, breeders and fans of the Morab all cite its intelligence and its dependable nature which makes them ideal mounts for children and novice riders, as well as more spirited competitive riders.

MORGAN

HEIGHT: 14.2–15.2 hh (1.45–1.55 m)

COLOURS: Bay, brown, black and chestnut

USE: Riding, driving, draught, competition

FEATURES: Medium sized, head with straight profile or just slightly dished – never Roman –nosed; large nostrils; well crested neck; clearly defined withers which are slightly higher than the point of the hip; strong, sloped shoulders; short, broad and well muscled back; large, rounded barrel; deep and wide chest; 'perfect' quarters; short cannon bones; short pasterns that are not too sloping; round feet of smooth, dense horn; long flowing tail that reaches the ground when horse is still.

The Morgan is one of America's first documented breeds and whose history, like that of the Quarter horse (see page 233) is part of the history of the country itself. Unlike the Quarter horse though, the Morgan owes its existence to a single, phenomenal stallion, Justin Morgan. This, the undisputed sire of the first American breed was a dark bay horse born sometime between 1789 and 1793, in West Springfield, Massachusetts and stood no more than 14 hh (1.43 m). He was also originally called Figure, until he came into the possession of Justin Morgan in 1795, a schoolmaster (although some say he was an innkeeper) who took the horse in lieu of debts owed to him and took him home to Randolph Center, Vermont, where he was put to work in the plough. Poor old Justin Morgan, it seems, was passed from owner to owner several times – and with each one he endured plenty of hard work – until he ended up with a farmer Levi Bean, who assigned the horse the duty of pulling a muck spreader.

Little is known of Justin Morgan's background: some claim he was a Welsh Cob (see page 168), while another account says he was sired by a celebrated, pre-Revolutionary racer called True Briton. The only true certainty is that Justin Morgan possessed an incredibly robust constitution, extraordinary strength, and great speed. For not only did he work all day on farms in the biting cold winters of the north-eastern states, he was a regular at weight-hauling matches and races. In saddle or in harness, it is claimed that Justin Morgan was never beaten. His reputation spread across the region and he was in great demand as a stud. Soon his descendants, who apparently inherited his qualities – including his diminutive size and dark colouring – were spread across New England. His most famous sons were Sherman, Woodbury and Bullrush, and all modern Morgans trace their ancestry to Justin Morgan through them.

The modern Morgan is no doubt a much more refined horse than Justin Morgan but it is still as spirited and courageous, intelligent, hard-working and versatile, powerful and as possessed of great stamina as their founding sire. The Morgan's compact size and happy nature has also helped to make it one of the most popular breeds in the USA.

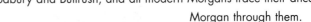

NATIONAL SHOW HORSE

HEIGHT: 14.3–17 hh (1.48 –1.70m)

COLOURS: Black, bay, chestnut, grey and pinto

USE: Riding, showing

FEATURES: Long neck without pronounced crest, set high on shoulders; small head with straight or slightly concave profile; pronounced withers; short back with relatively level top line; short cannon bones in front legs; long, well-angled pasterns in rear legs; high set tail.

The National Show Horse is a relatively new breed appellation: the result crosses between Arabs (see page 183) and American Saddlebreds (see page 190), these horses have been around for some time. But it was not until the 1980s that a group of American enthusiasts formed an organisation dedicated to the breed that the National Show Horse was formally established. Until 1982, the association allowed open registration to form a pool of horses that would become the foundation of the new breed. Today, there are specific rules regarding registration. Three types of stallions an three types of mares are permitted: these must be American Saddlebreds, Arabs or Nationa Show Horses, and they must also be registered with their appropriate registry. While any combination of the three breeds can be used to produce a National Show Horse, any result foals must meet blood content requirements ranging from 25-99% Arabian.

The qualities that are required in a National Show Horse include balance and power in the hindquarters and elevated front with the forelegs showing both flexion and extension. The relatively small head must have a straight profile or be slightly concave, but a 'Roman-nose' profile is discouraged. Thanks to its American Saddlebred ancestry, the National Show Horse also one of the newest gaited horse breeds an is shown in three- and five-gaited classes. Lik the Saddlebred, it can do the stepping pace: this takes its name from the fact th the horse's hind foot steps down just before the front foot of the same strid strikes the ground. The horse always has either one or two feet on the ground and suspension occurs first with th hind legs as they change places, then with the front legs and produces a very 'dainty' showy appearance. In some instances, th National Show Horse also performs the rack or 'singlefoot' – where only one foot is on the ground at any time and there is a moment o complete suspension when all four feet are off the ground.

In addition to gaited classes in the show rings, the National Show Horse is shown in Hunter, and Hunter Pleasure, English Pleasure, Pleasure Driving, Country Pleasure, Fine Harness, Western Pleasure, Show Hack and Equitation classes. Its all-round abilities and good look are set to make this, one of the newest American breeds, a firm favour across the world.

OLDENBURGER

HEIGHT: 16.2–17.2 hh (1.65–1.75 m)

COLOURS: All solid colours but chestnuts and greys are unusual.

USE: Riding, driving

FEATURES: Neck is long and very strong, reflecting coach horse ancestry; long shoulders; head is plain, with straight profile although there is a tendency to a 'Roman nose'; short-legged with plenty of bone; a strong back; good depth of girth; quarters and hind limbs exceptionally strong; tail is set and carried high; stallions are tested before licensing and particular attention is paid to the feet which must be well open at the heels, sound and in large enough proportions to the horse.

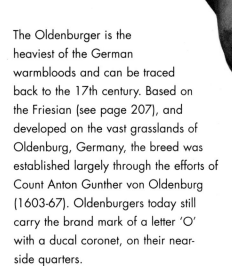

The Oldenburger is the heaviest of the German warmbloods and can be traced back to the 17th century. Based on the Friesian (see page 207), and developed on the vast grasslands of Oldenburg, Germany, the breed was established largely through the efforts of Count Anton Gunther von Oldenburg (1603-67). Oldenburgers today still carry the brand mark of a letter 'O' with a ducal coronet, on their near-side quarters.

The Count imported Spanish and Neapolitan horses – which both had backgrounds of Barb blood – along with his own grey stallion, Kranic, to develop a breed of good, strong and versatile carriage horses that could also be used for farm work. In the last part of the 18th century, half-bred English stallions were also introduced to refine the breed, and then, in the 19th century, breeders introduced Thoroughbreds (see page 188), Cleveland Bays (see page 199), Hanoverians (see page 1211), and French-Norman blood. The result was a karossierpferd, a heavily built coach horse standing 17 hh. In spite of its massive size and build, the Oldenburger was an early-maturing animal, a very unusual feature in such a large horse.

As the demand for heavy coach horses declined with the introduction of motor vehicles, the breed began to be developed for agricultural work. When demand for this type of horse collapsed after World War II, the emphasis shifted to producing a riding horse. A Norman stallion called Condor who carried 70% Thoroughbred blood was used along with a Thoroughbred called Lupus. Since then out-crosses have been mainly Thoroughbred but with some Hanoverian, in order to maintain the even temperament for which the breed is famous.

While still a big, powerful animal, the Oldenburger is not built for speed, but is well suited to dressage on account of its regular paces. The action is straight and rhythmical, although on account of its coaching ancestry, is inclined to be a little high. But this does not disadvantage the dressage horse, or indeed the show jumper, at which the Oldenburger can also excel. Strong stocky legs are needed to carry such a large-bodied horse: the joints are big, the cannons fairly short and the bone measurement is around 23 cm (9 in). Under Acts of 1819, which were amended in 1897 and 1923, the responsibility for the Oldenburger breed and the licensing of stallions lies with the Society of Breeders of the Oldenburg Horse. The society pursues a rigorous policy of careful selection and testing to ensure a uniformity of type in the breed.

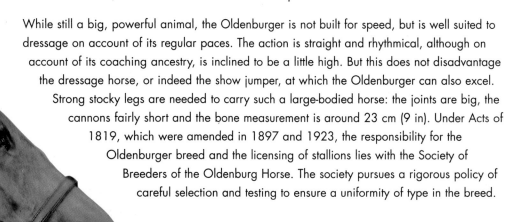

ORLOV TROTTER

HEIGHT: 16 hh (1.60 m)

COLOURS: Grey predominates, black and bay are also common, chestnut rare.

USE: Trotting, driving, riding

FEATURES: A tall, lightly built horse with strong shoulders; long 'swan neck' set high on shoulders; long back but plenty of depth in girth; low withers; strong legs with good bones and slight feathering; slightly heavy head.

The oldest and most popular breed in Russia, the Orlov Trotter dates back to 1778 when Count Alexei Orlov (1737-1808) began a breeding programme at the Khrenov Stud. The white Arab stallion, Smetanka, was used along with Dutch, Mecklenburg and Danish mares. Among the five progeny was Polkan I who was the sire of the Orlov breed's foundation stallion, a grey stallion called Bars I who was born in 1784. Bars I was described by contemporaries as a tall horse of elegant conformation with outstanding action, especially in the trot. He was mated with Arab, Danish, and Dutch mares, as well as English half-breds an Arab-Mecklenburg crosses. Thereafter, the policy was to inbreed Bars I and his sons to establish the desired type.

By the beginning of the 19th century the Orlov Trotters were widely known: an important par of their improvement came with the systematic tests of the breed on race courses. Trotting rac in Moscow had been held since 1799: these took place usually in winter with horses racing with light sleighs. From 1834, as a result of crossing Orlovs with American Standardbreds, a faster Orlov emerged. Although they were used on the race course, Orlov Trotters were neve purely for racing: they have also been used for drawing coaches, phaetons and of course, th famous Russian Troikas. The troika is the Russian method of harnessing three horses side by side. The centre horse works at a fast trot while the out-spanners are bent outward by tight si reins, and they must gallop or canter to keep up with the centre horse. For this reason, Orlov Trotters for breeding have always been chosen not only for speed, but for their other qualitie a good height, with a light but substantial frame, and an attractive conformation coupled wit a sound constitution.

There are five basic types of modern Orlov Trotter, with the type varying according to the stu at which the animals are bred. The best and most characteristic Orlovs are those which are bred at Khrenov, and these are regarded as the 'classical Orlov'. Others are bred at Perm in the Urals, Novotomnikov, and at Tula and Dubrov. The Orlovs bred here are closer to a heavier harness conformation than that of a harness racer, but they can still be used to improve a wide variety of stock which has also been a part of the Orlov's breeding policy.

HESSIAN

HEIGHT: 16–17 hh (1.60–1.70 m)

COLOURS: All solid colours

USE: Riding, competition

FEATURES: Strong horse, ideally suited to riding and sport

The Hessian is one of the less well-known German warmblood breeds. Hesse has been a centre for horse breeding for centuries, but the state stud at Dillenberg was not established until 1869, so consequently, local farmers concentrated on breeding light draught horses for which there was a great demand until the advent of mechanisation removed the need for horses in agricultural work.

The transition from the warmblooded horse with predominantly Oldenburger (page 227) bloodlines, and with its characteristic 'Dillenberg Ram nose' – a distinct convex head profile – into the modern sports horse began in the mid-20th century. Using Hanoverians (page 211), Westphalians (page 173), Trakehners (page 244) as well as English Thoroughbreds (page 188) and Anglo-Arabs (page 187) to add refinement, the modern Hessian emerged. A very elegant horse, its temperament makes it ideally suited to both sport riding and pleasure riding.

Breeding continues to take place at the Dillenberg Stud in tandem with private Hessian stallion owners who are organised into the Vereiningen Hessischer Hengsthalte.

PINTO AND PAINT HORSES

HEIGHT: Average for horses: 15–16 hh (1.52–1.63 m); for Pinto ponies, up to 15 hh (1.52 m)

COLOURS: Two patterns for Pinto (Overo and Tobiano), three patterns for Paints (Overo, Tobiano and Tovaro)

USE: Riding, ranch work, trail riding

FEATURES: Varied, see text

The Pinto and the Paint Horse, which have also been known as Calico, are academically colour types and only in the USA do they have breed status. In America these coloured horses come under the joint aegis of two societies: the Pinto Horse Association of America and the American Paint Horse Association. Most Paint horses are Pintos, but not all Pintos are Paints!

The Pinto Horse Association of America maintains a register for horses, ponies and miniatures which is divided into stock type: those with mainly Quarter Horse (page 233) background; Hunter (page 212), largely Thoroughbred (page 188), pleasure, Arab or Morgan; and saddle, based largely on Saddlebred (page 190), Hackney (page 210) or Tennessee Walking Horse (page 243).

The American Paint Horse Society register places an emphasis on bloodlines rather than simply colour or coat pattern: it registers stock-type horses and sets strict standards with regard to conformation, athleticism and temperament. This association requires Paint horses to be registered in one of four recognised associations: the American Paint Quarter Horse Association; the American Paint Stock Horse Association; the Jockey Club; or the American Quarter Horse Association.

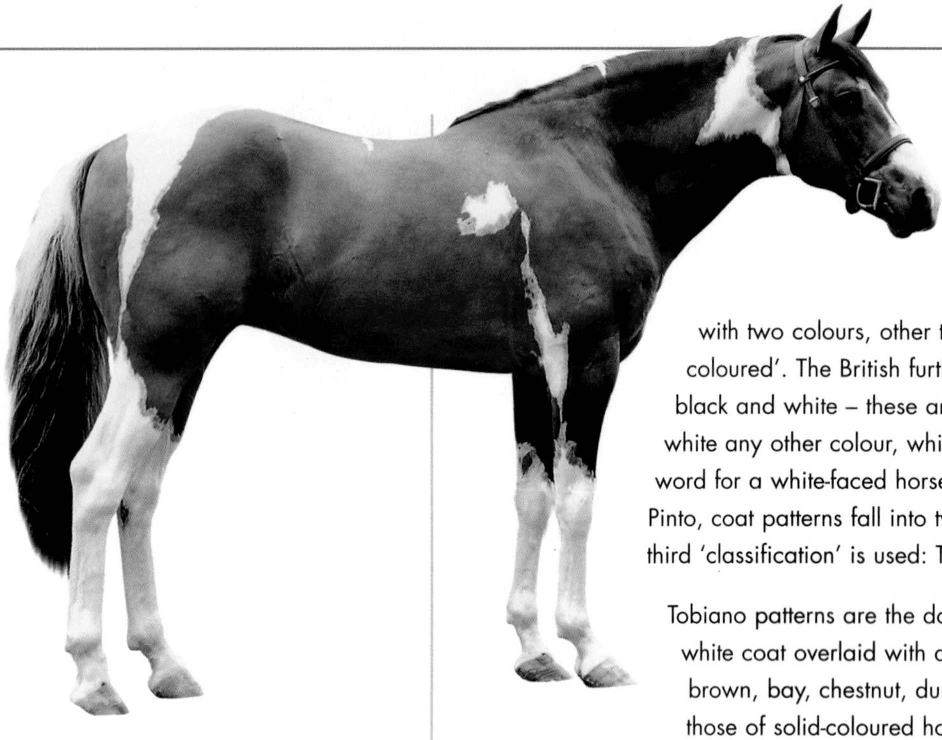

Both the Pinto and the Paint descend from th Spanish Horses brought to the New World b the Conquistadors in the 16th century. The name 'Pinto' comes from the Spanish word pintado which means 'painted'. In Europe hors with two colours, other than the spotted breeds, are called 'part', or 'od coloured'. The British further distinguish between coats with patches of black and white – these are called piebald – and those with patches of white any other colour, which are called skewbald. ('Bald' is the old English word for a white-faced horse). In the USA, more precise terms are used: in th Pinto, coat patterns fall into two types: Overo and Tobiano. In Paint horses, a third 'classification' is used: Tovaro.

Tobiano patterns are the dominant colouring, and are distinguished by a white coat overlaid with any basic colour common to horses, such as brown, bay, chestnut, dun, or grey. Tobianos may have head markings lik those of solid-coloured horses, such as a blaze, strip, star or snip. Generally, all four legs of Tobiano horses are white, at least below the hocks and knees. The spots of colour are regular and distinctly oval or round in shape and the tail, although sparse (which is a common trait in spotted horses) is often in two colours.

The Overo pattern is the recessive pattern in coats. This is a solid coat of colour with irregula patches of white. Typically, the white patches on an Overo will not cross the back of the hors between its withers and tail, and generally, all four legs will be dark and the tail will be of one colour.

But not all coat patterns fit neatly into the two: the American Paint Horse Association has expanded its classification to include 'Tovaro' which is used to describe a Paint horse with bo Overo and Tobiano characteristics. Whatever their colour or pattern, no two Pintos or Paints will look identical.

In any case, these distinctive coat markings are not achieved by mating a white horse with another of solid, darker colour. Two mono-coloured horses will not produce two-coloured offspring unless one or both of the parents has the specific spotting genes inherited from a Pinto or Paint ancestor. Breeding two Paint or Pinto horses does not result in a two-coloured foal each time, either. Consequently, Pinto and Paint foals can be rare and are extremely desirable.

The Sioux and Crow Indians considered Pinto and Paint horses advantageous not only because their coats provided perfect camouflage, but because they were very tough horses. Cowboys, too, held them in great esteem: many considered these horses to be especially lucky and were willing to pay a higher price for one. A recurring point in the testimony of many wranglers and cattlemen who swore by th supremacy of these horses was their characteristic ruggedness and their incredible ability to survive in the most rigorous of country. Powerful horses with strong bodies and back, robust quarters, a good head and neck, Paints and Pintos are carefully bred to ensure good conformation and correct limbs and feet. Their intelligence als makes them valued for ranch work and rodeos, as well as for pleasure and trail riding, and showing.

PERUVIAN PASO

HEIGHT: 14–15 hh (1.40–1.50 m)

COLOURS: Bay and chestnut predominate, but all solid colours may be found

USE: Riding

FEATURES: Well muscled, short, upright neck; notable muscled structure in chest; long, strong hind legs with flexible joints; hard feet; quarters are lowered, long mane and tail.

The Peruvian Paso, also known as the Peruvian Stepping Horse, is the most prominent of the Peruvian horse breeds and shares a common ancestry with the Criollo (see page 201) of Argentina, which is descended from Spanish stock – a mixture of Arab, Barb, and Andalucian brought to America in the 16th century. The first horses were imported to Peru in 1531-32 by Francisco Pizarro, and the Peruvian Paso is descended from these horses. Like the Criollo, the Peruvian Paso is a horse of great stamina: it has excellent bones and very hard feet, as well as relatively large heart and lungs, all of which make it well suited to working at high altitudes in the Andes mountains.

Over the centuries, the Peruvian Paso has been systematically and carefully developed for its characteristic lateral gaits, the paso llano and the paso sobreandando. Both of these gaits are natural and every pure-bred Peruvian Paso inherits them; training only serves to increase muscular development and flexibility (as well as teaching the horse to respond to riders' cues).

The paso llano is the most commonly seen of the two gaits and can be described as a 'smooth walk' which, while similar to the rack of the American Saddlebred (see page 190) or the running walk of the Tennessee Walking Horse (see page 243) and Missouri Fox Trotter (see page 223), in the Peruvian paso, it is marked by characteristically energetic, round, dishing action of the forelegs – an action called termino – supported by a very powerful movement of the hind legs overstepping the prints of the forefeet. An even 1-2-3-4 cadence can be heard, with the hind foot striking the ground just before the forefoot. The quarters are noticeably lowered and the back is held straight, level and rigid. The paso llano can be maintained at a steady 11 mph (18 km/h) for long periods over the roughest mountain trails and so smooth is the gait that it can reach speeds of 13 mph (21 km/h) without the rider suffering any discomfort whatsoever.

The sobreandando maintains the four beat cadence but is a little more of an 'overdrive' and perhaps, a little closer to the pace. In the show ring, judges will often ask for a Peruvian Paso to accelerate or slow down to see the range of speeds that can be achieved while maintaining the pure gait.

PALOMINO

HEIGHT: 14.1–16 hh (1.45–1.63 m)

COLOURS: Light gold with white tail and mane. Any white socks should not extend above the knees.

USE: Ranch work, rodeo, pleasure and trail riding

FEATURES: Variable height, skin either dark or golden colour; no smudges of colour on coat; mane and tail white with no more than 15% of darker hairs in either; hazel or dark eyes; white facial markings limited to blaze, snip or star; white socks can extend no higher than knees.

Like Pintos and Paints, the Palomino is descended from the Spanish Horses brought to North America in the 16th century by the Conquistadors. The origin of the name Palomino are uncertain: some say it is derived from the Spanish palomilla which apparently – and conveniently – means a 'cream-coloured horse with a white mane and tail'. Others maintain it is derived from paloma, the Spanish for dove. In Spain itself, the Palomino colouring is called Ysabella after the queen who encouraged horse-breeding in that colour.

The Palomino is a 'colour breed' – it is defined by colour rather than by conformation – although its physique is usually that of a riding horse. The Palomino is recognised as a breed only in the USA, although they are bred elsewhere. Even in the USA, because of variations in size and appearance, the Palomino does not have true breed status. It is also quite a different sort of colour breed to the Appaloosa (see page 194) or Pintos and Paints (see page 229): the gorgeous golden coat is not the result of a Palomino gene and so it can therefore appear in any breed or strain where the spotted gene has been bred out. The Palomino colour can therefore be found in other horse breeds, especially in the Quarter Horse (see page 233).

In 1936 the Palomino Horse Association Inc. was founded to perpetuate and improve the horses by recording bloodlines and registering horses which met their stringent 'breed standards'. The height may vary from 14.1–16 hh (1.45–1.63 m), but the colour requirement is very specific. The Palomino is a solid-coated horse which, much like any other single-coloured horse such as bays and chestnuts, should not have any areas of white at all on the body. The skin must be of an overall uniform colour: a dark, greyish black or a golden colour. The coat must be no more than three shades lighter or darker than a newly minted gold coin and must be free from smudges. There must be no hint of a dorsal stripe on the back – a usual feature of dun coloured horses, and any zebra marks on the legs (another sign of 'primitive' origins) are also unacceptable in the Palomino. The mane and tail should be white and may contain no more than 15% of darker hairs. The eyes must be hazel or dark: horses of Pinto, Paint, Albino or Appaloosa parentage, which may have pink, blue or wall eyes, are ineligible for inclusion in the Palomino register. White facial markings are also limited to a blaze, snip, or star, and white socks cannot extend above the knees and hocks.

To qualify for entry into the breeding register, stallions and mares must have one parent already in the register, while the other must be Quarter Horse, Arab or Thoroughbred.

While colour is a prime requirement, the Palomino Horse Association Inc. will not tolerate poor conformation in any horse. The conformation of Palominos is that of the predominant cross: consequently it may tend towards the working stock horse-type, or to the 'finer' parade-type horse.

Because the golden coat colour is not the result of a special 'Palomino gene', producing Palomino colouration is not difficult and can be deliberately brought about by at least four known crosses: Palomino to Palomino, which produces an average ratio of two Palomino offspring to one chestnut and one albino offspring; Palomino to chestnut, which

produces an average of one chestnut to one Palomino foal. This crossing tends to produce the richest and most dazzling golden colour in Palomino coats. The third crossing is Palomino to albino which produces on average, one Palomino to one albino offspring. The fourth crossing, chestnut to albino produces only Palomino foals. While this crossing is the most consistent, it can however, also produce a colour that is often flat, dull and 'washed out'.

The Palomino is in great demand, not only for its good looks, but also for its skill and aptitude in Western riding activities, for ranch and rodeo work, and for pleasure and trail riding.

QUARTER HORSE

HEIGHT: 15–16 hh (1.50–1.60 m)

COLOURS: All solid colours

USE: Riding, racing, ranch work, rodeo

FEATURES: Compact horse with a short head on a muscular, flexible neck; strong shoulders; well defined withers that extend back beyond top of shoulders; underline (belly)is longer than back; short cannons and hocks set low to ground; no play in joint other than directly forwards; oblong hoof with same degree of slope as in pastern, about 45 degrees; heavy muscular quarters

The Quarter Horse, or to give it its full and correct name, the American Quarter Running Horse, is the oldest all-American horse breed (although the Morgan, which came into being in the 18th century is the oldest documented American breed). The history of the Quarter Horse begins in the early 17th century in Virginia and the other early English colonial settlements on the east coast, where the inhabitants obtained 'native' mares – descendants of the Spanish horses brought earlier by the Spanish explorers – from the Chickasaw Indians which were crossed with imported English 'running horses'. The first import of English horses to Virginia was a cargo of 17 stallions and horses which arrived in 1611. These 'running horses' (which would later provide the basis for the Thoroughbred (see page 188) may have been the now extinct Galloways, swift ponies bred in the north of Britain between Nithsdale and the Mull of Galloway, and Irish Hobbies, a breed of pony found in Connemara in the west of Ireland in the 16th and 17th centuries and also noted for its speed.

The resulting offspring were ideally suited to the demands of early colonial life: they performed farm work, hauled goods and lumber at mills, conveyed churchgoing folk in carriages on

Sundays, and carried the master astride on a comfortable gait when he went on business. All this on a pretty meagre diet supplemented by what the horse could forage for. Compact, and 'chunky' – averaging 15 hh (1.50 m) with massive, muscular quarters, these horses had tremendous thrust and pull through the shoulders and haunches. It was this extraordinary power that would lead to the Quarter Horse becoming the master of the short-distance sprint. The love of racing was not diminished among the English in the New World, and while much of their time was spent building a new land – with little left for building race courses – nevertheless, any main street or clearing of a quarter of a mile in length (0.5 km) would suffice as a race track – and would eventually give the breed its name.

The rise of the Thoroughbred and the construction of the now familiar oval-shaped race tracks stimulated interest in long-distance racing so that the original quarter-mile sprints were eventually abandoned in the eastern seaboard states. When pioneers began moving westward, their efficient and versatile Quarter Horses went west too: its agility and speed made it a favourite cow pony. It is often said that the Quarter Horse could 'Turn on a dime and toss you back nine cents change' from a flat out gallop. Consequently, Quarter Horse racing was kept alive and well in the western states: the top prize in Quarter Horse racing is the All-American Futurity Stakes which are run annually in California and are worth in excess of half a million dollars.

In the 19th century, as the ranches grew in size, and cattle were being selectively bred for increased profitability, ranchers also began upgrading their horse stocks. Some were regrettably more concerned with the performance of their horses than pedigree, and bloodlines became confused. It was only in the early 1900s that the first serious attempts to trace the Quarter Horse's origins were made.

There are 12 principal Quarter Horse families, at the root of which are the breed's two most important foundation sires, Janus, an imported English horse who died in 1780 and was responsible through his son of the same name for the Printer line, and Sir Archy, the son of the first ever English Derby winner Diomed – who was also concerned with the beginnings of the American Saddlebred. The Shiloh, Old Billy, Steel Dust and Cold Deck families trace back to him. Through the diligent research of Robert Denhard, a Quarter Horse enthusiast, the American Quarter Horse Association was formed in 1940. The first horse to be registered was Wimpy, listed as P-1 in the stud book. Today, there are more than three million Quarter Horses registered, making it the largest horse breed organisation in the world.

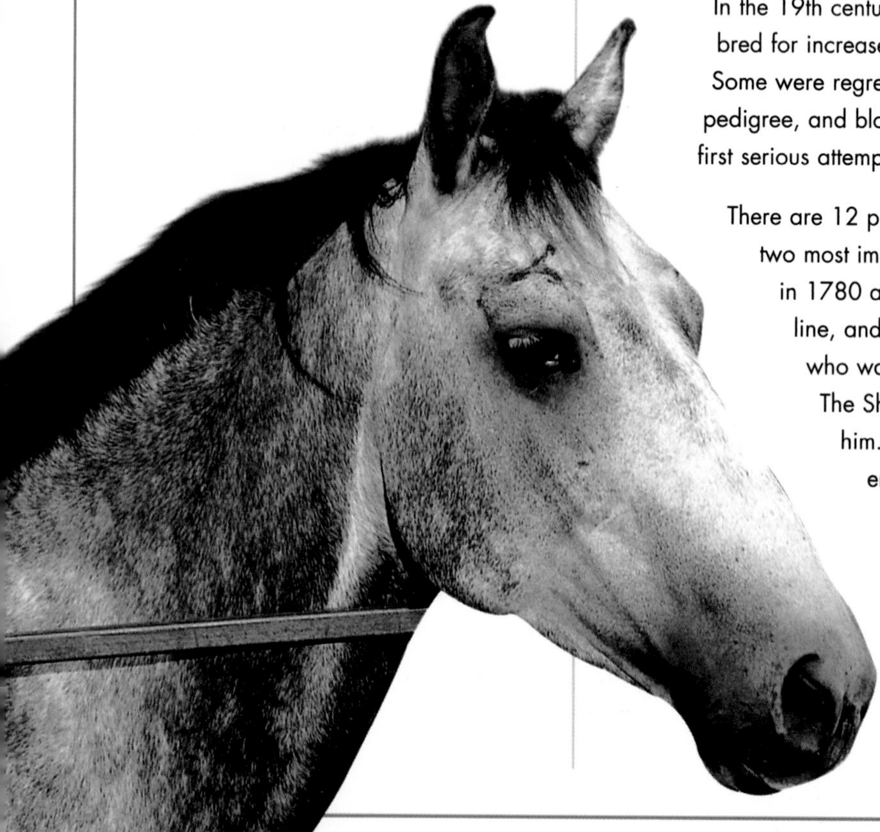

RACKING HORSE

HEIGHT: Average 15.2 hh (1.55 m)

COLOURS: All colours including spotted

USE: Riding, jumping and show ring

FEATURES: Long, sloping neck; well boned; smooth legs; finely textured hair.

The Racking Horse is famous for its beauty, stamina, calm temperament and most of all, for its smooth, easy lateral gait. The Racking Horse has its origins deep in Tennessee Walking Horse (see page 243) bloodlines and until 1971, it did not have a registry or a uniform set of breed rules. In the 1960s a detailed programme of research into the breed began and a group of Alabama business men, headed by Joe D. Bright formed a corporation and initiated the legal process with the Department of Agriculture (USDA) to designate the Racking Horse as a distinct breed. In May 1971 the USDA recognised the Racking Horse Breeders' Association of America, and allowed a registry to be established. The association chose the name 'racking' so that the new horse breed would not be tied to a specific American state or region, and eligibility for registration was determined by performance of the gaits that were natural to the breed. In the beginning, horses of all ages were registered because of their gait performance.

The Racking Horse is considered a 'light' horse, averaging 15.2 hh (1.52 m) and weighing around 1,000 pounds (450 kg). Colours are varied and can be black, bay, sorrel, chestnut, brown, grey, yellow, cremello, buckskin, dun, palomino (see page 232), champagne, roan, and spotted.

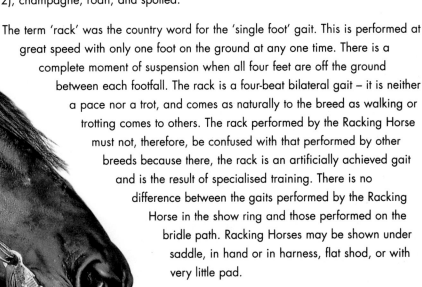

The term 'rack' was the country word for the 'single foot' gait. This is performed at great speed with only one foot on the ground at any one time. There is a complete moment of suspension when all four feet are off the ground between each footfall. The rack is a four-beat bilateral gait – it is neither a pace nor a trot, and comes as naturally to the breed as walking or trotting comes to others. The rack performed by the Racking Horse must not, therefore, be confused with that performed by other breeds because there, the rack is an artificially achieved gait and is the result of specialised training. There is no difference between the gaits performed by the Racking Horse in the show ring and those performed on the bridle path. Racking Horses may be shown under saddle, in hand or in harness, flat shod, or with very little pad.

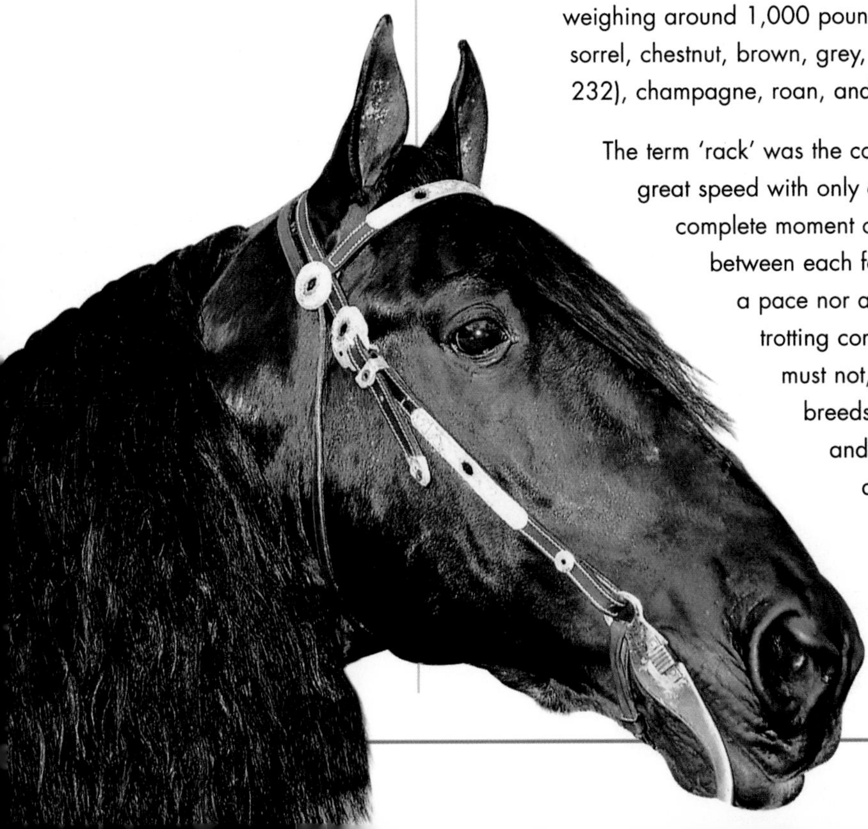

RHINELANDER

ALSO KNOWN AS: Rheinlander, Rheinish

HEIGHT: 16.2 hh (1.68 m)

COLOURS: All solid colours with chestnut predominant

USE: Riding

FEATURES: Plain head on short, thick but strong neck; strong shoulders are reasonable riding type but are heavy and lack depth; clean legs but feet seem small and narrow in relation to large body

The Rhinelander is a relatively new warmblood breed from Germany. Developed in the 1970 the Rhinelander is based on the old Rheinisch-Deutsches Pferd (Rhenish-German Horse), or Rhineland heavy draught horse which was once a very popular work horse in the Rhineland, Westphalia and Saxony regions. This horse's chief qualities were early maturity, efficient food conversion, and a very good temper. But, with modern agricultural practices, this heavy draught breed became redundant and is no longer recognised in Germany.

The Rhenish Stud Book, however, was never closed, and breeders, using the lighter specimen of the breed, worked towards developing a warmblooded riding horse. Stallions from the Hanover-Westphalia area were used on warmblood mares sired by Thoroughbred (see page 188), Trakehners (see page 244) and Hanoverians (see page 211) out of dams which claimed a relationship with the old Rhenish heavy horse breed.

From this mix of blood, the best half-bred stallions were selected to develop the Rhinelander breed. The result is a riding horse about 16.2 hh (1.68 m), often chestnut in colour. While the early examples lacked bone, breeders continued to concentrate on developing an improved conformation, an even temperament, and the straight action which distinguishes German breeds. The modern Rhinelander may not as yet be as distinguished as the Holsteiner (page 174) or the Hanoverian, but its qualities as a riding horse that is greatly suited to the average (even novice) leisure rider are highly recommended.

ROCKY MOUNTAIN HORSE

HEIGHT: 14.2–14.3 hh (1.45– 1.47 m)

COLOURS: Chocolate

USE: Riding and harness

FEATURES: Graceful, long neck flaxen mane and tail; excellent feet; strong hind legs; withers are not sharply defined, but back is good

The Rocky Mountain horse – which was formerly referred to as a pony – is a very distinctive animal. The Rocky Mountain horse is, in fact, a 'breed in the making': its history is less than 20 years old which is not enough time for it to acquire the fixed characteristics of a breed. Nevertheless, a registry was opened in 1986 and there are more than 200 horses registered. Careful and selective breeding will ensure that this very attractive, sure-footed horse with its ambling gait, achieves great success and popularity.

Like many American horses, the origins of the Rocky Mountain Horse lie in the Spanish horses brought to the New World in the 16th century and later Mustang (see page 240) stock. The credit for the modern development of this distinctive horse belongs to Sam Tuttle of Stout Springs, Kentucky, who ran the riding concession at the Natural Bridge State Resort Park. This offered visitors a unique opportunity to ride the rugged trails of the foothills of the Appalachian Mountains. A favourite horse with the visitors was a stallion called Old Tobe, who was famed for his sure-footedness and his comfortable ambling gait (a slow version of the pacing gait) which he had inherited from his distant Spanish ancestors. It may be also that Old Tobe had a genetic relation to the old Narragansett Pacer, a horse that was highly prized by 19th century plantation owners and which would exert a great influence on American gaited horse breeds. Narragansetts were said to be small horses – no bigger then the Rocky Mountain – smooth-moving, and sure-footed in the most rocky and rugged of terrain. They were also very hardy horses – a quality shared by the Rocky Mountain Horse.

Old Tobe was active on the trails – and on the mares – until he was 37 years old, and he passed on all his fine qualities to his offspring, among whom there were some unusual chocolate-coloured foals. This colour is not a prerequisite for registration, but it is a much-prized and very attractive attribute, especially when combined with the beautiful flaxen colour of the mane and tail. This chocolate colour is a little reminiscent of the 'bloodstone' colour that is very occasionally found in Highland Ponies (see page 161), but how it appears in the Rocky Mountain is something of a mystery. There are no records of this colour in horses in early Spanish or colonial horses, but the last of the Narragansett Pacers, a mare who died in 1880, was described as being an 'ugly sorrel colour'. It is possible that this 'ugly' colour somehow became refined over a century.

The Rocky Mountain Horse is currently judged principally on its natural ambling gait, a lateral gait rather than the conventional trot. This can carry the rider very comfortably at a steady 7 mph (11 km/h) over rough trails. Where the going is good, speeds of 16 mph (25 km/h) can be achieved.

RUSSIAN TROTTER

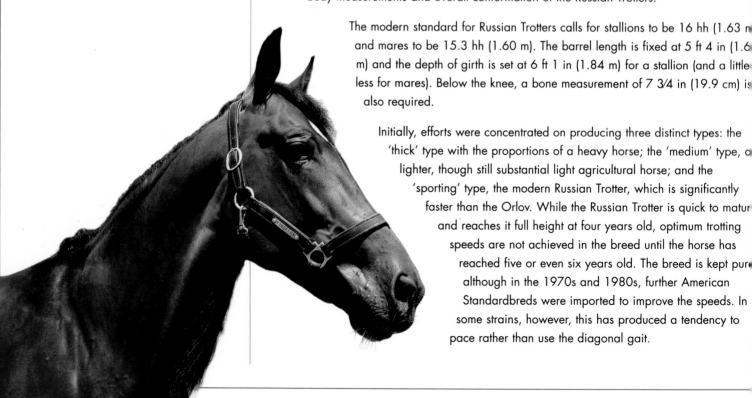

HEIGHT: 15.3–16 hh (1.60–1.63 m)

COLOURS: Black, bay, chestnut, grey

USE: Harness racing

FEATURES: Slightly convex head: pronounced muscular development; hard, clean limbs; sound, strong feet; short cannons; quick to mature, reaching full height at 4 years old; action is low and very long.

Trotting is one of the most popular equestrian sports in the countries of the former USSR, and harness racing horses, like the Orlov Trotter (see page 228) have been bred there since the 18th century. The Russian Trotter is a more recent breed: it has only been recognised as such since 1949. Breeding began in the second half of the 19th century when Russian racers and breeders realised that the Orlov Trotter was being outclassed in international events by the American Standardbred.

The obvious solution was to cross the Orlov with imported Standardbreds. Between 1890 ar 1914, 156 stallions and 220 Standardbred mares were imported. Among these were notab horses including General Forrest, who had trotted one mile (1.6 km) in 2 minutes and 8 seconds; Bob Douglas (2 minutes 4 seconds), and the reigning world-record holder at the tin Creceus, with a mile time of 2 minutes 2 seconds. The resulting offspring were indeed faster, but they were also smaller and less refined than the Orlov, and unlike the Orlov, these horse were not a suitable type for upgrading agricultural horses: the average mare stood around 15.1 hh (1.55) and had a girth measurement of 5 ft 9 in (1.75 m) with a bone measuremen below the knee of 7 1⁄2 in (19 cm). A new breeding programme of interbreeding the cross-breds was dedicated to increasing the trotting speed, as well as improving the height, frame body measurements and overall conformation of the Russian Trotters.

The modern standard for Russian Trotters calls for stallions to be 16 hh (1.63 n and mares to be 15.3 hh (1.60 m). The barrel length is fixed at 5 ft 4 in (1.6 m) and the depth of girth is set at 6 ft 1 in (1.84 m) for a stallion (and a little less for mares). Below the knee, a bone measurement of 7 3⁄4 in (19.9 cm) is also required.

Initially, efforts were concentrated on producing three distinct types: the 'thick' type with the proportions of a heavy horse; the 'medium' type, a lighter, though still substantial light agricultural horse; and the 'sporting' type, the modern Russian Trotter, which is significantly faster than the Orlov. While the Russian Trotter is quick to matur and reaches it full height at four years old, optimum trotting speeds are not achieved in the breed until the horse has reached five or even six years old. The breed is kept pure although in the 1970s and 1980s, further American Standardbreds were imported to improve the speeds. In some strains, however, this has produced a tendency to pace rather than use the diagonal gait.

SELLE FRANÇAIS

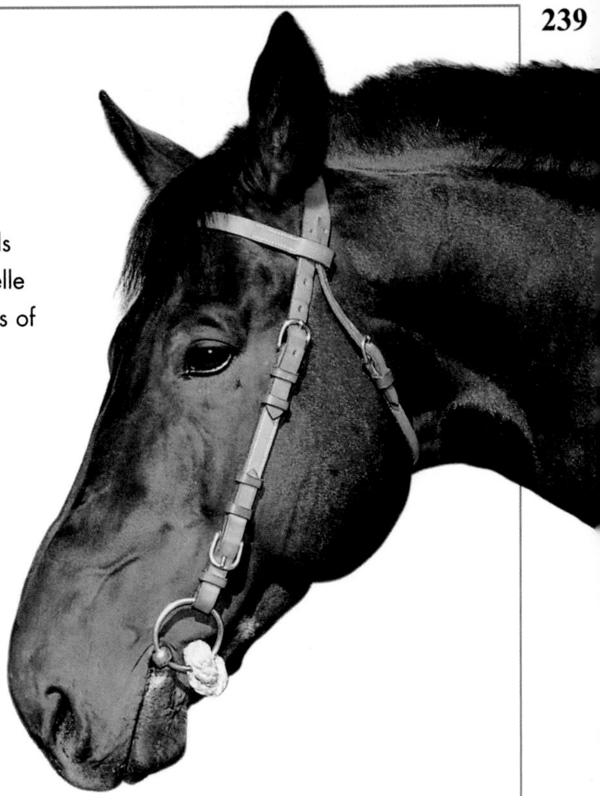

HEIGHT: 15.2 16.3 hh (1.55–1.67 m)

COLOURS: Predominantly chestnut, but all solid colours may be found.

USE: Riding, competition

FEATURES: Plain head on long, elegant neck; strong, compact body; powerful shoulders but not sufficiently sloped for great galloping; broad quarters; powerful limbs and strong hocks; bone measurement of at least 8 in (20 cm) below the knee; ideally suited to show jumping.

Le Cheval du Selle Français – the French Saddle Horse – is one of number of European warmbloods or 'half-breds', but what is significant about the Selle Français is the use of fast trotting stock. The origins of the Selle Français date back to the early 19th century in the horse-raising districts of Normandy, in northern France. Here the local Norman mares were crossed with imported English Thoroughbred (see page 188) and English half-bred stallions which had a background of the important and robust Norfolk Trotter. The French breeders produced two crossbreds: a fast harness horse which would eventually become the French Trotter, and, the Anglo-Norman, which was subdivided into a draught cob and riding horse. The riding horse was the prototype for the modern Selle Français, an all-round competition horse.

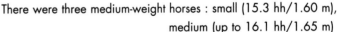

Throughout two world wars, French breeders were able to maintain a small stock of Norman mares and after World War II, further crosses were made with French Trotters (page 206), Arabs (page 183) and Thoroughbreds – including the notable stallion Furioso – to develop a quality horse that combined speed, stamina and jumping ability. The appellation Cheval de Selle Français came into use in December 1958 to describe French 'half-bred' competition horses. Before that time, all French riding horses other than Thoroughbreds, Arabs, and Anglo-Arabs were simply known as 'demi-sangs' ('half-bloods'). Most Selle Français stand over 16 hh (1.53 m), but until the 1980s, the breed was officially split into five classifications. There were three medium-weight horses : small (15.3 hh/1.60 m), medium (up to 16.1 hh/1.65 m) and large (over 16.1 hh/1.65 m) and two heavy-weights: small (under 16 hh/1.63 m) and large (over 16 hh/1.63 m). Today, show jumping is now the main specialisation of the breed, but a lighter Selle Français (which carries a greater amount of Thoroughbred blood) is bred for racing limited to non-Thoroughbred horses and is known as AQPSA (Autre que pur-sang Anglais).

MUSTANGS: SPANISH AND SUFFIELD

HEIGHT: About 14 hh (1.42 m)

COLOURS: All colours including appaloosa and zebra striped dun, grulla (slate grey) buckskin (ranges from light cream to dark brown), roan, paint, ysabella, palomino, cremello and perlino. All colour patterns accepted except Tobiano.

USE: Riding

FEATURES: Spanish type head with straight or convex profile; necks are quite well crested in mares and geldings, heavily crested in stallions; chests are narrow but deep, with front legs joining chest in an 'A' shape rather than straight across; short back; low withers; sloping croup; low set tails; 'mule feet' – concave sole which resists bruising; short canons, but a larger circumference than other breeds of comparable size and height; upper foreleg is long. Many are gaited.

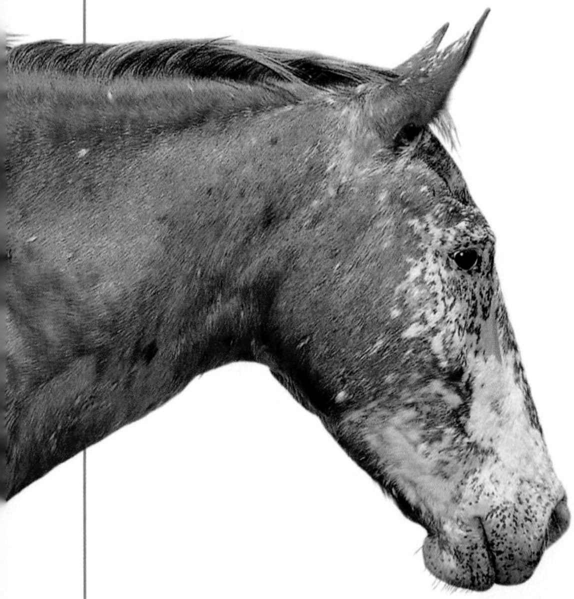

The term 'mustang' is derived from the Spanish word mestena which means a group or herd of wild horses. The Mustang is descended from Spanish stock introduced by the Conquistadors in th 16th century and was an important influence on a large number of American breeds. Mustangs come in all types of build, shapes, sizes and colours. The average size is about 14.2 hh (1.45 m but it is not uncommon to see shorter or taller examples. The most often seen colours are sorrel and bay, but any colour – and coat pattern including spotted and paint – is possible.

A number of Spanish horses either escaped or were turned loose and became feral and formed the nucleus of the once-great herds of wild horses that spread up from Central America into the western plains of the United States. At the beginning of the 20th century there were an estimated one million wild horses roaming the USA. By 1970, however, their numbers had dramatically fallen as the result of wholesale massacres for the meat market and fewer than 17,000 horses remained.

During the 1950s, in Nevada, Velma B. Johnston, later known as 'Wild Horse Annie' became aware of the ruthless manner in which these horses were being 'harvested' for commercial purposes. She led a grassroots campaign that brought the issue to public attention. The outrage that followed eventually led to a bill passed in 1959 (known as the 'Wild Horse Annie Act') whi prohibited the use of motorised vehicles to hunt horses and burros on all public lands. Regrettabl the law did not initiate a government programme to protect, manage and control the wild stock.

In the 1950s and 1960s, anxious to preserve their wild horse heritage, a number of enthusiasts formed societies to preserve, manage and improve Mustang stocks. These included the North American Mustang Association and Registry, and the Spanish Barb Breeders' Association. In 1971, the Mustang was declared an endangered species and was protected by law under the Wild Free-Roaming Horse and Burro Act. According to the US Bureau of Land Management (BLM there are approximately 48,624 Mustangs living in ten western states today.

There are now numerous groups which are involved in research and protection, such as the International Society for the Protection of the Mustang and Burros, the Wild Horse Organised Assistance; the National Mustang Group, and the National Wild Horse Association.

SPANISH MUSTANGS

The first Mustang 'support group' was founded by Mustang breeder Robert E. Brislawn of Oshoto, Wyoming, in 1957. This was the Spanish Mustang Registry which aimed to preserve the purest possible strains of early Spanish horses of both Barb and Andalucian type. Brislawn had in fact started his preservation project in 1925 with two full brothers called Buckshot and Ute, who had been sired by a Buckskin stallion named Monty out of a Ute reservation mare. Monty was captured in 1927 in Utah. Within every Mustang herd is a dominant stallion who is the leader of at least one mare or a group of mares. Among the mares there is also one dominant horse who leads the herd to graze, to water and to shelter, while the dominant stallion follows up in the rear, protecting his herd from intrusions by other stallions. Mustangs bond with each other within the herd, so when Monty escaped back to the wild in 1944, he also took his mares with him, and he was never recaptured.

In spite of this setback, Brislawn continued in his efforts, collecting individual horses he considered to be the best examples of the breed. Brislawn was looking for a small horse of about 14 hh (1.42 m) and weighing about 800 lb (360 kg), short in the back, low in the withers and with a low sloping croup. In 1957, 20 horses were registered; by 2001, the Spanish Mustang Registry contained 3,000 Spanish Mustangs. While it is still considered a rare breed by the American Rare Breeds Conservancy, the Spanish Mustang's future looks as bright as the horses are colourful. The Spanish Mustang is a medium-sized horse averaging around 14 hh (1.42 m) with a proportional weight. They are smooth muscled and short-backed, with rounded rumps and low-set tails. Long-strided, many Spanish Mustangs are gaited with a comfortable four-beat gait such as the 'single foot' or amble. Some are laterally gaited and can perform a 'paso' gait (see Peruvian Paso, page 211) but without the extreme knee action.

Because of their short backs, powerful quarters, and 'bruise resistant' hard feet, Spanish Mustangs are ideally suited to endurance and trail riding and can also do very well at advanced dressage movement. With their energy and precise footwork, they are popular as polo-playing ponies, while their sensible characters also make them ideal pony club mounts.

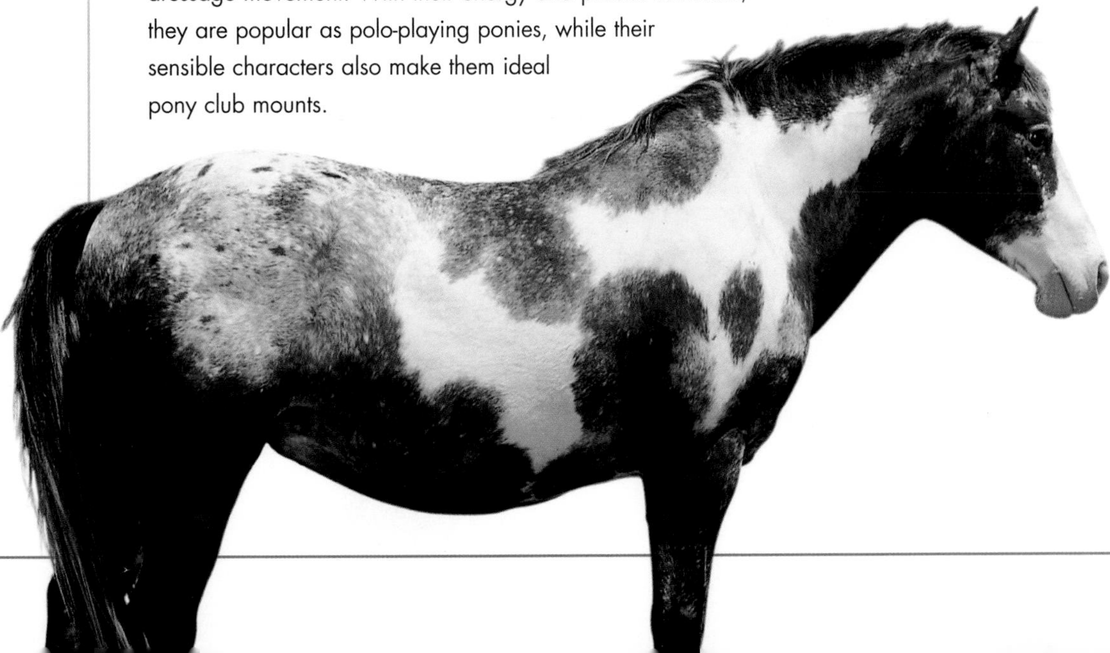

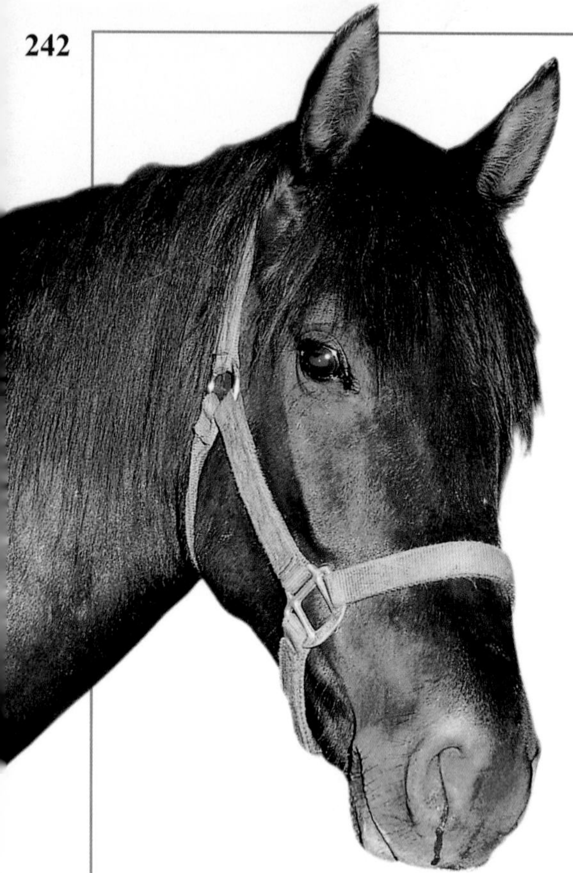

SUFFIELD MUSTANGS

The Suffield Mustang is a bloodline that has developed from domesticated stock that was subje to decades of natural selection. Some 1,200 horses, divided into small herds with a stallion at head, moved freely across one of the largest areas of natural prairie in southern Alberta, Cana until the military annexed the rangelands in 1941.

Throughout the 1950s and early 1960s, the wild horses on the Canadian Forces base at Suffie were loosely managed by the local ranchers and among the wild horses, some Thoroughbreds (see page 122) Quarter Horses (see page233) Morgans (see page 225) and Arabs (see page 183) were also turned out. In 1965 the military fenced off the Suffield base, effectively cutting access by the local ranchers to the horses, which now had to survive unmanaged by humans. From what started out as high quality stock, through interbreeding, and the process of natural selection, a horse of superb quality evolved.

But the Suffield Mustangs' ability to adapt, survive and reproduce on the open range, nearly caused their downfall: in the early 1990s the military authorities decided that the herds were damaging the grasses on the base and the number of horses needed to be controlled. In 1994 was decided to round up the Mustangs and to disperse them to anyone willing to take one. Th people who had the foresight to recognise the historical importance of these horses, adopted a Suffield Mustang and joined together to form the Suffield Mustang Association of Canada with aim to promote and preserve the bloodlines. Around 200 horses from the original 1,200 horse were registered as foundation stock and since 1994, 350 Suffield Mustang foals have been added to the register.

TERSKY

HEIGHT: 15 hh (1.50 m)

COLOURS: Silver-grey, white

USE: Riding

FEATURES: Head is of Arab-type with large eyes and straight profile; short back, deep chest, well sprung ribs; legs are clean and there is 7 1/2 in (19.4 cm) of bone below knee; feet are rounded; mane and tail are usually short and thin, hair is very fine and tail is carried high.

This elegant and athletic Russian horse was developed between 1921 and 1950 at the Ters and Stavropol Studs in the northern Caucasus as a deliberate attempt to preserve the old Strelets Arab which had nearly died out. The Strelets was an Anglo-Arab rather than a pure bred Arabian, the result of crossing pure-breds with Anglos from the Orlov and Rastopchin Studs. By the end of World War I only two Strelets stallions, Cylinder and Tsenitel had survived and both were the characteristic light-grey colour with a silvery sheen. But with no Strelets available to attempt pure-breeding, crossing with Arabs and cross-bred Don/Arab a Strelets/Kabardin began and the resulting offspring were carefully chosen for conformation. After 30 years of selective work, the type was sufficiently fixed f the new Tersky breed to be recognised.

The modern Tersky are distinctly Arab in appearance, although they are a little larger and heavier in build. They are characterised by a particularly light, elegant movement. Most are grey with a silver sheen, or white, often with a rosy sheen which is imparted by the pink skin beneath th coat. Immensely popular in circuses, they are also excellent jumpe and strong cross-country horses.

TENNESSEE WALKING HORSE

HEIGHT: 15–16 hh (1.50–1.60 m)

COLOURS: Black, bay, chestnut as well as part-coloured

USE: Riding, show ring

FEATURES: Quite large head carried low; large boned, deep and short-coupled with a square look to the barrel; clean, strong quarters legs; shoeing is critical to the unique pace: foot is grown long and fitted with shoes to give lift to the action; tail is set high, grown long and is usually nicked (according to US conventions).

One of the most popular breeds in America, the Tennessee Walking Horse, or Tennessee Walker, was once also called a 'Turn-Row' horse because it was used to inspect the crops on the plantations of 19th century Tennessee, Kentucky and Missouri, in rows. Speed was not important, but a strong and stylish horse that provided a very comfortable ride for the plantation owner through the fields was.

Like all the American gaited horse breeds, the Tennessee Walking Horse is descended from the old Narragansett Pacer of Rhode Island with later additional input from Thoroughbreds (page 188), Standardbreds (page 191) and Morgans (page 225). The most important influence on refining the previously quite stocky Walker was made in 1914 with the infusion of American Saddlebred (page 190) blood, introduced by Giovanni, who stood at Wartrace in Tennessee.

In 1935 the Tennessee Walking Horse Breeders' Association was formed at Lewisburg.In 1947, the breed was officially recognised by the US Department of Agriculture.

Primarily a show and pleasure riding horse, the Tennessee Walker is famous for two things. First, its steady and reliable temperament which makes it the ideal mount for even the most inexperienced novice rider. Second, the breed's soft, gliding gait which is virtually bounce-free and said to be the most comfortable ride in the world – an added bonus for first timers in the saddle.

The Tennessee Walking Horse has three gaits: the flat walk, the running walk (which is the predominant gait) and the rolling 'rocking-chair' canter marked by the horse's head nodding in a distinctive manner. Both of the walks are in four-beat time, with each foot hitting the ground separately at regular intervals. In the running walk, the hind feet overstep the print of the front feet by between 6 and 15 inches (15-38 cm). The result is a very smooth gliding motion accompanied by the nodding head – and at top speeds of 15 mph (24 km/h) over short distances, by clicking teeth as well.

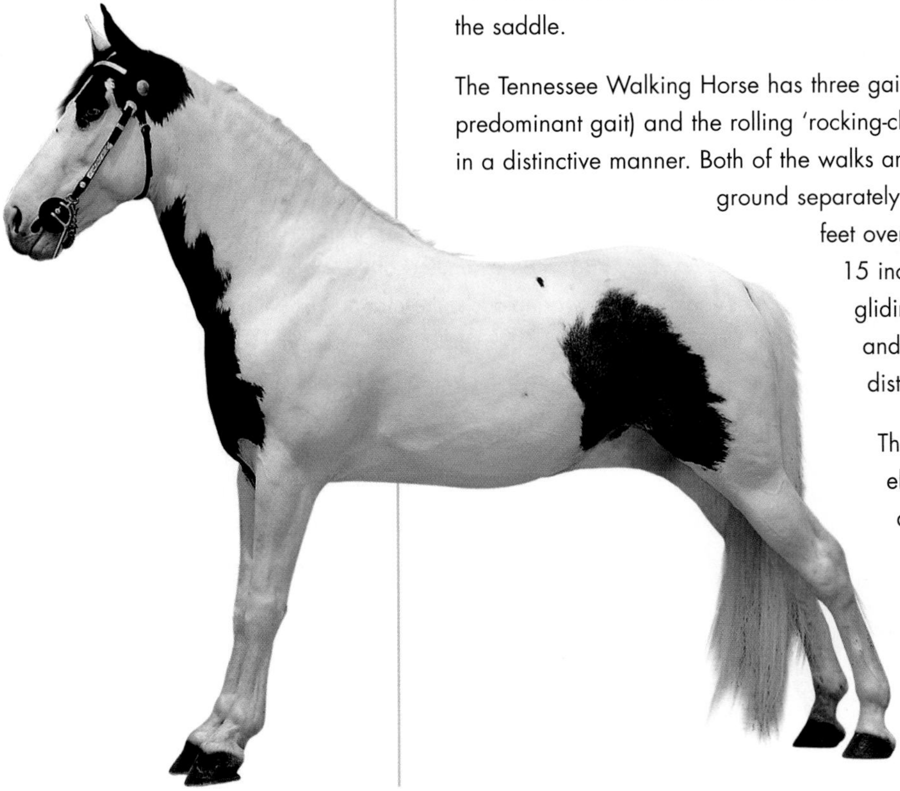

The gliding movement is accentuated by the elongated heels on the hind shoes. The front feet are also grown long and fitted with shoes that give lift to the action. While these may make the Walker's feet look 'artificial' they do not injure the horse in any way and rarely does the Tennessee Walker suffer from any tendon problems.

TRAKEHNER

HEIGHT: 16–16.2 hh (1.63–1.68 m)

COLOURS: All solid colours

USE: Riding, competition

FEATURES: 'Noble' head on long elegant neck; alert, mobile ears; width between very expressive eyes; good, well-shaped shoulders; powerful quarters; medium-long body, well-ribbed; good, strong limbs and hard hooves. Overall conformation is like a Thoroughbred of substance.

The Trakehner, also known as the East Prussian, is an ancient breed, based on the Schwieken and dating from the 13th century. In the area between Gumbinnen and Stalluponen (now in present-day Poland) the Teutonic Knights established a horse breeding industry using the Schwieken as its base. This horse was much used in farming and, as a descendent of the Tarpan, was a very strong and hardy horse. Using these horses, the Knights developed strong cavalry horses that carried them to the crusades. In 1732, Frederick William I of Prussia ordered the marshes drained and the Royal Trakehner Stud Administration was established. This was the main source of stallions for all Prussia and the area soon established a reputation for breeding elegant and fast, coach horses.

By 1787 the emphasis had shifted to breeding cavalry remounts and chargers, as well as horses which were capable of being used for agricultural work. The type of horse was developed at the beginning of the 19th century was an out-cross of Arabs (see page 113), b later, increasing numbers of English Thoroughbreds (see page 122) were used. Two of the most influential Thoroughbreds were Perfectionist (son of the winner of the 1896 Epsom Derb and St Leger, Persimmon, who was owned and bred by King Edward VII of England), and Tempelhuter (Perfectionist's son). Their blood appears in nearly all modern Trakehner pedigrees. Although by 1913, nearly all Trakehner stallions were Thoroughbred, Arab conte always remained a powerful balancing agent in the breed in order to offset any deficiencies either constitution or temperament caused by the Thoroughbred.

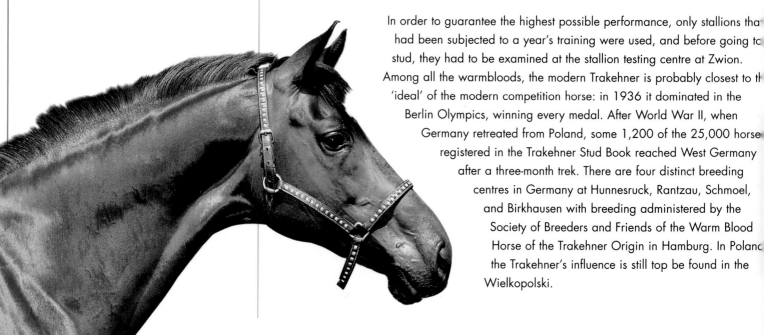

In order to guarantee the highest possible performance, only stallions tha had been subjected to a year's training were used, and before going to stud, they had to be examined at the stallion testing centre at Zwion. Among all the warmbloods, the modern Trakehner is probably closest to th 'ideal' of the modern competition horse: in 1936 it dominated in the Berlin Olympics, winning every medal. After World War II, when Germany retreated from Poland, some 1,200 of the 25,000 horse registered in the Trakehner Stud Book reached West Germany after a three-month trek. There are four distinct breeding centres in Germany at Hunnesruck, Rantzau, Schmoel, and Birkhausen with breeding administered by the Society of Breeders and Friends of the Warm Blood Horse of the Trakehner Origin in Hamburg. In Polanc the Trakehner's influence is still top be found in the Wielkopolski.

RUSSIAN TRAKEHNER

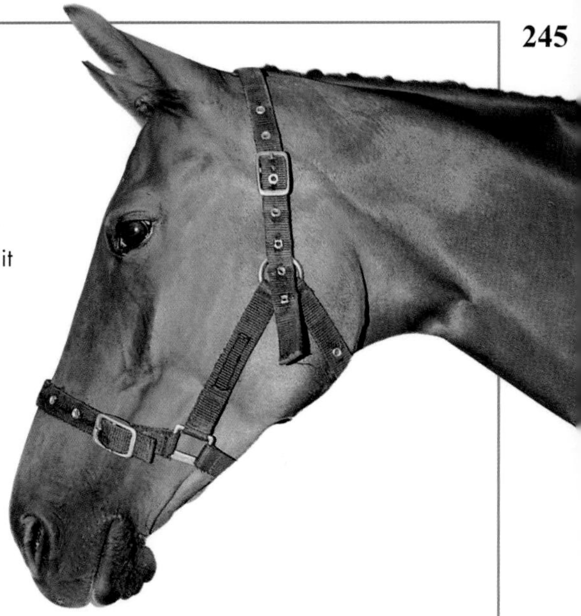

HEIGHT: 16–16.2 hh (1.63–1.68 m)

COLOURS: All solid colours

USE: Riding, competition

FEATURES: Shares the same characteristics as its European cousin but is a little rangier and lighter: a noble head on long elegant neck; alert, mobile ears; width between very expressive eyes; good, well shaped shoulders; powerful quarters; medium-long body, well ribbed; good, strong limbs and hard hooves. Overall conformation is like a Thoroughbred of substance.

The Russian Trakehner shares the same origins as its European cousin the Trakehner (see page 244), but it is a slightly rangier and lighter horse, that is very popular in Russia as a competition horse where it is raced on the flat and over hurdles. Trakehners first arrived in Russia in 1925 from what was then East Prussia. Most of these horses were used as remounts for the Russian cavalry. A second group arrived at the end of World War II: in October 1944 as the war was reaching its closing stages and the Soviet forces were closing in on the Trakehner Stud, about 800 horses were evacuated by rail and by foot.

They did not travel far enough west and eventually fell into the hands of the Russian occupation forces in Poland and were subsequently shipped to the USSR. These were concentrated on the Kirov Stud on the Don River and in 1947, the first volume (of seven) of the Russian Trakehner Stud Book was opened by the Russian Institute of Horse Breeding. Although the bulk of breeding still takes place at the Kirov Stud, since the break-up of the former Soviet Union, many Russian Trakehners are bred elsewhere at private studs, the largest of which is the Oros-L, near Kaluga, some 200 km from Moscow.

UKRANIAN RIDING HORSE

HEIGHT: 16–16. 2 hh (1.60–1.65)

COLOURS: Bay, chestnut, brown

USE: Riding, competition

FEATURES: Straight, long neck; prominent withers; long, flat back; solid, heavy body

Arctic Russia may well have been the first area in which horses were domesticated: the 'relic' horse of the Ice Age, Przewalski's Stallion still exists in a wild state on the Eastern frontier. Horses have been bred in Russia and its neighbouring states for generations, with an emphasis placed on using local breeds particularly suited to the needs and the land of each region.

The Ukrainian Riding Horse is highly regarded in its homeland. Development of the Riding Horse began in the Ukraine after World War II by crossing Nonius (page 221) Furioso-Northstar (page 208) and Gidran mares from Hungary with Thoroughbred (page 188), Trakehner and Hanoverian (page 211) stallions. Particular value was placed on individuals with a trace of Russian Saddle Horse blood, however. Breeding began at the Ukrainian stud at Dnepropetrovsk and later at the Aleksandriisk, Derkulsk, and Yagolnitsk studs where, to produce quality sports riding horses, pure breeding with corrective crossings with Thoroughbreds was undertaken. The most common colours in the Ukrainian Riding Horse are bay, chestnut and brown.

The Ukrainian Riding Horse is a large, heavy saddle horse with a solid build, that performs well in events such as dressage: CIS (Commonwealth of Independent States) equestrians riding Ukrainians have been repeatedly highly placed in international competitions including the Olympic Games, the World and European Championships.

BUCKSKINS

Like the Windsor Grey, Cremello (see page 247) and Palomino (see page 232), Buckskins are a 'colour' and can be found in all breed types. The Buckskin horse's colour is an indication of its ancestry: in the western states of America, the Buckskins, as well as dun, red dun, and grulla colours, trace back to the Mustangs (see page 240), the descendants of the Spanish Horses which were brought to the New World in the 16th century with the Spanish explorers. Other Buckskins can trace back to the Norwegian Dun, relatives of the primitive Tarpan horse.

There are societies dedicated to preserving particular strains, such as the American Buckskin Registry Association and the International Buckskin Horse Association. They maintain registries and work to preserve and promote these horses. Eligibility is based on colour: horses must be either buckskin, dun, grulla, red dun and brindle dun.

Buckskin-coloured horses have a body coat which is a shade of tan, but that can range from very light (called 'creme') to very dark (called 'bronze'). The points – the mane, tail, ears and legs – are black or brown, and overall, the buckskin is clean of any 'smuttiness' in colour. The guard hairs which are buckskin colour, grow through the body coat, up and over, the base of the mane and tail.

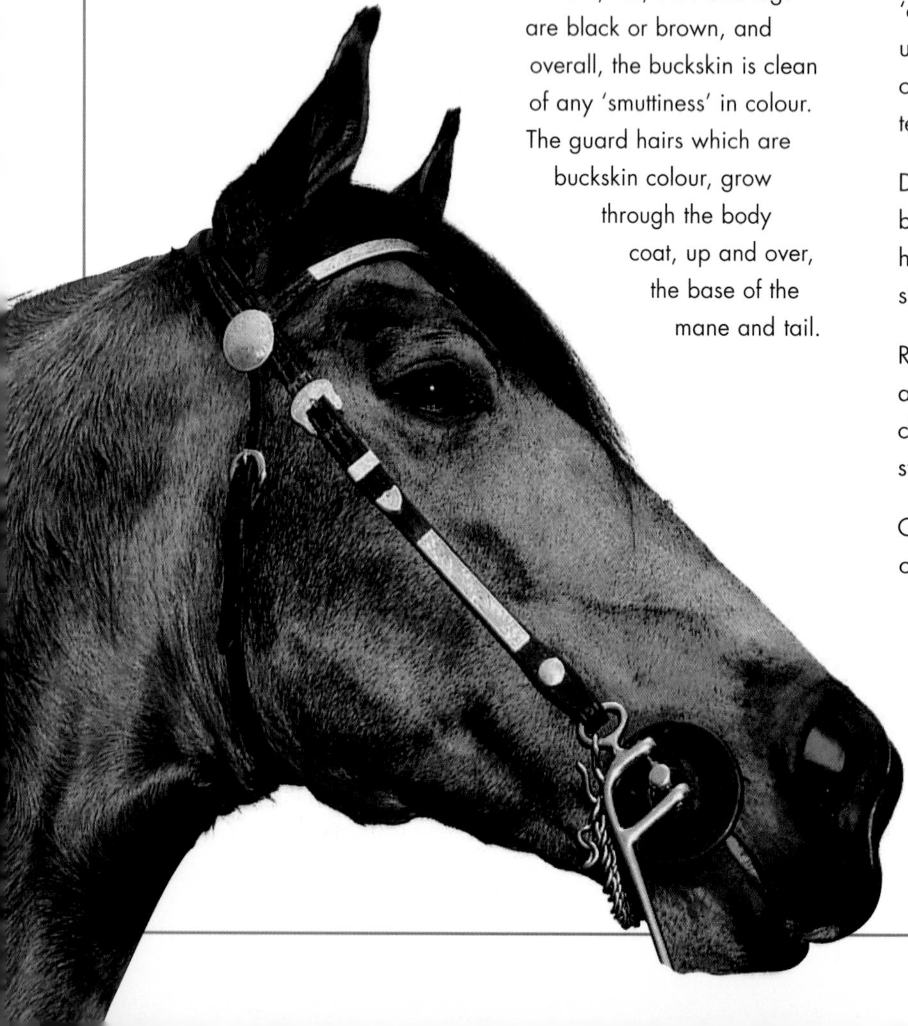

Brindle dun is buckskin with a dun factor. This is a buckskin-coloured horse but with a dorsal stripe, leg barring, ear 'frames', shoulder stripes, face masking and 'cob webbing' in a 'dirty black' or 'smutty brown' colour. Brindle dun horses show up in the Netherlands and are referred to as 'ancient dun colour'. The peculiar body markings can appear in the form of tear drops, or as zebra stripes.

Dun is an intense colour, but is generally a 'duller' shade than buckskin and may have a more 'smutty' appearance. Most dun horses have dark points of brown or black, and have a dorsal stripe along with shoulder stripes and leg bars.

Red dun can range from 'peach' to 'copper' to 'rich red' but in all shades, the accompanying points will be a darker red or chestnut and contrast with the lighter body colour. The dorsal stripe will usually be dark red and very evident.

Grulla (pronounced 'grew-ya') is the rarest of all horse body coat colours. The word 'grulla' is Spanish for crane or heron and like this bird, grulla is a slate colour which ranges from bluish-grey to a brownish colour but there are no white hairs mixed in the body hairs. A dorsal stripe, shoulder stripes and leg barring, in a dark-sepia to black, are also registry requirements in this colour.

WINDSOR GREYS

At the Royal Mews in London there are about 30 horses: the Bays (most of which are Cleveland Bays, although there are some Dutch Bay horses as well) and the Windsor Greys, which are the only horses used to draw the monarch's carriage. These grey horses, which are almost identical, are not a particular breed.

They are called Windsor Greys because, since before Queen Victoria's reign (1837-1901) they were always kept at Windsor Castle until, in the early 20th century, they were moved to the Royal Mews in London by King George V (1910-36).

The Windsor Greys wear the most opulent of the eight sets of state harness when they draw the State Coach. Made of red morocco, each harness weighs 110 lb (50 kg) and is richly ornamented with gold ormolu. The current harnesses were made in 1834 to replace sets made in 1762. By tradition, the manes of the 'state horses' are always plaited: Bays wear scarlet ribbons, while Windsor Greys wear purple ribbons with a matching brow band and rosette forming part of the bridle.

CREMELLO

Cremello horses, like Windsor Greys, are not strictly a breed, but a colour type. This means that the colour can appear in a number of horse breeds.

The colour of Cremello horses is the result of the complexities of genetics. Cremellos are 'double diluted' – they have two copies of the cream colour gene rather than one. A Palomino (see page 208) gets its colour from the fact that it has a single dilution of the basic red (chestnut or sorrel) base colour because it inherited one cream gene from one parent. The buckskin colour likewise, is a single dilution of the basic bay colour.

The Cremello has a double dilution of the cream gene on the red (chestnut or sorrel) base, because it inherited two cream genes – one from each parent. The resulting Cremello colour is a rich cream set off by a very pale white mane and tail. Underneath, the skin is a dark pink colour all over, while the eyes are blue. Most of the major registries accept Cremello – and Perlino, which is a creamy colour but with a darker mane and tail with tan, yellow or orange hues – except for the American Quarter Horse Association. As the rules currently stand, Cremello (and Perlino) horses cannot be registered with the AQHA – even if both its parents are registered. They can however, be registered with the American Paint Horse Association as breeding stock.

MINIATURE HORSES

HEIGHT: In UK (British Miniature Horse Society) not exceeding 34 in. (86.3 cm); in USA: not exceeding 34 in. for AMHA (American Miniature Horse Association). AMHR (American Miniature Horse Registry) registers 'minis' in two divisions:
'A' Division: 34 in. and under; 'B' Division 34 in. and up to 38 inches.

COLOURS: All colours

USE: Showing, companion

FEATURES: Miniature horses must possess the correct conformation that is required in other horse breeds, notably, symmetry, strength, agility, alertness. They are to be perfectly formed horses in miniature.

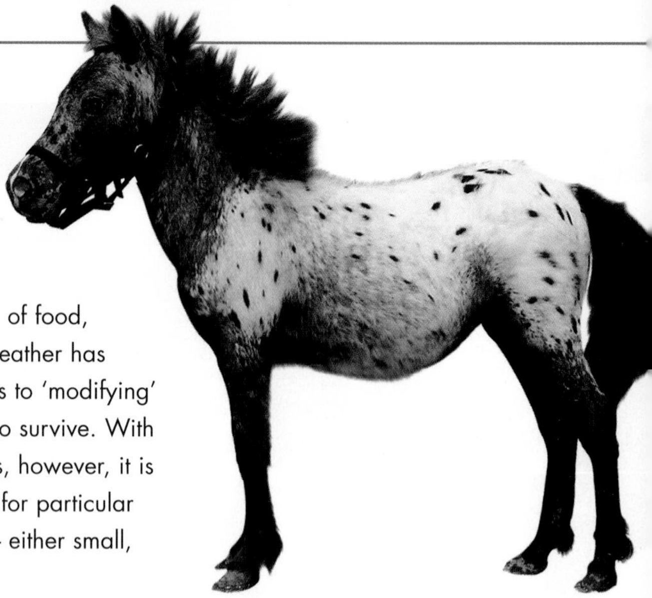

Small horses are usually the product of a harsh natural environment: scarce supplies of food, difficult terrain and severe weather has contributed over the centuries to 'modifying' their stature to enable them to survive. With an understanding of genetics, however, it is possible to selectively breed for particular characteristics such as size – either small, or indeed, very big.

The first true miniature horses originated in Europe and as early at the 17th century, they we bred as pets for the nobility, and for their curiosity value. Lady Estella Hope and her sisters continued breeding the English lines into the mid-19th century, and many of the Miniatures i America are descended from the 'Hope' line. Perhaps the best known of the miniature breec is the Falabella (see page 157) which, in spite of its size, it not a pony but a true horse, sharing a horse's characteristics and proportions.

Miniature horses are really a 'height breed': the features of Miniature horses are exactly the same as large-size horses: Miniature horses are 'scaled down' versions standing no taller th 34 in. at maturity. They must be healthy, sound, well-balanced and possess the correct conformation characteristics required of most breeds: the head must be in proportion to the length of the neck and the body; a straight or slightly concave profile; an even bite; a flexib neck blending into the withers; long, sloping shoulders; well muscled forearms.

There should be ample bone and substance to the body, neither overweight or artificially thi short back in relation to the underline; smooth and generally level top line; long well-muscle hip, thigh and gaskin; highest point of croup the same height as the withers; smooth roundir at the rump and the tail set neither excessively high or too low.

Legs are set straight and parallel when seen from the back, hooves pointing directly forwards; pasterns slope about 45 degrees and blending smoothly. Hooves should be rounded and there should be a fluid gait in motion. Any colour or marking is permissible: the hair is notably silky and lustrous.

Their small size and gentle, affectionate nature makes Miniature horses excellent companions. While they should never be ridden, they are adept at learning to drive and can often to be seen in performance classes at shows where their strength and natural athleticism delights the crowds. They take part in a range of classes, from hunter jumper to showmanship and driving.

BRITISH WARMBLOOD

The term 'warmblood' is a relatively recent addition to British breeders vocabulary.

'Cold blood' is used to describe the heavy draught horses such as the Suffolk Punch (see page 178), while 'pure blood' or 'hot blood' is used for the Thoroughbred (see page 188) and Arab (see page 183) horse. Consequently, any horse 'in-between' could be called a warmblood, as they are in Continental Europe. Because Britain had a tradition of hunting on horseback, these 'warmblood in-betweens' were termed Hunters. In Europe, however, which did not have the same hunting tradition, a catch-all term like 'warmblood' was needed to describe the many breeds of driving and riding horses being bred. There is, however, a significant difference between Hunters and Warmbloods: the studbook registration and the selective breeding process.

Nearly every European country imported English-bred carriage and riding horses as foundations for their warmblood breeds: the French developed the Anglo-Norman – the forerunner of their champion warmblood, the Selle Français (page 239) with Norfolk Trotters and Thoroughbreds, while most German warmbloods (except the Trakehner) are descended through Hanoverians and Holsteiners from the Yorkshire Coach Horses and Norfolk Trotters of the 19th century. Unlike in Britain, where they were kept for the 'best breeds', on the Continent, breeders were careful to maintain detailed stud books which allowed them to selectively breed different types of horses for different uses. This proved particularly useful when, after the Second World War, mechanisation took over from heavy horses in farming, and the demand for leisure and riding horses increased.

Meanwhile, in Britain breeders were basically breeding for the hunt field and the show ring and were unfamiliar with producing 'performance' or 'competition horses'. However, recently, British breeders have turned their attention to producing a British Warmblood. In many ways, the British can claim an advantage over their continental cousins: by importing foreign-bred stallions they will have the benefits of the same 'hybrid' effect just as much as they did in the past – and the British can pick and choose the stallions they think are the most useful. In effect, the British are able to reimport their own bloodlines in a more advanced formula. There is also the open and continuous grading system which makes for rapid improvement so it won't be very long before a British Warmblood will be competing alongside European Warmbloods at international-level competition.

AMERICAN WARMBLOOD

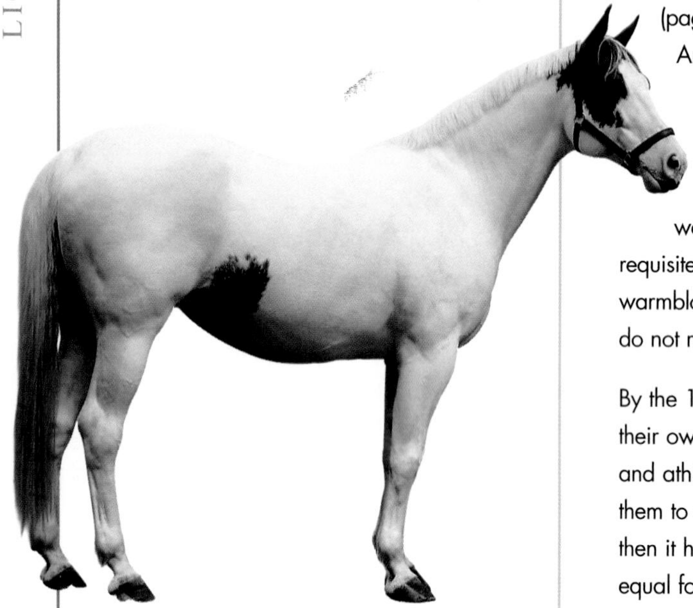

In Europe, the breeding of warmblood horses for work, sport and driving, has been a very organised undertaking, with breeding strictly controlled by government or federal rules which resulted in horses of extremely high quality. From the 1950s, European warmbloods started arriving in the USA, with more established breeds such as the Swedish Warmblood (page 203), the Bavarian Warmblood (page 196), and the Dutch Warmblood (page 202) finding early acceptance. There is now an American branch of almost every European warmblood breed.

But while the European breeders offered breeding guidelines, they did not consider the American groups to be part of their regional breeding programmes: if the 'American' horses are exported to Europe, they would have to be re-examined extensively before they would be allowed into the local breeding population. Since American breeders do not have the requisite allegiance to a specific European country, American breeders contend that all the European warmbloods are 'intermingled' – they are all from one big gene pool – and in American eyes, they do not represent distinct breeds, but rather, various different types of the Warmblood breed.

By the 1970s many Americans thought that the time had come for them to produce and promote their own sport horse, the American Warmblood. America already possesses a number of elegant and athletic horses that are also graced with agreeable temperaments and fluid gaits which allowed them to excel in competition. In 1981, the American Warmblood Registry was established and since then it has registered not only European imports, but their American offspring as well an on an equal footing.

IRISH SPORT HORSE

The Irish Sport Horse is essentially a cross between a Thoroughbred (page 188) and an Irish Draught Horse (page 218). The Thoroughbred-Irish Draught cross has for a long time been used to produce some of the finest Irish Hunters, but it has been further developed with the aim of producing a warmblood that was particularly suited to show jumping, eventing and dressage, and the combination of the blood produces horses of exceptional soundness, stamina and temperament.

The breeding programme requires that three-year-old stallions are inspected in spring when a number are selected for performance testing. This is done either through open competition, or through central testing. In open competition, the stallions are reassessed at four years and older, while in central testing, they undergo rigorous testing over an intense 12-week period from September to November. Mares are likewise inspected to be considered for premium status.

CANADIAN HORSE

ALSO KNOWN AS: Canadian Sports Horse

HEIGHT: 14–16 hh (1.40–1.60 m)

COLOURS: Black predominates, but browns, bays and chestnuts are also common

USE: Riding, harness, competition, ranch work, trail riding

FEATURES: Strong, arched neck; high, well sloping shoulders; long, deep body; rounded barrel; tail set high on powerful rump; mane and tail are long, thick and usually wavy; strong legs and feet.

Known affectionately as the 'Little Iron Horse', the Canadian Horse played a vital role in building the nation. Although listed as 'critical' by the American Livestock Breeds Conservancy with approximately 2,500 head mostly located in Eastern Canada, there has been a great deal of renewed interest in this once very popular breed.

The Canadian Horse traces its origins back to the royal stables of the French King Louis XIV: three shipments were sent from France to the New World: the first, in 1665 consisted of two stallions and 20 mares; the second, in 1667, around 14 horses were sent; and in 1670, a stallion and 11 mares made the transatlantic crossing. These horses were of Breton and Norman descent – the latter carrying Andalucian (page 192) blood which would manifest itself in the Canadian's trotting ability. It is also possible that there was Friesian (page 207) influence in the feathered legs and magnificent mane and tails, as well as, Arab (page 183) and Barb blood.

The 1670 shipment of horses from France was the last: the colonial governor, Intendant Talon now believed there were enough horses in the colony to supply a regular number of colts for the population. The breeding programme that followed was very successful: by 1679 there were 145 horses in the colony, and by 1698, there were 684.

The Canadian Horse worked the land, provided transport and entertainment in the form of racing. They endured the freezing winters and the blazing summers on little feed. Famed for their hardiness and stamina, they survived the rigours of life in Canada. But they did become smaller in size – hence their name 'Little Iron Horse' – and produced both trotters and pacers. Consequently, the Canadian Horse was popular in the United States where they contributed to the foundation stock of many American breeds. The demand for Canadian Horses was so great that in fact, by the end of the 19th century, the number of pure Canadians at home had decreased that the breed was in danger of extinction. In 1895 the Canadian Horse Breeders' Association was formed, but even by 1976, the breed was still struggling with only 383 registered Canadian Horses. Thanks to the efforts of a number of dedicated breeders, numbers began the slow climb back from virtual extinction.

The Canadian Horse is a very versatile horse: they are willing and adaptable and have a very even temperament. These qualities, combined with their good looks, have made the Canadian Horse a popular mount for both pleasure riding (their tough legs and hard feet make them very sure-footed trail-riding horses) as well as in harness, as show jumpers and in the dressage ring.

GLOSSARY

Action	The movement of the horse's body frame and legs at all paces,
Amble	The slow form of the lateral pacing gait,
Barrel	The body between the forearms and the loins,
Blood weed	A lightly built, poor quality Thoroughbred horse which lacks bone and substance,
Blue feet	Dense blue-black colouring of the horn,
Bone	The measurement around the leg just below the knee or hock The bone measurement determines the horse's ability to carry weight.
Breed	An equine group bred selectively for consistent characteristics over a long period, whose pedigrees are registered in a stud book.
By	A horse is said to be 'by' a particular sire. A horse is said to be 'out of' a mare.
Cannon bone	The bone of the foreleg between the knee and fetlock. Also called the 'shin bone'. The corresponding bone in the hind leg is called the shank.
Carriage horse	A light, elegant horse used for private or hackney carriage use.
Cavalry remount	Also called a 'trooper', a horse used for military service.
Charger	Military officer's mount.
Clean-bred	A horse of any breed of pure pedigree blood.
Clean-legged	Without feather on the lower limbs.
Close-coupled	Short back without a hand's width between the last rib and the point of the hip, with no slackness in the loins. Also called short-coupled.
Coach horse	A strong, powerfully built horse able to pull a coach.
Cold blood	The name for heavy European breeds descended from the prehistoric Forest Horse.
Conformation	The way the horse is 'put together' – the shape and proportions of its body.
Cow hocks	Hocks that turn inward at the points like those of a cow.
Cross-breeding	Mating individual horses of different breeds or types.
Dam	A horse's mother.
Depth of girth	The measurement from the wither to the elbow: 'good depth of girth' describes generous measurements between these two points.
Desert Horse	A term used to describe horses bred in desert conditions, or horsesbred from desert stock. Such horses are heat-tolerant and can survive on minimal water intake.
Dished face	The concave head profile as exemplified by the Arab horse.
Docking	Amputation of the tail purely for appearance. Illegal in the UK.
Dorsal stripe	A continuous strip of black, brown or dun-coloured hair extending from the neck to the tail. It is a feature of horses with a primitive connection and is most usually found in dun coloured horses. Also called an 'eel stripe'.
Draught	A word used to describe a horse which draws any vehicle, but generally applied to the heavy breeds.
Dry	A word used to describe the 'lean' appearance of the head of desert-bred horses. There is little fatty tissues and the veins stand out clearly under the skin.
Feather	Long hair on the lower legs and fetlocks.
Floating	The word used to describe the action of the Arab horse's trotting gait.
Forearm	The upper part of the front leg, above the knee.
Forelock	The mane between the ears which hangs over the forehead.
Gaited horse	The American term for horses schooled to artificial as well as natural gaits.
Gaskin	The second thigh extending from stifle to hock.
Girth	The circumference of the body measured from behind the withers around the barrel.
Hands	Height of horses in the UK and USA is measured in 'hands': 1 hand equals 4 inches (10.16 cm).
Harness	The equipment of a driving horse.
Harness horse	A horse used in harness, or with a harness type conformation: straight shoulders and with an elevated 'harness action'.
Haute école	The classical art of advanced horsemanship.
Heavy Horse	A large draught horse.
Hock	The joint in the hind leg between the gaskin and cannon bone – the equivalent of the human ankle.
'Hocks well let down'	Where a horse has short cannon bones, considered to give great strength. Long cannons are regarded as a conformational weakness.

Hogged mane	The mane clipped close to the neck.
Hot blood	Used to describe Arab, Barbs and Thoroughbreds.
Hybrid	A cross between a horse on one sid and a zebra or ass, etc. on the other.
In-breeding	Literally incest, e.g. the mating of a sire to a daughter, or dam to a son, or brother to a sister, in order to enhance or fix characteristics.
In hand	When a horse is controlled from the ground, rather than from the saddle.
Jibbah	The bulged formation on the forehead of an Arab horse.
Light Horse	A horse other than a heavy horse or pony suitable for riding and carriage work.
Line breeding	Mating individual horses which share a common ancestor some generations removed.
Loins	The area on either side of the back bone just behind the saddle.
Mitbah	Used to describe the angle at which the neck of an Arab horse enters the head. It gives an arched set to the neck and allows for almost all-round movement.
Native ponies	Another name for British Mountain and Moorland breeds.
Oriental horses	A term that is loosely applied to horses of eastern origin – either Arab or Barb – which were used in the formation of English Thoroughbreds.
Out-crossing	Mating unrelated horses; introducing outside blood to the breed
Paces	The walk, trot, canter and gallop.
Pacer	A horse that uses a lateral action at trot rather than the more conventional diagonal movement: i.e. near fore and near hind leg together followed by the offside pair.
Pack horse	A horse used to transport goods in packs carried on either side of its back
Palfrey	A medieval light saddle horse that could amble.
Parietal bones	The bones on top of the skull.
Part-bred	The offspring of a Thoroughbred and another breed.
Pedigree	Details of a horse's ancestry recorded in a stud book.
Piebald	The British term for a body colour of black with white patches.
Points	The various parts of the horse's body comprising its conformation. Also used in colour description: the mane, tail, legs varying in colour from the rest of the body.
Prepotent	Able to pass on a character or fixed type to offspring.
Primitive	A term used to describe the early subspecies of horses: the Asiatic Wild Horse, the Tarpan, the Forest Horse and the Tundra Horse.
Pure-bred	A horse of unmixed breeding.
Quarters	The body from behind the flank to the tail and down to the top of the gaskin.
Ram head	A convex profile like that of the Barb, similar to the 'Roman nose' that is found in Shire and other heavy horse breeds.
Rangy	A horse with size and scope of movement.
Riding Horse	Also called a Saddle Horse. A horse with the conformation associated with a comfortable riding action, as opposed to a draught or carriage horse.
Roached mane	The US term for a hogged mane.
Running Horse	The English racing stock, also called Running Stock, which provided the base for the English Thoroughbred when crossed with imported Oriental sires.
Second thigh	Gaskin.
Shoulders	The angle from the point of the shoulder to the withers should be 45 degrees in a riding horse. If the shoulder or the pastern is too upright, the horse's action will not be smooth and comfortable.
Skewbald	The British term for a body colour of irregular white and coloured patches other than black.
Slab-sided	Flat-ribbed.
Stud	A breeding establishment. Also a stallion (an uncastrated male horse of four years old or more).
Stud book	The book kept by a breed society in which the pedigrees of stock eligible for entry are recorded.
Top line	The line of the back from the withers to the end of the croup.
Type	A horse that fulfils a particular purpose, such as a cob, hunter or hack, but which does not belong to a specific breed.
Warmblood	In general terms, a half-, or part-bred horse, the result of an Arab or Thoroughbred cross with other blood or bloods.
Well-ribbed	A short, deep, rounded body with well-sprung ribs which gives ample room for lung expansion and is suitable for carrying a saddle.
Withers	The part of the horse where the neck joins the body.
Zebra bars	Dark, striped markings on the forearms and sometimes on the hind legs.

INDEX

CREDITS

BIBLIOGRAPHY:

Elwyn Hartley Edwards *The New Encyclopedia of the Horse* (Dorling Kindersley, 2000)

Elwyn Hartley Edwards *Ultimate Horse* (Dorling Kindersley, 2002)

Elizabeth Peplow (ed) *Encyclopedia of the Horse* (Hamlyn, 2002)

Collins Gem *Horses and Ponies* (Harper Collins, 1999)

Horse & Hound magazine

If you want to learn more about your favourite horse breed, log onto the internet and check out the various breed clubs and societies and click on the links to other sites to find out more.

ACKNOWLEDGEMENTS:

Vic Swift at the British Library, London, but special thanks to all the breed societies and associations, and to all the horse enthusiasts, around the world, who willingly shared their expert knowledge of breeds, history, types, colours and features on the internet.

ADDRESSES:

The Association of British Riding Schools
Old Brewery Yard
Penzance
Cornwall, TR18 2SL

British Horse Society
British Equestrian Centre
Stoneleigh
Kenilworth,
Warwickshire, CV8 2LR

National Pony Society
Willingdon House
102 High Street
Alton,
Hampshire GU34 1EN

International League for the Protection of Horses (ILPH)
Colvin House
Hall Farm
Snetterton
Norwich,
Norfolk, NR16 2LR

Riding for the Disabled Association
National Agricultural Centre
Stoneleigh
Kenilworth
Warwickshire CV8 2LR